DECISION SUPPORT SYSTEMS

DECISION SUPPORT SYSTEMS
Tools and Techniques

SITANSU S. MITTRA

System Development Corporation
Boston University

A Wiley-Interscience Publication

JOHN WILEY & SONS

New York · Chichester · Brisbane · Toronto · Singapore

Library of Congress Cataloging in Publication Data:

Mittra, Sitansu S.
  Decision support system

  "A Wiley-Interscience publication."
  Includes index.
  1. Decision-making. 2. management information
systems. I. Title.

T57.95.M57   1986   658.4'03   86-7816
ISBN 0-471-81641-8

To

Pranati
Partha
Ansu

the greatest assets in my life

PREFACE

A decision support system, DSS for short, is a computer-based information system that helps a manager make decisions by providing him or her with all the relevant data in an easily understandable form. As the user of DSS, the manager formulates the problem by using an interactive and probably menu-driven front end. The system then accesses a database to locate the necessary data, utilizes a repertoire of mathematical and/or statistical models, and finally produces the desired information at the user's terminal. The user can explore several "what if" scenarios in order to arrive at a decision. The DSS thus merely helps the manager make a decision; it does not and cannot make the decision for the manager. This shows that in order to design a DSS it is necessary to have a database supported by a sophisticated database management system, a set of mathematical tools in the form of optimizing and nonoptimizing models, and an online interactive system that can be used by the manager to tap the resources of the DSS.

DSS is a relatively new addition to the ever-expanding realm of computer science. Significant developments in DSS were made during the late 1970s and early 1980s. DSS is now included in standard computer science curriculums at the senior undergraduate and graduate levels in colleges and universities. However, not many comprehensive textbooks on DSS are currently available. I became aware of this situation for the first time when I gave a course on DSS at the graduate level at Bentley College for students in an M.S. program in computer information systems. As a result, I prepared a set of extensive notes during the summer of 1982 in order to teach the course in fall 1982. After repeating the course I decided to revise these notes into the form of a book. This text is the outcome of that effort.

The book is divided into four parts comprising 15 chapters.

Part I, Introduction, consists of Chapters 1 and 2. Chapter 1 provides background materials for introducing DSS. Chapter 2 discusses the detailed step-by-step process for the analysis and design of a decision support system.

Part II, Modeling Techniques, consists of Chapters 3, 4, and 5. Chapter 3 provides a background for model building. Chapter 4 treats the various linear and nonlinear optimizing models, using both deterministic and probabilistic methods. Chapter 5 deals with statistical models such as linear and nonlinear projection, time series analysis and forecasting, and qualitative forecasting using the Delphi method.

Part III, Simulation Techniques, consists of Chapters 6 through 11. Chapters 6 and 7 discuss general simulation concepts with queueing theory as a framework for studying discrete system simulation. Chapters 8 and 9 are devoted to a discussion of discrete and continuous system simulations, respectively. Chapter 10 gives an overview of GPSS as an example of a discrete system simulation language. Chapter 11 gives a similar treatment of DYNAMO II as an example of a continuous system simulation language.

Part IV, Examples and Contemporary Issues of Decision Support Systems, consists of Chapters 12 through 15. Chapter 12 discusses additional case studies in a manner similar to the treatment of SIMPLAN and CIS in Chapter 1. Chapter 13 explores some of the software packages that can be used as instructional materials to simulate a real-world DSS. Chapter 14 shows how a DSS can be built as a classroom project and is based on my experience in teaching a DSS course at the graduate level. Chapter 15 discusses future trends in DSS and describes some of the existing DSS packages. It concludes with comments on the impact of artificial intelligence on DSS.

From its contents it should be clear that the book is a hard core technical book and requires a good level of mathematical maturity on the part of the reader. As an absolute minimum, the reader must be thoroughly familiar with techniques of linear algebra and elementary statistics, which includes probability distributions (e.g., Poisson, exponential, normal), concepts of mean and variance, mathematical expectation, the sampling process, and correlation concepts.

The book is aimed at two categories of users:

☐ Computer science students who want to learn the analysis, design, and implementation of decision support systems.

☐ Computer system professionals (e.g., systems analyst, information systems specialist) who want to build a decision support system or are in the process of building one.

For the first group, the book can be used as a text for a one- or two-semester graduate level course on DSS. More details on this topic are given in the following paragraphs. For the second group, the book provides a "how to" compendium of information on building a DSS and as such can be used both as a step-by-step procedure manual and as a reference.

Any information system can be looked at in two ways: the user's view and the designer's view. The user's view describes the functional capabilities of the system: it explains *what* the system can do for its users. The designer's view then shows *how* these functional capabilities can be made available by the system. Obviously, the students must have a clear conception of the user's view of a system before they can formulate the designer's view of that system. A DSS is no exception to this general rule. In fact, my teaching experience indicates that the students' exposure to DSS in their workplaces is very limited. Accordingly, this book should be supplemented by an operational DSS package at the college or university so that the students can have hands-on experience with DSS. Chapter 15 lists nearly two dozen commercially available DSS packages.

The book contains enough material to support two one-semester courses at the graduate level. The first course could be labeled the user's view of DSS; it should include Chapters 1, 2, and 12–15 and should be supported by a DSS package to give the students some hands-on experience in the use of a DSS. The second course would then be a sequel to the first, concentrating heavily on Chapters 3–11 and concluding with a review of Chapters 12 and 15. Students would be required to design and implement a DSS on a team basis. The instructor could devote the first two-thirds of the course to explaining the DSS tools, i.e., Chapters 3–11, and the last third to discussing the two case studies, IDSS and D/T DSS in Chapter 12, to show how the mathematical tools are combined with database technology and interactive systems to design a DSS.

During the time that I was writing the book I got continuous support from my wife Pranati, to whom goes my deepest appreciation. My sons, Partha and Ansu, were too unsophisticated at this time to appreciate the continuing pressure of writing a book.

I acknowledge the help I received from my former students at Bentley College in shaping my ideas about DSS. I have included three papers written by some of them as case studies of DSS while they were my students.

It is a pleasure to acknowledge the friendly support of James T. Gaughan, Editor of Computer Science at Wiley-Interscience. I sincerely thank the staff of John Wiley & Sons for making this production job a success.

SITANSU S. MITTRA

Medfield, Massachusetts
September 1986

CONTENTS

PART II
MODELING TECHNIQUES

3 Models and Model Building   57

4 Models for Optimization   70

5 Statistical Models and Applications   **129**

13   DSS Games as Instructional Tools   356

14   Building a DSS as a Term Project   374

15   Current and Future Trends in DSS   407

DECISION SUPPORT SYSTEMS

INTRODUCTION

Part I of the book introduces the concept of a decision support system (DSS) and explains the process of building a DSS. After a discussion of the major issues involved in a DSS, Chapter 1 analyzes two examples of DSS: SIMPLAN, which is a corporate planning model, and CIS, which is a production planning model. Chapter 2 introduces the five phases of a system life cycle and correlates them with the development of a DSS. This chapter concludes with two case studies to illustrate the analysis phases required by a DSS study.

Introduction to Decision Support Systems

1.1   WHAT IS A SYSTEM?

The word *system* is used today in connection with a wide variety of phenomena in almost every possible field of activity. Alexander ([1], Chapter 1) lists nine different definitions of a general system in his discussion of general systems theory. These definitions show that a system need not be just a computer information system. We talk about the public welfare system, the health care system, the criminal justice system, the higher education system, and so on. Alexander has combined the various definitions to arrive at the following composite general definition of a system ([1], p.4):

> A system is a group of elements, either physical or nonphysical in nature, that exhibit a set of interrelations among themselves and interact together toward one or more goals, objectives, or ends.

This broad definition can be narrowed down to apply to a computer-based information system. Here the primary group of elements is *data,* the set of interrelationships refers to the *flow* of data through an organization and to the manner in which this flow is related to the operation of the organization, and the common *goal* is to have well-informed managers working in an efficient organization. In any information system, manual or automated, there is a basic objective which justifies the system's existence.

Different people view the information system differently, somewhat similar to the legendary six blind men describing an elephant. To a user or a customer, the system is a vehicle for generating periodic reports, both detailed and summary, which can be used by different levels of management in their

daily functions. In addition, the system enables management to access the data files through ad hoc queries to gather desired information which is not available through the periodic reports. To a systems analyst, the system represents the logical flow of data through the basic computer cycle of input–process–output whereby the requisite data can be collected, stored, processed to generate reports, and finally disseminated in useful form. To a programmer, the system is much more restricted in that it is reduced to individual modules which carry out some very specific functions such as updating a master file or printing invoices using data from sales receipts. To the computer operations staff, the system consists of detailed operations documentation that specifies how the system is run, how data should be entered and verified, what the control procedures and restart procedures are, and so on.

1.2 TYPES OF SYSTEMS

In general, we can distinguish among five types of computer-based systems:

1. Operating systems (OS).
2. Database management systems (DBMS).
3. Application systems such as payroll, customer invoice, and inventory.
4. Management information systems (MIS).
5. Decision support systems (DSS).

The *operating system* is the essential software that enables a computer to function, and it works in conjunction with the hardware. All application systems need the OS for efficient operation. The *DBMS* is a desirable feature in that it reduces data redundancy and ensures data independence. If an organization has many application systems whose file data overlap, then a DBMS is highly useful for integrating this multitude of files. The *MIS* in the organization provides a broad umbrella which includes all the application systems and the *DSS*, if any. However, the MIS does not include the OS or the DBMS, because the latter two are supporting software for running the MIS just as the computer equipment is the supporting hardware for the MIS. Finally, a *DSS* is a computer-based information system that helps a manager in making key decisions and thereby improves the effectiveness of the manager's problem solving process.

We therefore conclude that the OS and the DBMS fall outside the realm of MIS since they are both different kinds of systems. In an organization the managers are interested in the capabilities provided by an MIS. If the latter includes a DSS, then the managers get extra support from the DSS in improving their decision-making power. Hence we now explore the nature and contents of an MIS.

1.3 THE MANAGEMENT SUPPORT SYSTEM

The MIS in an organization is a collection of all the application subsystems (inventory, accounts payable, sales forecast, corporate planning, and so on) and the decision support system, if one exists. The MIS thus represents a philosophy or viewpoint that integrates all the existing systems in the company and makes information available to the managers in a readily accessible form. A true MIS should be supported by a versatile DBMS with a nonprocedural query language capability to retrieve data from the integrated database.

The MIS develops in response to the needs of management for accurate, timely, and meaningful data for planning, analyzing, and controlling the organization's activities and thereby maximizing its survival and growth. The MIS accomplishes this objective by providing means for input, processing, and output of data along with a feedback decision-making capability that helps management to respond to current and future changes in the internal and external environment of the organization.

A well-developed MIS in an organization should be able to respond to the following questions:

1. What information is needed?
2. When is the information needed?
3. Who needs it?
4. Where is it needed?
5. Why is it needed?
6. How much does it cost?

This list is often referred to as 5 W's and an H.

Initially the MIS gets a modest start and addresses a small set of management needs. Gradually more and more demands are made on the system, and these demands are addressed in a patchwork fashion. Eventually the system gets too many patches, and then the need arises to integrate all the components in a well-coordinated fashion. Formal, semiformal, and even informal reporting habits are standardized, definite procedures are set up, and schedules and priorities are established. Information flows are structured for early warning of problems, quick response to crises, and clear channels for communicating management directives. Finally, the organization gets its MIS.

Within recent years there has been increasing emphasis placed on helping managers make decisions on the basis of good information. As a result, the *decision support system* (DSS) has become an essential subsystem within the framework of MIS. The DSS has four primary characteristics:

1. It helps managers at the upper levels.
2. It is flexible and responds quickly to managers' questions.

3. It provides "what if" scenarios.
4. It takes into account the personal decision-making styles of managers.

A decision support system retrieves information from other parts of the MIS and interfaces with the other subsystems of the MIS. More specifically, the DSS can provide routine detail, summary, and exception reports. If a suitable database management system is available, then the DSS can provide nonroutine information through an ad hoc query facility of the DBMS. Finally, sophisticated optimizing techniques and statistical packages can be used to analyze available data and provide feedback capabilities to management.

1.4 DSS AND THE THREE LEVELS OF MANAGEMENT

In any organization there are three levels of management:

☐ Strategic or top.
☐ Tactical or middle.
☐ Operational or bottom.

Generally, as the list indicates, bottom level management deals with operational information, while the middle and top levels are concerned with tactical and strategic information, respectively. The required information should be more and more summarized the higher the level of managers who use it in this three-tier hierarchy of management (see Fig. 1-1). The MIS in the organization must keep track of the varying information needs.

The time spans for the reports that address the needs of the three levels of management differ significantly. Strategic level managers are concerned

Top (strategic) level	Summary reports Goal and planning oriented
Middle (tactical) level	Detailed technical reports Planning, control, and solution oriented
Bottom (operational) level	Detailed operational reports Daily operation and implementation oriented

FIGURE 1-1 Three levels of information needs.

TABLE 1-1 Information Need Characteristics

Management Level	Information Type	Time Span	Level of Uncertainty
Top	Strategic	1–5 years	High
Middle	Tactical	1 year	Medium
Bottom	Operational	Daily	Low

with the overall goals and planning for the company and want to compare the company's performance with that of its competitors. Their information needs normally span 1 to 5 years. The level of uncertainty in these reports remains high. Tactical level managers are involved with technical information and usually deal with a time span of 1 year. Accordingly, the level of uncertainty in such reports is lower. Operational level managers (foremen, first line supervisors, etc.) implement the work plan on a daily basis and thus deal with information having very little uncertainty. Table 1-1 summarizes the essential characteristics of the types of information needed by the three levels of management.

As a subsystem of the MIS, the DSS caters to the needs of all levels of management. However, it is oriented toward the needs of top and middle level managers, enabling them to experiment with different alternative and "what if" scenarios. The needs of the bottom level managers are normally met by the various application subsystems of the MIS.

1.5 REQUIREMENTS FOR A DSS

The following characteristics enable the DSS to achieve its objectives:

☐ It relies heavily on sophisticated quantitative techniques of model building (see Chapter 3).

☐ In cases where an analytic optimizing model cannot be solved, the DSS relies on simulation (see Chapter 6).

☐ It uses statistical analysis to collect data and to predict trends (see Chapter 5).

☐ It uses features whereby non-computer-oriented people can use it in an interactive mode.

☐ It is usually aimed at semistructured and unstructured tasks.

☐ It is designed to remain flexible and adaptable so that it can be modified to meet the specific decision-making style of the user.

A semistructured or unstructured task involves a decision process that is partly routine and partly judgmental. The routine part can be easily automated

but the judgmental part has to be developed by the manager. A DSS is developed by working mainly from the manager's perspective and accepting his/her implicit definition as to which components should be left to personal judgment. It provides a delicate balance between human judgment and automated procedures. It adopts a coherent strategy for going beyond the traditional use of computers in fairly structured situations while avoiding ineffectual efforts to automate inherently unstructured tasks. The DSS thus thrives best on semistructured tasks.

This leads us to the requirement that a DSS should be an adaptive system. It must adapt itself to changes of several kinds over three time horizons. Sprague and Carlson ([5], Chapter 1) comment as follows:

> In the short run, the system allows *search* for answers within a relatively narrow scope. In the intermediate time horizon, the system *learns* by modifying its capabilities and activities (the scope or domain changes). In the long run, the system *evolves* to accommodate much different behavior styles and capabilites.

1.6 TECHNICAL CAPABILITIES OF A DSS

We are now ready to attempt a formal definition of a decision support system. A DSS can be described as a computer-based information system that helps a manager make key decisions and thereby improves the effectiveness of the manager's problem-solving process. Like any other information system, a DSS consists of both hardware and software. However, a DSS always contains a feedback loop that helps the manager answer various "what if" questions. As a result, the DSS has to be implemented as an online interactive system where the user can easily begin and be guided by the system, preferably in a menu-driven manner. The DSS provides adequate HELP routines to enable its user to select his/her path. This is normally described by saying that the DSS should always have a user-friendly front end, since it is geared primarily toward users who are not very computer-oriented. A typical feedback loop in a DSS is depicted in Figure 1-2.

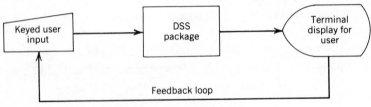

FIGURE 1-2 Feedback loop.

We can summarize a situation in which DSS can be useful as involving some or all of the following characteristics:

☐ Existence of a large database, so large that the manager has difficulty accessing and making conceptual use of it.
☐ Necessity of manipulation or computation in the process of arriving at a solution.
☐ Existence of some time pressure for the final answer.
☐ Necessity of judgment to decide upon available alternatives by asking many "what if" questions.

The DSS requires a unique approach to systems analysis and design. The usual process of designing and implementing a system has to be interfaced with rapid and frequent user feedback to ensure that the DSS being built will ultimately address the decision-making needs of the managers.

The first state in DSS development is decision analysis, with the manager defining the key decision problems. The manager can best recognize, with the system designer's help, the particular aspects that can be improved and the components that have the most overall impact on the effectiveness of decision making. There are four levels of support available from a DSS ([3], Chapter 4):

1. Access to facts or information retrieval. For a manager to find relevant information in a mountain of raw data can be a nontrivial job.
2. Addition of filters and pattern-recognition ability. The manager can selectively ask for information and give conceptual meaning to data.
3. Ability to perform simple computations, comparions, and projections.
4. Development of useful models for the manager. The model must be so designed as to provide the managers with answers they can and will act on.

The design and implementation of a DSS require sophisticated mathematical modeling techniques (e.g., linear programming and statistical forecasting), simulation methods, and high-powered computer support. Recent improvements in technology have made possible the implementation of such systems. In the past, traditional mathematical models and MIS were generally not allowed such interaction because of (1) the existence of a substantial gap between managers and MIS specialists, (2) the high degree of specialization of the computer world, and (3) the nature of decision making being not amenable to computerization.

1.7 OPERATIONAL SCENARIO FOR A DSS

Let us consider a hypothetical session involving a DSS. Suppose that you, as the director of personnel in your organization, have been asked by the president of the company to prepare a projection of staffing needs for the next 5 years. The company has a well-developed DSS supported by a sophisticated DBMS which provides a query language and graphics capability. We can visualize the DSS in operation as follows:

1. You begin as an authorized user via a CRT terminal with graphics capability.

2. The DSS displays a menu listing a set of options from which you must select one. You can also call for a HELP file or you can EXIT, if you so desire.

3. You select the option STAFFING NEEDS.

4. The DSS provides a series of prompts by which it collects data from you in order to perform the projection. Thus, you communicate to the system the time frame (i.e., 5 years), the frequency of projection (i.e., projection on an annual basis), the different job classifications, salary levels, and so on.

5. The DSS searches the personnel database to gather historical data on staffing. It then feeds these data to a statistical projection module to determine the annual staffing needs for the next 5 years. Finally it displays these data at your terminal in a report format.

6. If you are satisfied with this simple ad hoc report, you may want to get a printed hard copy of it. Otherwise, you may want to experiment with the projected data by changing your input. Herein is the typical "what if" capability of a DSS.

7. At the end you may even get a graphics display of the projected data and also be able to obtain a hard copy of the graph.

Figure 1-3 illustrates this situation graphically.

This scenario, though simple enough, embodies the essential features of a DSS session. In order to make this session possible, the designers of the DSS have used a set of sophisticated quantitative tools. We next formulate a list of such tools with a brief description and justification of each.

1.8 TOOLS FOR BUILDING A DSS

Conceptually a DSS consists of four modules:

1. Control
2. Data storage

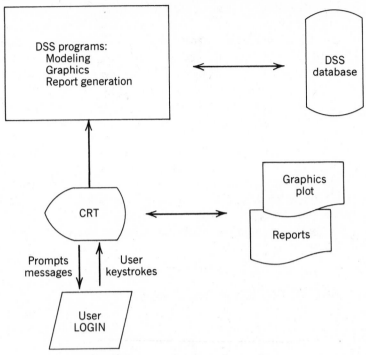

FIGURE 1-3 A DSS interactive session.

3. Data manipulation
4. Model-building

The *control module* (CM), also known as the DSS front end, is usually menu-driven and interfaces with the other three modules. It provides prompts and messages to guide the user in formulating the problem and generating the response. It accepts user keystrokes and interprets them as specific action-initiating commands. The CM has to be user-friendly in the sense that it can help a non-computer-oriented user utilize the DSS. The prompts and messages should be written in plain English as far as practicable and should avoid computer jargon.

The *data storage module* (DSM) contains all the data required by the DSS. It is really the complete database for the organization. The DSM should preferably be structured as a relational database instead of a network model, because generation of reports is comparatively simple when the database uses a relational model. The DSS provides all the current data as well as historical data required by the model-building module.

The *data-manipulation module* (DMM) is responsible for retrieving data from the DSM and producing reports and/or graphs using these data. The

DMM is supported by a nonprocedural query language, a report-generating package, and a graphics package. Normally the DBMS which supports the DSM provides all these features. As a minimum, the graphics capability includes such business tools as bar graphs, pie charts, and plots.

The *model-building module* (MBM) contains all the quantitative model-building software. It utilizes optimizing modeling principles, statistical analysis, forecasting algorithms, decision analysis methods, and simulation principles. Usually the MBM is the most difficult component in a DSS to design, since the selection of appropriate algorithms from the vast repertoire of mathematical models is a nontrivial job. In addition, if a specific modeling algorithm does not lead to an explicit solution, then the user must take recourse to the simulation method.

Figure 1-4 is a schematic of the four component modules of a DSS.

Since the control module provides interfaces to all the other modules, it should be designed and implemented first. The success of a DSS depends to a large extent on the efficiency of its control module.

1.9 IMPACT OF DSS ON MANAGEMENT

A DSS is designed and implemented with managers as the end users. Its impact is on decisions in which there is sufficient structure for computer tools and analytical techniques to be useful but where the manager's judgment

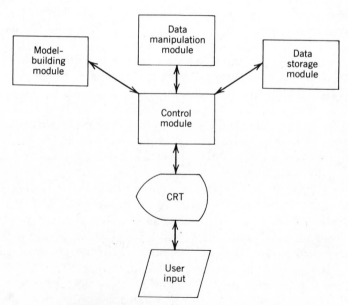

FIGURE 1-4 Component modules of a DSS.

is essential. The real payoff from the manager's viewpoint is in the degree to which the DSS extends the range and capability of his/her decision-making process to make it more effective. The manager sees the DSS as a supportive tool under his/her own control that does not attempt to automate the decision process, predefine objectives, or impose solutions. It accepts input from the manager, processes it, and then provides the output for review. If the output is not satisfactory, then the manager can repeat the process until the solution is satisfactory, as shown in Figure 1-2.

It must be clearly understood that no DSS can ever take the decision-making authority away from its users. Many managers, especially those who are not familiar with computer technology, have an inherent fear of the DSS. They fail to realize that it is just a tool to be used for making better and quicker decisions.

While managers play the role of end users of a DSS, analysts and designers get involved with the actual building of the system. These two groups are technical persons who usually belong to the middle management level in the company or are outside consultants from vendors of DSS. The analysts form a technical liaison between the managers and the designers. They must have some familiarity with the general problem area and must also be fairly comfortable with the information system technology components and capabilities. The designers are the really technical people who develop new analytical models, new databases to store data for easy access and retrieval, and appropriate prompts and display formats for user-friendly interaction with the DSS. In this task the designers use or even develop new hardware and software.

In order to get the flavor of a DSS, we shall discuss two examples: (1) SIMPLAN, a corporate planning model, and (2) CIS (Capacity Information System), a production planning model.

1.10 SIMPLAN: A CORPORATE PLANNING MODEL

Corporate planning models are one specific type of DSS that is widely used. They attempt to describe the complex interrelationships among a corporation's financial, marketing, and production activities in terms of a set of mathematical and logical relationships that have been programmed into a computer. Some of the reasons such models are becoming increasingly popular are:

☐ Risk and uncertainty in the business environment, especially in the financial area.
☐ Shortages of energy and basic raw materials.
☐ The leveling off of productivity.
☐ International competition.

☐ Tight money and inflation.
☐ Political upheavals.
☐ Environmental problems.
☐ New business opportunities.

The basic problem is that everything is related to everything else and therefore ad hoc plans which focus only on one functional area of the business are likely to be short-sighted and ineffective. Corporate planning models are thus an attractive and viable alternative to informal, ad hoc planning procedures.

SIMPLAN is one example of a corporate planning model. It is an integrated system that can be used by salespeople, marketing managers, production managers, and other administrative staff members to support the overall company goal of making profit forecasts and meeting them.

SIMPLAN was first introduced by Dr. Thomas H. Naylor in 1975 with the objective of helping corporate executives handle the uncertainty that is inherent in corporate planning. He attempted to describe the complex interrelationships among a corporation's financial, marketing, and production activities in terms of a set of mathematical and logical relationships that can be programmed into a computer.

SIMPLAN has three major types of components: financial models, marketing models, and production models.

The main purpose of the *financial models* is to show the effects of various assumptions on the company's financial position. This is normally accomplished by generating financial statements based on various trends and scenarios.

Marketing models are used to estimate the future size of the market and the possible share of the market the company can obtain. Uses of marketing models include:

☐ Analyzing the company's pricing policy and that of its primary competitors.
☐ Estimating the effect of a change in advertising expenditures.
☐ Evaluating the impact of a change in regional or national economic conditions.
☐ Determining the effect of a new product on the sales of existing products.

Production models are used to determine various cost and scheduling questions. They deal with

☐ Inventory policy
☐ Manpower requirements
☐ Raw material cost and availability
☐ Changes in plant and equipment capacity

SIMPLAN is a viable integrated system because it has the ability to link the various models together, allowing management to examine the overall impact of any action or circumstance that may require consideration during the planning process. As an example of this linking of functions, the sales forecasts from the marketing model may serve as initial production targets. The production model can then use this input to see if these targets can be met economically or whether the targets are too high or too low relative to current resources and capacity. The results of the models then serve as inputs to the financial model, which calculates the impact of the sales forecasts and production costs that were derived earlier and determine the final profit.

1.10.1 Technical Design and Capabilities of SIMPLAN

SIMPLAN incorporates seven basic functional areas needed by corporate planners:

1. Data management
2. Modeling
3. Report generation
4. Security control
5. Graphics displays
6. Forecasting
7. Econometric and statistical analysis

Data management involves the efficient storage and retrieval of large amounts of data in a form suitable for use in *any* aspect of the planning process. The SIMPLAN *modeling language* allows the user to express any type of financial, marketing, or production relationship in a form that can be understood by all types of users. In the *report-generation* area, results of SIMPLAN models can be printed in a form that exactly duplicates existing financial statements and management reports. This guarantees that the information generated can be easily understood by management members who may be totally unfamiliar with SIMPLAN. Also, since reports are generated independently of the modeling process, data may be taken from any source during the printing of a report. Forecasts, business plans, budgets, variance reports, and actual results can all be printed in the same format. The area of security, always a big concern, is dealt with in SIMPLAN by a multilevel *security control* system that limits access to data and information in varying degrees. Sensitive information can be stored along with data in the public domain with appropriate levels of security attached to each. SIMPLAN also has much to offer in the area of *graphics displays* that allow patterns and trends to be observed visually.

SIMPLAN's *forecasting* techniques range from simple linear time trends to adaptive forecasting with irregular patterns. Its *econometric and statistical*

techniques enable the user to identify any meaningful relationships that exist among the planning data. Finally, SIMPLAN allows the user to define new functions and to incorporate them directly into the system. In this way, the user is never "locked into" a system that is unable to fulfill new and different requirements.

SIMPLAN is organized in a "mode" structure, as can be seen from Figure 1-5. Conceptually, a mode is related to one or more of the functional areas discussed above. A mode provides the facilities required to accomplish individual steps that are logical and convenient for the user. The first mode entered by the user is the *control mode*. At this point certain start-up activities occur, and from this mode any other mode can be accessed. When activity is completed in any of the other modes, the user automatically returns to the control mode. The *data mode* includes the data management features to facilitate the collection and structuring of information. In the data mode, data are stored in the form of numeric values in logical groupings, that is, records. The *analysis mode* encompasses econometric and statistical analysis, forecasting, and the full SIMPLAN modeling language. The econometric and statistical techniques include least squares regression augmented by statistical and error analysis facilities. Forecasting includes time trends, exponential smoothing, and adaptive forecasting to provide estimates of future values. The modeling language allows simple recursive models as well as models that include linear or nonlinear simultaneous relationships.

The *report mode* is self-explanatory; it involves the formulating and printing of reports. The *edit mode* is designed to further simplify the creation and use of models and reports. The editor works with the text libraries in SIMPLAN, which contain such information as model specifications, report def-

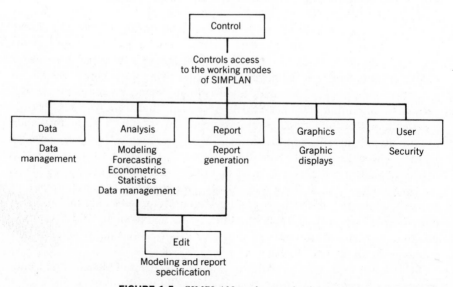

FIGURE 1-5 SIMPLAN mode organization.

initions, and graphics layouts. The *graphics mode* gives the user the ability to identify patterns in data used as the basis for forecasts, to examine the variance between actual data and forecasts or budgets, and to visually compare the results of models using different sets of assumptions. The graphics mode helps to increase comprehension of the information generated. Finally, the multilevel security controls discussed earlier are specified in the *user mode*.

All the information needed for SIMPLAN to function is stored in three permanent storage areas. These are the database itself, text libraries, and the user file. The database includes all numeric data as well as some additional information that describes the nature of the data (i.e., ''net sales'' or ''sales budget''). As mentioned before, the text library contains model specifications, report definitions, and graphics layouts. The user file contains the information to provide multilevel security control. This file is not normally noticed by the SIMPLAN user, as it is generally maintained by a key user in charge of system integrity and security.

1.10.2   Forecasting Techniques in SIMPLAN

SIMPLAN provides a number of techniques that can be used to develop forecasting and econometric equations. There are two primary types of forecasting methods: time trends and exponential techniques.

(a) Time Trends.   A time trend is exemplified by a smooth curve passing through existing data and extending into subsequent time periods to calculate future values for the series. There are three types of time trends that SIMPLAN can work with: linear, semilogarithmic, and quadratic. A *linear trend* is used when historical data increase or decrease by a nearly constant amount in each time period, a *semilogarithmic trend* is used when prior data change at a nearly constant rate, and a *quadratic trend* is used when prior data change at a changing rate. The primary result of each forecasting technique is an equation that can be used to forecast future values for the series.

In order for a forecast to be accepted, it should fulfill two important criteria. (1) The forecast must be accurate; that is, the forecast values must strongly resemble the corresponding historical values. (2) The forecast must be statistically valid, which means that the test statistics generated by SIMPLAN must show that the right type of forecasting method was used. Two methods are used to assess the accuracy of a forecast: a comparison of forecast values to historical data, and the R-squared test. The SIMPLAN validate command allows the user to compare actual to forecasted data.

To test whether the forecast is statistically valid, the user must see if certain test statistics fall within prescribed ranges. The three statistics used to determine validity are the F statistic, the t statistic, and the Durbin–Watson statistic.

The F statistic measures the predictive ability of the estimated equation. The larger the F value, the greater the predictive ability; and the general

rule of thumb is that a value over 4.0 shows that the equation is valid. The t statistic is calculated for each term on the right-hand side of a forecasting equation, including the constant term, and measures the contribution of each individual term to the overall forecast. Values of the t statistic (t values) may be either positive or negative, but the sign should be ignored. A t value greater than 2.0 (or less than -2.0) indicates that the associated term makes a significant contribution to the forecast, and absolute values between 1.0 and 2.0 indicate that the term may be significant. The final statistic to determine validity of the forecasting equation is the Durbin–Watson (D-W) statistic. This statistic has to do with the fact that the forecast errors (i.e., differences between the forecast values and the historical values for the same period) should be randomly distributed. The D-W statistic ranges from 0 to 4.0, with the middle values of 1.2–2.8 indicating that the forecast errors are approximately random and that the forecasting method used is statistically valid.

(b) Exponential Techniques. The second type of forecasting methods in SIMPLAN comprise the exponential techniques, which can be further classified as adaptive forecasting and triple exponential smoothing. The *adaptive forecasting* technique begins by passing a smooth curve through the historical data. The estimated equation is then adjusted by examining the forecast errors over time, with more recent errors receiving additional weight. There are 10 types of adaptive forecasting available in SIMPLAN. The user can select the appropriate pattern out of these options and also specify the relative weight to be given to more recent data by using a fast, normal, or slow option. The fast option is used for extremely irregular time series, while the slow option is appropriate whenever the historical data are very consistent. In employing *triple exponential smoothing,* the user assigns a weighting factor by specifying a smoothing constant.

1.10.3   Econometric Techniques in SIMPLAN

In addition to these forecasting methods, SIMPLAN offers econometric techniques that allow a user to develop equations that reflect cause-and-effect relationships. This is done by expressing the value of a variable in terms of the values of other variables. The first step in econometric analysis is the selection of the independent variables that will be used to explain the behavior of the dependent variable. This is done by examination of the correlation coefficients between the dependent and independent variables. The CORRELATE command prints out the correlation coefficient matrix along with the data for the variables involved in the correlation. Two advanced regression techniques provided by SIMPLAN allow a user to compensate for autocorrelation in the residuals and to estimate the coefficients of an equation using distributed lags.

Finally, SIMPLAN provides two commands that are used for statistical analysis. The MEAN command calculates a number of single-variable statistics such as the mean, median, and standard deviation. The ANOVA command is used to perform an analysis of variance among a number of time series. The analysis of variance determines whether a statistically significant difference exists among the means of two or more variables.

1.10.4 Creating and Solving Models in SIMPLAN

SIMPLAN allows the execution of recursive models as well as simultaneous models. With recursive models the value of each right-hand-side variable in an equation comes either from the database or from a previously executed assignment statement. On the other hand, simultaneous models require that the statements be processed all at once rather than in top-to-bottom order. As an example, the following is a simultaneous model:

$$10 \quad B = A + C$$
$$20 \quad C = B/A$$

This model cannot be solved recursively, because in line 10 the value of B cannot be calculated since the value of C is not yet known.

To give an idea of the modeling capability of SIMPLAN, a recursive financial assets model will be presented. Table 1-2 shows the data records that the model will need in order to produce a current assets portion of a comparative statement of financial position. The model itself is seen in Figure 1-6. The first two statements, lines 3 and 5, are called policy equations, because their contents represent a policy decision by management. Policy equations are always placed at the top of a SIMPLAN model so that they are easy to locate and modify. Lines 10–20 are examples of constants in the model, and line 30 is a basic assignment statement. Figure 1-7 is the output generated by running the model for a 4-year time span, 1977 to 1980. The top of the report lists all the policy assumptions of the model and their values for each year the simulation was run. It is important to identify the assumptions made, as the model can be run again and again using different sets of assumptions. The next portion of the report shows the results of the simulation model for the current asset variables under study.

The feedback control loop inherent in the model can now be understood. Let us refer to Figure 1-6, which represents the financial assets model. Equations (3) and (5) are policy equations and are input by management. By altering them, the "what if" scenario can be generated. Lines 10, 15, 20, and 80 are constants. Other lines are program statements, such as assignments and decisions, Figure 1-7 is a sample output. It can be changed by reinputting the policy assumptions. Thus, the model provides the user with feedback control capability. This feature makes SIMPLAN especially suitable for corporate planning.

TABLE 1-2 Records for the Financial Assets Model

Name	Abbreviation	Units
Accounts Payable	AP	$000
Accounts Receivable (Net)	AR	$000
Cash	CASH	$000
Cost of Goods Sold	COGS	$000
Accounts Receivable Collected	COLLECTION	$000
Total Current Assets	CURASSETS	$000
Dollar Value of Sales	DOLLARSALE	$000
Fixed Costs	FIXEDCOST	$000
Sales Growth Rate	GROWTHRATE	%
Cost of Labor	LABOR	$/unit
Raw Material Cost	MATCOST	$/unit
Raw Material Inventory	MATERIALS	000-lbs.
Current Value of Inventory	MATVALUE	$000
Reduction of Accounts Payable	PAYMENTS	$000
Selling Price	PRICE	$/unit
Production Volume	PRODUCTION	000-units
Additions to Inventory	PURCHASES	000-lbs.
Inventory Reorder Point	REORDER	000-lbs.
Sales	SALES	000-units
Production Cost per Unit	UNITCOST	$/unit
Variable costs	VARCOST	$000
Production Payroll	WAGES	$000

1.11 CIS: A PRODUCTION PLANNING MODEL

A production planning model is appropriate in a manufacturing environment. Its primary focus is on profits, and its output has to interface with the sales department, R & D operations, production engineers, and plant managers. An example of a DSS handling production is given by The Capacity Information System (CIS).

CIS is an interactive graphics DSS used by Ztrux, a major manufacturer of trucks, to assess the impact of changes in product plans on the company's overall manufacturing operations. Keen and Scott Morton have given a comprehensive discussion of CIS in their book [3]. The present treatment is adapted from their description.

The major decision supported by CIS is the creation and modification of the 1-year plan for design specifications of the key investment items in a truck: engine type, type of transmission axle size, and so on. It identifies any major bottlenecks that can arise from changes in an existing production

```
  3    GROWTHRATE = 7
  5    PRICE = 1.2
 10    MATCOST = .6
 15    REORDER = 3000
 20    LABOR = .285
 30    UNITCOST = LABOR + MATCOST
 40    PRODUCTION = SALES(-1)
 50    MATERIALS = MATERIALS(-1) - PRODUCTION
 60    WAGES = LABOR * PRODUCTION
 70    SALES = SALES(-1) * (1+GROWTHRATE/100)
 80    FIXEDCOST = 50
 90    VARCOST = UNITCOST * SALES
100    COGS = FIXEDCOST + VARCOST
110    DOLLARSALE = SALES * PRICE
120    IF MATERIALS   REORDER
130       PURCHASES = REORDER + 2 * PRODUCTION - MATERIALS
140       MATERIALS = MATERIALS + PURCHASES
145    ELSE
146       PURCHASES = 0
150    END
160    COLLECTION = 3/4 * AR(-1)
170    AR = AR(-1) - COLLECTION + DOLLARSALE
180    PAYMENTS = .6 * AP(-1)
190    AP = AP(-1) - PAYMENTS + (PURCHASES * MATCOST)
200    CASH = CASH(-1) + COLLECTION - PAYMENTS - WAGES
210    MATVALUE = MATERIALS * MATCOST
220    CURASSETS = CASH + AR + MATVALUE
```

FIGURE 1-6   Financial assets model.

schedule. For example, if, due to market fluctuations, it becomes necessary to change the production level of one item—say, the transmission system— then CIS can be used to identify the various ripple effects on the overall production plan of the company.

In a real-world environment, production planning interfaces with sales forecasting. The latter determines the total component product demand. Using a linear programming model it is then possible to allocate production volumes to individual plants. However, if the actual sales differ significantly from the forecast, then the production allocations must also be changed. The complexity and detail involved in generating modifications of production plans too often make it impossible to test the impact of changes in profit estimates. CIS, as used by Ztrux, was partly intended to speed up the process of analysis and thus to allow the planners to examine various "what if" scenarios.

POLICY ASSUMPTIONS

	1977	1978	1979	1980	AVERAGE
SALES GROWTH RATE (%)	7.00	7.00	7.00	7.00	7.00
SELLING PRICE ($/UNIT)	1.20	1.20	1.20	1.20	1.20
RAW MATERIAL PRICE ($/UNIT)	0.60	0.60	0.60	0.60	0.60
COST OF LABOR ($/UNIT)	0.28	0.28	0.28	0.28	0.28
INVENTORY REORDER POINT(000-LBS.)	3,000	3,000	3,000	3,000	3,000

RESULTS (ALL IN $000 UNLESS OTHERWISE NOTED)

	1977	1978	1979	1980	% GROWTH
CASH	1,432	1,997	1,860	2,346	17.88
ACCOUNTS RECEIVABLE (NET)	1,527	1,481	1,546	1,645	2.61
CURRENT VALUE OF INVENTORY	1,920	2,827	2,278	2,976	15.73
TOTAL CURRENT ASSETS	4,879	6,306	5,684	6,967	12.61
SALES (000-UNITS)	856	916	980	1,049	7.00
VARIABLE COSTS	758	811	367	928	7.00
FIXED COSTS	50	50	50	50	
COST OF GOODS SOLD	808	861	917	978	6.59
DOLLAR VALUE OF SALES	1,027	1,099	1,176	1,258	7.00
ACCOUNTS RECEIVABLE COLLECTED	(1,500)	(1,145)	(1,111)	(1,160)	(8.22)
ACCOUNTS RECEIVABLE (NET)	1,527	1,481	1,546	1,645	2.51
REDUCTION OF ACCOUNTS PAYABLE	840	336	987	395	(22.25)
ACCOUNTS PAYABLE	560	1,645	658	1,550	40.39
PRODUCTION PAYROLL	228	244	261	279	7.01
PRODUCTION COST PER UNIT($/UNIT)	0.885	0.885	0.885	0.885	
PRODUCTION VOLUME(000-UNITS)	(800)	(856)	(916)	(980)	7.00
ADDITIONS TO INVENTORY(000-LBS.)		2,368		2.144	
RAW MATERIAL INVENTORY(000-LBS)	3,200	4,712	3,796	4,960	15.78

FIGURE 1-7   Output of financial assets model.

1.11.1   An Example of a CIS Session

An interactive session using CIS requires a CRT terminal with the screen divided into three sections:

Work section.   This is the main area of the screen containing data and results from analysis.

System Commands.   These are the commands available for use.

Menu Selection.   This shows the various analysis options available to the user.

A light pen is used to select system commands or menu options.

Let us assume that a user wants to accomplish the following in a CIS session:

1. Get forecasts for light trucks.
2. Revise the forecasts.
3. Perform a capacity analysis on the basis of revised forecasts.
4. Obtain a summary of bottlenecks.
5. Save the proceedings of the session.

The user then proceeds as follows:

1. Select FORECASTS option from the menu, and specify light trucks as the line item.

2. Input new value for forecasts and use PROCEED as system command. This updates the previous forecasts to include the changes provided by the user.

3. Select an appropriate menu option to perform the capacity analysis by using the revised demand schedule. At this stage CIS uses a linear programming algorithm to determine the truck lines and products affected by bottlenecks and lists total demand and total capacity for each line item.

4. Display a summary of these bottlenecks by using the system command REDISPLAY.

5. Save the result of the session by using the system command HOLD and assigning a unique name to the revised demand allocation plan.

1.11.2 Technical Design of CIS

CIS has been designed in terms of the software interface between the user and the system. Keeping in mind the human engineering issues, the system design of CIS emphasizes a short response time. The allocation of component product demands to the manufacturing plants is computed by a linear programming algorithm that minimizes overtime and excess capacity utilization. The system uses the component product demand implied by sales forecasts and product plan as its set of constraints. It ensures that the cost is minimized by such allocations.

The linear programming model has two major limitations:

1. It ignores transportation costs so that demand may be badly misallocated.

2. When the demand for a line item exceeds its current supply, the model determines the impact on production of adding an extra assembly line by providing the added supply volume, which is computed as demand minus current supply. But it does not provide the cost of the additional plant equipment required to implement it.

In spite of these limitations, the linear programming model provides a believable allocation of demand, which in turn realistically identifies the major bottlenecks, which can then be examined in more detail.

1.11.3 Implementation of CIS

Nearly two full years were needed to design and implement the CIS. The entire package was written in FORTRAN. About 40,000 lines of code were used. The development and implementation involved a good deal of user interaction. This partially accounted for its success. As Keen and Scott Morton put it:

> The system has, on the whole, been a success. There are fewer infeasible plans accepted, and, in addition, the planners have been able to pinpoint bottlenecks much earlier in their analyses. There are virtually no complaints about the quality of the system; to a large extent, the planners take for granted its reliability and ease of use. Ztrux remains fully committed to CIS; no major design modifications have been proposed, and the general expectation is that the system will be used more and more as the product planners come to accept it as a tool of their trade.

1.12 ANALYTICAL TOOLS OF DSS

The two foregoing case studies (SIMPLAN and CIS) involved a number of analytical tools in the process of design and implementation of DSS:

☐ Linear programming and other optimizing models
☐ Statistical forecasting
☐ Econometric and statistical analysis
☐ Simulation in a discrete event system
☐ Computer-based system analysis
☐ Database systems
☐ Graphics capability
☐ Report generation—both interactive and batch

Such tools and techniques are needed for the design and implementation of any effective DSS. These techniques can be classified into three broad categories:

1. Mathematical modeling
2. Simulation using computer systems
3. Systems analysis and design

Items in categories 1 and 2 involve fairly sophisticated mathematical processes, which make the design and implementation of a DSS a more difficult

procedure than that of typical business application system such as customer invoicing, payroll, inventory management, or order processing. The rest of this volume will be devoted to an in-depth discussion of modeling and simulation principles, concluding with several examples of decision support systems and a look into the future. The topic of systems analysis and design requires a separate book for a comprehensive discussion. Knowledge of systems analysis and design is a prerequisite for the design of a DSS. However, since several excellent texts on systems analysis and design are currently available, this topic will not be discussed in this book.

1.13 OUTLINE OF THE BOOK

The book comprises 15 chapters grouped into four parts.

Part I, Introduction, consists of Chapters 1 and 2. Chapter 1 has set the stage by introducing DSS. Chapter 2 discusses the detailed step-by-step process of the analysis and design of a DSS.

Part II, Modeling Techniques, consists of Chapters 3–5. Chapter 3 provides a background for model building. Chapter 4 treats the various linear and nonlinear optimizing models using both deterministic and probabilistic methods. Chapter 5 deals with statistical models such as linear and nonlinear projection, time series analysis and forecasting, and qualitative forecasting using the Delphi method.

Part III, Simulation Techniques, consists of Chapters 6–11. Chapters 6 and 7 discuss general simulation concepts with queueing theory as a framework for studying discrete system simulation. Chapters 8 and 9 are devoted to a discussion of discrete and continuous system simulations, respectively. Chapter 10 provides an overview of GPSS as an example of a discrete system simulation language. Chapter 11 treats DYNAMO II similarly, as an example of a continuous system simulation language.

Part IV, Examples and Contemporary Issues of Decision Support Systems, consists of Chapters 12–15. Chapter 12 discusses additional case studies in a manner similar to the treatment of SIMPLAN and CIS in Chapter 1. Chapter 13 explores some of the software packages that can be used as instructional materials to simulate a real-world DSS. Chapter 14 shows how a DSS can be built as a classroom project. Chapter 15 examines current and future issues involving DSS.

1.14 SUMMARY

Sections 1.1–1.9 discuss the broad areas of the decision-making role of managers and their interaction with information systems. Sections 1.10–1.12 present two case studies to illustrate the scope and contents of a DSS. Section 1.13 discusses an outline of the book.

The chapter begins by describing what a general system is and how that definition is modified to apply to an information system. Different types of computer-based systems (e.g., operating system, DBMS, application system) are described. The role of managers as the end users of a management information system (MIS) is emphasized. It is pointed out repeatedly that a computer information system cannot replace a manager nor can it strip him/her of the human decision-making authority. Next, the chapter discusses the evolutionary nature of the MIS in an organization and how it can benefit the managers at all three levels—top, middle, and bottom. The view of an MIS as a concept or a principle whereby all the existing application systems are integrated under the broad umbrella of MIS becomes predominant.

The DSS appears as a subsystem within the MIS. Its aim is to help managers address semistructured and unstructured tasks, because the structured tasks can easily be handled by the application subsystems. In order to meet its goal the DSS has to be designed and implemented as an interactive system with a user-friendly front end. The prompts and messages given by this front end should be in plain English as far as practicable and should avoid computer jargon, because the users of a DSS are not always computer-oriented. The most important requirement for a DSS is to enable its users to experiment with "what if" scenarios. A manager always likes to examine alternatives before coming to a decision, especially when the decision has far-reaching consequences.

After describing a hypothetical operational scenario illustrating the use of DSS in action, the chapter provides a list of technical requirements for a DSS. Conceptually a DSS consists of four components or modules:

☐ Control module
☐ Data storage module
☐ Data manipulation module
☐ Model building module.

Each of these has been described briefly with respect to its function and justification.

The second half of the chapter gives an overview of two existing decision support systems: SIMPLAN, a corporate planning model, and Capacity Information System (CIS), a production planning model.

As a corporate planning model, SIMPLAN describes the complex interrelationships among a corporation's finanical, marketing, and production activities in terms of a set of mathematical and logical relationships that can be programmed into a computer. The characteristics of the three types of component models are then described, followed by an overview of the technical capabilities of SIMPLAN, which include trend analysis, econometric tools, graphics displays, and report generation. By way of an example, a financial assets model shows how SIMPLAN can handle "what if" questions from its user.

As a production planning model, CIS is described as an interactive graphics DSS that is used to assess the impact of changes in production plans on the company's overall manufacturing operations. A description of a sample CIS session is given exemplifying the capability of handling "what if" questions. Some comments about the design and implementation of the CIS are then presented.

The chapter closes with a brief outline of the rest of the book.

1.15 KEY WORDS

The following key words have been used in this chapter:

Capacity Information System (CIS)
corporate planning model
decision making authority
Decision Support System (DSS)
Management Information System (MIS)
model building
operational level of management
query language

semistructured task
SIMPLAN
simulation
strategic level of management
tactical level of management
time trend
unstructured task
user-friendly front end
"what if" questions/scenario

REFERENCES

1. M.J. Alexander *Information Systems Analysis,* SRA, Chicago, IL, 1974

2. J.B. Boulden, *Computer-Assisted Planning Systems,* McGraw-Hill, New York, 1975.

3. P. Keen and M. Scott Morton, *Decision Support Systems: An Organizational Perspective,* Addison-Wesley, Reading, MA, 1978.

4. T. Naylor, ed., *Simulation Models in Corporate Planning,* Praeger, New York, NY, 1979.

5. R.H. Sprague and E.D. Carlson, *Building Effective Decision Support Systems*, Prentice-Hall, Englewood Cliffs, NJ, 1982.

6. R.J. Thierauf, *Decision Support Systems for Effective Planning and Control*, Prentice-Hall, Englewood Cliffs, NJ, 1982.

7. J.C. Wetherbe, *Systems Analysis for Computer-Based Information Systems,* West Publishing, St. Paul, MN, 1979.

REVIEW QUESTIONS

1. Define a system. Take any social system (e.g., a health care delivery system) and identify the elements comprising the system, their interrelationships, and the goal of the system.

2. Describe how an operating system is different from a payroll system. Are there any similarities between them?

3. Explain the evolutionary process involved in the development of an MIS in an organization.

4. Take a particular organization, say, the company where you work. Identify the kinds of problems that are handled by the three levels of management and indicate their time spans. Your answer should be specific to the company you choose.

5. Distinguish between a structured, a semistructured, and an unstructured task. Why is a DSS more effective for the latter two types?

6. Explain the statement: "The structured tasks can be handled by the application subsystems of the MIS and do not need a DSS."

7. List the technical capabilities of a DSS.

8. Why do you need mathematical modeling and simulation for building a DSS?

9. Identify the four modules of a DSS and describe the function of each.

10. Do you think that a DSS can take some decision-making authority away from the managers using it? Explain your answer fully.

11. What are the three component models in SIMPLAN? Discuss how they interact.

12. Describe the two forecasting techniques used in SIMPLAN.

13. Refer to Figure 1-6. List the two policy equations from the model. Next list four constant equations. How do you interpret the program statements 60, 50, 90, and 100?

14. How does a CIS user utilize the menu selection feature in order to accomplish his/her objective?

15. What are the two major limitations of the linear programming model in CIS?

16. How do you measure the success or failure of a DSS? (The answer is *not* in the book!)

FORMULATIONAL PROBLEM

Rig Me Insurance Incorporated (RMII) is a unique Boston-based insurance company that was established 30 years ago to provide mandatory health and optional life insurance coverage to its small and selected clientele. RMII processes all claims from the claims processing system, which is completely automated and runs partially online.

RMII management wants to explore the possibility of building a DSS module to augment the existing automated system. This module should provide an interactive capability to the user whereby he/she can determine a

course of action to pursue in case of a sudden future increase in the volume of clientele. The course of action is limited to the following items:

☐ Enhancement of the computer system (more auxiliary storage, faster CPU, etc.)
☐ Increase in personnel (additional claim processors, programmers, data entry operators, etc.)

Now address the request for building a DSS module by performing the following tasks:

a. Prepare a step-by-step plan specifying the data collection, data processing, and data output functions.
b. Design a screen format showing a sample interactive session. Attach a narrative to describe the session.

2

Analysis and Design of a DSS

2.1 SYSTEM LIFE CYCLE

The development process of any application system undergoes five phases:

1. Problem definition and feasibility.
2. Systems analysis.
3. Preliminary system design.
4. Detailed system design.
5. Implementation, maintenance, and evaluation.

Since the development of a DSS follows the same life cycle, we shall discuss each of the five phases briefly and then relate each of them to the building of DSS.

2.2 PROBLEM DEFINITION AND FEASIBILITY

The origin of any systems study can always be traced to the existence of a problem. Often the user encounters difficulties and asks for help. At other times, a problem may have existed for quite some time before it was identified by management as an area of poor performance in the organization. As a result, a systems study is undertaken. In any case, a systems team is assigned the task of looking into the problem area and coming up with a proposed plan of action.

The first step in the problem-definition phase is to gather facts by reviewing existing documents, manuals, reports, and so on and by interviewing knowledgeable people in the organization. Subsequently, the systems team prepares a written statement describing the scope and objectives of the study and some preliminary ideas about the solution. Once management basically accepts the statement, the systems team examines the feasibility issues.

In general, three types of feasibility are considered:

1. *Economic feasibility* is usually the most stringent restriction imposed on the study, because the company cannot allocate an unlimited amount of funds to the project. The maximum available funds usually restrict the scope of the system.

2. *Technical feasibility* deals with the issue of whether the necessary technology exists to solve the problem. With today's computer technology, almost any business or scientific application system of everyday life can be technically implemented. In this sense, technical feasibility is subservient to economic feasibility.

3. *Operational feasibility* is related to the question of whether the proposed system can be implemented in the present organization. The systems team proposes modifications to be made to the existing operations if it feels that operational feasibility is lacking.

As indicated above, economic feasibility normally poses the most severe constraints.

At the end of this first phase, the systems team submits a report to the user for review. If the user agrees with the recommendations, then the systems team proceeds to the next phase, systems analysis. The user may suggest some changes, in which case the systems team will submit a revised report on problem definition and feasibility. This phase is usually short-term, and its main purpose is to enable the user and the systems team to come to an agreement regarding the scope and objectives of the proposed system. This helps to avoid future misunderstandings and consequent failure of the project.

2.3 SYSTEMS ANALYSIS

The systems analysis phase is an extension of the problem-definition phase. It involves a further in-depth study of *what* capabilities are required in the system. In order to ascertain these capabilities, the systems team interviews more people at the company to learn more about the existing system and to identify its deficiencies and bottlenecks. The team then designs a conceptual or logical system, taking a structured top-down approach. Thus, during the analysis stage the systems team works with the user to develop a logical model of the system.

The systems team examines the overall objectives of the system, then

breaks it into subsystems, and finally defines the interfaces between the subsystems. The interfaces are really the links between the component subsystems of the system. The graphics tool used during this process is the data flow diagram ([1], pp. 281–292), usually called the DFD. It describes the proposed logical system in terms of its component processes, data flows, and data stores. The DFD shows how data are captured at the point of entry into the system, how they are transformed under various processes such as EDIT, UPDATE, or GENERATE REPORT, and how, finally, the transformed data are distributed via reports.

Both the problem-definition and systems analysis phases deal with the "what" issues: what specific capabilities the system must have in order to meet the user's requirements. The difference between these two phases is one of degree only, not of kind. The outcome of the analysis phase is a logical model of the proposed system that consists of several data flow diagrams; an elementary data dictionary describing the component data flows, data stores and processes, and a brief cost/benefit analysis for the system.

As a result of phases 1 and 2 we have an in-depth understanding of the requirements of the proposed system. The end product is a report describing the following:

☐ Problems, deficiencies, and bottlenecks of the present system.
☐ Objectives of the proposed system.
☐ Description of the proposed system (only *what* functions will be achieved, not *how* to achieve them).
☐ List of subsystems.
☐ List of interfaces among the subsystems.
☐ Multilevel DFDs showing:
    Processes.
    Data flows.
    Data stores.
☐ Data dictionary providing entries for *all* processes, data flows, and data stores.
☐ Feasibility issues.
☐ Cost/benefit analysis.
☐ Alternatives and recommendations.

2.4 PRELIMINARY SYSTEM DESIGN

After the analysis phase, the systems team knows what capabilities are needed. The next step is to determine, in broad outline form, *how* to achieve the proposed system capabilities. We are therefore moving from the logical system to the physical system.

Any computer system consists of three components: input, processing,

and output. The users normally provide the necessary details of the output, because that is their concern. The systems team, in collaboration with the users, determines the input. The most important part of the design process, however, is to provide the link between the input and the output. This link may be regarded as a "black box" that is explored during the design phase. This black box constitutes the processing component of the system, as illustrated in Figure 2-1.

The design of processing starts with the conversion of each detailed data flow diagram into a system flowchart. One or more processes in the DFD are combined into a program, the data stores are changed into files, and it is determined whether the files are going to be sequential or random access. Appropriate data entry procedures are shown as inputs to the system. Reports produced by the system are shown as outputs in the system flowchart. Any screen displays are also indicated.

At the end of the preliminary design phase the systems team prepares a report consisting of the system flowcharts, input and output specifications, and screen formats. In addition, two or more alternative solutions are presented to show how the problem can be solved. Usually, three options are given to the user:

1. A low-cost solution that just does the job and accomplishes nothing more.
2. An intermediate-cost solution that solves the problem reasonably well and offers some extra features that are valuable to the user.
3. A high-cost system incorporating everything that the user may think of.

2.5 DETAILED DESIGN

The difference between this phase and the previous preliminary design phase is one of degree only. The situation is similar to the distinction between the first and second phases (see Section 2.3). A prerequisite for this phase is the identification by the user of one specific solution out of two or more submitted by the systems team. In the detailed design phase the team works with the solution selected by the user and prepares detailed design specifications

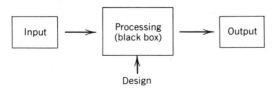

FIGURE 2-1 Overview of the design process.

showing how the system can be implemented. With these specifications, which are analogous to the engineer's blueprints for constructing a building, the programmers can write their programs and the team leader can prepare more precise cost estimates and an implementation schedule. Moreover, the user can conceptualize the proposed system in these specifications.

The detailed design specifications are normally split into two parts: system-level design specifications and program-level design specifications. The system-level design provides the following:

1. List of all data elements with format.
2. Record and file structure.
3. File organization—sequential, indexed sequential, or direct.
4. Schema structure, if a database is involved.
5. Space estimate for files.
6. Auxiliary storage estimate.
7. Design of data communication network and estimate of traffic volume, if applicable.

The program-level design provides the following:

1. Structure chart for each program.
2. Program flowcharts.
3. Input/output tables.
4. HIPO charts, as an alternative to the structure chart.
5. Pseudocodes for the programs, if deemed necessary.
6. Equipment or hardware specifications.
7. Personnel selection.

2.6 IMPLEMENTATION, MAINTENANCE, AND EVALUATION

Both detailed design and implementation deal with the "how" aspect of the system. But design shows only on paper and in concept how the proposed system will work, while implementation converts the "paper" system into an electronic system.Consequently, various issues related to the physical creation of the system are addressed during the implementation phase. All the programs are coded, tested, and debugged. New hardware is selected, ordered, and installed. Necessary operating procedures are prepared, and documentations are written. System conversion plans are made for changing from the old system to the new. The following is a checklist of the main issues addressed during this phase:

☐ Coding of programs using structured techniques.
☐ Testing and debugging of programs.

☐ Preparation of the physical site for hardware installation.
☐ User training sessions.
☐ Plan for system conversion: direct, partial, or parallel.
☐ Procedure for system backup and system recovery from a crash or natural disaster.
☐ Establishment of an audit trail.
☐ Preparation of software documentation and user manuals.
☐ Detailed implementation schedule.
☐ System handover plan.

Once the system is implemented, it requires ongoing maintenance. This is normally the responsibility of the computer operations staff rather than the systems team. If the systems team provides adequate documentation in the form of an operations manual and a programmer's manual, then the maintenance job becomes fairly straightforward. Minor modifications of the system can be made easily on an as-needed basis.

The system should be evaluated after it has been operational for some time, say, 6 months or more. During the evaluation, users of the system should be asked to comment on its usefulness. In case any deficiencies are noted, the users should be requested to suggest ways to improve the system. To assure anonymity of response, system evaluation questionnaires are sometimes circulated among the users. The operations staff can provide valuable insight into the system's operational status. If the use of the system is voluntary, then a high usage indicates that it is indeed worthwhile.

The five phases and their end products are summarized in Table 2-1.

2.7 SYSTEM LIFE CYCLE FOR A DSS

A DSS, being itself a system, undergoes the five phases of a typical system life cycle. However, the DSS is characterized by four distinctive features:

1. A DSS is always implemented for online interactive access and therefore requires a user-friendly front end.
2. A DSS accesses a vast amount of data and hence requires a database system for implementation.
3. A DSS relies heavily on model-building and simulation methods.
4. A DSS addresses "what if" questions that require sophisticated data manipulation via nonprocedural query languages.

These four special features are implemented by means of four component modules: the control module, the data storage module, the model-building module, and the data manipulation module, as discussed in Section 1.8. Consequently, the analysis, design, and implementation of a DSS are handled through the five activities listed in Table 2-2.

TABLE 2-1 End Products of System Development Phases

Phase	End Product
1. Problem definition and feasibility	Scope and objectives of the study
	Description of proposed system
	High-level data-flow diagram
	Feasibility issues
2. Systems analysis	Deficiencies of existing system
	Functional capabilities of the proposed system
	Detailed data-flow diagrams
	Data dictionary for processes, data flows, and data stores
	Cost/benefit analysis
3. Preliminary design	System flowcharts of proposed system
	Input and output of the proposed system
	Screen formats
	Alternative solutions and recommendations
4. Detailed design	Record and file structure
	Auxiliary storage estimate
	Schema design (if applicable)
	Data communication network and traffic volume (if applicable)
	Structure charts
	Program flowcharts or IPO charts
	Equipment specifications
	Personnel selection
	Detailed cost estimate
	Implementation plan
5. Implementation, maintenance, and evaluation	Structured coding
	Testing plan for programs
	User training
	System documentation manuals
	System backup, recovery, and audit trail procedures
	Maintenance procedures for computer operations staff
	Evaluation plan

We can see that the first two phases correspond to the problem definition and systems analysis, respectively, while the third and fourth phases together constitute the system design. The implementation consists of implementing the four modules mentioned above.

2.8 ENVIRONMENT FOR A DSS

There are a wide variety of environments in which a DSS can exist. Some possible examples follow.

Investment. A DSS handles portfolio management issues. Its objective is to provide maximal return on investments while maintaining liquidity of assets. It addresses the trade-off involved in selecting high-risk, high-return securities versus low-risk, low-return securities.

Manufacturing. A DSS handles the optimal allocation of available resources. A company wants to maximize its profits by manufacturing an optimal amount of products with limited amounts of labor, raw materials, equipment, and funds.

Marketing. A DSS helps the manager to decide on an optimal policy to maximize sales and maintain profits. The appropriate allocation of funds for advertising and sales promotion is determined by the DSS.

Customer Service. A DSS can be used to calculate the optimal number of employees for providing the required service to the customers. The un-

TABLE 2-2 Five Levels of Activity in Building a DSS

Activity	Issues Involved
1. Background and objectives	*Why* is the DSS needed? *Who* needs it? *When* is it needed?
2. Overall plan and outline	*What* capabilities are required? *What* are some typical scenarios?
3. Technical details of DSS design	*How* is the system designed? *What* modeling methods are used? *How* are the data collected, processed, and displayed and/or printed? *What* are typical reports?
4. Feedback control loop	*How* does the system handle "what if" questions?
5. Evaluations of DSS by management	*What* service does it provide the management? *What* additional capabilities, if any, are needed?

derlying principle used here is queueing theory. The DSS finds the optimal balance between the waiting cost for customers and the service cost for servers by minimizing the total cost, which is the sum of the two. A wide variety of problems belong to this category. Examples are: customers in line for a bank teller, students waiting for a computer terminal in a university computer center, and patients awaiting treatment in a hospital emergency room.

Planning and Administration. A DSS produces an optimal time schedule to meet deadlines with given limited resources. Various scheduling techniques using network methods (PERT, CPM, MOST, etc.) are used in these situations. The DSS identifies bottlenecks and critical task items, estimates the cost and completion times, and updates the plan as tasks are completed.

In order to design and implement a DSS in any of the above areas, the DSS team has to conduct a detailed analysis of the important and intricate decision-making process in the organization. It requires extensive sensitivity testing. Rarely, if ever, will a manager ask for a "single number" as the solution. Instead she/he will require a quantitative assessment of the various trade-offs to answer such questions as

What risks are associated with what actions?
What new policies are likely to yield more profits?
What new horizons should be explored?

A DSS should provide a recommended strategy rather than a single decision.

As with any systems study, the success of a DSS depends on the degree of user involvement. In addition, it depends on the economic and strategic stakes of the problem and the available data. Estimating how profitable or beneficial an application will be in an organization is central to the study of that application system. The same holds for a DSS. However, it must be pointed out that the initial phases of a DSS are often exploratory.

2.9 MANAGEMENT OF A DSS PROJECT

Project management is an essential part of the system life cycle. In managing a DSS the team leader must urge the decision-making managers to participate actively in the project's goal formulation, administration, and evaluation. Otherwise, there is a very high probability that the proposed DSS will not be sufficiently comprehensive and flexible to handle the managers' problems.

The following issues should be addressed throughout the planning, design, and implementation of a DSS project (adapted from Wagner [3], Chapter 22):

☐ Specific plans should be made to determine the broad and specific managerial decision-making areas.

☐ The model-building phase should be performed accurately, because if it is poorly done the outcome can be disastrous. This effort is directly related to the model-building module of the DSS.

☐ The data requirements should be determined early. Appropriate steps should be taken to organize the data-collection phase. This effort involves the data storage module.

☐ The decision-making areas must be properly coordinated with the modules to ensure smooth operation of the data manipulation module.

☐ Managers and operating personnel should be alert to any transitional difficulties that may arise during the testing and installation of the DSS. Any system conversion process is disruptive to some extent. The DSS implementation is no exception to this rule. Top management is likely to express dissatisfaction unless properly cautioned beforehand.

2.10   DOCUMENTATION OF DSS

The DSS design team should be careful in preparing documentation. At the conclusion of the project the team should provide the following documentations:

1. *User's Manual.*   This document describes for the user the procedures for using the system. In addition to showing the login, access, and logout processes, this manual should concentrate on the control module of the system, because the latter handles the user interface to the system. The manual should describe how the user can retrieve HELP files in case of necessity.

2. *Operational Manual.*   This document tells the computer operations staff how to run the DSS after it has been implemented. Consequently, the manual should contain a system flowchart identifying the component programs and the sequence in which they are executed. For each program, the manual should describe the input and output along with error conditions, messages, and operator responses. Ideally, the names of the programmers responsible for the different modules should also be included as resource persons to handle any major problems related to their modules.

3. *Design Documentation.*   This is the most comprehensive type of documentation for the DSS. It should state the scope and objectives of the DSS and provide a brief feasibility study and a hierarchical overview of the component modules. Next, it should describe in detail the scope and function of each module and the interfaces among these modules. The mathematical modeling used in the model-building module should be clearly explained, and all the algorithms should be included. The logical and physical views of the data used by the DSS should be adequately described, and their structure defined in the data storage module description. Adequate graphics (e.g., data flow diagram, system flowchart, and structure chart) should be used for system-level as well as program-level documentation.

The team leader of the DSS project has the responsibility of generating and maintaining adequate documentation for the project. He or she should adopt the principle that no software will be written and tested until a prior design of that software has been approved by the user. Once the software for an individual module has been successfully implemented, its documentation should be prepared. This procedure of continually updating the documentation should be handled by the technical writer or the program librarian assigned to the project. Various types of software packages are now available which can keep track of all the ongoing changes of the software being developed. Once it has been finalized, its most recent version can then be included in the software documentation. All the assumptions made in order to develop the module should be clearly stated along with a record of the input data and sources.

In a large-scale DSS project, assumptions made several months earlier are easily forgotten. Furthermore, as test results and new data are examined, the individual modules of the DSS are inevitably altered. Hence it is essential that the DSS team catalog each revision.

It is also desirable to keep a central program identifier library, especially since a DBMS package will be used in developing the DSS. The same data element should be known by the same identifier or variable name in all programs. This practice makes it much easier to debug and modify programs, especially if group programming is used.

2.11 USER TRAINING FOR DSS

The ultimate judge of the success or failure of any system is the user. The DSS is no exception to this rule. A good level of user interest and involvement results in a good public relation image for the DSS team. As a result, the managers become willing to allocate the time of their people for successful implementation of the project. In return, therefore, the DSS team must arrange for adequate user training. Well-informed users provide the greatest support to the project.

Most of the materials required for user training can be developed from the user's manual and the design documentation discussed in Section 2.10. If the DSS team includes one or more users, then these users should be involved primarily in writing the user-training materials. Normally user training should begin by looking at possible output of the system including the "what if" scenarios, because the users can best identify their own needs with this aspect of the DSS.

Having briefed the users on the output, the DSS team should discuss the input data and the files that are needed to produce the desired output. This is the main function of the data manipulation module of the DSS. Finally, the computer processing logic and other procedures that belong to the model-building module of the DSS should be discussed. Since most users are not

interested (and perhaps also not competent) in the technical details of the component mathematical models, reference to this area should be kept at a minimum in user training.

If the users are continuously involved in the DSS development process, then the subsequent training becomes relatively easy. Through their participation the users have reviewed all the relevant parts of the system and therefore are well prepared for training. If new problems arise during the training phase, then the DSS team should work with the users to solve them.

2.12   COST/BENEFIT ANALYSIS FOR DSS

A cost/benefit analysis forms an integral part of any systems study. As indicated in Section 2.2, the feasibility study examines the cost aspect in order to determine the economic feasibility of the system. The cost of a system is always balanced by the benefits it produces. There are two types of benefits that are considered:

Tangible Benefits.   These consist of all those benefits to which a dollar value can be assigned. For example, the salaries of employees who will not be needed after a system becomes operational will constitute a tangible benefit of the system.

Intangible Benefits.   These cannot be quantified to the extent that a dollar tag can be assigned. Improved public relations as a result of the new system can always be cited as an intangible benefit of the system. It is difficult, however, to weigh such a benefit against the cost incurred by the system.

Since the objective of a DSS is to provide a better decision-making environment for the managers, it is extremely difficult to justify its design and implementation costs by enumerating its tangible benefits. In most cases, the economic benefits of a DSS are not self-evident. To make matters more complicated, a reliable "before and after" comparison of a DSS project is very hard to perform. We can cite two reasons for this situation:

1. Appropriate data may not be available for past operations. Managers often cannot pinpoint the exact data they used to make their decisions before the DSS was implemented. Moreover, after the DSS has become operational, it may be difficult to identify the improvement in the decision-making process brought about by the DSS. The only way to overcome these difficulties is to let the DSS team design a controlled experiment that focuses on the impact to be evaluated.

2. Only in exceptional circumstances can the DSS team make a completely parallel comparison between two distinct environments: one pre-DSS and the other post-DSS. Further, since managers' decisions at one point in time may have a specific effect on business conditions later, it may be futile to attempt to show with great precision how anything short of an actually operational DSS behaves over an extended period of time.

As a result, it is hard to establish conclusively how much better the decision-making situation has become in the organization after the DSS has been implemented. Management has to understand that the DSS team cannot provide irrefutable evidence that improvements have indeed occurred as a result of the DSS project.

The only way that a DSS can establish its credibility is by anticipating what questions a manager may ask, what variations of those questions may exist, what data may yield answers, and how to manipulate those data to obtain accurate answers. The benefits of the DSS should be viewed from this standpoint. An open dialogue between the managers and the DSS team is essential to establishing the credibility of the DSS project.

2.13 TWO CASE STUDIES

We shall now discuss two case studies to illustrate the five-phase process of building a DSS (see Section 2.7). For each case study, we shall address the first two phases (i.e., background and objectives, and overall plan and outline) in this chapter. The technical design phases (phases 3 and 4, Section 2.7) will be discussed in later chapters after we have developed the necessary technical materials. Sections 2.9–2.12 have already addressed the issues involved with the implementation and management of a DSS project.

The two case studies to be discussed here are related to two different areas. One addresses investment and portfolio analysis and is called the Investment Decision Support System or IDSS. The other is related to the distribution of costs in automobile manufacturing and is called Distribution/Transportation Decision Support System or D/T DSS. Both projects were done by graduate students at Bentley College, Waltham, Massachusetts, under my supervision.

2.14 IDSS*

The Investment DSS is an interactive decision support system designed for financial managers. Its purpose is to help portfolio analysts select investments in corporate equities that will maximize return on investment while minimizing the risk of losses caused by declines in security values.

The system at its implementation stage is expected to be user-friendly, interactive, and powerful. It will not be designed for data processing professionals but rather for consultants who are skilled in financial analysis, stock trend theories, and/or statistical analysis. It will allow users to practice their skills in making projections of future price and yield trends by providing the necessary numerical and graphic displays, both video displays and/or hard

---

*The study was done by three of my students: Kathy Doucette, Joan McGonagle, and Randall Parr, all candidates for the M.S. degree in computer information systems.

copy. It will also allow the computer to calculate, project, and analyze future trends, providing feedback to the user.

2.14.1 Users of IDSS

The users of the IDSS are the investment managers of a large investment firm. The firm's clients vary in economic background. Their investment needs range from "safe" investments for long-range return to investing for high returns in a short period of time. The investment managers' information must be up to the minute to enable them to make the best investment decisions for the clients.

The manager's job involves keeping her/his clients informed about their current investments [future trends and return on investment (ROI)] as well as suggesting other investments that will meet the client's needs. This requires knowledge of how each investment will affect a portfolio's ROI, liquidity, and risk.

For a client with investments in many areas such as stocks, bonds, and precious metals, the manager must have a mass of information literally at his fingertips to be able to answer any questions the client may ask. Since market conditions fluctuate daily and even hourly, the task of keeping this information current is awesome. Yet, without the most current information the firm cannot operate.

2.14.2 Basic Capabilities of IDSS

The types of daily or even hourly changes that occur in an investment environment justify a DSS that can analyze vast amounts of data in a relatively short period of time. This necessitates an online system.

While the DSS can be used to clarify the complex array of daily changes in investment opportunities, it can also be used to track changes in a client's portfolio. Managers can then make new investments and/or liquidate investments to take advantage of sudden or unexpected shifts in the market. To support this function, the IDSS should forecast investments based on past performances and evaluate actual performance based on the projected forecasts. The DSS should also have capabilities to create hypothetical portfolios and then measure the actual performance against the forecast.

The rapid changes in the marketplace make it very difficult to predict with a high degree of accuracy which direction an investment will take. At the same time, the vast number of potential investments make rational analysis difficult. Traditionally the solution to this problem has been attempted through specialization. For example, one analyst may specialize in bank stocks and another may specialize in precious metals. Although a specialist may be highly competent in one area, he/she will not have a wealth of knowledge in all areas of the investment market.

The Dow Jones Industrial Average and the Index of Leading Economic

Indicators have been used as indices of the overall market. However, their applications are limited. An investment DSS can be used as a tool to overcome previous shortcomings through its abilities to examine large volumes of data, evaluate specific opportunities, and evaluate current portfolios in support of the investment manager's decision-making process.

2.14.3 System Cost as an Opportunity

It has been estimated that the initial investment for the proposed DSS will cost between 1 and 2 percent of the firm's annual revenues. The chief executive officer (CEO) feels that the cost of the system is fully justified by the ability of the DSS to provide more timely information essential for the firm's operation.

In addition, the investment managers view the implementation of a DSS as an asset offering great potential for supporting their daily activities, namely, making the necessary calculations for investment decisions and explaining their investment decisions to their clients.

2.14.4 Variables Affecting the Investment Market

Variables that can affect the investment market and must therefore be taken into consideration in order to design and implement the IDSS can be either quantitative or qualitative. The impact of the quantitative variables is easier to formulate, the incorporation of qualitative variables into the model-building module of IDSS poses a greater challenge.

We now provide a tentative list of variables of each of these types. During the technical design phase of IDSS we shall discuss in more detail the exact handling of these variables.

Quantitative Variables
Interest rates
Gross national product
Consumer prices
Prices of producer/wholesale goods
Industry trends
Money supply
Federal deficit/surplus
Individual security prices

Qualitative Variables
Mergers
Default on loans
International events

Tax laws

Government regulations

2.14.5 Overall Functionality of IDSS

To summarize, IDSS

- [ ] Hastens the retrieval of portfolio information of clients from files and records, thereby improving the investment counselor–client relationship.
- [ ] Improves decision making by more effectively accessing existing data and forecasting future price and yield trends.
- [ ] Allows managers to measure and compare security performance against the market averages and economic indicators.
- [ ] Tests out sensitivity of certain variables to highlight critical factors.
- [ ] Reduces unproductive communication by providing managers with concrete evidence in support of their decision-making process (i.e., graphs, tables, computed calculations).
- [ ] Once a model has been developed, it can be used in the future for continuous analysis.

2.14.6 Uses of IDSS in Daily Activities

The functional capabilities of IDSS are used on a daily operational basis as follows:

1. The security selection analysis has the capability to obtain information that can be valuable to the manager in making recommendations to the client. Some of the factors an investment manager may consider when analyzing securities are price trends, financial ratios, earnings per share, and price/earnings ratios. Values of these factors are made available to the manager through the screening function of the system. With this function the manager can list securities that meet specific user-defined criteria. An example is a list of the top 20 securities that have the highest earnings per share for the last 3 years.

2. The client portfolio module displays information concerning a client's investments. This information consists of ratios measuring the performance of each security (e.g., annual yield on investment) along with portfolio risk and return. A news function containing recent news that may be considered relevant to investment decision making is also available.

3. Investment timing analysis involves the use of mathematical methods for estimating future trends in stock and bond yields so that investment managers can more accurately predict security price movements.

4. The portfolio analysis module looks at investor's portfolios as a whole, giving managers a tool for creating hypothetical portfolios and comparing

them to actual market performance. Another capability of this module is to compare individual security performance with the market performance.

2.14.7 Operational Scenarios

Three scenarios follow to illustrate different situations where IDSS can be used. Assuming that IDSS is implemented as an online system with a menu-driven front end, each situation is described as a session where the user logs in and continues to work interactively via the terminal.

Scenario 1. The investment consultant is asked to review a client's portfolio to ensure that expected yields have kept up with a changing marketplace. The manager logs on to the system using an appropriate password and user ID #. A main menu appears, giving the manager a list of the system's general functions.

```
1)   SECURITY ANALYSIS
2)   INVESTMENT TIMING
3)   PORTFOLIO ANALYSIS
4)   MANAGER-CLIENT INFORMATION
•
•    (graph/table display follows)
•
>
```

The manager requests the manager-client information:

```
CLIENT'S NAME: > Collette Adae
PRIMARY KEY: > Current yield - ascending
SECONDARY KEY: > <CR>
INVESTMENT TYPE RESTRICTED TO > 1 (common stock)
```

The report containing information on the value, yield, purchase price, and date for the common stock owned by Collette Adae is displayed. The stocks are listed in ascending order of current yield.

At this point the manager is prompted with CLIENT'S NAME again. Hitting a carriage return ⟨CR⟩ will get the manager back into the main menu.

The manager is able at any time to key in a question mark (?) to receive instructions on how to use a particular function.

Scenario 2. The investment consultant is called by a client with questions about his investment. The consultant needs quick access to the client's portfolio with information regarding recent performance and comparison of the portfolio with the market, to answer his questions.

Again the main menu is displayed after the investment manager logs on to the system. Portfolio analysis is selected this time.

```
> PLOT PORTFOLIO FRONTIER
CLIENT'S NAME: > Lowin Octane
> PLOT FRONTIER
•
•
•       (graph/table display follows)
>
```

   The efficient frontier and the market line are plotted for the client's portfolio along with the frontier and market line of the market (estimated by Standard and Poor's 500).
Note that if previous to plotting the portfolio frontier a CHANGE command was used to change a client's portfolio, then the PLOT command would assume that the changed portfolio was to be plotted and CLIENT'S NAME would be supplied.

```
> CHANGE PORTFOLIO
CLIENT'S NAME: > Lowin Octane
SECURITY CODE: > <CR> (for all securities)
RISK > + 2%
RETURN > <CR> (no change)
> PLOT PORTFOLIO
CLIENT'S NAME: LOWIN OCTANE > <CR> (correct name)
•
•
•               (graph/table display)
>
```

Scenario 3.   The manager is considering investing a client's money in security XYZ. In recent weeks the security price has been falling. The manager is interested in finding out if this price trend is about to reverse.
   This time the manager selects security analysis from the main menu:

```
>BREADTH
SECURITY NAME: > XYZ
START DATE > 11/12/81
END DATE > <CR> (present date)
•
•
•       (graph/table display)
>
```

The manager can view the displayed graph of the breadth of market and note any indications of a price trend reversal.

   These three scenarios refer to a variety of modeling methods such as the

efficient frontier model, the market line for the portfolio, and price trend analysis. These will be discussed in detail in Chapters 4 and 5.

IDSS also requires a wide range of historical data in order to build the models. Examples of data that should be included in the data storage module of IDSS are

Company income statements
Balance sheets
Stock prices
Industry composite data
Economic data

2.15   D/T DSS†

D/T DSS stands for Distribution/Transportation Decision Support System. It is designed for use in the manufacturing area in the automobile industry. Its principal objective is to provide accurate feedback to the managers to enable them to evaluate the performance of the total distribution system.

2.15.1   Background and Objectives

The distribution of finished products to end customers is a fundamental concern of any manufacturing business. Distribution costs can include any money spent to deliver products from the manufacturer to the final consumer. These costs incurred can impact total company profits as much as manufacturing.

The objective of the D/T DSS is to provide accurate feedback to aid in evaluating the performance of the total distribution system. Performance can be evaluated by using three measurements:

1. Total costs, compared to a target cost level.
2. Market coverage and market share, that is, the extent to which market areas are being serviced and how effectively.
3. Cost minus charges to customer, or gross profit.

Depending on management philosophy, any of these could be used to evaluate performance against established management goals.

Controlling the distribution system is very important. A study revealed that U.S. industry spends 20% of the GNP on the physical distribution of goods from producer to final consumer.‡ The distribution system must be

---

† Like IDSS, D/T DSS was done by three of my students: David Janigan, Stephen Lindberg, and Richard Wenner, all of whom were candidates for the M.S. degree in computer information systems.

‡ National Council of Physical Distribution Management, Chicago, 1978.

reviewed in its entirety, since reducing costs in one area may result in higher costs in another area. Distribution costs include transportation, warehousing, and inventory carrying costs. Each of these has an element of internal (company-owned) or external (privately owned) alternatives. Further decisions must be made as to carrier, distribution routes, optimal lot size, mix of special-order models, warehousing locations, optimal inventory levels, and method of financing. In order to form an economical decision, all these areas must be integrated into a functional model.

The DSS must also remain valid as the environment changes. An established DSS can be affected by poor performance of carriers, new or closing dealerships, transportation rate changes, and reduced sales. New distribution lines may have to be established or existing lines modified to maintain an acceptable performance level.

Since the distribution of products impacts several areas of the organization, several functions can have input into controlling distribution costs. These areas of middle management would also benefit by information made available by the distribution model.

☐ Marketing needs information to determine the inventory levels necessary to avoid selling out or overstocking of inventories.

☐ Physical distribution/traffic requires information to analyze the efficiency of delivery routes and carrier performance.

☐ Accounting needs information to report to management and evaluate financing costs.

☐ Production needs information in order to forecast inventory levels and make appropriate production plans.

Information may be most useful when it is provided on the basis of a particular time period (i.e., monthly), since profitability may be erratic and thus be significantly measured only over a period of time. A quicker by-carload analysis may not be meaningful, since the distribution costs may be difficult to allocate over a single carload. The effect of changes to the system may not be recognized for some time; they may not be felt until the entire distribution cycle is complete (from plant to consumer). A longer time interval for normal reporting may be sufficient to evaluate the effectiveness of decisions.

Certain data such as warehousing costs and in-transit reports can be received daily. Therefore, the model should also be available on an as-needed basis to provide timely and relevant information.

In summary, since manufacturers are vitally concerned with distribution costs, it is necessary for them to have access to a flexible DSS model that can provide useful feedback and a measure of performance that can be used by middle management in various departments.

2.15.2 Overall Plan

In general, the D/T DSS will serve to provide information to middle managers throughout the particular company that will enhance the managers' ability to make decisions and to make them correctly. More specifically, the purpose of modeling is to provide a means to test the probable effects of various alternative courses of action proposed to improve current operations. Once the model is complete, Marketing, Physical Distribution/Traffic, Accounting, and Production will be submitting different scenarios to attempt to lower costs or improve performance. Modeling will allow each department to estimate the cost reduction or performance improvement without putting each alternative course into actual operation. Furthermore, because of the speed of the computer, millions of calculations can be performed accurately in a short period of time, enabling the modeler to deal with the vast number of alternatives within each scenario submitted to the model.

2.15.3 Operational Scenarios

The scenarios submitted to the model may originate in a single department or from several departments wishing to analyze a more complex situation. For example,

☐ Marketing may wish to know the effect of introducing or discontinuing a model line. In a depressed economy, where reduction in demand translates into dealer closings, the number of final distribution points in the model would be reduced.

☐ Production may wish to know the effect of changes in the number or location of plants. Also, temporary shutdowns would affect the results of the model. It would be very valuable to know beforehand what impact these shutdowns would have on the overall distribution system. Production might also wish to modify plant capacity or production mix to respond better to actual demand.

☐ Physical Distribution/Traffic might want to change the number of warehouses or the location or capacity of each warehouse. These changes would have a direct impact on the distribution model.

☐ Management might be negotiating a new contract with the transport unions, and need payroll information from Accounting. Thus Accounting becomes a potential user of the model.

☐ Finally, anticipated government regulations might greatly modify the results of the model within a given scenario.

A scenario may include only one of the above problems or may have a myriad of factors modified or introduced. Modeling is the only practical method to produce results based on such a complex environment. However,

each scenario will produce results that must be tempered with judgment, experience, trends in the industry, or economic arguments beyond the scope of the model. All relevant factors must be included when making recommendations or decisions based on the output of a scenario.

The D/T DSS will provide information to the marketing manager that will facilitate the determination of the proper amount of inventory levels to be maintained. The system will also provide the distribution/traffic manager with the information necessary to determine the most cost- and time-efficient delivery routes. Furthermore, it will provide the accounting manager with information that will allow tracking and monitoring of the costs incurred, thereby allowing Accounting to provide top management with management reports. And, finally, the system will provide the production manager with enough information to establish forecasts and production plans based on inventory levels.

2.15.4   Measurements for Performance Evaluation of D/T DSS

In order to determine whether or not the overall objective of the model— to provide accurate feedback for evaluating the performance of the total distribution system—is being accomplished, the model's performance can be evaluated by using the following three measurements as indicated:

1. Total costs can be measured to determine if they exceed a target cost level. The company can project an estimated target cost level for any particular distribution cost by using previously incurred costs to arrive at an average cost over a specified period of time, and then applying a reasonable escalation factor. By arriving at a target cost level for a particular distribution cost in this manner, the system will provide feedback to the middle manager that allows him/her to make any corrections deemed necessary to ensure that the target cost will not be exceeded.

2. A market share/coverage measurement can be provided to determine if all market areas are being serviced and serviced effectively. The company will determine which market areas are to be covered and what market share can be anticipated based on that coverage. The marketing manager can then use the system to determine whether or not the company has attained its market share objectives. If it has not, the system can be used as an aid in making decisions as to how the objectives can be accomplished.

3. A measurement providing a comparison of total distribution costs versus charges to the customer, or gross profit, can be made. Here, the accounting manager will use information derived from the model to convey information to top management in the form of various management reports.

In summary, the distribution/transportation decision support system will provide information to both upper and middle management in such a way

as to allow the various managers to make more appropriate decisions than might have been possible had they not had access to such a system.

2.16   SUMMARY

The chapter begins with an introduction to the concept of system life cycle. It describes briefly the five phases of a systems study: problem definition and feasibility; systems analysis; preliminary design; detailed design; and implementation, maintenance, and evaluation.

It then gives in tabular form the end products of each. The phases are then correlated with the system development process that is undertaken to build a DSS. It is shown that due to the special feedback orientation of a DSS the system design phase is concerned with the design of the four basic modules: the control module, the data storage module, the model-building module, and the data manipulation module.

Next the chapter addresses some of the issues related to the implementation of a DSS and the overall management of a DSS project. Like any other system, a DSS must be adequately documented. As a minimum, a user's manual, an operations manual, and a design documentation report are essential. These provide a sound basis for user training in DSS. The importance of involving the users from the very inception of the project is continuously emphasized. The discussion closes with a description of cost/benefit analysis of a DSS. It is pointed out that it is very difficult to cost justify a DSS project since its benefits are primarily intangible.

The later sections of the chapter are devoted to the discussion of two case studies in DSS, an Investment Decision Support System (IDSS) and a Distribution/Transportation Decision Support System (D/T DSS).

IDSS concerns portfolio analysis and the selection of an optimal investment policy. D/T DSS is related to manufacturing in the automobile industry. Its objective is to provide accurate feedback to management for determining how distribution costs should be allocated in the delivery of cars from the manufacturer to the final consumer. In both of these case studies only the first two phases of a DSS project are discussed, namely, the background and objectives of a DSS and sample operational scenarios of a DSS. The latter uses a variety of modeling techniques that will be discussed in Chapters 4 and 5.

2.17   KEY WORDS

The following key words are used in this chapter:

control	data flow diagram (DFD)
cost/benefit analysis	data manipulation module (DMM)

data storage module (DSM)
design documentation
distribution system
D/T DSS
feasibility
IDSS
intangible benefit
interface
logical system
model-building module (MBM)
operations manual
physical system
portfolio analysis
portfolio information for client

program level design
sensitivity testing
subsystem
system analysis
system backup
system design
system evaluation
system implementation
system level design
system life cycle
system maintenance
system recovery
tangible benefits
user's manual

REFERENCES

1. W. Davis, *System Analysis and Design: A Structured Approach,* Addison-Wesley, Reading, MA, 1983.
2. H. Lucas, Jr., *Tha Analysis, Design and Implementation of Information Systems,* McGraw-Hill, New York, 1981.
3. H.M. Wagner, *Principles of Operations Research,* Prentice-Hall, Englewood Cliffs, NJ, 1975.

REVIEW QUESTIONS

1. Explain the concept of system life cycle. What are its five phases?

2. What is meant by the statement: Analysis deals with "what" issues of a system, whereas design addresses the "how" issues?

3. Both design and implementation phases of a systems study deal with the "how" issues. In what respect, then, do they differ? Explain the need for each of them.

4. Enumerate the five phases of a systems development process and identify the end products of each phase.

5. Describe the four distinct features of a DSS. Explain how they are related to the four component modules of a DSS.

6. How would you handle the user training for a DSS project?

7. What difficulties does a DSS team face in performing a cost/benefit analysis of a DSS? Can you justify the cost of a DSS project quantitatively?

8. What are the basic capabilities of the DSS discussed in this chapter?
9. Describe an operational scenario of the IDSS that is different from the three described here.
10. What are the main objectives of the D/T DSS discussed here?
11. Select any one operational scenario of the D/T DSS discussed here and convert it into the prompt-driven format used for IDSS.
12. Discuss the three measurements that can be used to evaluate the performance of the total distribution system in D/T DSS.

MODELING TECHNIQUES

Part II discusses the techniques of mathematical modeling, because model building forms an essential component of a decision support system. Chapter 3 explores the concept of model formulation and then classifies models into two types: optimizing and nonoptimizing. Chapter 4 describes four major types of optimizing models: mathematical programming, inventory, portfolio analysis for investment, and marketing. Chapter 5 describes the nonoptimizing statistical models. The main emphasis is on forecasting using both quantitative and qualitative methods. The concluding sections provide a brief discussion of decision trees and decision analysis models.

3

Models and Model Building

3.1 WHAT IS A MODEL?

Mathematicians have an aptitude for giving everyday words a highly technical meaning. The words group, ring, and field, for example, are used in a very special technical sense in abstract algebra. While it is true that a ring can be lost (mathematicians prefer to say "embedded") in a field under this technical algebraic connotation, none of the familiar implications of the words ring and field are retained. To make matters worse, the word "field" has three different technical meanings depending on the subject in which it is used. Thus, the meaning of field in the expression "field of real numbers" (algebra) is quite different from its meaning in the expression "electromagnetic field" (physics), which is still different from its meaning in the expression "employee name field" (data processing).

The word "model" is a good example of a word with dual connotations. When mathematicians talk about a model, no reference, explicit or implied, is made to any fashion show or parade. A *model* in mathematics is just a representation of a real-life situation by means of variables and equations or inequalities. This perhaps sounds simplistic, but various examples can be given to illustrate this point.

3.2 EXAMPLES OF MODELS

3.2.1 Statistical Projection Model

Let us suppose that a company has the following annual sales data for the last five years:

Year	Sales (in thousands)
1978	$105
1979	$110
1980	$109
1981	$ 98
1982	$112

The vice president for sales wants a projection of annual sales for the next 3 years based on the past 5 years' data. He calls the statistician in his team and gives her this assignment. What does she do in response?

Her very first reaction is to plot the given data and determine their trend. Noticing that the five data values are scattered around a straight line, which in statistical terminology means that the data exhibit a linear trend, she uses the technique of linear regression to fit a least-squares line to these data values. We shall discuss the linear regression method later in Chapter 5. However, for the present we need to point out that the statistician builds a linear projection model to project the future sales values. Her model consists of the following:

1. Equation of a straight line in the form

$$y = a + bx \tag{3.1}$$

where the constants a and b are determined by solving two other linear equations involving a, b, and the given data values.

2. Two variables x and y, where x represents time with one year as the unit and y represents sales dollar value with $1000 as the unit.

3.2.2 Optimizing Model Using Linear Programming

A garment manufacturer makes two types of dresses for women: type A and type B. It makes a profit of $10 per type A dress and a profit of $8 per type B dress. To make one dress of type A, the company uses 2 hours of skilled labor and 4 hours of unskilled labor. To make one dress of type B, the company requires 9 hours of skilled labor and 3 hours of unskilled labor. During each day a total of 36 worker-hours of skilled labor and 42 worker-hours of unskilled labor are available. How many dresses of each type should the

company produce each day in order to maximize its profit subject to the limitations of available skilled and unskilled labor?

This problem can be formulated as a linear programming problem and can be solved either manually or through a software package using the simplex method. The detailed techniques and the actual solution of this problem will be discussed in Chapter 4. However, a mathematical model for solving the problem can be formulated as follows.

Since we need to determine the number of dresses of each type to be produced daily, we start the design of the model of defining two nonnegative variables x and y, where

$$x = \text{number of type A dresses to be produced daily}$$
$$y = \text{number of type B dresses to be produced daily}$$

The next step in the model design is to determine the maximizing objective function and then to give it a mathematical formulation. Since the manufacturer makes a profit of $10 for each type A dress and a profit of $8 for each type B dress, the total profit arising out of x dresses of type A and y dresses of type B is calculated as

$$(10x + 8y) \text{ dollars}$$

The manufacturer wants to maximize this profit.

We next notice that there is a limitation on the supply of total skilled and unskilled labor available daily. These are represented by the two inequalities

$$2x + 9y \leqslant 36 \qquad\qquad (3.2)$$
$$4x + 3y \leqslant 42$$

The linear programming model thus consists of the following:

1. Two variables x,y which are nonnegative.
2. A function $10x + 8y$ to be maximized.
3. Two inequalities

$$2x + 9y \leqslant 36$$
$$4x + 3y \leqslant 42$$

3.2.3 Inventory Management Model

For any company, inventory management poses the problem of setting up the correct amount of items to be stocked so that neither too much capital is tied up in the form of unused inventory nor too few items are kept in inventory so that customers are back-ordered. The company thus faces two

contradictory goals in inventory control. It would like to determine the most profitable balance between the two goals: to keep the inventory as low as possible so that capital can circulate while still maintaining an adequate supply to meet its customers' orders. In addition, the company wants to determine an optimal reorder cycle to avoid stockouts or back-ordering.

An inventory management model addresses this type of problem. To take an example, suppose that a bicycle manufacturing company wants to institute an optimal inventory policy that will determine an optimal order quantity Q and an optimal reorder period T for each item in the inventory in such a way that the sum of the ordering cost and the carrying cost is minimum. Assuming that the company has a policy of continuous review of its inventory status and that the demand for each type of bicycle is fairly uniform, the economic lot size model can be used to provide the answer. This model will be discussed in detail in Chapter 4. Here the model consists of the following items:

1. Two variables Q and T representing the optimal reorder quantity and the optimal reorder period, respectively.
2. A function representing the total cost per unit time, which is minimized.

3.3 BASIC INGREDIENTS OF A MODEL

With the examples of Section 3.2 for reference, we can formulate the primary characteristics of a model and its main components. Models can be used to address real-life business problems. With the advent of high-speed computers, their solution can be done very quickly.

The process of model building can be characterized as follows:

1. Model building starts with a real-life situation that is observable, measurable, and systematic or nonarbitrary. Thus, there must exist a set of causes and a set of effects interacting in a complex manner.

2. Depending on the boundary of the problem, it is necessary to formulate a set of causes that are responsible for the situation observed.

3. At the very center of the model lies its objective. This usually is translated into a formal mathematical objective function, which must be properly manipulated to yield the solution.

The main branch of mathematics that deals with model building is usually called *operations research* or *management science*. Model building normally consists of five steps:

1. Formulating the problem.
2. Constructing a model.
3. Deriving a solution.

4. Testing and controlling the solution.
5. Implementing the solution.

Clearly this is a cyclical process. It closely resembles the analogous process of systems analysis and design, which is also a cyclical process. Both processes have some overall objectives to start with and then go through continual analysis, formulation, change, and reformulation until the solution is reached. Of course, there is no unique "best" model for any management situation.

We can philosophize about the purely mathematical concept of a model and claim that a *model* is a convenient way of representing the total experience we possess, deriving from that experience the existence of some pattern or law, and finally showing how such patterns and laws can be used to predict the future. It has been said that human history is a history of model building. It is a history of constant search for pattern and for generalization.

It is in this more generalized sense that we must view a model to understand its proper role in an organization. The mathematical equations or inequalities, which are called the *constraints* of a model, arise out of the limitations imposed by the organization within which the model must function.

3.4 CONSTRAINTS IMPOSED BY THE ORGANIZATION

Since a model must interact with an organization, we must understand the nature and scope of the organization and the constraints within which it must work. It is wrong to think that even a commercial organization is devoted solely to maximizing profits. The industrial company will act within a complex environment. There are several layers of interaction ([3], Chapter 2):

1. The local community or a series of local communities. Decision making is influenced by the need to act as a good neighbor.
2. The nation and its needs. The company must be concerned with national well-being as well as its own organizational well-being.
3. Interest of the shareholders. Nominally the organization is responsible to its owners as shareholders.
4. Financial analysts. Companies preserve their relations with financial analysts to be aware of any apparent decline in company performance in any one year.
5. Labor force. The company must deal with professional and non-professional labor.
6. Customers/consumers. The company may deal directly with consumers or lawyers or deal with them through customers, for example, wholesalers and retailers.

7. **Suppliers.** The company depends on suppliers for raw materials and services.
8. **Rivals.** Relations with rivals are not always hostile. There can be explicit alliances or even unspoken implicit alliances.

Figure 3-1 illustrates this situation graphically.

3.5 GENERAL STRUCTURE OF A MODEL

Referring to the three examples of models given in Section 3.2, we find that all of them contain the following two components:

1. Variables; for example, x and y in Sections 3.2.1 and 3.2.2.
2. Equations and/or inequalities; for example (3.1) and (3.2) in Sections 3.2.1 and 3.2.2.

If the model is an optimizing one, as in Sections 3.2.2 and 3.2.3 then it contains a third component:

3. The function to be optimized; for example $10x + 8y$ in Section 3.2.2.

Proceeding from these particular examples to the general situation, we can say that any *nonoptimizing model* always has the first two components that is, variables and equations and/or inequalities, while an *optimizing model* always has all three components, that is, variables, equations and/or inequalities, and an optimizing function. Thus, a mathematical model always has a fixed structure.

We now introduce the formal terms and notations that represent the com-

FIGURE 3-1 Constraints on an organization.

ponents of a model. The three basic sets of elements for an optimizing model are:

1. *Decision Variables.*   These are the unknowns that are to be determined from the solution of the model. They represent real-world entities in abstract mathematical form. For example, in Section 3.2.2 the two decision variables are x and y, which represent, respectively, the number of type A and type B dresses to be produced daily. The decision variables are written as x, y, z or as $x_1, x_2, \ldots x_n$, when more than three are involved.

2. *Objective Function.*   This represents the ultimate goal of the model and is expressed as a mathematical function of the decision variables. For example, if the objective of the model is to maximize the total profit, as in Section 3.2.2, then the objective function must express the profit in terms of the decision variables. Thus, in Section 3.2.2, the profit is expressed as the function $10x + 8y$ of the two decision variables x and y. If the decision variables are $x_1, \ldots x_n$, then the objective function can be written as $f(x_1 \ldots x_n)$.

3. *Constraints.*   These are restrictions imposed on the model by the boundaries of the problem. They are expressed as equations and/or inequalities involving the decision variables. For example, (3.1) and (3.2) of Section 3.2 represent constraints for the respective models.

The final aim of an optimizing model is to derive an optimum solution of a given problem. It is said that the optimum solution to the model has been obtained if the corresponding values of the decision variables would yield the best value of the objective function while satisfying all the constraints. This means that the objective function acts as an indicator for the achievement of the optimum solution. Consequently, a poor formulation of the objective function can only lead to a poor solution to the problem.

A common case of poor formulation of the objective function occurs when some aspects of the system are neglected. For example, in determining the optimal inventory level of a certain commodity, the objective function may reflect the goals of the sales and finance departments only while neglecting that of the production department. In such cases, the model will yield what is called a suboptimal solution, with the disadvantage that it may not serve the best interests of the entire operation.

In general, optimization of the objective function signifies either a maximization or a minimization of this function. For example, in an industrial plant the objective may be viewed as maximizing profit or productive time or as minimizing cost or idle time. Optimization in this sense has received wide acceptance among researchers and practitioners because it reflects the common goal of obtaining the best solution to the model. Moreover, the tremendous advances in the mathematics of optimization have offered unifying approaches for tackling such problems.

The structure of a nonoptimizing model includes the decision variables

and the constraints. A statistical model like the one discussed in Section 3.2.1 is an example of a nonoptimizing model. Thus, in that example, x and y are the decision variables and (3.1) is the constraint involving x and y. However, it should be noted here that in statistical models, the term *random variable* is used instead of decision variable.

Some authors ([3], Chapter 1) distinguish between two types of decision variables: controllable and uncontrollable. According to them, a *controllable* variable refers to real-world factors that are under the control of the model builder. In general, it can refer to what goes on in the company at two levels below the model builder and also to what occurs at one or two levels above. An *uncontrollable* variable may belong to nature or society or government, or else it can be within the jurisdiction of the competitor.

The objective function is closely related to the overall goals and objectives of the organization. An *objective* is an end status toward which the organization should proceed. It may be unobtainable, but it provides standards by which to judge if the company is making the right decisions.

Goals are measured states in which we want the organization to be at or during a specific period of time. The goals are thus directly related to the objectives.

Current *criteria* of performance are those measures which we use currently to check on the progress of the organization toward its goal.

In a typical company it is necessary to classify the objectives into several groups to determine if the company is achieving its goals. For example, a manufacturing firm may divide its objectives into diverse functions such as purchasing, production, marketing, personnel, and finance. Subsequently, a variety of models may be constructed to optimize the objective functions in each of these areas. Such models will, of course, be subject to the constraints in the respective branches of the company.

Essentially a model is an attempt to extract from the richness of a real situation a concept that can be manipulated and controlled. Hence, every model is a many-one transformation in which the many variables of the real situation are classified and then either ignored or treated in groups or treated singly. It is one of the tasks of model building to try to understand the real situation and to formulate in a hypothetical form the logical patterns of causes and effects that link together the controllable and uncontrollable variables.

3.6 TRADE-OFFS IN OPTIMIZING MODELS

As indicated in Section 3.5, an optimizing model seeks to *maximize* or *minimize* the objective function subject to a set of constraints. In doing so, the solution algorithm first determines a *feasible solution,* which is a set of values of the decision variables that satisfy all the constraints. However, this solution does not necessarily yield an optimum value of the objective function. The solution algorithm of the model then proceeds with the feasible solution and

eventually arrives at an *optimal solution,* if one exists, through a set of it-
erative processes. At each stage of iteration the current values of the variables
are changed and the objective function is recomputed to test whether the
optimum value has been reached.

If we analyze this algorithmic iteration, we can discern an implicit trade-
off situation. The mathematical process of changing current values of decision
variables to achieve a more optimum value of the objective function corresponds to the real-life physical process of changing some resource allocation, say, in order to achieve a higher profit or a lower cost. This latter
situation indeed is a trade-off process. Thus, an optimizing model always
involves a trade-off. We now illustrate this situation with several examples.

To start with, the example in Section 3.2.2 shows a trade-off between the
cost of available skilled and unskilled labor and the amount of profit that the
company can make by manufacturing the two types of dresses. If the company
manufactures more dresses, then it can get more money by selling them,
assuming that there is always enough demand in the market for the dresses.
However, not all of the sales revenue can be realized as profit, because the
company has to pay for its establishment, the wages of its labor force, raw
materials, marketing expenses, and so on. The net profit is determined by
deducting all expenses from the total revenue. Therefore, a mere increase
of production volume does not ensure a higher profit. The optimizing model
handles such a trade-off scenario in a mathematical manner and derives an
optimal solution.

In an inventory model, as discussed in Section 3.2.3, one looks for a trade-
off between maintaining a huge unused inventory and back-ordering too often.
A large unused inventory is expensive owing to carrying costs of items and
is undesirable owing to lack of liquidity of the company's capital. The company certainly prefers a better cash flow and investment policy than just
tying up its capital in the form of unused inventory items. On the other hand,
the company cannot lower its inventory level too much to get more liquid
capital, because thereby it may be forced to place too many customers on
back-order and get a bad name in the market. In fact, many customers may
choose to go to a different company. The inventory management model helps
the company to set up the proper balance.

In a portfolio analysis model, the user wants to determine an optimal combination of investment items (stocks, bonds, real estate, etc.) so as to receive
an optimal return on investment. The greater the probability of default on
the part of the issuer of securities, the higher the investment return is going
to be. For example, a government bond is regarded as totally risk-free, and
consequently it normally carries the lowest return rate. On the other hand,
stocks with a highly volatile market offer a much higher yield. The underlying
reason is quite easy to determine. An investor does not want to take a higher
risk unless there is the possibility of getting a higher yield in return. In other
words, we are back to the trade-off situation. Ideally the portfolio analysis
model provides the investor with a highly diversified combination of securities

so as to strike a balance between the amount of risk and the amount of return. Diversification of securities usually achieves this balance.

Finally, let us look at an example of a queueing model. This model is characterized by the fact that a limited number of servers provide some service to the customers. If a server is not available when a customer comes for the service, the customer joins a queue for the next available server. Since nobody likes to wait in a line, the immediate tendency is to think that the objective for the queueing model should be to minimize the customer waiting time. However, the situation is not that simple and can best be understood by taking a concrete example.

We all have the experience of going to a bank and standing in line for service. If the bank management decides to hire enough tellers to eliminate queues even during the peak hours, say 11:00 a.m. to 2:00 p.m., then some of these tellers will remain idle during the nonpeak hours, although customer satisfaction would be maximized. On the other hand, if few enough tellers are employed to ensure no idle time for tellers, then there will be long customer lines during the peak hours. This will raise customer dissatisfaction and may even result in loss of some customers for the bank. We thus have here a trade-off situation to analyze.

The cost incurred by the bank in hiring enough tellers to provide immediate service is called the *service cost*. The cost of losing customers who do not want to wait too long in line because of an insufficient number of tellers may be labeled the *waiting cost*. It is easy to see that the service cost and the waiting cost vary inversely; that is, when one increases, the other decreases. The objective of a queueing model is to find the optimal balance so as to minimize the total cost, which is the sum of the service cost and the waiting cost.

It should be noted here that a nonoptimizing model such as a linear regression model does not involve any such trade-off considerations.

3.7 IMPLEMENTATION AND INTERPRETATION OF MODELS

In Section 3.3 a five-step process was described as basic to model building. The last two steps there involve the implementation of a model and interpretation of its results. We now discuss these two issues.

After the solution is derived from a model, it is necessary to interpret the decision variables as representing the real-world entities and to follow the course of action prescribed by the model. For example, the solution of the problem in Section 3.2.2 is given by

$$x = 9, \quad y = 2$$
$$\text{Objective function} = \$106$$

This means that the company should produce 9 dresses of type A and 2 dresses of type B to realize a total profit of $106. However, a manager may

find that some physical situations in the company prevent her from producing exactly 9 dresses of type A daily. In that case, she modifies the solution of the model and implements only what is practical within the company environment.

The scenario described above raises an important issue. Since a model is just a tool for replicating a modified version of a real-world situation, users should use their own judgment in implementing the solution. For instance, there are optimizing models that indicate that one of their decision variables should be zero ([1], Chapter 7). If the real-world interpretation of the model does not permit that, then the manager must modify the final solution to implement it. The new solution will no longer be optimal, but the manager has decided to accept a near-optimal solution to fit reality. A decision support system merely helps the manager to make good decisions by providing them with appropriate analytic information. The managers reserve the final authority to use that information or to modify it before implementation. Owing to practical business considerations, a solution that is mathematically optimal is not necessarily optimal in practice. It is up to the manager to decide how to interpret and implement the final outcome of a model.

3.8 CLASSIFICATION OF MODELS

Models are classified in two ways: by technique used and by type of application. Since a model replicates a real-world situation, the classification tells us which technique to use in what application. Of course, there are overlaps between these classifications in the sense that a single technique can be used in more than one application, and the same application can use more than one technique. For example, a manufacturing problem can use linear programming, an inventory model, or statistical projection. Similarly, linear programming techniques can be used in financial applications, determination of marketing policy, and so on.

3.8.1 Classification by Technique

Models can be built using one or more of the following techniques:

- ☐ Inventory analysis, which handles an optimal policy determination for reorder quantities and reorder frequency.
- ☐ Mathematical programming, which includes linear, nonlinear, dynamic, and parametric programming.
- ☐ Queueing theory, which handles a wide variety of problems where "customers" vie for service from "servers."
- ☐ Statistical analysis, which includes linear and nonlinear regression, asymptotic growth curves, game theory, decision analysis, and other techniques.

Note that the first three techniques use optimizing models while the last one uses nonoptimizing models.

3.8.2 Classification by Applications

Models can be used to handle the following applications:

- ☐ Production or manufacturing.
- ☐ Financial (including econometric).
- ☐ Marketing.
- ☐ Network computations (e.g., data communication, PERT, CPM).
- ☐ Census and actuarial studies.

3.9 SUMMARY

This chapter discusses the concept of a model as used in operations research. A model is defined as mathematical representation of a real-world situation. The model builder analyzes the situation and extracts from it the essential components that represent the characteristics of the model. In doing so he/she strips the real-world problem of many nonessential features.

A model can be optimizing or nonoptimizing. In both types, however, the model builder defines mathematically the decision variables whose values are given by the solution of the model and the constraints imposed on these decision variables by the model. A statistical model is of the nonoptimizing type. An optimizing model contains a third ingredient known as the objective function, whose optimization is the goal of the model. For example, in a business environment the objective function usually concerns profit or cost, and the goal is either to maximize the function, as in case of profit, or to minimize it, as in case of cost. In any optimizing situation a trade-off issue is always involved. The notion of trade-off is discussed with a variety of examples to show exactly why this issue arises and how it is solved in a model.

Several examples are given to illustrate an optimizing as well as a nonoptimizing model. The issue of implementation and the role of a manager's decision-making authority to determine the implementation procedure are emphasized. No model can ever replace human judgment. The chapter ends with a brief discussion of classification of models.

3.10 KEY WORDS

The following key words are used in this chapter:

classification of models	decision variable
constraint	feasible solution

model

nonoptimizing model

objective function

optimal solution

optimizing model

trade-offs in model

REFERENCES

1. S.C. Hanna, and J. C. Saber, *Linear Programming and Matrix Algebra*, Babson College Press, Wellesley, MA, 1978.
2. F.S. Hillier, and G.J. Lieberman, *Introduction to Operations Research*, Holden-Day, San Francisco, 1979.
3. P. Rivett, *Model Building for Decision Analysis*, Wiley, New York, 1980.
4. H.M. Wagner, *Principles of Operations Research*, Prentice-Hall, Englewood Cliffs, NJ, 1975.

REVIEW QUESTIONS

1. Define a model. What are the two main types of models used to solve real-life problems? Specify the basic ingredients of each type.

2. Why is it said that model building is more an art than a science?

3. List and explain the five steps to follow in building a model. Do you find any similarity between these steps and those followed in the systems analysis, design, and implementation process? Explain your answer.

4. Is model building a cyclical process like the systems life cycle?

5. Why is a statistical model always of the nonoptimizing type? What is an alternative name for a decision variable in a statistical model?

6. Explain clearly the issue of trade-offs encountered in an optimizing model. Give an example of the trade-off situation other than the ones given in the book.

7. How do you interpret the solution of an optimizing model that includes a zero-valued decision variable?

8. Who, in your opinion, should have the final say in implementing a model?

4

Models for Optimization

4.1 INTRODUCTION

In Chapter 3 we discussed the overall process of building a mathematical model. As we saw there, there are two types of models: optimizing and nonoptimizing. In this chapter we shall consider optimizing models.

An *optimizing model* has three components:

1. Decision variables, for example, $x_1, x_2, \ldots, x_n$.

2. An objective function expressed in terms of the decision variables, for example, $f(x_1, \ldots, x_n)$.

3. Constraints expressed as equations or inequalities involving the decision variables $x_1, \ldots, x_n$.

We shall discuss here four types of optimizing models:

☐ Mathematical programming models
☐ Inventory models
☐ Portfolio analysis model for investment strategies
☐ Marketing models

Of these four categories the mathematical programming models are the most extensive. These comprise three major classes: linear programming, nonlinear programming, and dynamic programming. The linear programming models are most widely used. They address a wide variety of problems such as resource allocation, optimal scheduling, network flow analysis, and transportation or routing problems.

Figure 4-1 shows the four categories of optimizing models discussed in this chapter and the subdivisions within mathematical programming. Queueing models are also optimizing models and will be discussed in Chapter 7.

4.2 MATHEMATICAL PROGRAMMING MODELS

Of the three categories of mathematical programming models, we shall treat four types of linear programming models in some detail. Then we shall comment briefly on nonlinear and dynamic programming models.

Under linear programming (LP) models we shall consider the following cases:

☐ Resource allocation
☐ Scheduling
☐ Network flow analysis
☐ Transportation or routing

First let us study the general formulation of an LP model.

4.3 GENERAL FORMULATION OF AN LP MODEL

In general mathematical form, an LP problem can be stated as follows:
Let $x_1, \ldots, x_n$ be n *decision variables*.
Define the *objective function:*

$$Z = c_1 x_1 + \ldots + c_n x_n$$

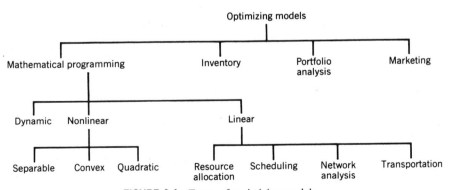

FIGURE 4-1 Types of optimizing models.

subject to the *constraints*

$$a_{11}x_1 + \ldots + a_{1n}x_n \leq b_1$$
$$a_{21}x_1 + \ldots + a_{2n}x_n \leq b_2$$
$$a_{m1}x_1 + \ldots + a_{mn}x_n \leq b_m$$

where $x_1 \geq 0$, $x_2 \geq$, $\ldots$, $x_n \geq 0$, and a_{11}, a_{21}, $\ldots$, a_{mn} are constants.

The model is called a *linear* programming model because the objective function Z and all the constraints are linear, that is, of first degree, in the decision variables $x_1, \ldots, x_n$. The input constants a_{ij} and c_i are often called the *parameters* of the LP model.

Let

$$A = (a_{ij}) \text{ be an } m \times n \text{ matrix}$$
$$C = (c_1, \ldots, c_n) \text{ be a } 1 \times n \text{ matrix}$$
$$X = \begin{pmatrix} x_1 \\ \vdots \\ x_n \end{pmatrix} \text{ be an } n \times 1 \text{ matrix}$$
$$B = \begin{pmatrix} b_1 \\ \vdots \\ b_m \end{pmatrix} \text{ be an } m \times 1 \text{ matrix}$$

Then, in matrix notation, the LP model is stated as follows:

Maximize or minimize $Z = CX$ subject to the constraints $AX \leq B$ and $X > \mathbf{0}$, where $\mathbf{0}$ represents the $n \times 1$ zero matrix.

Similarly, we can have an LP model with the constraints $AX \geq B$, everything else remaining the same.

Any set of values of $x_1, \ldots, x_n$ is called a *solution*, regardless of whether it is an allowable or desirable choice. If all the constraints are satisfied, then the solution is called *feasible*. Given that there are several feasible solutions, the goal of linear programming is to select the solution that is "best," as measured by the value of the objective function of the model. An *optimal* solution is a feasible solution that gives the optimum value of the objective function.

Usually, the LP model is solved by the *simplex method*. If the decision variables are constrained to be integers, then the problem becomes an *integer linear programming* (ILP) model.

Very rarely does one solve a real-life LP or ILP problem manually, because the number of variables and constraints usually runs over 50 or even 100. Several packages are available to solve LP problems on computers by means of the simplex method. IBM uses their MPSX (Mathematical Programming

System) software package. A separate package is available for the CDC 6600 to solve ILP problems. Such software can handle LP models consisting of as many as 10,000 variables and 1000 constraints.

LINPRO, LINDO, and P1P2 (Phase 1/Phase 2) software packages enable the user to solve an LP model interactively. Each package prompts the user for the parameters of the model, the type of objective function (i.e., maximizing or minimizing), the number of decision variables, and the number and type (equality, less than, or greater than) of constraints, and then provides the optimal values of the decision variables and the objective function. If, however, no optimal solution exists, then the model prints a message to that effect.

4.4 COMPUTATIONAL CONSIDERATIONS OF THE SIMPLEX METHOD

Three factors determine how much time the general simplex method will require to solve an LP model:

1. *Number of Constraints.* Computation time tends to be proportional to the *cube* of this number. Hence if the number of constraints is tripled, then the computation increases nearly 27 times.

2. *Number of Decision Variables.* Computation time is very slightly affected by this number. Thus, doubling the number of decision variables may not even double the computation time.

3. *Density of the Coefficient Matrix (a_{ij}).* The term "density" here means the ratio of the number of nonzero matrix elements to the total number of matrix elements. The density of the coefficient matrix affects the computation time per iteration of the simplex method. Normally, the total number of iterations needed to solve the LP model is about twice the number of constraints.

A large LP model requires the manipulation of massive amount of data. Consequently, it is advisable to use a *matrix generator* program to perform the following functions:

☐ Convert the basic raw data into constraint coefficients in a format appropriate for the simplex method.

☐ Fill in the zero entries in the coefficient matrix, since in large LP models most of these entries are zero.

☐ Print out the key input data in an easily readable form so that they can be shown to various people for checking.

☐ Scale the coefficients to approximately the same order of magnitude to avoid significant roundoff error.

In addition, an *output analyzer* or a *report writer* program can be used to achieve the following goals:

☐ To compile and summarize relevant information for debugging the model.
☐ To provide useful data for analyzing the sensitivity of the optimal solution to the various estimated parameters of the model.
☐ To develop a well-organized report describing the proposed solution of the model.

4.5 RESOURCE ALLOCATION PROBLEMS

A resource allocation problem arises whenever there is a set of resources and a number of ways in which they may be used. The allocation of particular group of resources to a particular activity will make a contribution toward the achievement of an objective, namely to devise a way in which the use of the resources should be split among the tasks such that the objective function will be maximized or minimized. In general, allocation problems are deterministic in nature. Often the relationship between the degree of attainment of the objective and the extent to which resources are deployed is linear, and thus linear programming is most often used to solve the problem.

The example of Section 3.2.2 is a resource-allocation problem. Here the company wants to determine how the available skilled labor can be optimally allocated in order to maximize its profit, which is expressed by the objective function. Running this LP model with a software package such as LINPRO will show that the optimal solution is

$$x = 9, \quad y = 2, \quad z = 106$$

That is, the comapny should produce 9 dresses of type A and 2 dresses of type B so as to make a profit of $106.

We now describe two more resource-allocation models of two different types.

4.5.1 The Homemaker's Problem

The following description is adapted from Dantzig ([2], p. 4).

A family of five lives on the modest income of the husband. A constant problem is to determine the weekly menu after due consideration of food prices and the family's taste preferences. The husband must have 3000 calories daily, the wife is on a diet of 1500 calories daily, and the three children need 3000, 2700, and 2500 calories, respectively, per day. These calories must be maintained by eating not more than a specified amount of fat and carbohydrate and not less than a certain amount of protein daily. The problem

is to assemble menus on a weekly basis so as to minimize food costs according to food prices published in the Sunday paper.

Here the decision variables are the quantities of food items of different types (x_1 = dozens of eggs, x_2 = gallons of milk, x_3 = number of apples, etc.). The constraints are the calories of the various food items and the limits imposed on amounts of fat, carbohydrate, and protein to be consumed. The objective function is the total cost of the food items and so must be minimized. We need a table of food prices to complete the formulation of the model.

This model was actually implemented in the early 1970s by the Pennsylvania Bureau of Correction ([8], pp. 174–176). The operations division of the bureau started a project in 1971 with consultant help from Pennsylvania State University Main Campus. Their computer package on linear programming was used to plan the menu at each institution for the staff and the residents. The program was then field tested and its success was later closely monitored by Pennsylvania State University. The plan is now fully operational with high success. In 1973 the New York City Department of Correction started a similar program on food service planning and inventory control system.

The plan gives consideration to age and sex, economy of foods as sources of nutrients, and suitability of foods in relation to meal patterns common in the United States. Through application of this plan, each state correctional institution has an individual set of food allowances in 11 food groups, based on the needs of its own particular population. Cards are punched with food allowances in "edible portion" pounds, inventory balances and costs, food receipts and costs, food issues (all in units of purchase), the number of rations served, and conversion and equalizing factors. This program enables the computer to:

1. Convert units of purchase into pounds.
2. Apply a factor and to convert pounds to edible portion weight.
3. Compute a unit cost per pound, per edible portion pound, and per serving when desired.
4. Determine the percentage of usage of each item and of each food group.
5. Determine the edible portion pounds per ration and the cost per ration.

Foods and costs are identified by method of procurement and by food group. Total amounts issued and differentials in food and cost allowances and issues can be determined. All these computations are reflected in the monthly report. The totals are printed at the end of each food group, with a recapitulation of all totals on the last page of each institution's report. A second report, prepared from inventory balance, food receipts, costs, and food issues, reflects current inventory balance by food item and shows the number of months' supply on hand and the dollar value of inventory.

The conversion factor converts units of purchase, which vary according to the many packaging sizes, into pounds; and the equalizing factor converts pounds of food as purchases to edible-portion pounds, that is, weights of food ready to cook or ready to serve. Where applicable, the average number of servings per pound is also indicated.

A complete food list is prepared for the participating institutions, and this information is keypunched on a set of IBM cards and in turn transferred to magnetic tape for computer use. The entire computer package consists of five decks of cards:

1. The *object program* deck gives the computer its instructions.
2. The *food master* deck lists all food items for all institutions, with each card carrying the item code, food item, unit of purchase, size of unit, conversion factor, and equalizing factor.
3. The *food allowance* data include the institution code and food allowances by food group.
4. The *inventory* deck shows the balance on hand in quantity and value, total issues to date and months involved, item code, and institution code.
5. The *food receipt and issue* deck includes item code, source of procurement, quantity of food received and its cost, quantity of food issued, total rations, and date.

The system provides an excellent management tool and the necessary information to compare unit costs of food items per edible portion pound as well as portion costs within and among institutions, to determine accurate food and budgetary requirements and maintain controls, and to ensure a nutritionally adequate diet for the people living in state institutions. The potential of the system is unlimited, since statistical information may be stored and used as needed. The code is complete enough to make it possible to separate food items in any way desired.

4.5.2 Capital Budgeting

A firm has n projects to be completed during one fiscal year. Due to budgetary constraints, not all of the projects can be selected. Assume that project j has present value c_j and requires an investment of a_{ij} dollars during month i. The capital available during month i is b_i. Then the ILP model can be set up as follows:

Maximize

$$Z = \sum_{j=1}^{n} c_j x_j$$

such that

$$\sum_{j=1}^{n} a_{ij}x_j \leqslant b_i, \quad \begin{array}{l} i = 1, \ldots, 12, \text{ corresponding} \\ \text{to the 12 months of the fiscal year} \end{array}$$

$$x_j = \begin{cases} 1 & \text{if project } j \text{ is selected} \\ 0 & \text{otherwise} \end{cases}$$

The solution of the model determines which specific x_j variables are 1 in order to maximize Z, which represents the total present value. Each unit value of x_j determines a project that is to be undertaken. Thus, the solution shows the individual projects that the firm will handle during one fiscal year.

4.6 SCHEDULING PROBLEM

The scheduling problem arises when a given limited amount of personnel is to be utilized in an optimal fashion so as to maximize profit or minimize cost. For example, such a model can be used to design an optimal schedule pattern that will minimize the amount of overtime. The objective function then represents the total overtime cost.

The following example describes an actual application of this model ([8], pp. 171–172), as used by the Pennsylvania Bureau of Correction.

The bureau had been paying a large amount of money in the form of over-time pay to the correction officers in eight state correctional institutions. Sometimes an officer could earn more than twice his/her regular salary in the form of overtime pay. To eliminate this situation, a model called the Scheduling Model for Correction Officers was designed under contracted consulting help from Dr. James Maynard, a faculty member in mathematics at The Pennsylvania State University—Capitol Campus. The model aims at finding the optimal number of correction officers that should be working on a specific day on a specific shift under the regular rate, the time-and-a-half rate, and the double-time rate so as to minimize the amount of overtime paid. The model also detenrmines the breakeven point beyond which hiring additional officers would be more economical than paying overtime to the existing staff.

To accomplish this, we divide the week into 21 time cells corresponding to 3 shifts a day for 7 days a week. Three sets of decision variables are assumed:

X_{kj} = number of officers to be assigned at regular rate on week k, shift j

Y_{ij} = number of officers to be assigned at time-and-a-half rate on day i, shift j

Z_{ij} = number of officers to be assigned at double-time rate on day i, shift j.

$$i = 1, 2, \ldots, 7$$
$$j = 1, 2, 3$$
$$k = 1, 2, \ldots, 7$$

The objective function W is constructed as

$$W = \sum_{ij} (1.5Y_{ij} + 2Z_{ij})$$

so that W represents the total overtime paid in 1 week.

The mathematical constraints are designed to ensure the following facts:

1. Total number of correction officers to be assigned at a regular rate over one week equals the total workforce in the institution.

2. Total number of correction officers to be assigned to a specific day and a specific shift at the regular rate and the two overtime rates equals the number of correction officers actually working on that day shift.

3. Total number of correction officers working overtime and chosen from X_{kj} must not exceed X_{kj}.

4. Time-and-a-half overtime is paid to correction officers for any work in excess of 8 hours in any one work day and in excess of 80 hours in any biweekly pay period.

5. Double-rate overtime is paid to any correction officer working the second scheduled day off provided he/she has worked overtime on the first scheduled day off.

The complete mathematical model contains 819 variables and 232 constraints. A computer package program in MPS III available from The Pennsylvania State University—Main Campus is being used to solve the integer programming model outlined above. The weekly computer printouts indicate the optimal structure of the correction officer staff at each institution. More specifically, the printouts indicate how many officers are to be optimally assigned to work at their regular pay rate on a specific day and shift, how many to work overtime at time-and-a-half, and how many at double-time. The printouts further show which group of officers should be selected to work overtime in order to keep the overtime cost at a minimum.

The system has been built to be flexible enough for posoptimality analysis. For example, if it is decided in the future that no two consecutive overtimes can be allowed or that no overtime can start immediately following regular work hours for an officer, or that an officer can work overtime only at the same shift where he/she is regularly assigned, then the model can be adjusted accordingly.

4.7 NETWORK FLOW ANALYSIS

There are two major areas for this application: design of a data communication network and project scheduling and monitoring.

4.7.1. Data Communication Network

Factors considered in the design of a data communication network are:

☐ Timeliness of data transmission.
☐ Response time for the corresponding requests.
☐ Availability of the line.
☐ Cost of data communication.

A typical optimizing model will minimize the total cost subject to the constraints of timeliness of data, response time, and the availability of the line. This will result in a network topology showing the nodes where data are generated and arcs along which the data are transmitted. As a minimum, the following parameters are specified for any data communication network:

☐ Network type (star, ring, tree structure, etc.).
☐ Speed of transmission (low, medium, high).
☐ Mode of transmission (asynchronous, synchronous).
☐ Type of transmission (simplex, half-duplex, full-duplex).
☐ Line configuration (point-to-point, multidrop).
☐ Equipment (terminal, modem, channels, controller, multiplexer, concentrator, etc.).

Due to the increasing use of transaction-oriented processing supported by CRT terminals and microprocessors, the data communication network design is a major aspect of almost any system design.

4.7.2 Project Scheduling and Monitoring: Generalized PERT System

Three fairly well-known management techniques currently used to plan and schedule projects are: PERT (Program Evaluation and Review Technique), MOST (Management Operation System Technique), and LOB (Line of Balance). Historically, PERT was designed by the U.S. Department of Defense in connection with launching the Polaris missile in the late 1950s. It has been used widely since then in private industry and in governmental agencies. MOST was designed much later to improve some aspects of PERT and is used mostly in production-oriented businesses. LOB was developed by the

U.S. Navy as a graphic method of industrial programming and is helpful in a production setting.

It is possible to combine some of the aspects of PERT with those of MOST to design a more informative network. Such a system can be augmented by using the graphic techniques of LOB, which are very helpful to top management in visualizing the current status of a project. Such a combined package can be thought of as a *generalized PERT system.*

In order to prepare a PERT network for a project, two steps are needed:

1. Analyze the project thoroughly and determine what subprojects or tasks must be accomplished to reach the final goal.

2. Determine the proper sequential order of the various tasks; for example, decide which tasks are to be done first, which tasks next, and so forth.

Most of the time, some tasks can proceed simultaneously; but some cannot start until certain others are finished. These considerations must be kept in mind in determining the sequential order mentioned in step 2.

In PERT language, each task is called an *activity* or a *job,* and the beginning and end of an activity are called *events.* Simultaneous activities are called *parallel activities.* When several activities have the same beginning event, the latter is called a *burst point.* Similarly, when several activities have the same end event, the latter is called a *node.*

Each event is represented by a circle with a number inside it. The number simply serves as a convenient reference point for the event. Each activity is represented by an open arrow. At the beginning of each activity there is a flag; five figures are written beside the upper portion of the flag. These figures indicate, respectively, the number of work hours involved in the activity, a cost estimate, and three time estimates of how long the activity will take. In order to keep track of progress, spot checks are made at regular intervals. A vertical line is inserted in the network to indicate when and at what event number the check is made. The date of the spot check is written on the line. If the activity is finished when the spot check is made, the blank space inside the activity arrow is filled in. This shows immediately whether the project is behind, on, or ahead of schedule.

At the top of each flag you can indicate other relevant data pertaining to the activity. Using three time estimates you can also predict the probability of completing the project on time. The network also can indicate the *critical activities* in the entire project. A critical activity is one that would cause a delay in the completion of the project if it were delayed. On the other hand, there are *noncritical* activities that have some *slack time* available; you can delay these activities until their slack time is used up without delaying the project as a whole. The concepts of *early start, early finish, late start,* and *late finish* times are also available in this network.

Along with a generalized PERT network, a LOB graph is designed to

represent the progress of the project. This is done by determining what percentage of the whole project each activity entails. The activities are then plotted on a graph showing the time frame. A solid-line graph is used to indicate the *anticipated delivery schedule,* and a broken-line graph to indicate the *actual delivery schedule.* A deviation between the two graphs indicates whether the project is behind or ahead of schedule.

In Section 4.6 we discussed a scheduling model to minimize overtime pay. The generalized PERT system described above was used to plan and monitor the progress of this project. The first step was to determine principal activities.

1. Design a linear programming model for the problem.
2. Design a form to gather field input on the actual roster of the officers.
3. Gather field input on the form.
4. Prepare a computer program to solve the problem.
5. Make computer runs to check the validity of the solutions.
6. Deliver the finished package as a scheduling model.

Figure 4-2 gives the generalized PERT network for the project. Each of the arrows a through f represents one activity, and each of the circles 1 through 8 is an event. Activities c and d are parallel, since they occur simultaneously. Event 3 is a burst point, since activities c and d originate from it. Event 6 is a node, since two activites end there. The critical path consists of events 1-2-3-4-6-7-8, and the total project takes 33–46 working days. The total cost of the project is $1000, and it requires 782 work hours.

A spot check was made on January 23, 1974, and everything was on schedule. Consequently, arrows a–d were filled in.

This is obviously a very small project. However, for large projects with 100 or more activities, you can use a computer to determine the critical path and slack times.

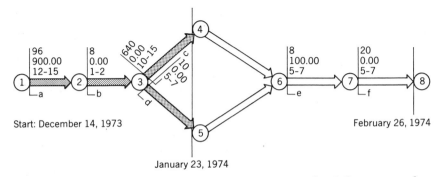

FIGURE 4-2 Generalized PERT network. The figures against top of each flag represent, from top to bottom, the number of worker hours involved in the activity, the cost estimates, and the most likely and most pessimistic time, measured in days.

Figure 4-3 is the LOB graph of the same project. The following percentages were assigned to activities a–f, depending on the time needed to perform each of them:

(a) 40 percent
(b) 15 percent
(c) 15 percent
(d) 10 percent
(e) 10 percent
(f) 10 percent

A spot check on January 14, 1974, indicated that the project was running nearly 1 day and 4 percent behind schedule. (The length of the horizontal gap between the end of the actual delivery schedule and the vertical line representing the day of check measures the number of days—or weeks, months, or other time units—that a project is behind or ahead of schedule. Similarly, the length of the vertical gap between the end of the actual delivery scheduling curve and the anticipated delivery schedule curve measures what percentage of the total project is running behind or ahead of schedule.) Consequently, the work was accelerated, and by January 23, 1974, the project was back on schedule.

The generalized PERT system is a package consisting of a list of all the activities in the project with percentages assigned to each, a generalized

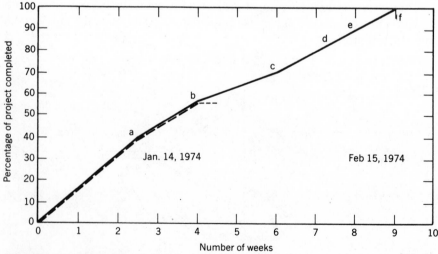

FIGURE 4-3   LOB graph. (——) Cumulative delivery schedule; (– – –) actual delivery schedule.

PERT network, and a LOB graph. The advantages of a generalized PERT system include the following:

☐ Direct spot checks can be made at regular intervals of time.

☐ The system's user can indicate visually, both on the network and on the LOB graph, whether the project is running behind, on, or ahead of schedule.

☐ Built-in cost figures indicate how much the total project will cost. These figures can be revised at the time of each spot check to determine whether the project is running below, above, or in accordance with the budget. If the project is costing more than was originally expected, new estimates can be prepared to indicate the projected cost overrun computed on the basis of the current cost overrun.

☐ The system indicates what percent of the total and how much actual time the project is behind or ahead of schedule when spot checks are made. The time difference and the difference in the percent of the project completed can be shown on a graph.

☐ The system can indicate how many work hours are needed for each activity.

☐ The blank space inside the open arrow for an activity can be colored in and a color code developed to indicate which division or department has the responsibility to finish that activity. A color-coded PERT network can be a great visual aid since the responsibilities of different departments are clearly shown. When a color-coded network is used, the arrow can be filled in with black tape when the activity is finished.

The generalized PERT network and the LOB graph can be used for planning and controlling a large variety of projects:

Any research and development project
Construction of a building or highway
Opening of a new facility
Installation and debugging of a computer system
Manufacture and assembly of large equipment
Design of a training program
End-of-the-month closing of accounting records

All such projects have the following characteristics in common:

1. The project consists of a well-defined collection of activities whose completion marks the end of the project.

2. The activities can be started and stopped independently of each other, within a given sequence.

3. The activities must be performed in a sequential order.

The generalized PERT system is useful at several stages of project management—from the early planning stages when various alternative programs or procedures are being considered, to the scheduling phase when time and resource schedules are laid out, and finally to the operational phase when it is used as a control device to measure actual versus planned progress. The network graph displays in a simple and direct way the complex interrelationships of activities that make up a project. Managers of various subdivisions of the projects may quickly see from the graph how their portion affects, and is affected by, other parts of the project. Network calculations focus attention on the relatively small subset of activities in a project that are critical to its completion. Managerial action is thus focused on exceptional problems, a feature that contributes to more reliable planning and more effective control.

Since network analysis models are special examples of LP models, it is possible to give a linear programming formulation of a PERT network. To do so, we take as decision variables the early occurrence times of the individual events and define the objective function as the difference between the early occurrence times of the initial and final events. The LP model seeks to minimize the objective function.

Wiest and Levy ([14], pp. 68–80) have given detailed algorithms for the LP formulations of network problems.

4.8 TRANSPORTATION OR ROUTING PROBLEMS

This class of problems relates to the situation where a company has several manufacturing plants, warehouses, sales territories, or distribution outlets. Each location is either a supply point or a demand point. A supply point can supply a given amount of a certain product, while a demand point needs a shipment of a required amount of the same product. The company wants to determine a delivery route so as to minimize the total transportation cost. The model's primary usefulness is for planning. The solution of the model helps the managers to make strategic decisions involving the selection of the transportation routes to meet the requisite demand subject to the supply from the production plants.

Let us assume that a large firm producing gasoline has m refineries located throughout a region. Refinery i produces at most S_i gallons of gasoline daily, where $i = 1, 2, \ldots, m$. Also, the firm must furnish its n distributing warehouses on a daily basis with at least D_j gallons of gasoline to meet the demand requirements, where $j = 1, 2, \ldots, n$. The model must determine which re-

fineries will furnish which warehouses so as to meet the supply and demand constraints and minimize the total transportation cost.

The mathematical formulation of the model is as follows:

Let

$$x_{ij} = \text{number of gallons of gasoline shipped from refinery } i \text{ to warehouse } j; i = 1, 2, \ldots, m; j = 1, 2, \ldots, n$$

$$c_{ij} = \text{cost associated with shipment of } x_{ij}$$

Then we want to minimize the total cost represented by the objective function

$$Z = \sum_{i=1}^{m} \sum_{j=1}^{n} c_{ij} x_{ij}$$

Two sets of constraints arise out of the supply and demand restrictions:

Supply restrictions: $\displaystyle\sum_{j=1}^{n} x_{ij} < S_i, \qquad i = 1, 2, \ldots, m$

Demand restrictions: $\displaystyle\sum_{i=1}^{m} x_{ij} > D_j, \qquad j = 1, 2, \ldots, n$

In addition, $x_{ij} > 0$ for all i and j.

Figure 4-4 describes the model graphically.

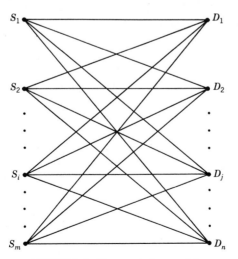

FIGURE 4-4 Transportation model.

4.9 NONLINEAR PROGRAMMING

Nonlinear programming, as the name implies, is applicable to the situation where the objective function is a nonlinear function (e.g., quadratic) of the decision variables. The general nonlinear model is formulated as follows:

Maximize or minimize $Z = f(X)$ subject to

$$\left.\begin{array}{r} g_i(X) \leq b_i \\ X \geq \emptyset \end{array}\right\} i = 1, 2, \ldots, m$$

where

$$X = \begin{pmatrix} x_1 \\ x_2 \\ \vdots \\ x_n \end{pmatrix}$$

is an $n \times 1$ matrix of decision variables and $\emptyset$ is the $n \times 1$ zero matrix. At least one of the functions $f(X)$ and $g_i(X)$ is nonlinear.

Because of the irregular behavior of nonlinear functions, no general algorithm exists for solving a nonlinear programming problem. However, a number of algorithms are available to handle special cases:

Separable Programming. Here the objective function and the constraints are separable functions; that is, they can be expressed as sums of linear functions.

Quadratic Programming. Here the objective function is quadratic in x_1, $x_2, \ldots, x_n$, but the constraints are all linear.

Convex Programming. Here it is assumed that $f(X)$ is a concave function while each $g_i(X)$ is a convex function. As a result, any local optimal solution is also a global optimum solution. Hence, rather than having to find and compare a large number of local optima, it is only necessary to find one local, and therefore global, optimum.

Nonlinear programming remains a very active research area.

4.10 DYNAMIC PROGRAMMING

Dynamic programming is a mathematical technique often useful for making interrelated decisions. There is no standard mathematical formulation of dynamic programming models. Particular equations must be formulated to fit

each situation. Nevertheless, all dynamic programming models have certain characteristics:

1. The problem can be divided into stages with a policy decision required at each stage.
2. Each stage has a number of states associated with it.
3. The effect of the policy decision at each stage is to transform the current state into a state associated with the next stage (possibly according to a probability distribution).
4. Given the current state, an optimal policy for the remaining stages is independent of the policy adopted in the previous stages.
5. The solution procedure starts by finding the optimal policy for each state of the final stage.
6. A recursive relationship that identifies the optimal policy for each state at stage n, given the optimal policy for each stage $n + 1$, is available.
7. Using the recursive relationship, the solution procedure moves backward stage by stage—each time finding the optimal policy for each state of that stage—until it finds the optimal policy when starting at the initial stage.

A dynamic programming model is *deterministic* if the state at the next stage is completely determined by the state and the policy decision at the current stage. The model is *probabilistic* if the state at the next stage is to be selected by a probability distribution.

4.11 INVENTORY MODELS

An inventory model is used when there is a need to uncouple fluctuations of supply from fluctuations of demand. Constant conflict occurs between stockpiling items, which ties up capital, and back-ordering customers' orders. The problem of inventory is the problem of manipulating existing stocks of items so that the combination of the cost of manipulating the stock against that of failing to meet the demand will be minimized.

Inventory control system application is related to this problem. The solution of an inventory model determines the reorder amount and the reorder time for each item in the inventory.

Inventory for a company consists of two parts: an amount of merchandise on hand to handle the regular volume of orders and an amount of safety stock to handle unforeseen situations arising from a sudden increase in demand or the unreliability of vendors. In order to determine the optimal in-

ventory level, many companies use a scientific inventory control procedure. This may be broken down into the following three steps:

1. Analyze the nature of demand for the merchandise and the review process that takes place for requesting a reorder.
2. Formulate a mathematical model in accordance with the demand analysis and the review process.
3. Develop an optimal inventory policy according to the solution of this model.

Inventory models are classified according to (1) whether the demand for a period is known (deterministic demand), or whether it is a random variable having a known probability distribution (stochastic demand); and (2) whether the inventory is reviewed continuously and an order is placed as soon as the stock level falls below the prescribed reorder point, or whether it is reviewed periodically and an order is placed only at the time of the review, even if the inventory level falls below the reorder point during the preceding period.

An optimal inventory policy determines an optimal order quantity Q and an optimal reorder period T for each item in the inventory in such a way that the sum of the ordering cost and the carrying cost is minimum. *Ordering cost* is the total of operating expenses for the receiving department and the expenses involved in paying invoices including the data processing cost, if any. *Carrying cost* is the total of all expenses incurred in retaining the merchandise in inventory. It is customary to compute the carrying cost as a fraction of the unit cost of the merchandise in the inventory. For most industries the carrying cost is between 5% and 25% of the unit cost.

The inventory model is inherently related to the purchasing system in the company, because inventory can be replenished only by purchasing new items. Consequently we now discuss briefly the issues underlying a purchasing system.

4.11.1 Purchasing System Analysis

The standard purchasing process in a company is to purchase raw materials, supplies, manufactured goods, and so on through a combination of purchase requisitions and purchases on contract. The purchasing department in the company supervises the process and follows a uniform policy described in a purchasing manual. The manual defines purchasing authority and procedures in writing, clarifies relationships with other departments and with vendors, and provides standards for evaluating performance. An efficient and effective purchasing system must be keyed to the ideal of providing the company with materials available at the lowest cost and at the proper time. Properly coordinated purchasing systems can provide top managers with a variety of information on which to base decisions.

The purchase requisition system is based upon the preparation of a pur-

chase order at the time of each purchase. This order is the legal authorization to the vendor to provide the requested materials. Generally speaking, the purchase requisition system has the following eight control points:

1. Preparation of purchase order by a formal requisition authority.
2. Value analysis check by the purchasing manager regarding the proper authorization and completeness of specifications in the purchase order.
3. Evaluation of competitive bids.
4. Supervision of the mechanics of transaction as spelled out in the purchase order.
5. Verification of agreement among the original requirement (represented by the office copy of the purchase order), the actual shipment (represented by the executed receiving copy of the purchase order), and the audited invoices, as prerequisite for payment.
6. Purchasing manager's review of the transaction to verify compliance with the company's purchasing policy and procedure.
7. Preparation of check for payment and posting of records by accounts payable.
8. Treasurer's review of the transaction and actual signing of the check for payment.

Purchasing on contract (also called systems contract) is helpful for stock replacement of routine items. A blanket purchase order is prepared describing in general terms the conditions of the purchase and, briefly, the materials covered. The company can draw down on this contract as the demand arises. The purchases on contract may be compared to a marriage between the company and the vendor in that the contract is mutually beneficial as long as both parties are willing to work together. Purchases on contract have the following advantages for the buyer:

1. Reduction of paperwork, since a single purchase order suffices for the entire purchase cycle.
2. Reduction of inventory and dollars invested, since the number of items stocked is less.
3. Reduction of obsolescence and availability of extra floor space, since fewer items are stocked.
4. Improvement in delivery of raw materials to the plant, resulting in a more efficient production operation.
5. Availability of extra time for the purchasing manager, since he/she is relieved of much of the routine paper handling.

In order to achieve maximum efficiency the company should maintain a good balance between centralized and decentralized purchasing systems. The

degree of centralization should be greater if the materials and equipment for a multiplant company are fairly uniform. However, if the materials and equipment are highly diversified over a varied line of production and if the plants are scattered throughout a wide area, then a centralized purchasing system may lead to difficulty in achieving proper controls and obtaining the best services from vendors. Hedrick has described the relative advantages of both systems ([4], pp. 81–84).

The purchasing system in a company must be closely coordinated with the inventory control procedure in that company. The goal is to get the highest possible efficiency in the purchasing department by providing the lowest possible cost consistent with customer requirements. As Hedrick puts it, "This is done by purchasing the right quantity at the right time and at the right price, from the right source, for delivery at the right time." The right quantity and the right time to purchase are determined by the inventory policy.

4.11.2 The Economic Lot Size Inventory Model

The economic lot size model uses continuous review and deterministic demand assumptions. The formulas for computing the optimal order quantity Q and the optimal reorder period T are given by

$$Q = \text{optimal order quantity} = \sqrt{\frac{2ak}{h}}$$

$$T = \text{optimal reorder period} = \frac{Q}{a} = \sqrt{\frac{2k}{ah}}$$

where a is the annual usage rate, k is the fixed setup cost for order, and h is the carrying cost.

It is possible to do sensitivity analysis on the above model. If instead of using Q, one uses a different quantity Q' such that $Q' = cQ$, with c a positive constant, then the ratio $r = (1 - c^2)/2c$ is used as a measure of sensitivity. For example, if $c = .5$, then $r = 1.25$, which means that the additional cost as a result of deviating from the optimal value Q is 25% of the optimal cost. Several values of the sensitivity measure r are available, corresponding to different values of c.

In addition to determining Q and T, the company must consider the lead time, that is, the time between the reorder point and the arrival of the shipment. The lead time is usually handled by keeping an adequate amount of safety stock. If the lead time increases, then the company should order the same quantity Q, but more frequently than before so the volume of inventory will not increase.

The safety stock for a commodity depends on the fluctuation of its usage rate, which is determined by the standard deviation of the frequency distribution of the usage rates. If the standard deviation is high, then the usage

rate fluctuates widely and a safety stock of one standard deviation proves adequate 68% of the time. It is cost ineffective to have a higher safety stock. For items with a highly stable usage rate, the standard deviation will be small, and a safety stock of two to three standard deviations will be adequate 97% or more of the time.

An Application of the Economic Lot Size Model. The application concerns a case study using the economic lot size model for the Industries Division of the Pennsylvania Bureau of Correction. There the purchasing delays were analyzed and an improved inventory policy for three of its garment plants were outlined.

The Industries Division operates 18 production plants in eight state correctional institutions in Pennsylvania. These plants produce furniture, upholstery, mattresses, garments, cardboard, shoes, underwear, hosiery, soap, detergent, lumber, metal shelves, bookcases, automobile license plates, coffee, tea, and printed government forms. During the fiscal year 1975–1976 there was a total workforce of 163 civilians and 1502 inmates. The total payroll for the civilian employees during this period was $2.94 million, and for the inmate workers it was $738, 911. The total average dollar value of the monthly raw material inventory during the same period at the three garment plants at Dallas, Graterford, and Huntingdon was $1.13 million. The total operating fund for the division during this period was $11.06 million. Accordingly, these three plants were criticized for tying up a large amount of cash in the form of unused raw materials. The Planning and Research Division of the Bureau of Correction was then asked to analyze the problem and suggest a solution.

On analysis it appeared there were two types of purchases made by the Industries Division: purchases through purchase requisition (90%) and purchases on contract (10%). For commodities purchased on contract, the division issued a field-limited purchase order for the raw material needed and bought directly from the vendor. The contracts were renewed every 6 months and could be drawn on as needed. For commodities purchased through purchase requisition, the division prepared the purchase order and sent it to the comptroller's office and then to the Department of General Services— Bureau of Purchase (subsequently referred to as "Bureau of Purchase"). Next, the Bureau of Purchase initiated the bid procedure and selected a vendor; the vendor shipped the material to the designated warehouse of the Industries Division; the warehouse sent samples of the material to the Department of General Services—Bureau of Standards (subsequently referred to as "Bureau of Standards"). If the Bureau of Standards approved the sample, then the Industries Division could start using the material. Otherwise, the purchasing cycle had to be repeated with the Bureau of Purchase selecting another vendor or negotiating with the current vendor for a discount on the disapproved material. Figure 4-5 shows the detailed system flowchart for the purchase requisition cycle.

Except for the control as indicated in the footnote of Table 4-1, all other

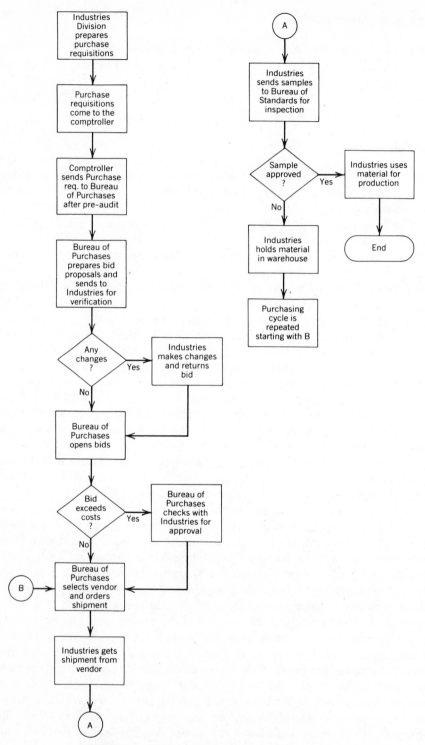

FIGURE 4-5 Industries Division purchasing system.

TABLE 4-1 Major Bottlenecks in Industries Division Purchasing System

From Time When	To Time When	Average Time[a] (in days)	
Industries Division generates purchase order	Purchase order arrives at comptroller	10	(12)
Bureau of Purchase receives purchase order from comptroller	Bureau of Purchase mails bid proposals to vendors	16	(0)
Bureau of Purchase mails bid proposals to vendors	Bids are opened at the Bureau of Purchase	19	(14)
Bureau of Purchase opens bids from vendors	Bureau of Purchase releases order to vendor for shipment	22	(0)
Bureau of Purchase releases order of vendor for shipment	Shipment arrives at Industries Division warehouse	76	(23)
Industries Division sends samples to Bureau of Standards	Bureau of Standards approves samples on testing	10	(0)

[a] Numbers in parentheses represent the corresponding time for purchasing "on contract," where the Industries Division has total control.

factors in both procedures remain the same. The average time was determined through work sampling over a 2-year period from July 1974 through June 1976.

Table 4-1 indicates that the total time an order remains in the purchase requisition cycle averages 153 days, ranging from a minimum of 108 days to a maximum of 214 days. For purchases on contract, that average is only 49 days. Clearly, the Industries Division is severely handicapped in its purchasing efforts by the time-consuming practices of the Bureau of Purchase and the Bureau of Standards. The main reason for the difference in time between the two purchasing procedures is that for purchases on contract the Industries Division deals directly with the vendor through a field-limited purchase order instead of involving the Bureau of Purchase. Negotiations for a discount on raw materials not meeting specifications take less time when the Industries Division deals directly with the vendor instead of going through the Bureau of Standards.

Personal interviews with the Industries Division supervisors at eight state correctional institutions revealed a general dissatisfaction ranging from moderate to intense with the present purchasing system. They further indicated that the government is not a welcome customer for many manufacturers of raw materials because the final payment is often delayed due to paperwork and the manufacturer has to provide a 10% bond for the materials supplied. As a result, Industries Division often has to buy from brokers instead of from the manufacturers. This increases both the price and the delay in receiving shipment.

To improve the purchasing system the following recommendations were made:

☐ Persuade the Department of Services to permit the purchase of more raw materials on contract.

☐ Encourage the policy of buying directly from the manufacturers instead of from the brokers.

☐ In view of the multiplant operation over a wide variety of products, encourage the decentralization of the purchasing system to the extent practicable.

In the next phase of the project, inventory control procedures were analyzed and coordinated with the purchasing system to develop an improved inventory policy.

Since the highest levels of inventory appeared in those items that were to be purchased through the Bureau of Purchase, attention was focused on those raw materials at the three garment plants at Dallas, Graterford, and Huntington that could not be bought on contract. At each plant the inventory system was found to involve a continuous review and uniform demand of the raw materials throughout the year. The monthly usage rate of each raw material was computed on the basis of data ranging over a 2-year period from July 1974 to June 1976. The following improved inventory policy was suggested for the garment plants:

Policy.   For each raw material place an order equal to the amount of the optimal order size at the frequency implied by the reorder period. Keep one month's supply as a safety stock.

Using the formulas given before, the quantities Q and T were computed for each raw material. Table 4-2 shows a sample of the results for the Graterford garment plant. As prerequisites of these computations, the quantities a, k, and h were estimated. In order to determine a, the average annual usage rate for a given raw material, the monthly usage rates for the period July 1974 through June 1976 were averaged. The result was then multiplied by 12 to provide an annual usage rate. The computation of k, the fixed setup cost for ordering a raw material, was based on all controllable costs associated with placing the order. Such costs included the operating expenses of the purchasing unit at the three institutions, of the shipping and receiving units at these institutions, and of the invoice payment unit at the Industries Division; overhead costs were a part of these expenses. Values of k at Dallas, Graterford, and Huntingdon were $2,267, $404, and $600 per year, respectively. Finally, the carrying cost h per year included the cost of capital tied up in idle merchandise, price of obsolescence, losses due to depreciation and deterioration, and losses resulting from an inability to use the cash involved in other ways. Due to the nature of the correctional industries op-

TABLE 4-2 Graterford Garment Plant's Monthly Inventory

Raw Material	Actual Inventory		Suggested Inventory		Reorder Period
	Quantity	Value	Quantity	Value	
65/35 Broadcloth	5,448 yd	$ 6,241	30,186 yd	$ 34,610	1.8 mo
Sunset Mfg. Mat.	157,359 yd	185,572	29,678 yd	35,311	1.9 mo
Poplin	9,623 yd	15,658	7,125 yd	11,586	7.6 mo
¾ oz. twill	13,299 yd	32,325	6,000 yd	14,584	3.8 mo
65% Wool lining	29,902 yd	101,124	5,024 yd	1,701	5.0 mo
Sellesia	16,265 yd	13,576	5,991 yd	5,000	16.1 mo
w/w Officer suiting	1,281 yd	16,739	1,453 yd	19,351	4.4 mo
s/w Officer suiting	1,397 yd	10,991	1,453 yd	12,303	7.2 mo
60/Polyspun	1,858 yd	6,826	1,276 yd	4,688	12.1 mo
Filco thread 12000	2,080 spools	18,161	360 spools	3,146	27.7 mo
Total Value		$407,213		$142,280	

eration, h for a raw material was estimated at 12–15½ % of the unit cost of that material.

In order to implement the suggested inventory policy, each plant was asked to delay the order of each raw material for 3 months, to draw down on their existing inventory so as to reduce the stocks, and subsequently to start the ordering. Since the purchasing cycle stretched over 5 months on an average, this policy provided additional time to use up the existing overloaded inventory.

Some estimates of the benefits available from the improved inventory policy were computed. On the basis of work sampling over a 2-year period from July 1974 through June 1976, it was found that the Graterford garment plant maintained, on an average, a monthly inventory of raw materials amounting to $407,213. However, the optimal inventory size (see Table 4-2) would reduce it to $142,280 a month. This indicated a monthly average reduction of $264,933, or 65% in the raw material inventory value at Graterford alone. The Dallas and Huntingdon plants indicated similar savings. Table 4-2 shows the actual and optimal monthly inventory sizes, their respective dollar values, and the reorder periods for materials at the Greaterford garment plant.

As a result of the recommendations on the purchasing procedure, additional materials were included on contract, and a significant amount of decentralization took place starting July 1, 1977. Instead of controlling every purchase item from a central office, the eight superintendents of the eight state correctional institutions took care of their individual purchasing needs. The Industries Division then played a coordinating role in this decentralized purchasing system. However, the suggested inventory policy was only partially adopted. The shop manager at each institution stopped ordering new raw materials and was asked to reduce the inventory by 30% within a 3-month period.

4.11.3 Other Inventory Models

The economic lot size model, though very widely used, represents only one type of inventory model. As noted in the introduction to Section 4.11, three other situations are possible:

☐ Continuous review and probabilistic demand.
☐ Periodic review and deterministic demand.
☐ Periodic review and probabilistic demand.

In practice, however, a periodic review policy can be used to approximate a continuous review policy by making the time interval sufficiently small. Thus, the real distinction pertains to a deterministic demand versus a probabilistic demand.

In a probabilistic inventory model the demand for a given period is a random variable having a known probability distribution. It is more difficult to

handle than a deterministic model. The principal source of the difficulty lies in the fact that a representation of the probability distribution is often quite hard to find, especially when the demand ranges over a large number of possible values.

Wagner and Whitin ([5], pp. 483–487) gave a dynamic version of the economic lot size model. They used the principle of dynamic programming to handle a periodic review situation where the demand varies from one period to another but is not representable by a known probability distribution. The solution provides a production planning model that assumes a variable demand requirement, a fixed setup cost, and linear production and holding costs.

Hillier and Lieberman ([5], pp. 492–494) have presented a solution of the above production planning model by formulating it as an ILP problem.

4.12 PORTFOLIO ANALYSIS MODELS FOR INVESTMENT STRATEGIES

A *portfolio* is a combination of securities such as common stock, bonds, real estate, and precious metals that an investor uses as the vehicles of investment. Each security provides a certain rate of return and is associated with a certain level of risk. The risk of a security is related to the probability of its default, that is, the probability that an investor can lose money by investing in that security. For example, a high-risk stock has a high probability that its value may go down due to market fluctuations, and consequently an investor must keep a close watch on the market. Normally the higher the risk of a security the higher its return.

The main objective of a portfolio analysis model is to determine a combination of securites belonging to the portfolio so that either the total portfolio risk is minimized for a given level of return or the total portfolio return is maximized for a given level of risk. Both situations involve the typical trade-off issues. A widely accepted technique to achieve the stated goal is to diversify the securities belonging to the portfolio, to let the portfolio consist of a wide range of securities of different types and of varying degrees of risk and return.

In recent years portfolio management techniques have entered a critical and innovative phase of activity. Faced with increasing pressure for high rates of return, with advances in performance measurement techniques, and with the glare of academic inquiry, portfolio managers have been forced to develop new decision-making procedures. They are now using sophisticated mathematical models to improve their performance on portfolio management. The efficient frontier model introduced by Markowitz uses sophisticated optimizing methods to address the problem of portfolio selection. In addition to discussing this model we shall also make brief comments about two other less mathematical models: the capital asset pricing theory model and the random walk and the efficient market model.

A portfolio analysis starts with information concerning individual securities. It ends with conclusions concerning portfolios as a whole. The purpose of the analysis is to find portfolios that best meet the objectives of the investor.

Various types of information concerning securities can be used as the raw material of a portfolio analysis. One source of information is the past performance of individual securities. A second source of information is the beliefs of one or more securities analysts concerning future performances. When past performances of securities are used as inputs, the outputs of the analysis are portfolios that performed particularly well in the past. When beliefs of securities analysts are used as inputs, the outputs of the analysis are the implications of these beliefs for better and worse portfolios.

4.12.1 Performance of Portfolio Managers

Cohen, Zinbarg, and Zeikel ([1], pp. 660–662) have discussed the history of modern portfolio theory and have shed some significant light on the past versus present performance records of portfolio managers. Their comments can be summarized as follows:

1. Traditionally, portfolio managers have made comparisons of rates of return for their portfolios with broad market averages.
2. These managers have been unable to discover whether extra return has been achieved through the assumption of risk.
3. Risk was at best a fuzzy notion.
4. Modern theory has had slow acceptance from practitioners for the following reasons:
   (a) Academicians are unable to communicate with practitioners.
   (b) Practitioners have not looked for methods that might demonstrate how ineffective they are.
   (c) The theories themselves have been challenged and modified frequently.
5. Modern theory is now available to
   (a) Measure risk quantitatively
   (b) Focus attention on the entire portfolio rather than on detailed analysis of individual securities

4.12.2 Markowitz's Assumptions for Portfolio Analysis

The foundation of the modern portfolio analysis models was laid by Dr. Harry M. Markowitz in 1952. His model provided a theoretical framework for selecting an investment portfolio such that an optimum balance could exist

between the level of risk that the investor was willing to assume and the level of return that might be expected from the portfolio. The model used the techniques of quadratic programming so that given an expected level of return, the risk could be minimized. The portfolio could select from hundreds of individual securities and used input from portfolio managers.

Markowitz made the following two assumptions in establishing his model:

1. Investors are risk averse and desire extra compensation in the form of higher return for assuming additional risk in investment.
2. Risk is measured by the standard deviation σ of the possible yield of a portfolio.

Using assumption 1, he demonstrated that diversification of securities can accomplish risk reduction as long as the various securities are uncorrelated. For example, let x_1 and x_2 be the possible returns from two securities so that their respective risks are given by σ_{x_1} and σ_{x_2}. Then the risk $\sigma_{x_1 + x_2}$ of the portfolio consisting of the securities x_1 and x_2 is given by the formula

$$\sigma^2_{x_1 + x_2} = \sigma^2_{x_1} + \sigma^2_{x_2} + 2\,\rho\sigma_{x_1}\sigma_{x_2}$$

where ρ is the correlation coefficient between x_1 and x_2.

For simplicity suppose that

$$\sigma_{x_1} = \sigma_{x_2} = \sigma$$

Then we get, from the above

$$\sigma^2_{x_1 + x_2} = 2\sigma^2 + 2\rho\sigma^2$$

If the securities are totally correlated so that $\rho = 1$, then the risk of the portfolio is given by

$$\sigma_{x_1} + x_2 = \sqrt{4\sigma^2} = 2\sigma$$

If, however, the securities x_1 and x_2 are uncorrelated so that $\rho = 0$, then the portfolio risk is

$$\sigma_{x_1} + x_2 = \sqrt{2\sigma^2} = \sqrt{2}\,\sigma < 2\sigma$$

that is, the risk of the portfolio becomes less. Also, as ρ decreases from 1 to 0, securities become less and less correlated and $\sigma_{x_1} + x_2$ continues to decrease.

4.12.3 The Efficient Frontier Model

A portfolio is *efficient* if it is not possible to obtain higher returns for a given level of risk or lower risk for a given level of return. Otherwise, the portfolio is defined as *inefficient*. The *efficient frontier* is the locus of points showing the maximum return for each degree of risk. Portfolios that lie below the efficient frontier curve fail to represent optimal diversification that can be achieved through a different distribution of securities.

Let us suppose that a portfolio consists of n securities $Y_1, Y_2, \ldots, Y_n$. Suppose that security Y_i has an expected return μ_{Y_i} and a risk (i.e., standard deviation of expected return) σ_{Y_i}, $i = 1, 2, \ldots, n$, over the time period under review. Then the portfolio yields n points $(\sigma_{Y_i}, \mu_{Y_i})$, $i = 1, 2, \ldots, n$. If we plot them on a two-dimensional graph and join them by a curve, as in Figure 4-6, then the resulting graph is called the *efficient frontier* for the portfolio.

Figure 4-6 shows that portfolio P is less optimal than either Q or R, because Q gives the same return as P (since P and Q have the same μ value) but assumes a lower risk (since $\sigma_Q < \sigma_P$), whereas R has the same risk as P (since $\sigma_R = \sigma_P$) but yields a higher return (since $\mu_R > \mu_P$).

In general, portfolios falling in the middle range of the curve are highly diversified while those lying near the extremes (like S and T) are much less so. An optimal or efficient portfolio yields the highest possible expected return for a given risk level that the investor is willing to assume. All other portfolios having the same or lower risk will yield a lower expected return.

(a) Mathematical Formulation of the Efficient Frontier Model. A portfolio is represented by a vector

$$x = \begin{pmatrix} x_1 \\ x_2 \\ \vdots \\ x_n \end{pmatrix}$$

where x_j is the fraction of the portfolio invested in security j, and $j = 1, 2, \ldots, n$. The decision variables $x_1, x_2, \ldots, x_n$ are subject to the constraint

$$\sum_{j=1}^{n} x_j = 1$$

so that the total portfolio is accounted for. Now let μ_j be the expected return on security j and let σ_{ij} be the covariance between the variables x_i and x_j, where $i, j = 1, 2, \ldots, n$. Then the expected return Z on the portfolio is given by

$$Z = \sum_{j=1}^{n} x_j \mu_j$$

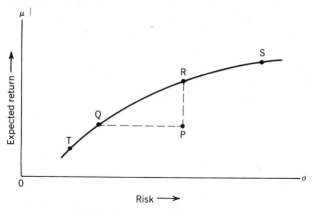

FIGURE 4-6   The efficient frontier.

A typical constraint involving Z is of the form $Z > C$, where C is a constant. It means that the expected return on the portfolio must be greater than C.
    The variance of return on the portfolio is

$$V = \sum_{i=1}^{n} \sum_{j=1}^{n} \sigma_{ij} x_i x_j$$

where $\sigma_{ij} = \sigma_{ji}$ for all i and j. Then V represents the risk of the total portfolio and is the objective function of the model.
    The solution of the model consists of variables $x_1, x_2, \ldots, x_n$ such that Z exceeds a given value C subject to the constraint $\sum_{j=1}^{n} x_j = 1$, and V is minimized. Since V is a quadratic function in the decision variables, the model uses the technique of quadratic progamming.
    Markowitz extended the above model to a more general form ([7], pp. 170–186) that is beyond the scope of our discussion. He also indicated that the critical line method of quadratic programming can be used to solve his efficient frontier model ([7], pp. 330–332).

(b) Solution Requirements of the Efficient Frontier Model.   In order to apply the efficient frontier model, it is necessary to have the following information.

1. Projected expected rate of return from security i
2. Projected range of variation in possible rate of return
3. Covariance σ_{ij} between the expected rates of return from every pair of securities i, j belonging to the portfolio

    Having given all the above information, the model can be run to provide the most probable rates of return on numerous possible portfolio combinations

TABLE 4-3   Sample Model Solution

Portfolio	Expected Return	Expected Standard Deviation (Risk)	Expected Range of Return at One Standard Deviation	
			$\mu - \sigma$	$\mu + \sigma$
1	4%	0.5%	3.5– 4.5%	
2	7%	1.5%	5.5– 8.5%	
3	10%	4.5%	5.5–14.5%	
⋮	⋮	⋮	⋮	
10	20%	16%	4–36%	

of individual securities and the associated possible ranges of deviation from these most likely returns, Table 4-3 shows a typical solution derived from the model.

The model user can change the last two columns by indicating how many standard deviations are to be included in the range.

The model was run first in 1962 using an IBM software package. Various modifications have been made since then to improve the model's performance.

After the model was introduced, several criticisms were leveled at it. These are summarized below ([1], pp. 667–668):

Being based on estimates of individual securities, it contains a subjective element and still requires detailed analysis of individual securities.

Investors may not be risk averse.

The variance of short-run performance may not be the proper measure of risk for long-run objectives.

Practitioners have difficulty in assessing individual σ_{ij}'s for every pair (i, j).

Each change in outlook for any security can require much buying and selling to change the portfolio to optimum.

There is a great deal of output, and many calculations are required.

Before concluding this section it should be noted that often near-optimal solutions are achieved by using the efficiet frontier model. To clarify this issue, let us look at Figure 4-7. Usually the portfolio is at P and the following four choices are possible:

1. At A, minimize portfolio risk at the maximum level of expected return.
2. At B, maximize expected return at the existing level of risk.
3. At C, minimize portfolio risk at the existing level of expected return.
4. At D, maximize expected return at the minimum risk level.

Portfolio managers must make the choice on the basis of a variety of portfolio constraints. Usually it involves a high degree of diversification among common stocks, long-term bonds, and U.S. Treasury bills.

4.12.4 Capital Asset Pricing Theory

Capital asset pricing theory, or capital market theory, details the character of the market's pricing mechanism when all investors act as if they were governed by the principle of risk aversion and the desire to optimize portfolio composition through diversification. The main assumptions of this theory are:

1. Investors are risk averse and want efficient diversification of their portfolios.
2. An individual investor's actions will not affect the prices of securities.
3. The market is a composite view of all the investors balancing their different opinions.
4. Investors have similar time periods for investments and similar concerns.
5. There is unlimited availability of risk-free borrowing and investing.
6. Securities are perfectly divisible, that is, an investor can use as small or as large a denomination as he/she chooses.

Assumptions 4–6 are unique to capital asset pricing theory and are not found in the efficient frontier model. Also, many of the six assumptions do not coincide with the actual state of the working-day securities market price mechanism.

The capital asset pricing theory claims that due to the above assumptions the market is a complete universe of all risky investments and is priced "fairly" in relation to the risk associated with the ownership of its securities. In order to represent the *capital market line* graphically, the investor calculates the return μ and its associated risk σ for the complete market. Normally,

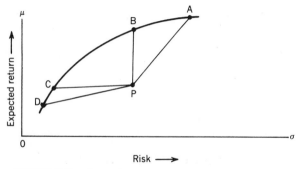

FIGURE 4-7 Alternative points on the efficient frontier.

Standard and Poor's 500 stock price index is used as a proxy for the market universe.

Figure 4-8 illustrates the capital market line. Line $R_f M$ in this figure is determined by joining the point (O, R_f), which corresponds to risk-free investment, and the point $M = (\sigma, \mu)$, which represents the complete market. In the figure, R_f is the rate of return from investment in a risk-free portfolio and segment $R_f M$ indicates the various returns available through commitments in a combination of risk-free assets and risky assets. In order to get an expected return greater than market, we need a point between M and A. The investor then is assumed to borrow at the risk-free rate and leverage the portfolio by reinvesting the borrowed funds in the market. This theoretical portfolio of greater than market risk to produce greater than market return is not available to most investors.

Capital asset pricing theory departs somewhat from the efficient frontier model in the following sense. In the latter, the level of risk (i.e., σ_Y for security Y) is adjusted by moving up or down the efficient frontier of alternative portfolios of different individual securities. However, under capital asset pricing theory, risk is adjusted by borrowing or lending against a single optimal risky portfolio, which happens to be the entire market.

The following criticisms are made against the capital asset pricing theory:

1. The assumption that all investors can lend or borrow unlimited sums at a risk-free rate is untenable.
2. Risk-oriented investors tend to exaggerate in their mind the returns from high-risk stocks, and thus realized returns are not commensurate with the risks involved.
3. Performance measurements for mixed funds (bonds and stocks) must separate the stock and bond components rather than compute a single market risk.
4. The use of correlation to measure diversification is inadequate.
5. There is no appropriate or preferred time interval over which to meas-

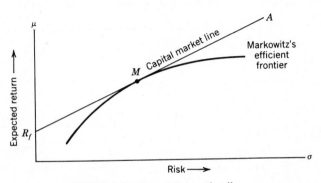

FIGURE 4-8   The capital market line.

ure the market risk. It is suggested that this risk should be related to the investor's time horizon. Choosing a very short time period for measuring risk leads to serious statistical problems.

4.12.5 Random Walk and the Efficient Market

The random walk hypothesis of stock price movement is based on the following assumptions:

1. The market is efficient; that is, the price is the best composite estimate of its value (it is not systemically under- or overvalued).
2. Successive price changes are independent of previous price changes and are caused by new information, which occurs in random fashion.
3. Prices conform to some frequency function.
4. Information affecting stock prices is immediately available to all investors.

The theory seems to have been borne out by statistical tests of independence and indicates that no mechanical rules do any better than random chance. An example of a mechanical rule is given by Alexander's filter technique, which states that an investor should:

☐ Sell when price completes its upward move (determined by a specified drop from the previous high).
☐ Buy when price completes its downward move (determined by a specified rise from the previous low).

Random walk theory claims that any such rule is as good as taking a random chance in stock investment, so that any technical approach is worthless. The theory thus poses a serious challenge to the use of mathematical models for optimizing portfolio returns. However, the following arguments can be made in favor of a more analytical approach:

1. It is remotely possible that generally unknown information can be discovered by analysis.
2. Improved research might provide a more accurate forecast of future earnings and greater awareness of critical factors.
3. It appears to take time for knowledge to filter through the market, so that a sophisticated analyst might move faster than competitors who lack analytical tools.
4. Random walk theory would imply that analysis can concentrate more on portfolio composition than on seeking out improperly valued securities.

Random walk theory is not an optimizing model and in reality tends to argue against using such a model. It seems to reinforce the following remark of Mark Twain

> October. This is one of the peculiarly dangerous months to speculate in stocks. The others are July, January, September, April, November, May, March, June, December, August and February.

4.13 PROBABILISTIC MODELS IN RISK ANALYSIS

As we have seen in the portfolio analysis models, the notion of probability is crucial here. Variance in general increases as the investment returns move further into the future. Consequently, some form of weighting coefficient must be used on the investment. For example, weighting the return inversely as the variance will have the effect of giving less credibility to returns in years far ahead.

In using probabilistic models we make two stringent assumptions: (1) Deviations from the expected return yielded by the investment each year are going to be independent of those in the other years, and (2) the form of prior probability distributions can be estimated.

Investment decision outcomes are strongly dependent on probability and cannot be calculated in a deterministic way. However, the major problem appears in estimating the prior probability distribution.

4.14 MARKET RISK AND SPECIFIC RISK

There are two types of risk associated with any security, market risk and specific risk. *Market risk* is associated with the movement of the market as a whole. *Specific risk* is the risk associated with the specific asset and consists of a part attributable to industry characteristics and another part attributable to the issuing company.

Consider the monthly returns from a security for a 12-month period. Each monthly return can be split into two parts, x and y, where

$$x = \text{market return for the month measured by the S\&P 500}$$
$$\text{Index as a representative of the overall market}$$
$$y = \text{specific return for the month on that security}$$

Let us fit a regression line through these twelve points: (x_i, y_i), $i = 1, 2, \ldots, 12$, and let its equation be

$$y = \alpha + \beta x$$

Then

$$\beta = \text{slope of regression line}$$
$$\alpha = \text{intercept of regression line on } y \text{ axis}$$

Hence β measures the rate of change of y with respect to x, that is, the amount of security return per unit of market return. We can distinguish among three different cases:

a. If $\beta = 1$, then, *on the average*, every 1% return on the market is associated with a 1% return on the security.

b. If $\beta < 1$, then *on the average*, every 1% return on the market is associated with less than 1% return on the security.

c. if $\beta > 1$, then, *on the average*, every 1% return on the market is associated with over 1% return on the security.

High-β stocks are more volatile; β measures the market component of a stock's return, and is usually positive. α measures the specific component of a stock's return and can be positive, zero, or negative.

As an example, suppose that for a certain stock $\alpha = 0.75$ and $\beta = 2$. Then the line of regression has the equation

$$y = 0.75 + 2x.$$

If the market return for the stock for a particular month is 8%, then the return for the stock for that month is expected to be

$$(0.75 + 2 \times 8)\% = 16.75\%$$

Finally, let ρ be the coefficient of correlation between x and y. As observations deviate from the line of regression, ρ declines. Also, if ρ is zero, then no linear relation exists between the market return and the stock return.

For a highly diversified portfolio, α is close to zero and ρ is close to one.

There is skepticism about these concepts and techniques. Many think that α and β cannot be separated in reality. Some practitioners claim that β relates only to relative stock price movement and not to the fundamental business and finanacial features of the company.

Merrill Lynch notes that by proper diversification, specific risk can be reduced to 5–15% and the market risk to 85–95%. The value of β for a portfolio is computed as the weighted average of the β values of the component securities.

4.14.1 Properties of the Beta Coefficient

☐ β values tend to regress toward the mean value of 1.0.

☐ β values of individual stocks are not very stable over time, and the same applies to β values for industry groups.

☐ β tends to be more stable when the portfolio contains a large number of issues.

☐ High-β securities normally earn less on average than low-β securities.

☐ High-β securities do better than market in a rising market and worse than market in a falling market.

☐ Risk and return for portfolios with $0.8 \leq \beta \leq 1.5$ (the range for most portfolio managers) are not mutually correlated to any discernible degree.

4.15 ACTIVE AND PASSIVE PORTFOLIO MANAGEMENT

Active portfolio management is the attempt to profit from stock selection, market timing, or both. It is an attempt to achieve an investment return about the capital market line. There are two major requirements for success; the portfolio

1. Have a good idea about how others view alternative investments.
2. Disagree with the consensus about the direction and magnitude of price movement.

Active portfolio management requires that the manager either concedntrate funds in a fairly small number of issues, continuously reassessing alternatives, or move in and out of well-diversified portfolios. Most professional portfolio managers are not very successful in these efforts.

Charles Ellis in an article in *Financial Analysts Journal* (July/August, 1975) suggests four rules for success:

Know your policies very well and play accordingly.

Make fewer but better investment decisions.

Concentrate on selling instead of buying, because it is too difficulty to outperform others in buying.

Be prepared to lose the same, for it is tough.

Passive portfolio management implies the creation of a well-diversified portfolio, usually with $\beta = 1.0$, and holding it relatively unchanged for the long run. Index funds (see Section 4.15.1) are examples of passive portfolio management.

Passive portfolios have very low turnover and hence minimum transaction

costs, reduced management expenses, and a low risk level. Most traditional portfolios contain both active and passive parts.

4.15.1 Index Funds

An *index fund* is a portfolio designed to mirror the movement of a selected broad market index by holding commitments in the same portfolio as those that comprise the index itself. An index fund, by definition, has $\beta = 1$. β can be moved up or down from the value 1.0 by adding or deleting risky assets to or from the portfolio. Once established, the portfolio need not be disturbed except to accommodate cash flows, to reinvest dividend income,a nd to adjust for issues added to or deleted from the market index. Once the fund is established, the transaction costs are minimal and there is no need for extensive security analysis.

With the growing dissatisfaction over the performance of conventionally managed portfolios, index funds are particularly attractive to pension fund trustees.

4.15.2 Apparent versus Actual Diversification

A carefully selected sample of stocks can provide about the same diversification as would be obtained by owning all the stocks in the index fund. About 90% of the market's movement can be achieved by holding about 32 stocks. The impact of diversification increases with the number of holdings at a rapidly decreasing rate, becoming asymptotic at approximately 35 holdings. Viewed from this perspective, most portfolios would seem to contain far too many securities.

On the other hand, some observers content that diversification improves a portfolio's predictability. For this purpose, 50 or even 100 holdings would be too few. A larger number of issues are needed in a high-risk portfolio to achieve the same level of diversification as in a low-risk portfolio.

4.16 MARKETING MODELS

Marketing is often called a function of management, although it is more than that. For many companies it is almost synonymous with corporate planning strategy. Marketing goals are viewed as overall company goals. Accordingly the marketing policy has to work within the broad purview of macroeconomics and must take into account the interaction between consumers and producers in a free market. The individual consumer runs through a cycle of produce purchase, product use, and exposure to outside influences. The influences on the consumer represent business expenditures, while the behavior of the consumer represents potential income to the business. A qualitative data analysis is needed to explore this relationship.

The first issue to resolve is what the *market* is. We need to know its boundaries and who the competitors are. The definition of a market affects the entire competitive strategy. Even within a single product the definition of market may not be straightforward; for example, sales of a particular brand of TV may relate to:

Sales of all brands of TV.
Sales of all brands of TV, radios, and video cassette recorders.
Sales of all electronic appliances.
Sales of all entertainment facilities.

The most competitive situations arise in the marketing of finished products. Two major issues involved are:

1. How to best utilize the sales force and how to evaluate the impact of promotional efforts on sales.
2. How to determine the optimal fund allocation to advertising and how to assess the effect of advertising on sales.

The marketing models to be discussed here will address these two issues.

4.16.1 Quantitative Measurements of Sales Performance

Using the results of an industry survey, we can list the following quantitative factors to measure the effectiveness of the sales force in a company ([11], pp. 215–217):

Turnover Rate. This is the ratio of the number of salespersons who quit or were discharged to the average size of the total sales force during a period of time.

Performance Index. This is the growth rate of the sales force over a given period of time. It thus represents the increase in sales volume per salesperson during the specified time period.

Compensation Rate. This represents the average compensation paid to a salesperson and is classified as low, medium, or high.

Span of Control. This is the average number of salespersons on a force divided by the average number of field supervisors.

Opportunity Rate. This is measured by the percentage of salespersons transferred out and promoted from the sales force.

Earnings Opportunity Ratio (EOR). This is the ratio of the compensation of the highest-paid salesperson on a sales force to that of the average-paid salesperson.

A marketing model designed to identify the exact goals that a sales ex-

ecutive should pursue in order to optimize sales performance must often cope with conflicting issues. Ideally the model should maximize the performance index and minimize the turnover rate subject to the constraints imposed by the company. However, these are not always compatible goals. Realistically, therefore, a sales executive should decide what turnover rate is tolerable and maximize performance subject to that level.

4.16.2 Major Findings on Performance Measures

Newton ([11], pp. 217–219) listed the following strong conclusions pertaining to the quantitative measurements listed in Section 4.16.1:

- ☐ The turnover rate of a sales force does not directly influence its performance index.
- ☐ A turnover rate of 10% or more is extremely costly in all classifications and should be avoided.
- ☐ The turnover rate is directly influenced by the opportunity rate.
- ☐ Turnover rate is also directly influenced by the compensation rate.
- ☐ The compensation rate does not directly influence the performance index.
- ☐ The performance index is directly influenced by the character and effectiveness of the reporting system used to control the force.
- ☐ Job content is a critical factor affecting both performance index and turnover rate.

4.16.3 Effect of Promotional Effort on Sales

Sales management always wants to know how much advertising, selling, or promotional effort can be economically justified. A response to this question requires at least an intuitive knowledge of the relation between sales volume and promotional efforts. A marketing model addressing this issue must provide an objective measure of the relative efficiency of the distribution of promotional efforts. Such a model can be set up as follows:

1. Study the effects of the existing promotional effort on sales.
2. Select an optimal goal and examine how close to this goal the current level of promotional efforts are.
3. Design a strategy to achieve the optimal goal.
4. Perform a trade-off analysis to determine whether the additional cost incurred in following the proposed strategy can be justified by the increase in sales. The justification may not always be economic in nature. For example, improved public relations is a valid justification.

(a) Impact of Advertising on Sales. The classic hypothesis here is: All other things being equal, there will be a direct relationship between the

amount of sales and the amount spent on advertising. The functional relationship should be a monotonically increasing function with an asymptotic approach to an upper limit. Figure 4-9 illustrates the shape of this function.

In an industry study done by Vidale and Wolfe ([3], pp. 29–42), three parameters are listed as helpful in describing the interaction between advertising and sales: sales decay constant, saturation level, and reponse constant.

(b) Sales Decay Constant. In the absence of advertising efforts, sales tend to decrease due to product obsolescence, competing advertising, and other factors. Under relatively uniform market conditions the rate of decrease is, in general, constant. Accordingly, the *sales decay constant* λ is defined as an exponential parameter. The sales rate $S(t)$ of a product at time t is given by

$$S(t) = S(0) \, e^{-\lambda t}$$

The parameters λ ranges from values as large as 1000 for products that become quickly obsolescent or products in a highly competitive market to nearly zero for noncompetitive, well-established products.

(c) Saturation Level. The saturation level M measures the practical limit of sales that can be generated. In Figure 4-9, the line $y = M$ is the asymptotic upper limit. M depends both on the product being advertised and on the advertising media used. It represents the fraction of the market that the specific advertising can capture. M can often be increased by other advertising media.

(d) Response Constant. The response constant r is the volume of sales generated per advertising dollar when initially the sale volume S is zero. We note that the number of new customers who are potential buyers decreases

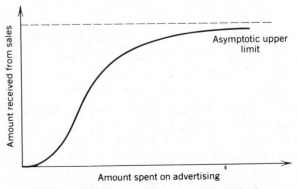

FIGURE 4-9 Relation between advertising and sales.

as sales approach saturation. When advertising is directed indiscriminately to both customers and noncustomers, the effectiveness of each advertising dollar in obtaining new customers decreases as sales increase.

4.17   MATHEMATICAL MODEL OF ADVERTISING EFFECT

Vidale and Wolfe ([3], p. 37) have proposed the following mathematical model to explain the relation between advertising expense and sales volume:

$$\frac{ds}{dt} = \frac{r\, A(t)(M - S)}{M} - \lambda S$$

where $S = S(t)$ is the volume of sales at time t, $A(t)$ is advertising expense at time t, r is the response constant, M is the saturation level, and λ is the sales decay constant.

A first approximation to the solution of the above differential equation is provided by the steady-state solution corresponding to $dS/dt = 0$. We then get

$$A(t) = \frac{\lambda S M}{r(M - S)}$$

Here $A(t)$ is the advertising expense needed to maintain sales at a steady predetermined level of S. We note that when M approaches S so that $M - S$ tends to zero, the denominator decreases. Hence the closer sales are to the saturation level K and the larger the ratio λ/r, the more expensive it becomes to maintain the required sales volume.

Once $A(t)$ is determined from the model, sales managers must allocate the total budget $A(t)$ among different products that are to be sold in the market. Advertising is a form of investment, so the whole or a part of $A(t)$ should be allocated to only those products whose sales will result in a return on capital invested equal to or greater than the returns from other possible investments, such as new equipment and research.

4.17.1   Remarks on the Advertising Model

Following Vidale and Wolfe we can make the following comments:

1. When carefully designed and executed, advertising experiments give results that are both reliable and reproducible. The degree of accuracy attainable is, however, considerably less than would be considered acceptable in many other fields of research. Product advertising gives quick results; the pretesting of proposed product advertising campaigns, therefore, is especially attractive.

2. The response of sales to advertising varies widely from product to product, but some generalizations are possible. The response of individual products to an advertising promotion may be characterized by two parameters: the response constant and the saturation level. A third parameter, the sales decay constant, gives the rate at which customers are lost.

3. A mathematical model of sales response based on these three parameters has proved useful in the analysis of advertising campaigns. By means of this model one can compute the quantities needed to evaluate and compare alternative promotional campaigns.

4. A knowledge of sales response to advertising for each product permits one to evaluate the return that can be expected from capital invested in advertising for each product. With this information it is then possible to select profitable advertising programs and to estimate the optimum total size of the advertising budget.

4.18   LINEAR PROGRAMMING MODEL IN MEDIA SELECTION

Bass and Lonsdale ([3], pp. 43–61) have formulated an LP model that allows the user to select the best set of media alternatives for advertising from a given range of such alternatives in order to maximize the media exposure for a given budget. The alternatives include not only media but also specific choices within a given medium. For a given magazine, for example, the model can select page size, color or black and white, and so on. Thus, the choices include all media vehicles capable of carrying an advertisement.

For the purpose of the model, we define a *media vehicle* to be any carrier of advertising. Each media vehicle then yields a certain number of exposures per dollar. The exposure is so defined as to allow comparison among various alternative media vehicles. We can now formulate the LP model.

Assume that the model wants to select from n media vehicles. The decision variables are defined as $x_1, x_2, \ldots, x_n$, where

$$x_j = \text{number of units of media vehicle } j, \quad j = 1, 2, \ldots, n$$

Also, let

$$c_j = \text{number of exposures per insertion in vehicle } j, j = 1, 2, \ldots, n$$

Then the objective function Z is defined as

$$Z = c_1 x_1 + c_2 x_2 + \cdots + c_n x_n = \sum_{j=1}^{n} c_j x_j$$

and Z is to be maximized.

The model includes three types of constraints:

Operational. This constraint restricts the model so that no more than one advertisement appears in each issue of a given medium.

Budgetary. Assume that h_j is the cost per unit of vehicle j and that B is the total budget available. Then we must have

$$\sum_{j=1}^{n} b_j x_j \leq B$$

In addition, the advertiser may want to restrict the proportion of budget spent in a certain media class—magazines, newspapers, television, and so on. For instance, he may insist that at most 25% of the budget be allocated to newspaper advertising and at most 40% to television.

Market Segment. The target audience for the product that is being advertised may belong to different market segments, say, men, women, and teenagers. If twice as many women as men buy the product, then the advertiser may want to impose a constraint that allocates twice as many exposures to women as to men.

4.18.1 Comments on Media Selection Model

We quote the following comments of Bass and Lonsdale on the above LP model for media selection ([3], pp. 54–55, reprinted with permission from the publisher, *Journal of Marketing Research,* American Marketing Association, Chicago.):

Linear models are crude devices to apply to the media selection problem. The linearity assumption itself is the cause of much of the difficulty. Justifying an assumption of linear response to advertising exposures on theoretical grounds would be difficult. In applying linear programming to media selection problems, it has been observed that a restraint must be imposed which is essentially judgmental. The restraints are fundamental judgements about the nonlinearity of response. Hence, restraints are imposed on media, or on the allocation of exposures to market segments, in order to express some judgement about limits of effectiveness within these categories.

On the basis of the investigation presented in this paper, it appears that attempts to impose meaningful restraints on the linear model would probably be unfruitful. When only the budget restraint and operational restraints on each vehicle are employed, the model is reduced to a simple cost per thousand model. The distribution structure of the media audiences makes it difficult to develop useful

restraints which allocate exposures to market segments. Finally, the weighting system used to adjust audience data for variations in "quality" and audience composition does not seem to influence solutions greatly.

Crude as these models are, they suggest possible avenues for examining alternatives. As a point of departure, these models serve a useful purpose. It is clear, however, that much more theoretical and empirical work will be necessary in order to permit significant improvement in media selection. Assumptions about the nature of response to advertising cause most difficulties in models of the types examined in this article. Models with non-linear response functions, although empirically demanding, would diminish most problems associated with the imposition of judgement restraints on a linear structure.

4.19   CASE STUDY OF LP MODEL FOR MEDIA SELECTION*

COMPANY: The Cormier Shoe Company, Paul J. Cormier, President.
PRODUCT: High fashion men's shoes.
STATEMENT OF PROBLEM: As President and Chief Financial Officer, I have just completed my budget for 1982. I have approved an advertising expenditure of $450,000 and I want the highest return on my investment for these advertising expenditures. In other words, what media vehicles should we choose and how many dollars should we spend on each?

I   MARKETING BACKGROUND
(A) *Primary Target.*   Men 18+ years. Since this target represents about one-third of all the people in the country. 100 percent of our advertising weight should be toward this target.

Adult Men

Age	% of U.S. Men	% of Our Market Weight
18–23	33%	40%
35–49	30%	40%
50+	37%	20%
Total U.S.	100%	100%

(B) *Occupation.*   Through our market studies it is felt the occupation of the market is important.

*The following study was done by Mr. Paul J. Cormier, a graduate student of mine at Bentley College, Waltham, Massachusetts, under my guidance and supervision. The paper is reproduced in full with only minor editing.

	Adult Men	
	% U.S. Men	% of Our Market Weight
Professionals, execs., etc.	22%	50%
Clerical and sales	10%	40%
Craftsmen and laborers	40%	10%
Misc. (Retired, unemployed, students, etc.)	28%	-0-
Total	100%	100%

(C) *Household Groups.* Certain household groups are more important than others. Higher weight is placed in the following areas:

1. Education

2. Income

3. Size of area population

II MODEL SELECTION

My team of managers decided that the objectives of our media selection could best be expressed in terms of exposures of advertising messages to our target audience. The exposure value is expressed as a function of the number of units of space (or time if vehicle is TV or radio) in each of the alternative advertising media vehicles available. Thus the objective function can be expressed:

$$\text{Total exposure value} = e_1 \text{ (units of vehicle 1)}$$
$$+ e_2 \text{ (units of vehicle 2)} + e_3 \text{ (units of vehicle 3)} \cdots + e_n$$

In essence, we decided to design a linear programming model for media selection as a mathematical procedure for maximizing the exposure value subject to certain conditions imposed by the attributes of the media itself, the budget available, and our own judgments imposed via our marketing policies.

III QUANTIFYING MEDIA EXPOSURE VALUES

A basic requirement of our linear programming model was an estimate of the exposure value of a unit of space or time in a given media vehicle. These values would show how much one unit in each vehicle contributes to the total exposure values so we can best decide how to spend our advertising dollars.

We decided to quantify media exposure values based on certain criteria deemed most important to myself and my marketing and advertising managers.

☐ Audience size; defined as how many people may be exposed to our advertisements: the total circulation of a magazine, total number of people estimated to be tuned into a television show, and so on.

☐ Audience composition, defined as "type" of audience reached: for example, *Fortune* magazine would reach more executives than *People* or *Woman's Day*.

☐ Advertisement exposure; defined readers or viewers actually seeing the advertisements. For example (unlike audience size), many people may leave the room when a commercial comes on, and not all readers of a magazine look at every page.

☐ Quantitative value; defined as media "class." In other words, some media may be more appropriate than others for a more creative approach. For example, Cormier Shoes believes that color added substantially to the impact of the advertisement.

Taking these four factors into account we defined the concept of "exposure value." We estimated an exposure value for each alternative media unit and the overall value of a media schedule measured in terms of exposure units (Exhibit A). Thus, for three media vehicles, the total exposure units is shown in the following algorithm.

Total exposure units = number of units in vehicle 1 × exposure value of one unit in vehicle 1 + number of units in vehicle 2 × exposure value of one unit in vehicle 2 + number of units in vehicle 3 × exposure value of one unit in vehicle 3

IV   THE LINEAR PROGRAMMING SOLUTION

The audience estimates for each advertising vehicle were compiled, yielding the table presented in Exhibit A.

CONSTRAINTS

A. All media units must be at least zero:

$$X(1) \geq 0, \qquad X(2) \geq 0, \qquad X(3) \geq 0, \qquad \ldots , X(20) \geq 0$$

B. The number of insertions in each of the print media must not cover a time span greater than the combined fall and spring seasons, which covered a total of 26 weeks for 6 months.

$X(1) \leq 6$	$X(5) \leq 26$	$X(9) \leq 6$	$X(13) \leq 6$
$X(2) \leq 6$	$X(6) \leq 26$	$X(10) \leq 6$	$X(14) \leq 26$
$X(3) \leq 6$	$X(7) \leq 26$	$X(11) \leq 26$	$X(15) \leq 26$
$X(4) \leq 6$	$X(8) \leq 26$	$X(12) \leq 6$	$X(16) \leq 26$

EXHIBIT A   Alternative Media Vehicles with Units, Costs, and Exposure Values per Unit for Cormier Shoes

| | | Per Unit | | Ratio of |
| | | Cost | Exposure Value | Exposure Value to Cost |
Vehicle and Unit		Cost	Value	to Cost
Magazines (all 4-color)				
Esquire, 1 page	X(1)	$ 9,650	193.0	.0200
½ page	X(2)	5,650	91.5	.0162
Fortune, 1 page	X(3)	50,140	882.5	.0176
½ page	X(4)	29,750	470.4	.0158
Look, 1 page	X(5)	48,170	751.7	.0156
½ page	X(6)	31,850	477.8	.0150
New Yorker, 1 page	X(7)	4,950	81.6	.0165
Newsweek, 1 page	X(8)	13,055	155.3	.0119
Playboy, 1 page	X(9)	11,300	209.1	.0185
½ page	X(10)	6,550	98.9	.0151
Time, 1 page	X(11)	23,050	246.6	.0107
True, 1 page	X(12)	13,450	150.6	.0120
½ page	X(13)	8,010	79.4	.0100
Newspapers:				
1,000-line advertisements in				
Top 10 markets	X(14)	15,500	261.9	.0169
Top 30 markets	X(15)	30,200	546.7	.0181
Top 50 markets	X(16)	40,000	662.7	.0166
Network Television:				
Participation in two 1-hour spectaculars-four commercial minutes	X(17)	148,000	1,296.5	.0088
Spot Television:				
Fringe evening time, 60-sec commercials, two commercials per week in:				
Top 10 markets	X(18)	11,800	132.2	.0112
Top 30 markets	X(19)	18,600	249.2	.0134
Top 50 markets	X(20)	23,000	259.7	.0113

C. Because they were considered "essential" media, *Esquire* and *Fortune* should receive at least one insertion each.

$$X(1) \geq 1, \quad X(3) \geq 1$$

D. We believe that it is essential to run at least one newspaper advertisement in each of the top 20 cities.

$$X(15) \geq 1$$

E. On the basis of past experience, we feel that at least one-half the total budget ($225,000) should be spent in magazines.

$$C(1)X(1) + C(2)X(2) + C(3)X(3) + \cdots + C(13)X(13) = \$225,000$$

where $C1, C2$, etc., are the costs per unit for the magazine units.

F. The total expenditures on media are restricted to the total budget.

$$C(1)X(1) + C(2)X(2) + \cdots + C(20)X(20) \leqslant \$450,000$$

G. We voted to undertake sponsorship of a television "spectacular."

$$X(17) \geqslant 1$$

The objective is to maximize the exposure value within the total budget constraint and subject to all the other constraints. Step number one is to satisfy the constraints by including in the solution the minimum number of units of each advertising vehicle for which a minimum has been specified. In this case, a minimum of at least one unit be used of $X(1)$, $X(3)$, and $X(15)$. Each of these is set to 1, thus satisfying all minimum restrictions.

The next step is to maximize the total exposure value by buying as many units as possible of the advertising vehicle with the highest exposure value per dollar up to the limits (the constraints) imposed for the specific units.

If any budget remains, it should be used on the advertising vehicle with the next highest exposure unit value per dollar, and so on until the budget is exhausted or until constraints restrict further use of a particular media vehicle.

In this case, the highest exposure unit value per dollar is $X(1)$; thus we selected the maximum permissible number of units of $X(1)$, which is 6. The next best unit is $X(9)$, so the maximum of 6 units is employed here also. A problem arises when we reach the next best unit, $X(15)$. Enough units of $X(15)$ could be bought to exhaust the rest of the budget without exceeding the maximum of 26; but we cannot do that because constraint E would be violated. Since over $175,000 has already been committed to media other than magazines under constraints D and G, only one additional unit of $X(15)$ could be utilized. We then selected the next best unit, $X(3)$, and an additional unit of this vehicle was selected. This brings our total expenditure to $434,380, so we then proceeded to select the unit with the highest exposure unit value among those with costs less than the remaining budget. Thus 3 units of $X(7)$ were selected to complete the solution.

The solution we computed was as follows:

$$X(1) = 6 \quad X(6) = 0 \quad X(11) = 0 \quad X(16) = 0$$
$$X(2) = 0 \quad X(7) = 3 \quad X(12) = 0 \quad X(17) = 1$$
$$X(3) = 2 \quad X(8) = 0 \quad X(13) = 0 \quad X(18) = 0$$
$$X(4) = 0 \quad X(9) = 6 \quad X(14) = 0 \quad X(19) = 0$$
$$X(5) = 0 \quad X(10) = 0 \quad X(15) = 2 \quad X(20) = 0$$

Total expenditures = $449,230
Total exposure units = 6812.3

SYSTEM SIMULATION *CORMIER SHOE COMPANY*

To facilitate our forecasting, I have created the program Trend. Bas. in BASIC. This program will compute the "line of best fit" using the formula $Y = A + B(x)$. The previous five years will be used, and the algorithm then carries the formula out ten years from the present.

As an example we will use the following data as sample. The output follows.

Data:

	Ratio of Exposure Value To Cost	
Year	*Esquire*	*Fortune*
1978	.0160	.0089
1979	.0173	.0100
1980	.0189	.0121
1981	.0197	.0141
1982	.0200	.0176

Output:

```
CORMIER SHOE COMPANY
***TREND DATA FOR ESQUIRE MAGAZINE***
YEAR          VALUE
=======       =======
1978          .0160
1979          .0173
1980          .0189
1981          .0197
1982          .0200

   VALUE A = -1.9620
   VALUE B =  0.0010
```

```
***REGRESSION ANALYSIS TREND***
YEAR          VALUE
=======       =======
1978          .0160
1979          .0170
1980          .0180
1981          .0190
1982          .0200
1983          .0210
1984          .0220
1985          .0230
1986          .0240
1987          .0250
1988          .0260
1989          .0270
1990          .0280
1991          .0290
1992          .0300

CORMIER SHOE COMPANY
***TREND DATA FOR FORTUNE MAGAZINE***
YEAR          VALUE
=======       =======
1978          .0089
1979          .0100
1980          .0121
1981          .0141
1982          .0176

  VALUE A = -3.9470
  VALUE B =  0.0020

***REGRESSION ANALYSIS TREND***
YEAR          VALUE
=======       =======
1978          .0090
1979          .0110
1980          .0130
1981          .0150
1982          .0170
1983          .0190
1984          .0210
1985          .0230
1986          .0250
1987          .0270
1988          .0290
1989          .0310
1990          .0330
1991          .0350
1992          .0370
```

```
100   REM    PROGRAM-ID. TREND.BAS
200   REM    AUTHOR.      P.J. CORMIER
300   REM    CORMIER SHOES - REGRESSION ANALYSIS
400
500   DIM.#1%,    Y(50),V(50)
600   DIM         S(5)
700   N = 1
800   OPEN 'TREND.DAT' FOR INPUT AS FILE 1%
900   OPEN 'TRENDB.REP' FOR OUTPUT AS FILE 2
1000  REM
1100  INPUT #1,Y(N),V(N)
1200  ON ERROR GO TO 1500
1300  N = N + 1
1400  GO TO 1100


1500  E = Y(1)
1600  L = V(1)
1700  N = N - 1


1800  FOR C = 1 TO N
1900  IF Y(C + 1) = 0 THEN 2700
2000  IF Y(C) < Y(C+1) THEN 2300
2100  IF E < Y(C+1) THEN 2300
2200  E = Y(C+1)
2300  IF Y(C) > Y(C+1) THEN 2600
2400  IF L > Y(C+1) THEN 2600
2500  L = Y(C+1)
2600  NEXT C


2700  REM   REGRESSION COMPUTATION STARTS HERE


2800  FOR C = 1 TO N
2900  S(1) = (Y(C) * V(C)) + S(1)
3000  S(2) = Y(C) + S(2)
3100  S(3) = V(C) + S(3)
3200  S(4) = (Y(C) * Y(C)) + S(4)
3300  NEXT C
3400  S(5) = S(2) * S(2)


3500  REM CALCULATION FOR A AND B


3600  B = (S(1)-((S(2) * S(3)) / N)) / (S(4) - (S(5) /
      N ))
3700  B = INT((B * 1000) + .5) / 1000
3800  A = (S(3) / N) - (B * (S(2) / N))
3900  A = INT((A * 1000) + .5) / 1000
```

```
4000   REM WRITE ROUTINE STARTS HERE

4100   Z$ = '======='
4200   PRINT #2, '***TREND DATA***'
4300   PRINT #2, 'YEAR','VALUE'
4400   PRINT #2, Z$,Z$
4500   FOR C = 1 TO N
4600   PRINT #2 USING '###          .####',Y(C),V(C)
4700   NEXT C
4800   PRINT #2
4900   PRINT #2
5000   PRINT #2 USING ' VALUE A =    ###.#### ',A
5100   PRINT #2 USING ' VALUE B =    ##.#### ',B
5200   PRINT #2
5300   PRINT #2
5400   PRINT #2, '***REGRESSION ANALYSIS TREND***'
5500   PRINT #2, 'YEAR','VALUE'
5600   PRINT #2,Z$,Z$
5700   PRINT #2 USING '####          .####',E,A+(B *E)
5800   FOR C = 1 TO N
5900   IF Y(C) = E THEN 6200
6000   IF Y(C) = L THEN 6200
6100   PRINT #2 USING '####          .####',Y(C),A+(B *)
       Y(C)
6200   NEXT C
6300   PRINT #2 USING '####          .####',L,A+(B * L)
6400   FOR C = (L +1) TO (L + 10)
6500   PRINT #2 USING '####          .####',C,A+(B * C)
6600   NEXT C

6700   CLOSE #2

6800   END
```

After the data base is updated for all media vehicles, we will develop our forecast based on the output.

In the sample run (attached) for *Esquire* and *Fortune* magazines, note that in the current year, 1982, *Esquire* was considered a better advertising vehicle for Cormier Shoes. However, in 1985 *Fortune* begins to overtake *Esquire* as a better advertising vehicle, and thus we will forecast accordingly. There could be many reasons for *Fortune* overtake:

☐ The cost of advertising in *Esquire* is expected to soar.

☐ *Fortune Magazine's* readership is expected to increase substantially in the future.

☐ *Esquire's* circulation is expected to drop.

☐ *Fortune* has hired a dynamic new young marketing executive known throughout the industry.

☐ *Esquire* has taken an off-beat stand on the equal rights amendment, which is expected to retard circulation.

☐ Etc., etc., etc. . . . .

4.20 SUMMARY

This chapter discusses a variety of optimizing models used in diverse areas of applications such as manufacturing, investment strategy, inventory, and marketing. Since linear programming is the most widely used optimizing technique, this topic is treated in detail.

After presenting a mathematical formulation of a linear programming (LP) model, the chapter discusses four major application areas of an LP model: resource allocation, scheduling, network flow analysis, and transportation or routing. Specific case studies of the first three are given, based on the author's experience and research. The discussion of LP models is followed by a brief review of nonlinear and dynamic programming.

The next category of models consists of inventory models. It is pointed out that the purchasing system and inventory policy are closely related. The economy lot size model is treated in detail, followed by a case study.

The next major category of models addresses the portfolio analysis for investment strategies. The principal model discussed here is Markowitz's efficient frontier model, which uses the quadratic programming technique. Since standard texts of operations research do not treat portfolio analysis, an attempt is made here to present a comprehensive and self-contained treatment of portfolio analysis. In addition to the mathematical model of the efficient frontier, two other models, capital asset pricing and the random walk hypothesis, are discussed. These are less mathematical and are treated accordingly. To complete the discussion of portfolio analysis, the impact of risk on investment is discussed. The two types of risk, market risk and specific risk, are described. This section closes with some comments on portfolio management and index funds.

The final sections of the chapter treat marketing models. Using some of the quantitative studies done in the area of sales management and advertising models, the chapter introduces a mathematical model to treat advertising effects on sales. Next, an LP model is provided to determine the best set of media alternatives for advertising to be selected from a given range of alternatives in order to maximize the media exposure for a given budget. The chapter closes with a case study using this model.

4.21　KEY WORDS

The following key words are used in this chapter:

activity
actual delivery schedule
advertising models
Alexander's filter technique
anticipated delivery schedule
beta coefficient
burst point
capital asset pricing theory
capital market line
carrying cost
constraints
convex programming
critical activities
data communication network
decision variable
diversification of securities
dynamic programming
early finish time
early start time
economic lot size model
efficient frontier model of
　Markowitz
efficient portfolio
event
feasible solution
homemaker's problem
index fund
integer linear programming
inventory model
late finish time
late start time
linear programming
LOB (line of balance)
market risk
marketing model

mathematical programming
media exposure
media selection
media vehicle
MOST (Management Operation
　System Technique)
network analysis
node
objective function
optimal order quantity
optimal reorder period
optimal solution
optimizing model
ordering cost
parallel activity
parameters of LP model
PERT (Program Evaluation and
　Review Technique)
policy decision
portfolio
portfolio analysis
portfolio management
purchases on contract
purchasing system
quadratic programming
random walk hypothesis
recursive relationship
resource allocation
response constant
return of a security
risk-free security
risk of a security
safety stock
sales decay constant
sales performance measures

saturation level
scheduling model
securities
separable programming
setup cost

simplex method
slack time
specific risk
transportation or routing
problem

REFERENCES

1. J.B. Cohen, E.D. Zinbarg, and A. Zeikel, *Investment Analysis and Portfolio Management,* Richard D. Irwin, Homewood, IL, 1977.

2. G.B. Dantzig, *Linear Programming and Extensions,* Princeton University Press, Princeton, NJ, 1963.

3. R.L. Day and L.J. Parsons (eds.), *Marketing Models: Quantitative Applications,* Intext Educational Publishers, Scranton, PA, 1971.

4. F.D. Hedrick, *Purchasing Management in the Smaller Company,* American Management Association, New York, 1971.

5. F.S. Hillier and G.J. Lieberman, *Introduction to Operations Research,* Holden-Day, San Francisco, 1974.

6. A.L. Iannone, *Management Program Planning with PERT, MOST, and LOB,* Prentice-Hall, Englewood Cliffs, NJ, 1971.

7. H.M. Markowitz, *Portfolio Selection: Efficient Diversification of Investments,* Wiley, New York, 1959.

8. S.S. Mittra, "Applications of Operations Research Methods to Correctional Problems," *Criminal Justice and Behavior.* 2, 169–179 (1975).

9. S.S. Mittra, "PERT, LOB and MOST: United for More Efficient Project Scheduling, *Supervisory Management,* 30–35 (November 1976).

10. S.S. Mittra, "Purchasing and Inventory Management for Public Productivity Improvement," *Akron Business and Economic Review,* Spring 1978, pp. 44–49.

11. D.A. Newton, "Get the Most Out of Your Sales Force" *Harvard Business Review on Management,* Harper & Row, New York, 1975, pp. 214–236.

12. P. Rivett, *Model Building for Decision Analysis,* Wiley, New York, 1980.

13. H.M. Wagner, *Principles of Operations Research,* Prentice-Hall, Englewood Cliffs, NJ, 1975.

14. J.D. Wiest and F.K. Levy, *Management Guide to PERT/CPM,* Prentice-Hall, Englewood Cliffs, NJ, 1969.

REVIEW QUESTIONS

1. What are the basic components of an optimizing model? Why is such a model called optimizing?

2. What is a feasible solution, and what is an optimal solution of an LP model?

3. Why is it necessary to consider the purchasing system in a company in designing an efficient inventory policy?

4. Distinguish between deterministic and probabilistic inventory models.

5. What is an investment portfolio? What is the objective of a portfolio analysis model?

6. Why is Markowitz's efficient frontier model classified as a quadratic programming model?

7. Geometrically, what does the efficient frontier curve represent?

8. Explain the capital asset pricing theory. How does it differ from the efficient frontier model?

9. Define the terms *market risk* and *specific risk*. How are the concepts related?

10. Enumerate the properties of the beta coefficient

11. Explain the concept of an index fund.

12. What trade-off issues are involved in the design of an advertising model?

5

Statistical Models and Applications

5.1 Nonoptimizing Models

A *nonoptimizing model* is characterized by two entities: parameters and constraint equations. As indicated by its name, such a model does not optimize any function. The parameters in a nonoptimizing model may be regarded as the counterparts of the decision variables in an optimizing model in the sense that the final solution of the model provides values of model parameters. Unlike the constraints in an optimizing model, which may be either equations or inequalities, the constraints in a nonoptimizing model are always stated as equations. We shall use the more widely used term *statistical model* to refer to a nonoptimizing model.

A statistical model can be either quantitative or qualitative. There are more quantitative models, however, and they are more widely used. In this chapter we shall discuss both of types of statistical models.

In a quantitative statistical model, we first define a set of parameters extracted from the physical description of the problem. Next we formulate a set of equations that these parameters must satisfy. The final solution of the model is obtained by solving the equations to determine the parameters.

5.2 REGRESSION ANALYSIS

Regression analysis is widely used to make predictions on the basis of historical data. Let us take an example to explain this process.

Suppose that Table 5-1 gives the advertising expenses (as a percentage

TABLE 5-1   Data for Regression Analysis

Advertising Expense	Net Operating Profit
1.2	2.7
0.7	2.4
1.5	2.7
1.8	3.3
0.5	1.1
3.4	5.8
1.0	2.2
3.0	4.2
2.8	4.4
2.5	3.8

of total expenses) and net operating profits (as a percentage of sales) for 10 small companies. We want to predict the net operating profit corresponding to a given value of advertising expense. First we examine the relationship between advertising expense and profit by plotting the given data on graph paper, labeling the advertising expense as X and the net operating profit as Y. Figure 5-1 shows this plot.

Since the data points are located on or near the dotted line in the graph, we assume that X and Y are related by a linear equation of the form

$$Y = a + bX$$

We then determine a and b from constraint equations for the model. This equation "predicts" the value of Y (i.e., advertising expense). In fact, as we shall see later in this chapter, X and Y are connected by the equation.

$$Y = 0.96 + 1.2485X$$

that is, $a = 0.96$, and $b = 1.2485$.

There are two major types of regression: linear and nonlinear. If the graph of X and Y is approximately a straight line, then the regression is called *linear* and the straight line is called the *line of regression*. If, however, the X, Y graph is not a straight line, then the regression is called *nonlinear* and the graph is called the *curve of regression*. A curve of regression can be a parabola, an exponential curve, an asymptotic growth curve, and so on.

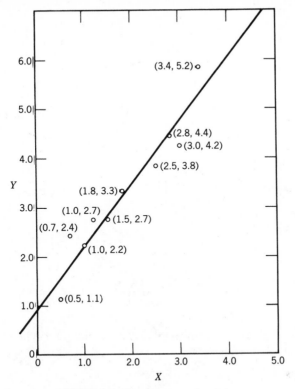

FIGURE 5-1 Plot for regression data.

5.3 LINEAR REGRESSION

Linear regression assumes that the two random variables X and Y are connected by a linear equation

$$Y = a + bX \tag{5.1}$$

which is called the line of regression L. Let us assume that there are n observed data values (X_1, Y_1), (X_2, Y_2), ..., (X_n, Y_n). Form the sum of the squares of the vertical distances of these n points from the line L and call this sum S. Then, as shown in Figure 5-2, S is given by

$$S = \sum_{i=1}^{n} [(a + bX_i) - Y_i]^2$$

Since S is a function of the parameters a and b, we can formulate two equa-

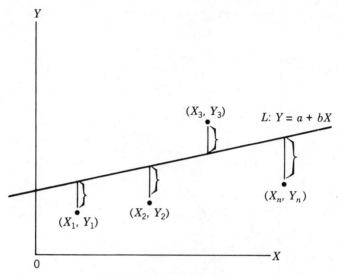

FIGURE 5-2   Curve of best fit.

tions involving a and b by requiring that S be a minimum. The two equations determining a and b are

$$na + b \left(\sum_{i=1}^{n} X_i \right) = \sum_{i=1}^{n} Y_i \tag{5.2a}$$

$$a\left(\sum_{i=1}^{n} X_i \right) + b\left(\sum_{i=1}^{n} X_i^2 \right) = \sum_{i=1}^{n} (X_i Y_i) \tag{5.2b}$$

The line L is called the *curve of best fit,* and the regression technique is often called the curve-fitting technique. Since S represents the sum of the squares of the vertical distances, and since we minimize S, this method is usually known as the *method of least squares.*

In order to simplify the calculations, we can choose the origin in a suitable manner so as to make $\sum_{i=1}^{n} X_i = 0$ always. This is done as follows:

1. If n is odd, label the middle point of the X values as $X = 0$ and relabel the X values as

$$\ldots, \quad -4, \quad -3, \quad -2, \quad -1, \quad 0, \quad 1, \quad 2, \quad 3, \quad 4, \quad \ldots$$

so that $\sum_{i=1}^{n} X_i = 0$ always.

2. If n is even, relabel the X values as

$$\ldots, \quad -5, \quad -3, \quad -1, \quad 1, \quad 3, \quad 5, \quad \ldots$$

so that $X = 0$ is the midpoint of the segment joining the two central values $X = -1$ and $X = 1$. As before, we get $\sum_{i=1}^{n} X_i = 0$ in this case.

Under this special choice of the origin, the equations to determine a and b are

$$na = \sum_{i=1}^{n} Y_i, \qquad b \left(\sum_{i=1}^{n} X_i^2 \right) = \sum_{i=1}^{n} X_i Y_i \qquad (5.3)$$

These yield the solutions

$$a = \frac{1}{n} \left(\sum_{i=1}^{n} y_i \right), \qquad b = \sum_{i=1}^{n} X_i Y_i / \sum_{i=1}^{n} X_i^2$$

5.3.1 Correlation

Under linear regression it is assumed that Y *depends* on X according to the relatinoship

$$Y = a + bX$$

However, a part of this dependence can be attributed to chance and is accordingly called a *chance variation*. The other part is called a *regression variation*. The *total variation* is then defined as the sum of the chance and regression variations.

We define the coefficient of determination γ^2 as the ratio

$$\gamma^2 = \frac{\text{regression variation}}{\text{total variation}}$$

Its square root γ is called the *coefficient of correlation*. The formula for γ is

$$\gamma = \frac{n \left(\sum_{i=1}^{n} X_i Y_i \right) - \left(\sum_{i=1}^{n} X_i \right) \left(\sum_{i=1}^{n} Y_i \right)}{\left\{ \left[n \left(\sum_{i=1}^{n} X_i^2 \right) - \left(\sum_{i=1}^{n} X_i \right)^2 \right] \left[n \left(\sum_{i=1}^{n} Y_i^2 \right) - \left(\sum_{i=1}^{n} Y_i \right)^2 \right] \right\}^{1/2}}$$

The quantity $100\gamma^2$ gives the percentage of the total variation of Y values that is due to their relationship with X values. Thus, if $\gamma = .8$, then $100\gamma^2 = 64$; that is, only 64% of the variation in Y is accounted for by its relationship with X. While low values of γ indicate the absence of causal dependence of Y upon X, high values of γ need not imply a strong dependence. There are many studies available to confirm this statement.

It should further be noted that γ measures only the strength of the *linear relationship* between X and Y. In fact, γ can be zero despite a strong curvilinear relationship between X and Y ([2], p. 460).

5.4 FORECASTING

Forecasting is a systematic process to predict the future by an analysis of the past. The forecaster studies the past through historical data to determine the existence of trends and/or seasonal variations. The main purpose of making forecasts is to gain knowledge about uncertain events of the future that are important for our present decisions.

The importance of forecasts cannot be overemphasized. Any agency, private or governmental, needs forecasts. Most large corporations are deeply involved in attempting to forecast opportunities for new products, sales, profit margins, personnel requirements, and so forth. Since factors affecting business activity are complex, the management of any company needs increasing amounts of information that shed light on the future. Successful forecasting gets its payoff in additional profits.

There are two types of forecasting: short-term and long-term. Usually, when the time span of the forecast is at most one year, it is called *short-term*, while a forecast extending to more than one year is termed *long-term*. Short-term forecasts are needed for the daily operation of the company, whereas long-term forecasts are used in the area of planning.

True forecasting is a blend of science and art that defies precise definition for a successful application. Preparation of a forecast entails more than just using historical data and mathematical formulas to project into the future. The key to realistic forecasting is the incorporation of informed judgment and intuition into the methodological framework being employed in order to minimize uncertainty associated with the future development, or event, in question. Most forecasting techniques or methodologies are founded on replicable scientific relationships. The art of forecasting is learned by experience rather than by academic study.

It must be stressed that a forecast is useful if it reduces the uncertainty surrounding an event and by doing so results in decisions that have increased value (because of the forecast) in excess of the cost required to produce the forecast.

Some basic characteristics of forecasting are:

☐ Forecasts are usually incorrect.
☐ A forecast should give the predicted value along with a range indicating the estimated error involved in the forecast.
☐ Forecasts become less and less accurate as they move further into the future.
☐ Forecasts are more accurate for a group of items (e.g., total sales of a company) than for individual items (e.g., sales of a specific product).

5.5 TIME SERIES ANALYSIS

The standard method used for forecasting is time series analysis. This can be regarded as a special case of regression analysis where the X variable represents the time and is written as t, and the Y variable represents the quantity to be forecast. Thus, $Y(t)$ represents the value of the forecast at time t.

$Y(t)$ consists of four components.

$$T(t) = \text{long-term or secular trend at time } t$$
$$C(t) = \text{cyclical fluctuation at time } t$$
$$S(t) = \text{seasonal variation at time } t$$
$$I(t) = \text{irregular variation at time } t$$

The first component is fairly stable, while the latter three denote the fluctuating parts of the time series for $Y(t)$. We assume that the four components are independent of one another so we can measure each of them separately.

There are two basic forms of time series: multiplicative and additive. Thus, we can represent the time series for $Y(t)$ in either of the following two forms:

$$Y(t) = T(t) \times C(t) \times S(t) \times I(t) \quad \text{(multiplicative)}$$
$$Y(t) = T(t) + C(t) + S(t) + I(t) \quad \text{(additive)}$$

Most analysts believe that the multiplicative model is more appropriate than the additive for analysis of business and economic time series. Under either form, the trend component is isolated by fitting a trend curve using linear or nonlinvear regression and is measured in terms of absolute magnitudes. In the multiplicative form the other three components are measured by ratios, usually percents.

The trend curve measuring the secular trend T can be linear or nonlinear. In any case, using given historical data and drawing a scattergram (SPSS can be used) we get an approximate idea of the shape of the curve. Then

we use regression techniques to determine that curve. If it is linear, we use the linear regression method. Otherwise, we use par-abolic or exponential or another type of growth curve. Various mathematical methods are available to determine the exact curve for the secular trend. Possible examples of trend curves are:

Straight line: $Y = a + bt$.

Quadratic, usually parabola: $Y = a + bt + ct^2$ (see Section 5.6.2).

Exponential: $Y = ae^{bt}$.

Growth curves: Gompertz and logistic (see Section 5.6.2).

The growth curves, when plotted on graph paper, indicate some type of absolute growth; that is, an asymptote to the curve exists giving the maximum value that $Y(t)$ can reach for any t. Gompertz and logistic curves are heavily used for mortality projections, with the upper limit of Y being taken as 100 years, the expected maximum life span of a human being.

In time series analysis one extrapolates into the future the trend and cycle from past observed data. Standard computer programs such as SPSS and Minitabs are available to perform the mechanical part of trend fitting. However, there are more important considerations:

☐ Time period—Ensure that the past pattern is relevant to the period ahead.

☐ Choice of appropriate curve—Determine the curve that is the best for trend projection.

☐ Assumptions—Specify the assumptions made for the future course of events. It is not necessarily true that the past pattern will be repeated in the future. Assumptions must be relevant and realistic.

The cyclical and seasonal fluctuations are determined from a study of past patterns and are of a short-range nature. These usually resemble irregular wavelike cycles varying in both length and amplitude. Sometimes business indicators of a known and related phenomenon can be used to estimate these two variations.

There are three types of business indicators: leading, coincident, and lagging. The National Bureau of Economic Research (NBER) publishes a list of such indicators. Examples are:

Leading: Average hourly work week for production workers, index of new building permits, corporate profits after taxes—quarterly.

Coincident: GNP in current dollars, personal income, unemployment rate.

Lagging: Business expenditures—new plant and equipment, bank rates on short-term business loans.

The seasonal patterns often lead to the calculation of seasonal indices, which are applied to the secular trend and cyclical variations to determine the forecast quantity. The irregular or random fluctuations are the most difficult to measure and are sometimes ignored due to lack of data.

5.5.1 Trend Curves and the Moving Average Method

The dominant factor in a multiplicative time series is the long-term or secular trend $T(t)$. This function provides the underlying pattern of the time series and is called the *trend curve*. There are two main types of trend curves: linear and nonlinear. Nonlinear trend curves may be further classified as quadratic, cubic, exponential, growth curves, and so on.

When the raw data are plotted to determine the overall trend visually, many sharp corners may appear on the graph. These often make the estimation of the shape of $T(t)$ quite difficult. To avoid this problem, the *moving average* method is often used. A moving average is obtained by replacing each value in a series by the mean of itself and some of the values directly preceding and directly following it. For instance, in a 3-year moving average calculated for annual data, each annual figure is replaced by the mean of itself and the annual figures for the two adjacent years. In a 5-year moving average of annual data, each annual figure is replaced by the mean of itself and the data for the two preceding years and the two following years.

The main difficulty in constructing a moving average lies in choosing an appropriate period for the average. The choice depends largely on the nature of the data and the purpose for which the forecast is made. Normally, the purpose of using data from the moving average method is to eliminate insofar as possible some of the "noisy" part of the raw data. This method merely smooths out certain fluctuations from the time series and does not and should not completely eliminate such fluctuations.

In estimating the secular trend over a long period of time it is possible that different trend curves will fit different groups of data values. Some kind of smoothing is needed at the junction points of two different curves used in such a situation. The resulting trend curve $T(t)$ then appears as a piecewise continuous function. In Section 5.8 we shall examine a case study that uses this technique.

5.6 METHODOLOGY FOR COMPUTING A TREND CURVE

In this section we shall describe a step-by-step method to compute the equation of a trend curve for a given set of data.

Step 1. Gather historical data. The forecaster collects suitable data on a time basis (e.g., monthly or weekly). The instrument to gather such data,

whether manual or automated, must be designed with extreme caution so as to yield usable and meaningful data.

Step 2.   Smooth the historical data by the moving average method. For example, in a 3-year moving average method, the value for each year is replaced by the average of the data for the preceding year, the year in question, and the following year. Thereby, much of the "noisy" part of the data is eliminated and the data start to show a definite trend. Table 5-2 gives an illustration of this principle.

Step 3.   Plot both sets of data on graph paper. The forecaster can then determine how the smoothed data provides a much better trend picture than the actual data. Figure 5-3 illustrates this for Table 5-2.

Step 4.   Determine any trend and/or cycles exhibited by the smoothed data. Figure 5-3, for instance, indicates a parabolic trend for the smoothed data that is not very obvious from the actual data.

Step 5.   Fit a linear or nonlinear curve to the smoothed data.

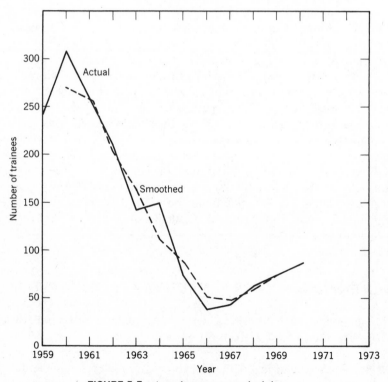

FIGURE 5-3 Actual versus smoothed data.

TABLE 5-2 Enrollment in a Course

Year	Actual Data	Smoothed Data (3-Year Moving Average)
1959	242	
1960	308	270
1961	260	258
1962	207	203
1963	141	166
1964	149	121
1965	74	87
1966	38	51
1967	41	47
1968	62	59
1969	74	74
1970	85	

Step 6. Use this curve to predict future data values.

We now explain step 5 under two separate categories: linear trend and nonlinear trend.

5.6.1 Linear Trend

This is really a special case of linear regression (see Section 5.3), where $X = t$, the time variable. Then the regression line is given by

$$Y = a + bt$$

and the parameters a and b are given by (5.3), assuming that the origin is so chosen as to make $\Sigma_i t_i = 0$, where n is the total number of data points (t, Y) used.

As an example, let us consider the data in Table 5-3. Plotting both sets of data on graph paper and solving Eq. (5.3) for a and b, it is found that

$$y = 77.31 + 5.75x \tag{5.4}$$

Figure 5-4 presents three curves: actual data, smoothed data, and the linear trend data. The predicted values for 1976 through 1980 are, respectively, 175, 187, 198, 210, and 222, as determined by Eq. (5.4).

5.6.2 Nonlinear Trend

If the data graph does not indicate a linear trend, then the forecaster has to try a quadratic curve or some asymptotic growth curve. It is generally true

TABLE 5-3 Sample Data with Linear Trend

Year	Actual Data	Smoothed Data (3-Year Moving Average)
1959	23	
1960	16	14
1961	4	10
1962	10	26
1963	63	43
1964	56	52
1965	37	43
1966	37	36
1967	33	32
1968	25	44
1969	74	61
1970	85	103
1971	150	119
1972	123	145
1973	162	152
1974	171	175
1975	192	

that a cubic or any other higher degree curve does not provide any significant improvement over a quadratic curve. Accordingly, the discussion here will be limited to quadratic curves and asymptotic growth curves.

(a) Quadratic Curves. The equation of a quadratic curve is of the form

$$y = a + bx + cx^2$$

where a, b, and c are constants to be determined from the given data. Assuming that there are n sets of observed x,y values as discussed before, the three equations to determine a, b, and c are

$$\Sigma y = na + c(\Sigma x^2) \tag{5.5}$$
$$\Sigma xy = b(\Sigma x^2) \tag{5.6}$$
$$\Sigma x^2 y = a(\Sigma x^2) + c(\Sigma x^4) \tag{5.7}$$

The origin must be specially chosen depending on whether n is odd or even, as explained in Section 5.3. Then (5.6) determines b, and (5.5) and (5.7) together determine a and c.

As an example, consider the data in Table 5-4. Plotting both sets of data on graph paper and solving Eq. (5.5) – (5.7) for a, b, and c, it is found that

$$y = 64.98 - 5.4x + 0.54x^2 \tag{5.8}$$

Figure 5-5 gives three curves: actual data, smoothed data, and the quadratic (parabolic) trend data. The projected values for 1976 – 1980 are 71, 86, 105, 129, and 157, as determined by Eq. (5.8).

(b) Asymptotic Growth Curves.
There are three types of asymptotic growth curves:

Logistic curve: $y = k/(1 + 10^{a+bx})$.
Gompertz curve: $\log y = \log k + (\log a)b^x$.
Modified exponential curve: $y = k + ab^x$.

Here a, b, and k are constants to be determined from the given x,y values of the data. The logarithm in the equation for a Gompertz curve is taken to the base 10. All these curves are used mostly for data with an increasing trend that approach an upper limit represented by the asymptote $y = k$ of the respective curve.

In order to fit the logistic curve to given data values, select three x values equidistant from each other and call them x_0, x_1, and x_2 : x_0 near the beginning, x_1 in the middle, and x_2 near the end. The origin on the x axis is at x_0; let y_0, y_1, and y_2 be the corresponding y values obtained from the data. If there

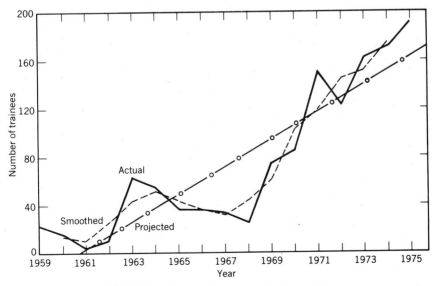

FIGURE 5-4 Sample data curves for Table 5-3.

TABLE 5-4 Sample Data for a Quadratic Trend

Year	Actual Data	Smoothed Data (3-Year Moving Average)
1965	180	
1966	97	152
1967	178	124
1968	97	118
1969	78	80
1970	66	48
1971	0	35
1972	38	33
1973	61	62
1974	87	59
1975	30	

are n sets of observed x,y values, then k, a, and b are determined from the equations

$$k = \frac{2y_0 y_1 y_2 - y_1^2(y_0 + y_2)}{y_0 y_2 - y_1^2} \tag{5.9}$$

$$a = \log \frac{k - y_0}{y_0} \tag{5.10}$$

$$b = \frac{1}{n} \log \frac{y_0(k - y_1)}{y_1(k - y_0)} \tag{5.11}$$

In order to fit the Gompertz curve to given data values, divide the data into three equal sections. Let Σ_1, Σ_2, and Σ_3 represent summations taken over each section, and let n be the number of x values in each section. Then b, a, and k are determined from the equations

$$b^n = \frac{\Sigma_3 \log y - \Sigma_2 \log y}{\Sigma_2 \log y - \Sigma_1 \log y} \tag{5.12}$$

$$\log a = (\Sigma_2 \log y - \Sigma_1 \log y) \frac{b - 1}{(b^n - 1)^2} \tag{5.13}$$

$$\log k = \frac{1}{n}(\Sigma_1 \log y - \frac{b^n - 1}{b - 1} \log a) \tag{5.14}$$

In order to fit the modified exponential curve, proceed exactly as for the

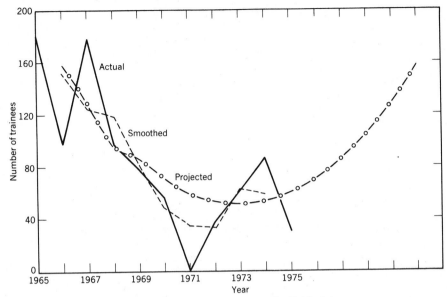

FIGURE 5-5 Sample data curves for Table 5-4.

Gompertz curve but replace log y, log a, and log k in Eqs. (5.12) – (5.14) by y, a, and k, respectively. The corresponding equations are

$$b^n = \frac{\Sigma_3\, y - \Sigma_2\, y}{\Sigma_2\, y - \Sigma_1\, y} \tag{5.15}$$

$$a = (\Sigma_2\, y - \Sigma_1\, y)\frac{b - 1}{(b^n - 1)^2} \tag{5.16}$$

$$k = \frac{1}{n}(\Sigma_1\, y - \frac{b^n - 1}{b - 1}\, a) \tag{5.17}$$

As an example, consider the data in Table 5-5. Plotting these data (Figure 5-6), it is found that the data from 1960 to 1966 are approximated by the parabola

$$y = 166.6 - 38.6x - .37x^2$$

while the data from 1967 to 1975 are approximated by the logistic curve

$$y = 269.44/(1 + 10^{.57 - .28x})$$

This illustrates the case where different parts of the data set can exhibit different trends. The projected values for 1976 – 1980 are, respectively, 264, 267, 268, 269, and 269.

TABLE 5-5   Sample Data for Growth Curve

Year	Actual Data	Smoothed Data (3-Year Moving Average)
1959	242	
1960	308	270
1961	260	258
1962	207	203
1963	141	166
1964	149	121
1965	74	87
1966	38	51
1967	41	47
1968	62	58
1969	71	77
1970	97	108
1971	156	197
1972	338	298
1973	399	347
1974	303	291
1975	170	

5.7   ERRORS OF FORECASTING

The only thing that is certain about a forecast is that it will be wrong. The question is, how wrong can we afford to be! Usually, once a time series has been designed, an error margin (projected − actual) is computed for the past data. If the error margin is "tolerable," then the time series is accepted. Here the hypothesis is that what worked well in the past will also work well in the future. This is not always true. Legal, social, and economic changes can be significant enough to make the future drastically different from the past. The extent to which past patterns are relevant to future prediction is a vital issue.

Normally forecasting will make use of quantitative data and, where necessary, will moderate them by judgment and intuition. Economic indicators can be used as descriptors of the present and the short-range future (e.g., up to 6 months). In using such indicators we are utilizing the well-established structural relationships of different parts of the economy as a basis to remove some uncertainty. The basic approach should be to form scenarios that give qualitative and quantitative descriptions of the world at a particular future time. These scenarios should be made flexible enough to answer "what if" questions, and the model should be capable of incorporating such changes.

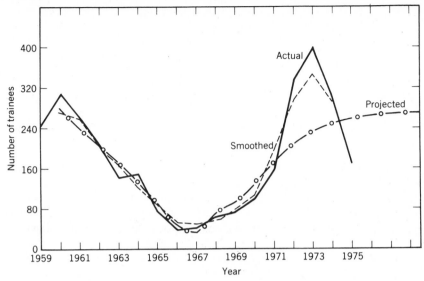

FIGURE 5-6 Sample data curves for data in Table 5-5.

5.8 POPULATION FORECASTING MODEL: A CASE STUDY

We now present a detailed case study done in 1974–1975 for the Pennsylvania Bureau of Correction. We used time series analysis, both linear and parabolic trends. In addition, the model was made flexible enough to handle "what if" questions relative to populaton forecasting.

5.8.1 Introduction

In a journal article published in 1975, Dr. John Flanagan mentioned the upward trend in the prison population all over the country. According to Dr. Flanagan, "Every indicator — economy, policy, public attitudes, crime rates, prison rates, exhaustion of alternatives and population at risk — points to higher prison populations, greater budget and building needs."

The Pennsylvania state prison system had been no exception. The population began to soar in late 1974, thereby leading to the problem of insufficient physical spaces (cells) to accommodate new prisoners. Accordingly, the Planning and Research Division of the Pennsylvania Bureau of Correction began to design a sophisticated model of population projection under my supervision.

The main objectives were two fold:

1. To project population figures.
2. To compare these figures with the number of usable cells in each state

correctional institution in order to determine if the institution would be able to hold all the future prisoners.

Here we look at the methods of the model and how it was made sensitive to "what if" questions. In view of the nationwide problem of high inmate populations, this model could prove useful to other states. The contingency plans can be made to tackle overcrowding by using the projected population figures determined by the model.

5.8.2 Methodology Used

After examining various forecasting models such as time series analysis, exponential smoothing, and autoregression, we decided to use the difference equation for steady state model. We received guidelines from the model used by the Georgia Department of Offender Rehabilitation:

The basic principle of the model can be expressed as:

Population during month M of year $Y =$
Population during month M of previous year $(Y - 1)$
+ Total number of admissions during past 12 mo
− Total number of releases during past 12 mo

Any population growth is affected by two separate factors: a long-term trend and a short-term seasonal variation. In order to capture the long-term trend a large amount of historical data had been collected, giving the total population figures by month dating back to January 1960. The method of "5-month moving average" was used to get rid of much of the "noisy" part of the collected data.

Plotting the data on graph paper showed that the curve indicated a very slow decrease during the 8 years ranging from January 1960 through December 1967. However, over the next 7 years, January 1968 through December 1974, some definite repetitive trends were visible. This coupled with the fact that the Omnibus Crime Control and Safe Streets act passed in 1968 had a significant impact on the entire criminal justice system prompted us to use the data starting in January 1968 to design the model.

The monthly population figures from January 1968 to March 1975 indicated a definite parabolic trend over a 20-month cycle. Each parabola had an absolute minimum point, although the overall trend in going from one cycle to the next was along a linear path with nonnegative slope (see Figure 5-7).

The parabolic trends equation was used to determine each cycle. This made it necessary to do some "smoothing" at each junction point of two consecutive cycles.

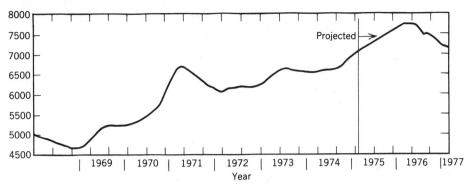

FIGURE 5-7 Monthly inmate population figures.

5.8.3 Factors

The inmate population in any system is affected by the prevalent legal and socioeconomic conditions. Accordingly, the forecast must be sensitive to these factors. In fact, the last 20-month cycle of the inmate population as mentioned in Section 5.8.2 started in August 1973 and should have ended by March 1975.

Under normal conditions the population should have leveled off and then should have started a slow decrease by April or May 1975. However, because of economic downturns and high unemployment, this did not happen. Instead, the population figures kept rising. It is generally agreed that faced with the choice between incarcerating an individual or placing him/her on probation or parole, a judge will decide in favor of the former if no employment is available. A similar criterion applies in granting paroles to incarcerated offenders; paroles are often withheld when no gainful employment awaits the inmate outside the institution.

Analyzing the number of monthly court admissions and monthly parole releases from October 1973 through March 1975, it was found that an average 5–7% increase showed in the former and an average 8–10% decrease in the latter. The combination effect was to push up the inmate population. Accordingly it was decided to make the model somewhat amenable to these external conditions.

5.8.4 "What If" Questions

The formula of the model (see Section 5.8.2) depends on admissions and releases. Pennsylvania has four types of admissions: court, revocation, return after escape, and transfer. The six types of releases are maxout, parole, escape, court discharge, transfer, and miscellaneous.

The total monthly admission figure is the sum of four numbers corresponding to the four admission types. The total monthly release figure is the sum of six numbers corresponding to the six release types.

Accordingly, if, for example, we want to know what happens in cases where there is a 10% increase in court admissions, we must take the court admission figures, project them by using the parabolic trend along with the 10% increase, and finally arrive at a new set of projections. A similar method can be used to answer "what if" questions in relation to other types of admissions and releases.

Table 5-6 gives projected population figures of Pennsylvania state correctional institutions showing a 10% increase in court admissions and a 10% decrease in parole releases over a 15-month period (April 1975 through June 1976). Column (1) includes a 10% increase in court admissions, and column (2) includes an additional 10% decrease in parole release. Looking at the table we find that until July 1975 the actual population was close to projected population (2), while in August 1975 it became close to projected population (1). This indicates that the Pennsylvania inmate population did not rise as high as was expected. Consequently, column (1) of the table is currently used to predict the future population through June 1976.

TABLE 5-6   Population Figures for Pennsylvania Bureau of Correction

Month/Year	Projected (1)	Population (2)	Actual Population
April 1975	7,080	7,120	7,142
May 1975	7,144	7,176	7,157
June 1975	7,168	7,232	7,211
July 1975	7,195	7,291	7,265
Aug. 1975	7,219	7,347	7,202
Sept. 1975	7,243	7,403	7,174
Oct. 1975	7,267	7,459	7,263
Nov. 1975	7,291	7,515	7,334
Dec. 1975	7,316	7,571	7,237
Jan. 1976	7,340	7,627	7,264
Feb. 1976	7,364	7,680	
Mar. 1976	7,388	7,736	
April 1976	7,396	7,732	
May 1976	7,420	7,724	
June 1976	7,445	7,701	

5.9 FORECASTING MODELS IN CENSUS AND ACTUARIAL STUDIES

Demographic statistics deals with the quantitative aspects of the population of a community, as related to social, economic, and health characteristics and geographic distribution. Demographic statistics are gathered by enumeration of a population, as in a census; by registration upon the occurrence of certain events, such as birth, marriage, or death; and by sample surveys of cross sections of the population. This brings census and vital statistics into the realm of demography.

Census statistics are used for forecasting in three major areas:

1. Intercensal estimates, that is, estimates for years between two consecutive censuses.
2. Postcensal estimates, that is, estimates for current years following the latest complete census.
3. Population projections for future years.

5.9.1 Intercensal Estimates and Postcensal Estimates

(a) Component Method. Assume two successive censuses t years apart. Let P and P_t be the population counts; and let B, D, and M be the births, deaths, and migrations, respectively, during these t years. Then the equation

$$P_t = P + B - D + M$$

should hold. However, due to errors in count, $P_t - P$ is, in general, different from $B - D + M$.

Let $C_t = (P_t - P) - (B - D + M)$. Then C_t is called the *error of closure*. The true intercensal estimate can be obtained by adding to P_t the appropriate signed (positive or negative) fraction of C_t. The U.S. Bureau of Census uses two procedures, known as procedure A and procedure B, to adjust the error of closure C_t. The basic idea behind either of these procedures is explained below. Figure 5-8 shows three population figures P_0, P_i, and P_t for years 0,

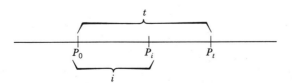

FIGURE 5-8   Census estimates of population.

i, and t, respectively. Assuming that C_t is the error of closure for t years, we have the relation

$$P_i = P_0 + \frac{i}{t} C_t$$

that is,

$$P_i = P_0 + \frac{i}{t} [(P_t - P_0) - (B - D + M)] \tag{5.18}$$

In (5.18), if P_0 and P_t are given, then P_i is determined as an intercensal estimate of the population for year i, which is less than t. If, on the other hand, P_0 and P_i are given, then P_t is computed as the postcensal estimate of the population for year t, which is greater than i. In either case, the error of closure C_t is proportionately allocated.

(b) Mathematical Method.   This method is very similar to the component method, but it does not use the error of closure. Assume that census population data P_1 and P_j are available for years 1 and j and that the intercensal estimate P_i is needed for year i (Figure 5-9). Then use the equation

$$P_j = P_1 + \frac{j}{i}(P_i - P_1)$$

which uses linear interpolation and assumes that the population changes rather uniformly. For intercensal estimates, P_1 and P_j are given and we determine P_i, whereas for postcensal estimates, P_1 and P_i are given and we estimate P_j.

If the population grows geometrically at an annual growth rate r, then the equations are

$$P_i = P_1 (1 + r)^i$$
$$P_j = P_1 (1 + r)^j = P_i(1 + r)^{j-i}$$

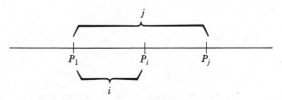

FIGURE 5-9   Census estimates of population.

5.9.2 Population Projection

Classical time series analysis can be used here by expressing the population $P(t)$ in year t as a polynomial

$$P(t) = a + bt + ct^2 + dt^3 + \cdots$$

and then solving for $a, b, c, \ldots$, using the least squares method.

Another method assumes that the small growth $dP(t)$ in population is a function of $P(t)$ itself and sets up the differential equation

$$\frac{dP(t)}{dt} = \phi\,(P(t))$$

If we set $\phi\,(P(t)) = \mu\,P(t)$, then we get the solution

$$P(t) = Ce^{\mu t}$$

where C is the constant of integration and μ is the uniform rate of increase of the population. This is known as the *Malthusian law*.

In 1838, Verhulst used the form

$$P(t) = uP(t) - ua[P(t)]^2$$

and got the logistic curve

$$P(t) = \frac{1/a}{1 + (b/a)e^{-ut}}$$

where b is the constant of integration and $1/a$ is the ultimate population, that is, $\lim_{t \to \infty} P(t) = 1/a$.

For a more detailed discussion, see [8], Chapter 14.

5.9.3 Mortality Theories

In actuarial science the statistical forecasting technique using asymptotic growth curves is extensively utilized. The objective is to predict the mortality rate for a given age. These values are then used to prepare mortality tables for all ages between 0 and 99 years, say. Insurance premium rates are based on such mortality tables.

Let us now define the variable l_x as the number of persons surviving to age x. Then the force of mortality μ_x is defined as

$$\mu_x = \frac{dl_x}{dx}$$

Various mortality theories estimate μ_x as a function of x by using statistical forecasting methods.

In 1825 Gompertz used the form

$$\mu_x = BC^x$$

where μ_x is the force of mortality at age x, and B and C are constants to be determined from the mortality experience to which the model is applied. The formula does not quite apply to the early childhood ages during which mortality is usually falling.

In 1860 Makeham improved the formula by writing

$$\mu_x = A + BC^x$$

where A represents the effect of chance independent of age. However, both Gompertz's and Makeham's laws produce excessively high mortality rates at advanced ages, say 90 and above. This defect was subsequently removed by Perks in 1932 in the logistic curve

$$\mu_x = \frac{A + BC^x}{1 + DC^x}$$

The effect of the denominator is to reduce the rate of increase of mortality at the very advanced ages to conform more closely to observation.

Spiegelman ([8], Chapter 6) is an excellent source of more information on mortality theories used in actuarial science.

5.10 QUALITATIVE FORECASTING

The methods of forecasting discussed so far use quantitative approaches based on historical data. As a result, the forecast works well only if the future is a close replica of the past. However, such an assumption does not always hold. In fact, events may occur that are poorly understood or completely unanticipated. Governmental regulations may introduce some completely new variables; an economic disaster may have happened in the past that will not be repeated; and so on. To handle such situations we rely upon the qualitative methods of forecasting.

Forecasts carefully derived from judgment can provide a coherent structure for evaluating contemplated actions, for "red flagging" other actions that should be considered or avoided, and for placing bounds on what might be reasonably expected in a world characterized by constant change. With these observations in mind, we now describe three methods that have been widely

utilized to develop forecasts in situations where subjective information is a principal input to the forecasting problem:

1. The Delphi method.
2. Subjective probability methods (including their use in conjunction with Bayes' law.
3. The cross-impact method.

In the following pages, these techniques are presented as systematic methodologies for eliciting subjective data essential to predicting the behavior of some uncertain quantity.

5.10.1 The Delphi Technique

The principle underlying the Delphi technique is the fact that a forecast made collectively by a group of people is better than one made by a single individual. Accordingly, this process draws upon the advice of experts as they form their judgments. The Delphi technique was developed during the 1940s by the RAND Corporation. It evolves forecasts from a group of people but avoids face-to-face discussion and confrontation in which the strongest personality or the loudest mouth might prevail. Forecasts are made anonymously and are then exchanged and criticized, with a gradual movement toward a consensus view.

In practice, Delphi coordinators might submit questionnaires to the individuals of a group and report back to them individually in the form of edited reports and fresh information. From such a series of questions and answers, the group and the coordinators move to a series of forecasts, opinions, and scenarios. The opinions of the participants can be focused upon the provision of a series of scenarios stretching into the future.

Two premises underlie the Delphi technique:

☐ Experts in a particular field make the most plausible forecasts.
☐ The combined knowledge of several persons is at least as good as that of one person.

Results from the Delphi method have been generally satisfactory.

The proponents of the Delphi technique claim that this method can be regarded as

☐ A structured means of studying the process of anticipating future events.
☐ A teaching tool leading people into thinking about the future in more directions and dimensions than they normally would.
☐ An aid to probing into goals and priorities of members of an organization.

However, the critics point out that the method has the following disadvantages:

- ☐ Questionnaires may be crudely designed.
- ☐ Opinion analysis and pilot testing may lack minimal professional standards.
- ☐ The selection of "experts" may be faulty.
- ☐ The method is virtually oblivious to reliability measurements and scientific validation of findings.
- ☐ Answers may often be quick but poorly formulated.
- ☐ The method capitalizes on forced consensus based on group suggestions.
- ☐ The method often confuses aggregations of raw opinions with systematic predictions.

In conclusion, the Delphi technique should be regarded as a vehicle to help discover and explore vague and unknown future issues that would be otherwise difficult to address. It should be used with the realization that its results are more in the nature of a structured brainstorming session than a highly scientific exercise in forecasting.

5.10.2 The Subjective Probability Methods

The subjective or personalistic interpretation of probability was first introduced by L. J. Savage, R. Schlaifer, and H. Raiffa ([9], pp. 153). Their main idea was that probability is a measure of one's personal belief in a particular outcome of an "experiment," and thus a rational approach to studying events that have not yet occurred can be developed. The method can be summarized as follows:

1. Use historical data for a specific period of time (e.g., 3 years).
2. Develop a questionnaire asking respondents to give their best (probability = .99), worst (probability = .01), and average (probability = .50) estimates of the projected value of the random variable. Call these estimates A, B, and C, respectively.
3. Ask respondents to estimate values D, E, F, G, H, and I as follows:
$$D = \text{median value of } A \text{ and } C$$
$$E = \text{median value of } C \text{ and } B$$
$$F = \text{median value of } B \text{ and } E$$
$$G = \text{median value of } E \text{ and } C$$
$$H = \text{median value of } C \text{ and } D$$
$$I = \text{median value of } D \text{ and } A$$

4. After a personal interview with each respondent to clarify any ques-

tions, prepare a frequency distribution of the random variable for the entire group of answers.

5. Select the *median* of the resultant frequency distribution as the *estimated forecast*.

The frequency distribution mentioned in point 4 is thus based on the subjective estimates provided by the respondents. Accordingly, the cumulative distribution function of this frequency distribution uses the notion of subjective probability. Any such subjective probability satisfies the two basic axioms of probability:

1. The probability p_i of an event i satisfies the inequality

$$0 \leq p_i \leq 1, \qquad \text{for all events } i$$

2. $\Sigma_i p_i = 1$, where the summation is taken over all events i in the event space.

After the forecasts are made, we can gather actual data and compare them with the forecasts to determine how good the forecasts are. Three statistical measures are used for this purpose, the mean absolute deviation (MAD), Systematic error E_s, and the mean deviation about the correction for systematic error (MD_{CSE}). These measures are calculated as follows:

$$\text{MAD} = \frac{\Sigma_{i=1}^n |F_i - A_i|}{n} \qquad \text{(measures accuracy)}$$

where n is the total number of data values, F_i is the forecast for the period i, and A_i is the actual data for period i.

$$E_s = \frac{\Sigma_{i=1}^n (F_i - A_i)}{n} \qquad \text{(measures bias)}$$

and

$$\text{MD}_{cse} = \frac{\Sigma_{i=1}^n |F_i - A_i - E_s|}{n} \qquad \begin{array}{l}\text{(measure of} \\ \text{consistency after} \\ \text{bias has been removed)}\end{array}$$

In general, bias is more acceptable than inconsistency, because we can correct our forecasts for the bias effect. We strive for a small value of MD_{CSE}, since otherwise the forecasts will become highly inconsistent.

It may be noted that the Delphi and subjective probability methods both

use questionnaires and informed judgment, but the former deals with actual values of forecast while the latter deals with the probability that a forecast will have a specified value. Also, the Delphi method usually involves a series of questionnaires, while the subjective probability method involves only one.

5.10.3 The Cross Impact Method

The Delphi technique can be utilized to collect and analyze expert opinion. However, it cannot be used to determine interrelationships among events shaping the future. Such interrelationships are called *cross impacts*. In 1968, T. J. Gordon and H. Hayward developed the cross-impact method to address the following type of problem.

Suppose that dependencies are suspected among future events. Then the probability that a potential event will actually occur is influenced by the occurrence or nonoccurrence of related events. The cross-impact method allows us to estimate each event's probability of occurrence based on interrelationships that exist between events included in the analysis.

A more rigorous formulation of the type of problem that can be handled by the cross-impact method is the following. Consider a set of developments forecast to occur prior to some year in the future with various levels of probability. If these developments are designated $D_1, D_2, \ldots, D_m, \ldots, D_n$ with associated probabilities $P_1, P_2, \ldots, P_m, \ldots, P_n$, then the question can be posed: If $P_m = 100\%$ (i.e., D_m will definitely happen), how do $P_1, P_2, \ldots, P_n$ change? If there is a cross-impact, then the probability of the individual items will vary positively or negatively with the occurrence or nonoccurrence of the other items.

If the occurrence of D_m increases P_n, then we say that there is a *positive cross impact*, or an *enhancing linkage*, between D_m and D_n, because the occurrence of D_m increases or enhances the probability of the occurrence of D_n. On the other hand, if the occurrence of D_m decreases P_n, then there is a *negative cross impact*, or an *inhibiting linkage*, between D_m and D_n, because the occurrence of D_m decreases or inhibits the probability of the occurrence of D_n. Finally, if the linkage is neither enhancing nor inhibiting, then there is an *unrelated* linkage between D_m and D_n, that is, the occurrence of D_m has absolutely no impact on the probability of the occurrence of D_n.

Now, if P_n is the probability of D_n before the occurrence of D_m, and P'_n is the probability of D_n after the occurrence of D_m, then P_n and P'_n are connected by the equation

$$P'_n = P_n + KSP_n(P_n - 1)$$

where P_n = the probability of occurrence of event D_n by time t prior to the occurrence of event D_m

P'_n = the probability of occurrence of event D_n some time after the occurrence of event D_m

K = -1 or $+1$, depending on whether the occurrence of D_m enhances or inhibits the occurrence of D_n. K is -1 for the enhancing linkage and $+1$ for the inhibiting linkage

S = a number between 0 and 1, a larger number representing a stronger effect of D_m on D_n and zero designating unrelated events

Gordon and Hayward, who were the originators of the cross-impact method, are uncertain about the accuracy of the above equation and suggest that other equations should be tried. However, as indicated by the equation, the relationship between P_n and P'_n is indeed nonlinear.

In order to apply the cross-impact method to a real problem, experts in the relevant field are requested to estimate the subjective probabilities P_1, $P_2, \ldots, P_m, \ldots, P_n$ and also to indicate the direction and strength of the cross impacts by estimating the values of KS in the above equation for different developments $D_1, D_2, \ldots, D_m, \ldots, D_n$, respectively. Next, the corresponding modified probabilities $P'_1, P'_2, \ldots, P'_m, \ldots, P'_n$ are computed. This experiment is repeated a large number of times and the cumulative number of occurrences for each development is kept. This number divided by the total number of trials provides an estimate of the modified probability for each event that reflects all interrelationships among the developments.

5.11 SOCIAL AND POLITICAL FORECASTING

In the area of social forecasting we are dealing with an ephemeral but pervasive effect. It is ephemeral because of the rapidity with which social factors ebb and flow. However, it is also pervasive because it affects society profoundly. Among the social constants we can include geography (e.g., layout of towns and cities) and permanence of man-made urban environment. Because of the slow process of social change, quantitative techniques prove quite useful in social forecasting. For example, in order to project on an annual basis the proportion of population changing residence, historical data prove to be adequate. In fact, during the past 30 years, this proportion has stayed almost constant at 20% annually.

Political forecasting has become popular during the last 20 years. Typical examples are the growth of polling and studies of the reasons why election campaigns have been held the way they were. Public opinion polling has become increasingly common. However, most of these studies take place during elections. Thus, there are few continuing studies showing the way in which political views are changing within the population and the reasons for those changes.

5.12   OTHER TYPES OF STATISTICAL MODELS

The statistical models discussed so far deal with forecasting, both quantitative and qualitative. But there are other types of statistical models such as estimation of parameters, hypothesis testing, analysis of variance, and decision analysis, not all of which are relevant to the design and implementation of decision support systems. In this chapter we shall consider two more categories of statistical models: financial models and decision tree models.

A nonoptimizing *financial model* is highly statistical and econometric in nature. It deals with investment of funds in interest-earning securities. Its basic ingredients are the initial amount a_0, say, invested at time $t = 0$ and the cash returns or reinvestments $a_1, a_2, \ldots, a_n$ at equal intervals of time $t = 1, 2, \ldots, n$, respectively. The investment generation method addresses this problem by allocating the interest or reinvestment income from a specific class of funds to the year in which that class of funds was first made available. Insurance companies use this technique to help assure equity among policyholders and to minimize adverse financial selection.

In a *decision tree* we take a sequence of decisions such that after each decision is undertaken there is a result and once that result is known there is the opportunity of making a further decision (see Figure 5-10). If there are only two possible decisions, then we get a *binary decision tree;* otherwise it is an n-*ary decision tree.* To arrive at a specific decision route, the expected value of the outcome is used as the deciding factor. Assume that each activity node has a probability and a profit value attached to it; then if we follow a specific route we can calculate the expected profit for that route. The optimal path to be taken is the one that maximizes the expected profit at the end of the route. Decision tree analysis presupposes a knowledge of the prior probability estimates and the profits associated with each outcome. In the real world, this is very difficult to achieve.

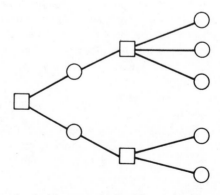

FIGURE 5-10   Example of a decision tree. (□) Decision node; (○) possible consequences or activity node.

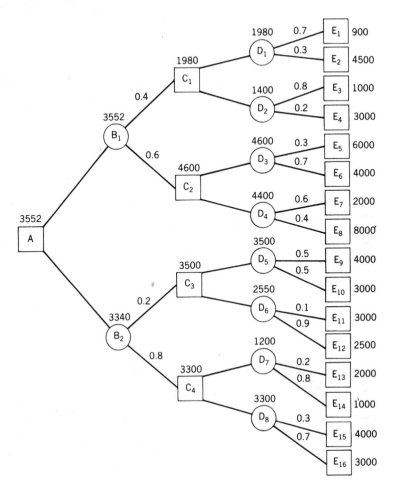

FIGURE 5-11 Multilevel decision tree.

5.13 DECISION TREES

In this section we shall discuss an example of a binary decision tree, that is, one in which each decision node has only two possible consequences.

Figure 5-11 shows a multilevel decision tree. Here the final decision node is A. Other decision nodes are $C_1, \ldots, C_4$ and $E_1, \ldots, E_{16}$. Activity nodes are B_1, B_2, and $D_1, \ldots, D_8$.

Assume that the whole tree is laid out with prior probabilities along the branches B_1C_1, B_1C_2, B_2C_3, B_2C_4, D_1E_1, D_1E_2, D_2E_3, D_2E_4, D_3E_5, D_3E_6, D_4E_7, D_4E_8, D_5E_9, D_5E_{10}, D_6E_{11}, D_6E_{12}, D_7E_{13}, D_7E_{14}, D_8E_{15}, and D_8E_{16}. The value of the prior probability estimate of each branch is noted along that branch. Thus, for example, the probability of the event denoted by branch B_1C_1 is 0.4, that of the event represented by D_1E_2 is 0.3, and so on.

We next assume that the profits are known at the decision nodes $C_1, \ldots,$ C_4 and $E_1, \ldots, E_{16}$. These profits are indicated against the corresponding nodes. Thus, the profit at E_1 is 900, that at E_2 is 4500, and so on.

In order to determine the optimal decision path, we start with the final decision nodes $E_1, \ldots, E_{16}$ and work backwards to determine which nodes should be selected from $D_1, \ldots, D_8$. The selected nodes then become the prior decision nodes $C_1, \ldots, C_4$. We repeat the process of calculating backwards to select the node B_1 or B_2. Finally, node A becomes the maximum of B_1 and B_2.

The selection process proceeds by first calculating the expected value at each activity node, then designating the pairwise maximal nodes as the next level decision nodes, and continuing this process until we reach the final single decision node. The expected value at D_1 is then

$$
\begin{aligned}
E(D_1) &= 900 \times 0.7 + 4500 \times 0.3 \\
&= 630 + 1350 \\
&= 1980
\end{aligned}
$$

Similar computations yield

$$
\begin{aligned}
E(D_2) &= 1000 \times 0.8 + 3000 \times 0.2 \\
&= 1400 \\
E(D_3) &= 6000 \times 0.3 + 4000 \times 0.7 \\
&= 4600 \\
E(D_4) &= 2000 \times 0.6 + 8000 \times 0.4 \\
&= 4400 \\
E(D_5) &= 4000 \times 0.5 + 3000 \times 0.5 \\
&= 3500 \\
E(D_6) &= 3000 \times 0.1 + 2500 \times 0.9 \\
&= 2550 \\
E(D_7) &= 2000 \times 0.2 + 1000 \times 0.8 \\
&= 1200 \\
E(D_8) &= 4000 \times 0.3 + 3000 \times 0.7 \\
&= 3300
\end{aligned}
$$

Therefore,

$$
\begin{aligned}
C_1 &= \max (E(D_1), E(D_2)) \\
&= \max (1980, 1400) = 1980
\end{aligned}
$$

Similarly,

$$
\begin{aligned}
C_2 &= \max (E(D_3), E(D_4)) = 4600 \\
C_3 &= \max (E(D_5), E(D_6)) = 3500 \\
C_4 &= \max (E(D_7), E(D_8)) = 3300
\end{aligned}
$$

Next, we repeat the cycle of computing expected values and then taking the maximum in pairs. Thus,

$$E(B_1) = 1980 \times 0.4 + 4600 \times 0.6 = 3552$$
$$E(B_2) = 3500 \times 0.2 + 3300 \times 0.8 = 3340$$

Therefore,

$$A = \max(E(B_1), E(B_2)) = 3552$$

Analyzing Figure 5-11, we now find that the optimal decision path is

$$A \ B_1 \ C_2 \ D_3 \ E_5$$

In other words, if the decision maker follows this route, then he makes the maximum profit of $3,552.

Since the probabilities used here are mere estimates, they will possibly be changed. In that case, path $AB_1C_2D_3E_5$ may not remain optimal. However, we can repeat the algorithm illustrated above for the new set of values and recompute the new optimal decision path.

5.14 DECISION ANALYSIS IN MARKET RESEARCH*

Funds are often appropriated for market research studies without consideration of either (1) monetary consequences of various possible acts and states of nature or (2) the probability of choosing the "wrong" act. The decision theory approach outlined here provides a convenient method of formally analyzing all the relevant variables to decide whether or not to collect additional information before acting, and if so, how much the additional information is worth.

The model permits the decision maker to utilize all the "information" he has at his command and to summarize this information in probability assignments and conditional profit estimates. One of the more important advantages of the formal analysis is that it provides a decision rule for each possible outcome of the proposed market research study.

In examining market research cases one is often struck with the fact that regardless of the outcome of the research project, the decision choice is unaffected or unclear. Formal analysis prior to the research may not only provide a better basis for evaluating a specific research proposal but may also suggest a research design that would provide information that is more germane to the decision that the management faces.

As indicated in Sections 5.12 and 5.13, decision analysis under uncertainty utilizes the expected value concept. It recognizes that the outcome of a de-

*The material depends heavily on a paper by Bass ([1], pp. 188–206).

cision depends upon deciding which of the several possible options is the best according to the user's judgment. Thus, having adopted the expected value decision criterion, the decision choice depends upon the assignment of probability to each possible outcome.

5.14.1 Assignment of Subjective Probability

In Section 5.10.2 we discussed the subjective probability method. The probability assigned to each option in a decision tree is subjective because the outcome of each option is mostly unknown and therefore dependent upon the user's intuition. This is more so in the area of market research where the objective is to decide upon the most profitable option to market a new product for which the possible consumer reactions are either unknown or not known very well. Bass ([1], p. 190) provides the following comments on the propriety of using subjective probability in this situation:

1. Many, if not most, business decisions are once-and-only decisions and consequently no objective (i.e., relative frequency) statistics are available. Hence insistence upon objective probability measures precludes rigorous analysis of the most common and most important class of business problems.

2. Use of subjective probabilities permits the incorporation into the decision model in a formal way of the many nonobjective variables business executives usually take into account in making decisions informally. The end result of "experience," "knowledge of the market," and so on, is summarized in the subjective probabilities assigned by the decision maker.

3. The purpose of the analysis in which subjective probabilities are employed is to permit the decision maker to arrive at a decision that is consistent with his/her explicitly stated beliefs about the "state of nature" and values assigned to consequences, not "truth," whatever that is.

5.14.2 Cost of Refinement of Subjective Probability

The determination of subjective probability for different possible outcomes in market research normally involves a cost factor. Therefore, the obvious question that arises is whether it is cost justifiable to ascertain such subjective probabilities for an added expense. Since we use these probabilities to compute the expected value of the optimal decision, we can use the following criterion:

If the sum of the expected value of the optimal decision before market research and the cost of the market research is less than the expected value of the optimal decision after the market research, then the cost is justified; otherwise it is not.

Thus, for example, suppose that the expected value for an optimal decision

in a decision tree is P dollars and that it costs an additional Q dollars to refine the previous subjective probabilities. With the refined subjective probabilities, the new expected value of the optimal decision is R dollars. Only if

$$P + Q < R$$

is the expenditure of Q dollars justified.

5.14.3 Prior Probability Distribution

In decision analysis the expected value of an optimal decision depends crucially on the prior probability distribution of possible outcomes in a decision tree. These outcomes can be discrete or continuous. Let us illustrate this issue with an example.

Suppose that an insurance company wants to introduce a variable life insurance policy in the market and has accomplished some market penetration through advertising. The company then comes up with the following estimates of market share:

p_1 = probability that 30% of the target audience will buy the policy.

p_2, p_3, p_4 are similar probabilities for 20%, 10%, and 1% of target audience, respectively.

In this case the outcomes are discrete, since they assume the four discrete values 30%, 20%, 10%, and 1%.

On the other hand, let us define p_1 as the probability that 20–30% of the target audience will buy the policy. Similarly, let p_2, p_3, and p_4 correspond to the ranges 10–20%, 1–10%, and 0–1%, respectively. In this case, the outcomes vary continuously from a lower limit to an upper limit. Realistically, the outcomes should be of the continuous type.

Theoretically, the decision maker can select the appropriate prior probability distribution from an infinite variety. The selection should reflect his/her best judgment and knowledge of the market. The normal distribution, with the proper choice of parameters μ and σ, can fit a large number of situations.

5.14.4 Case Study on Market Research Expenditures

Frank M. Bass performed a case study ([1], pp. 188–206) using the decision analysis model discussed in Section 5.14.1. His main objective was to determine whether market research would be worthwhile preceding the introduction of a new product. He considered two potential market research activities: test marketing and a consumer panel test. For test marketing he assumed the outcomes to be discrete, while for the consumer panel test he

considered both discrete and continuous outcomes. For both test marketing operations and the consumer panel test he provided detailed decision tree diagrams.

5.15 CRITICISMS OF THE DECISION ANALYSIS MODEL

In the real business world, numerous branches are possible in a decision tree rather than only two at each node. As a result, the combinatorial problem of computing all possible outcomes may be overwhelming. However, that can be handled through computer programs and thus is not insurmountable. The real problems are as follows:

1. *Timing of sequences of actions.* Decisions and results take place in a continuum of time, but in decision tree analysis we use an arbitrary breakdown of time into points of decision, which may not be realistic.

2. *Estimate of profits at each decision node.* This depends on accounting conventions in the office and therefore is subjective in nature.

3. *Estimate of prior probabilities.* This is the most difficult part in a decision analysis situation and, as already noted, is subjective.

In addition, the verdict of following the path of maximum expected value may not always be realistic. A decision maker may be willing to take extra risk to follow a different path leading to a higher profit but with with a lower probability of realization.

The decision maker should explore different possible tree logics rather than one tree; make a decision to follow one path, perhaps the path of maximum expected value; then reassess the possible future courses of action before proceeding any further. Thus, the decision tree should be dynamic rather than static.

5.16 SUMMARY

This chapter discusses nonoptimizing statistical models. The major emphasis is placed on forecasting models of different types, both quantitative and qualitative.

First regression analysis using the least squares method of curve fitting is introduced. Linear regression and correlation are treated in some detail, followed by briefer reference to nonlinear regression. Forecasting then appears as a special case of regression where the independent variable is labeled t (i.e., time) instead of X. If the historical data show a linear trend, then the trend curve is a straight line; otherwise, the trend curve can be a parabola, an exponential curve, or an asymptotic growth curve. Detailed procedures are given with equations in order to compute the coefficients of the trend

curve to fit the past historical data. This is followed by a case study using a population forecasting model that shows how a model can be made flexible to handle "what if" questions. As further examples of forecasting, several topics from census and actuarial studies are also introduced.

The next set of topics deals with qualitative forecasting. Here the prediction depends not only on past historical data but also on the subjective judgments and personal beliefs of experts. Three methods of qualitative forecasting are treated: the Delphi technique, subjective probability methods, and the cross-impact method.

The chapter then introduces two other areas in which statistical models are used: financial models and decision tree models. The remainder of the chapter then deals with decision trees and decision analysis. Decision analysis uses the notion of expected value in statistics as well as subjective probability. The estimation of prior probability is crucial to the application of decision analysis to market research. A case study done by Frank M. Bass is heavily used to explain how marketing policy makers can use decision analysis. The final section of the chapter addresses some of the criticisms brought against the use of decision trees and decision analysis.

5.17 KEY WORDS

The following key words are used in this chapter:

additive time series
asymptotic growth curve
coefficient of correlation
coefficient of determination
cross-impact method
curve-fitting technique
decision analysis
decision tree
Delphi technique
enhancing linkage
forecasting
Gompertz curve
inhibiting linkage
intercensal estimate
investment generation method
least squares method
line of regression

linear regression
linear trend curve
logistics curve
moving average method
multiplicative time series
nonlinear regression
nonoptimizing model
postcensal estimate
prior probability distribution
quadratic trend curve
qualitative forecasting
quantitative forecasting
regression analysis
statistical model
subjective probability
time series analysis
trend curve

REFERENCES

1. R.L. Day and L.J. Parsons (eds), *Marketing Models: Quantitative Applications*, Intext Educational Publishers, Scranton, PA, 1971.
2. J.E. Freund and F.J. Williams, *Elementary Business Statistics*, Prentice-Hall, Englewood Cliffs, NJ, 1982.
3. E.A. Green, "The Case for Refinement in Methods of Allocating Investment Income," *Transactions of the Society of Actuaries, 13, 308–319 (1961)*.
4 D.M. McGill, *Fundamentals of Private Pensions*, Richard D. Irwin, Homewood, IL, 1979.
5. S.S. Mittra, "Population Forecasting Model," *American Journal of Correction*, July–August 1976, pp. 19, 42.
6. S.S. Mittra, "Forecasting Techniques," *Quality*, May 1977, pp. 26–28.
7. P. Rivett, *Model Building for Decision Analysis*, Wiley, New York, 1980.
8. H. Spiegelman, *Introduction to Demography*, Harvard University Press, Boston, 1973.
9. W.G. Sullivan, and W.W. Claycombe, *Fundamentals of Forecasting*, Reston, Reston, VA, 1977.

REVIEW QUESTIONS

1. Why is a statistical forecasting model described as a nonoptimizing model?

2. Explain the method of least squares used for curve fitting.

3. Does a very small value of the coefficient of correlation necessarily mean that X and Y are not causally related?

4. What are the two alternative models for time series analysis? Describe each one.

5. For what types of forecasting would you use the asymptotic growth curve as the trend curve? What does the asymptote represent?

6. If the forecast is bound to be wrong, then what is the value of forecasting?

7. Is it possible that different parts of the given data fit different trend curves? How do you then handle the junctions of two different trend curves? (Hint: Use your knowledge of the continuity concept in calculus. The answer is not in the book.)

8. For a certain community the following population totals are given:

$$P_{1960} = 100,000$$
$$P_{1970} = 110,000$$
$$P_{1980} = 121,000$$

(a) Project the population to the year 2000 (i) by linear regression; (ii) by geometric projection.

(b) How many of the given population totals does (i) the least
     squares line pass through? (ii) the geometric curve pass through?

 9. The following information is given for a certain community:

Year	Population January 1
1970	100,000
1980	117,000

Vital Statistics

	Number of Recorded Occurrences	
Occurrence	Jan. 1, 1970 to Jan. 1, 1980	Jan. 1, 1970 to Jan. 1, 1975
Births	18,000	1500
Deaths	10,000	850
Net migration	6,500	350

The annual number of occurrences of births, deaths, and net migra-
tion were assumed to increase by the same amount during each year
of the 10-year period. Determine:

(a) The error of closure for the 10-year period.

(b) The intercensal population on January 1, 1975 by (i) the com-
     ponent method distributing the error of closure evenly over the
     whole period; (ii) using linear interpolation.

(c) The population January 1, 1981 by (i) linear extrapolation; (ii)
     geometric extrapolation.

10. Discuss the advantages and disadvantages of the Delphi technique
of forecasting. Why is it called a qualitative method?

11. What are enhancing linkage and inhibiting linkage in the cross-impact
method?

12. In the cross-impact method, how does the equation connecting P_n
and P'_n indicate that P'_n depends on P_n in a nonlinear manner?

13. What is a binary decision tree?

14. How is subjective probability used in decision analysis?

15. Why is the prior probability distribution so crucial in decision analysis?

16. What are some of the criticisms that are leveled against decision
analysis models?

SIMULATION TECHNIQUES

Part III discusses the techniques of simulation. This process is used when an explicit mathematical model of the system cannot be built. Simulation is essentially a systematic trial and error process. There are two types of simulation: discrete and continuous. Chapter 6 introduces the basic concepts of simulation. Chapter 7 discusses the principles of queueing theory, which forms the basis of discrete system simulation. Chapter 8 then discusses discrete system simulation. Chapter 9 provides a brief overview of continuous system simulation. Chapters 10 and 11 describe two simulation languages for handling a discrete model and a continuous model, respectively. Chapter 10 is an introduction to GPSS and Chapter 11 is an introduction to DYNAMO II.

6

Simulation Concepts

6.1 LIMITATIONS OF MATHEMATICAL MODELS

In chapter 3 we discussed the basic concepts of mathematical models, both optimizing and nonoptimizing. In Chapter 4 we introduced a variety of optimizing models that are used in operations research. In Chapter 5 we described a set of nonoptimizing statistical models. In all these models a set of variables that satisfy a system of equations and/or inequalities are introduced. The model is solved explicitly by using mathematical techniques, and the solution gives the values to be assigned to the variables defined in the model. While such models can address a wide variety of problems, they have significant shortcomings. In fact, not all models can be solved in terms of explicit analytic functions.

There are three fundamental limitations to the use of mathematical models:

1. A model may be so complex or involve such functions that an explicit solution is not possible even with the use of computers.

2. A mathematical programming model, which happens to be the most widely used and is applicable to a highly diversified category of problems, provides solutions (e.g., planning strategies) for a prescribed time period. However, the solution does not indicate how the plan is to be implemented on a time span that is shorter than the time period assumed in the model. For example, if the planning horizon used in the model extends over 6 months to a year, then the solution leaves implicit the resulting implementation plan for week-to-week and month-to-month operations.

3. All models rely on past historical data and assume that the past conditions will continue into the future. However, this need not be the case always. Consequently, some amount of uncertainty pervades a model. Al-

though statistical models can be made sensitive to "what if" situations (see Chapter 5) and linear programming models can be modified by using sensitivity or postoptimality analysis, the scope of such techniques is limited.

Because of these limitations, many important managerial decision-making problems cannot be handled by mathematical modeling techniques in spite of the great diversity of models. The simulation technique is especially useful in these situations. It starts by building an experimental model of a system in analytic terms. However, instead of solving the model explicitly, the simulation approach evaluates various specific alternatives with respect to how well they fare in test or simulated runs of the model. Essentially we can regard simulation as a systematic trial-and-error approach to solving a problem. It is very well suited to answer "what if" questions.

Many operations research analysts regard the simulation process as a method of last resort. In his operations research book, Wagner ([8], Chapter 21) begins the chapter on simulation with a rather provocative expression, "When all else fails . . . ."

6.2 WHAT IS SIMULATION?

In the simplest form, any make-believe model of a real-life situation can be described as a simulated environment. For example, a toy train set is a simulated version of a real train; a programmable model car simulates a real-life automobile; a planetarium shows a simulated version of space; and so on. However, we shall use the term simulation in a more formal sense. Thus, a *simulation* of a real-life problem is a model that consists of variables and constraints as in any mathematical model. But instead of an explicit analytical solution, the simulated model uses several test values of the variables and derives the corresponding solutions. The manager can examine the results to see if they are satisfactory. If they are not, the simulation model is run again. A computerized simulation program is a prerequiste to running any simulation model.

Simulation should not be regarded as a panacea. A simulation model includes uncertain events. Hence the answers it provides should be regarded as approximations subject to statistical error. Moreover, the model incorporates a complicated problem that is unsolvable by standard operations research tools. As a result, an analysis of the simulated solutions is often difficult. To accommodate "what if" scenarios, a large number of simulation runs are necessary, which makes the experiment a fairly costly proposition. Computer simulation is often an expensive way to study a complex system, but it is virtually impossible to perform a simulation experiment manually in any reasonable period of time. Finally, simulation only compares alternatives instead of generating an optimal solution.

6.3 THE NEED FOR SIMULATION

The process of simulation is used in a business or scientific environment in an attempt to estimate the outcome of an event or to predict the impact of a future course of action when the problem to be addressed cannot be handled by means of a mathematical model. Some examples of such problems are:

Design of information-feedback scheduling and operations rules; for example, scheduling rules for a job-shop manufacturing plant, or user services available at a computer center.

Selection of facilities in providing services; for example, the number of tellers in a bank.

Marketing of a new product; for example, a variable life insurance plan marketed by an insurance com

Choice of investment strategies for strategic planning; for example, corporate planning models such as SIMPLAN and EXPRESS.

An explicit solution represented by mathematical functions does not exist for such problems.

The combined effect of uncertainty, the dynamic interactions between decisions and among the variables in the system, and the need to use either finely divided time intervals (e.g., multiprogramming in a computer system) or a long-term horizon (e.g., long-range planning) make the problem too big and intricate to be solvable with explicit functions. This leads us to the technique of *simulation*. Computer simulation serves a management scientist or an operations research analyst in the same way as a laboratory experiment serves a physical scientist.

Simulation as a separate discipline started around 1959 with several jobshop simulators developed by large industrial corporations. In 1962 the simulation languages GPSS and SIMSCRIPT were introduced to handle simulation models.

6.4 THE PROCESS OF SIMULATION

A simulation model is built with one or more of the following objectives in mind:

☐ To describe a current system.
☐ To explore a hypothetical system.
☐ To design an improved system.

The steps involved in building a simulation are as follows:

Step 1. Formulate the model. This is similar to the mathematical mod-

eling process. However, do not include too much detail in a simulation model lest you consume an excessive amount of computer time in performing the experiment. For example, if the model's objective is to decide between two different locations for a new warehouse, simulate activities on a week-to-week basis rather than on a day-to-day or hour-to-hour basis. If the model decides between one or two loading docks at a new warehouse, then simulate activities on the basis of 5–15-minute intervals.

Step 2. Design the Experiment. Work out the details of the experimental procedures. For example, what characteristics of the simulated system should be measured? What are the scope and detail involved? Usually the broader the scope of the system, the less detail is likely to be included.

Step 3. Develop the computer program. Use a standard language such as FORTRAN or a simulation language such as GPSS, DYNAMO, or SIMULA.

Steps 1 and 2 are usually combined into the single but involved procedure of simulation model building and validation.

6.5 BUILDING A SIMULATION MODEL

The general process of building a simulation model consists of the following four steps:

1. *Determination of model components.* The model is described in terms of its *dynamic* phenomena and *entities* that are regulated according to some *decision rules.* For example, suppose we want to simulate the flow of customers to bank tellers in order to determine an optimal number of tellers to be assigned. Then the dynamic phenomenon would be the flow of customers through the bank, and the entities would be the individual tellers who are assigned to their jobs according to some decision rule established by management, such as that no teller should remain idle for more than 10% of his/her time. At any instant of simulation the model is in a particular *state.* For example, the number of customers and the number of available tellers at the beginning of a day describe the state of the simulation model at the beginning of a simulation run.

2. *Data Gathering.* There are three types of data used in a simulation model:

☐ Timing
☐ Resource utilization and queueing
☐ Historical

The analysis of the output from a simulation model depends on what type of data are gathered. Timing data normally include the time required to com-

plete a job, the time allocation to a system user, and so on. Resource utilization data describe how the customers and the servers are handled in the
model. These data are particularly useful when the simulation model handles
a queueing process. The output gives the number of customers in the model,
the average waiting time for a customer, the average fraction of time that
the servers remain busy, the maximum length of the queue during the simulation run, the average length of the quene, and so on. Historical data are
represented by a chronological event-by-event trace for entire or partial simulations.

3. *Model Validation.* If a system is simulated in parts, then once the
system is completely built, all the parts should be linked together and tested
for overall systemwide validity. It should not be assumed that merely because
each of the component parts seems adequate when considered in isolation,
the entire simulated system is sufficiently accurate. A similar situation arises
in the link testing of computer programs; for example, an edit program must
conform to the specifications of an update program. The model validation
is usually a complicated statistical process and can be accomplished in several
alternative ways.

4. *Time Incrementation.* The model views the simulated time as elapsing
period by period. The simulated clock is up-dated at the conclusion of each
time period. The clock may increment the time in fixed lengths (e.g., from
t to $t + k$) or in variable lengths. Accordingly, we may have a *time-oriented*
simulation or an *event-oriented* simulation.

In a time-oriented simulation, the simulated time changes in fixed increments and thus the model is deterministic in nature. In an event-oriented
simulation, the simulated clock is updated at the arrival of the next event.
If the events occur at fixed intervals of time, then the event-oriented simulation becomes time-oriented and can be handled in the same deterministic
manner, by incrementing t by constant amount. If, however, the arrival times
of the events follow a given probability distribution, then the simulated clock
has to be updated by variable time increments and the simulation becomes
truly event-oriented and probabilistic. The arrival time of the next event is
computed by an algorithm applied to the probability distribution, and the
simulated clock is changed to that time value. The exact algorithm will be
given in Chapter 8.

Let us illustrate the situation with an example. The flow of customers coming
to a bank and being served by a teller can be simulated by using a queueing
model and discrete system simulation technique (see Chapter 7 for details).
The flow is characterized by two probability distributions—one representing
the arrival times of customers and the other representing their service times.

In addition, the model specifies how many tellers are available and in
what order the customers are served (first in first out, ramdon, etc.). By
using the means and the variances of the probability service times, we compute the arrival time of the next event and update the simulated clock accordingly. Thus, the heart of the typical simulation model is the "next event"

file, which maintains a list of all events to be processed and also serves as the "clock," allowing simulated time to be updated. An entry in the next-event file is made whenever the arrival time for a future event is established. The file handles simulation events, reporting events, and end of simulation.

6.6 CLASSIFICATION OF SIMULATION MODELS

There are two types of simulation models: discrete and continuous. In a *discrete* system simulation model the simulated time changes in a stepwise discrete fashion, while in a *continuous* system simulation the time changes occur smoothly.

A continuous system is normally expressed by a set of mathematical equations, algebraic or differential, and during the simulation the variables are updated by a continuous process. Historically, continuous system simulation was in general use for studying complex systems long before discrete system simulation was similarly applied. Many continuous system simulation studies are concerned primarily with the study of *servomechanisms,* which is the general name given to devices that rely upon feedback for their operation. The field of *control theory* provides the theoretical background with which to design such systems, but continuous system simulation is extensively used to carry out detailed studies. Continuous simulation is used mostly for scientific and engineering applications rather than in the business environment. It presupposes a mathematical model of the problem and thus an understanding of physical or chemical laws. As a result, it is necessary to perform a number of experiments or measurements to derive the coefficients of the model.

Discrete system simulation assumes that the simulated time changes in a stepwise manner, although, as indicated in Section 6.5, the time increments can be constant or variable. One or more variables are used to describe the *state* of the system at any given instant. As the simulation proceeds and the simulated time changes in a discrete manner, the state descriptors change their values. It is possible that two different events in the discrete system simulation occur simultaneously so that changes of state descriptors occurring simultaneously do not necessarily correspond to a single event. The simulation proceeds by executing all the changes to the system descriptors associated with each event as the events occur, in chronological order.

As was noted in Section 6.5, a discrete simulation is called *time-oriented* if the clock representing the simulated time is updated at regular time intervals. On the other hand, if the simulated clock is updated at scheduled occurrences of events, then the simulation is *event-oriented*. For event-oriented discrete simulations, the occurrence of events takes place according to a probability distribution that can be *uniform* or *nonuniform*.

In a uniform probability distribution the random variable can take a set of values with equal probabilities. For example, if a balanced die is rolled,

then the probability that a given face shows up is ⅙, since there are six faces and each face can appear with the *same* probability because the die is balanced. In a nonuniform probability distribution the probability that the random variable assumes a particular value is usually different in each case. Accordingly, the probability is expressed as a function $f(x)$ of the random variable x. The function $f(x)$ can be a *discrete* function or a *continuous* function. Binomial and Poisson distributions are examples of nonuniform discrete probability distributions, while exponential and normal distributions are examples of nonuniform continuous probability distributions.

The various types of simulation can be represented as in Figure 6-1.

For the sake of completeness it must be mentioned that some authors talk about a third type of simulation and call it a *hybrid simulation* (see [2], Chapter 4). The form taken by a hybrid simulation depends upon the application. It is possible that the system being simulated is an interconnection of two subsystems, one discrete and the other continuous. Such a hybrid simulation model must contain appropriate links to join the outcomes from the two components.

6.7 OUTPUT OF A SIMULATION MODEL

Any system simulation is concerned with changes in the system with respect to time. However, the observation of the system response relative to time is particularly important for continuous system simulations. Accordingly, the nature and contents of the output of a simulation model depend on the type of simulation. The output of a discrete system simulation would be

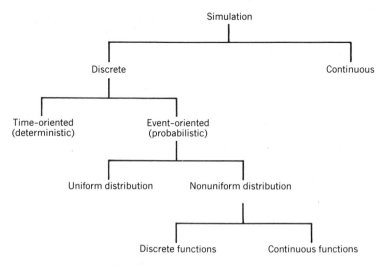

FIGURE 6-1 Types of simulation.

specific measures relative to time, such as the average waiting time in a queue, the average fraction of time that a server remains idle, and so on. On the other hand, the result of a continuous system simulation often involves such factors as the boundaries and oscillations of the system parameters. Consequently, visual inspection of the output is very important. For this reason, most of the continuous system simulation languages, such as DYNAMO, include various graphic features whereby graphs, bar charts, and so on can be displayed on the screen or printed with a plotter. To make such graphics easily changeable, the user should be able to work inter-actively via keystrokes on a CRT terminal or with a light pen. Interactive graphics is the appropriate tool in these cases.

6.8 SIMULATION LANGUAGES

Simulation languages, as distinguished from general purpose programming languages, are problem-oriented. Such languages are usually written in a largely computer-independent notation for a particular problem area and contain statements or constructs appropriate for formulating solutions to specific types of problems. Of course, general purpose languages like FORTRAN or PASCAL are also used. A recent survey estimates that 75% of all discrete event simulation is performed using FORTRAN or PASCAL, while most of the remaining 25% is performed using GPSS and SIMSCRIPT. A language like FORTRAN has a wide range of applications and therefore imposes the least bias upon the model to be programmed. However, such a language does not provide the control features available from a simulation language, such as data aggregation, event timing routines, data collection and presentation, random variable generation, and reporting of collected statistics.

Discrete simulation languages can use block-type structures as in GPSS, or they can use FORTRAN-like statements as in SIMSCRIPT. Continuous simulation languages include DYNAMO and CSMPIII (Continuous System Modeling Program, Version III). In Chapters 10 and 11 we shall take a glimpse into GPSS and DYNAMO to understand how simulation languages work. The graphics made available through DYNAMO help in exploring a continuous system. GPSS automatically generates and prints a variety of system statistics that describe the characteristics of the discrete system being simulated and are useful in identifying an optimal or near-optimal solution of the problem.

6.9 SUMMARY

This chapter introduces the concept of simulation. It is first pointed out that mathematical models are not always solvable in terms of explicit analytical values. Consequently, there exist a large group of business and scientific problems which cannot be addressed by the modeling technique. Simulation

provides the method of last resort to be tried in these situations. It is essentially a systematic trial-and-error method by which several test values are used to explore possible solutions of the model and the one that appears to be optimal or satisfactory is accepted. It provides a capability to run different "what if" scenarios from which a manager can make decisions. Three main limitations of a simulation model are (1) results are only approximate and are subject to statistical error so that model validation is necessary in all cases, (2) simulation merely compares alternatives and does not provide an optimal solution, and, (3) simulation models are costly to run and require a computer because manual simulation is virtually impossible.

Next, the chapter describes some general situations where simulation is used. It outlines a four-step process for building a simulation model. Time incrementation is essential in such a model. The simulated time can be incremented in fixed amounts, in which case we get a time-oriented deterministic model, in variable amounts, for an event-oriented probabilistic model. In either case, the simulated clock in the model is updated at the occurrence of the next event. The simulation is called discrete or continuous according as the time increments occur in a stepwise manner or continuously.

Computer programs to implement a simulation model can be written in a high-level scientific language like FORTRAN or PASCAL or in a special-purpose simulation language like GPSS or DYNAMO. A simulation language is especially designed to generate as output various statistical data from the simulation as well as to plot graphs. The latter technique is a special feature of DYNAMO.

6.10   KEY WORDS

The following key words are used in the chapter:

continuous simulation	nonuniform distribution
decision rule	simulated clock
discrete simulation	simulation
dynamic phenomenon	simulation language
entity	state
event-oriented simulation	state descriptor
job-shop simulator	time-oriented simulation
model validation	uniform distribution

REFERENCES

1. W.G. Bulgren, - *Discrete System Simulation*, Prentice-Hall, Englewood Cliffs, N. J., 1982.

2. G. Gordon, *System Simulation*, Prentice-Hall, Englewood Cliffs, N. J. 1978.

3. F.S. Hillier and G.J. Lieberman, *Introduction to Operations Research*, Holden-Day, San Francisco, 1974, Chap. 15.

4. Ralston, A. ed., *Encyclopedia of Computer Science,* Van Nostrand, New York, 1976, pp. 1259–1278.

5. G.P. Richardson and A.L. Pugh - *Introduction to System Dynamics Modeling with DYNAMO,* MIT Press, Cambridge, MA, 1981

6. P. Rivett, *Model Building for Decision Analysis,* Wiley, New York, 1980.

7. T. Schriber, *Simulation Using GPSS,* Wiley, New York, 1974

8. H.M. Wagner, *Principles of Operations Research,* Prentice-Hall, Englewood Cliffs, N. J., 1975, Chapter 21.

REVIEW QUESTIONS

1. Explain some of the limitations of a mathematical model. How does simulation address these limitations?

2. Comment on the statement: "Simulation should not be regarded as a panacea."

3. Identify the four steps involved in the process of building a simulation model. Describe each step briefly.

4. Explain clearly time incrementation as used in a simulation model. Why is this step so vital in the simulation process?

5. Define discrete system simulation and continuous system simulation. Why is continuous simulation more suitable for scientific problems?

6. Define a discrete probability distribution and a continuous probability distribution. Why is Poisson distribution called discrete? (*Caution:* The answer to the last question is not in the chapter! Consult a statistics text, or see Chapter 7 of this book.)

7. Describe the advantages and disadvantages of using a simulation language instead of a high-level scientific programming language for implementing a simulation model.

FORMULATIONAL PROBLEM

The following list of applications of simulation method is taken from Hillier and Lieberman ([3], p. 649). For each application, indicate (a) whether the process of simulation is discrete or continuous; (b) if discrete, whether it is time-oriented or event-oriented; and (c) if event-oriented, whether the probability distribution should be given by a discrete function or by a continuous function.

1. Simulation of the operations at a large airport by an airlines company to test changes in company policies (e.g., amounts of maintenance capacity, berthing facilities, spare aircraft, and so on).

2. Simulation of the passage of traffic across a junction with time-sequenced traffic lights to determine the best time sequences.

3. Simulation of a maintenance operation to determine the optimal size of repair crews.

4. Simulation of the flux of uncharged particles through a radiation shield to determine the intensity of the radiation that penetrates the shield.

5. Simulation of steel-making operations to evaluate changes in operating practices and the capacity and configuration of the facilities.

6. Simulation of the U.S. economy to predict the effect of economic policy decisions.

7. Simulation of large-scale military battles to evaluate defensive and offensive weapon systems.

8. Simulation of large-scale distribution and inventory control systems to improve their design.

9. Simulation of the overall operation of an entire business firm to evaluate broad changes in the policies and operation of the firm and also to provide a business game for training executives.

10. Simulation of a telephone communications system to determine the capacity of the respective components that would be required to provide satisfactory service at the most economical level.

11. Simulation of the operation of a developed river basin to determine the best configuration of dams, power plants, and irrigation works that would provide the desired level of flood control and water-resource development.

12. Simulation of the operation of a production line to determine the amount of in-process storage space that should be provided.

7

Queueing Theory and Simulation

7.1 THE QUEUEING PROCESS

In Chapter 6 we discussed the two types of simulation: discrete and continuous. Discrete system simulation involves the queueing process. In Chapter 3 we briefly referred to the queueing model while discussing the issue of trade-offs in an optimizing model. Let us now explore the concept of a queueing model more deeply. The example of customers coming to a bank for the service of a bank teller and forming a queue when a teller is not immediately available illustrates the concept of a queueing process.

Examples of queueing models abound in real life. Customers standing in line at a checkout counter of a supermarket or a department store, passengers waiting at an airline reservations counter, patients coming to the emergency room of a hospital for treatment, inmates waiting at a diagnosis and treatment center of a prison before being admitted into the prison are all examples that can be dealt with in queueing models. The customers in a queue need not be human beings. Thus, machines waiting to be serviced in a repair shop, cases pending in a court, jobs waiting for the attention of the CPU in a time-sharing environment are illustrations of inanimate "customers" forming a queue.

A queue is formed whenever there is congestion for service, that is, when more customers arrive than can be served by the available servers. Thus a queue is characterized by the following four features:

1. *Arrival pattern*, which describes statistically the frequency of customers arriving for service.

2. *Service pattern,* which describes statistically how the customers are served.
3. *Capacity* of the service, that is, the number of servers who can serve simultaneously in the system.
4. *Queueing discipline,* which specifies the rule by which the customers are served: first in first out (FIFO), last in first out (LIFO), round robin algorithm, and so on.

A queue always exhibits an element of uncertainty. For instance, we do not know exactly *when* the next customer will arrive at the bank or exactly *how many* customers will come during the next half hour. Similarly we do not know exactly *how long* it will take for a server to serve a given customer. Accordingly, the arrival and service patterns of a queue are given by a probability distribution instead of by definite numbers. For this reason a queueing model is called a *probabilistic* or *stochastic* model.

7.2 ARRIVAL PATTERN

An arrival pattern is described in terms of the interarrival times, that is, by the amount of time elapsed between two consecutive arrivals. If an arrival pattern is completely uniform, then the interarrival time is a constant. For example, if a customer comes to a bank every half hour, then the interarrival time equals 30 minutes constantly. However, realistically speaking, such is not the case. Based on an analysis of historical data pertaining to the arrival times of customers at a bank, an opeations research analyst can formulate the probability that x number of customers will arrive during a given time interval of length t, say. Such a mathematical function is called a *probability distribution* and can be used to describe the arrival patterns.

The probability distribution uses the following notation and terminology:

T_a = mean interarrival time, the time elapsing on the average between two consecutive arrivals

λ = mean arrival rate, the number of customers arriving on the average per unit of time

It is always true that

$$\lambda = 1/T_a$$

Note that since T_a represents the mean time, the actual time elapsing between two successive arrivals can be greater than, equal to, or less than T_a. As an example, suppose that during one week of 34 work hours in a bank (9:00 a.m. to 3:00 p.m. daily from Monday to Friday and 9:00 a.m. to 1:00 p.m.

on Saturday), a total of 1190 customers arrived. Using 1 hour as the unit time, it then follows that

$$T_a = 34/1190 \text{ h} = 1/35 \text{ h} = 1.7 \text{ min (approx.)}$$
$$\lambda = 1/T_a = 1190/34 = 35$$

In other words, on the average a new customer arrived every 1.7 minutes or 35 customers arrived per hour.

The probability distribution for the arrival pattern is usually written as follows:

$f(x,t)$ = probability that there are x arrivals during
a time interval of length t

The function $f(x,t)$ is expressed in terms of the parameter x.

It is assumed that the arrivals occur in a completely random manner so that the time of the next arrival is independent of that of the previous arrival. Such a random arrival pattern is called a *Poisson arrival pattern,* and the function $f(x,t)$ is called a *Poisson distribution* and is defined by the formula

$$f(x,t) = \frac{(\lambda t)^x \, e^{-\lambda t}}{x!}$$

where $x = 0, 1, 2, \ldots$, and t is a continuous variable. Here $x!$ is defined as the product $x(x - 1)(x - 2) \ldots (3)(2)(1)$. The Poisson distribution is said to be *discrete* since its argument x can assume only nonnegative integer values. This distribution is commonly applied to processes involving demands for service.

7.3 SERVICE PATTERN

As with arrival patterns, a service pattern is characterized by the time required to serve a customer in the system. The total time taken for serving a given customer is called the *service time* for that customer. Frequently the service time is a constant. However, if it is not constant, it will be determined by an appropriate probability distribution. On the basis of historical data, an operations research analyst can determine the frequency distribution of the service time and then compute the function that gives the probability distribution of service times. This distribution is expressed in terms of service time or the mean service rate.

Let us now introduce the following notation and terminology:

T_s = mean service time, the time taken on the average to
serve a customer

μ = mean service rate, the number of customers served
per unit time on the average

It is always true that

$$\mu = 1/T_s$$

As with T_a, T_s does not represent the actual time required to serve a customer. This latter time may be greater than, equal to, or less than T_s. For example, in continuation of the example given in Section 7.2, suppose that the total service time (in minutes) actually used to serve the 1190 customers of the bank during a week was 5593 minutes, Then

$$T_s = 5593/1190 \text{ min} = 4.7 \text{ min}$$
$$\mu = 1/T_s = 1190/5593 = 0.21 \text{ (approx.)}$$

This means that on the average a teller needed 4.7 min to serve a customer, and that on the average 0.21 customer was served per minute.

The probability distribution of the service time is given by a function

$g(t)$ = probability that the service time of a customer
is t units

$g(t)$ is expressed in terms of the parameter μ.

If the service time is constant, then T_s, and therefore μ, are constant. If the service time is completely random, then it may be represented by an exponential distribution, in which case we have

$$g(t) = \frac{1}{\mu}e^{-t\mu}$$

where t is a continuous variable. Note that the exponential distribution is *continuous* while the Poisson distribution is *discrete*. The reason for this difference is as follows:

The random variable x in $f(x,t)$ represents the number of arrivals during a time interval t and hence must be a nonnegative integer $0,1,2,\ldots$, depending on whether no customers, or one customer, or two customers, etc., arrive during time t. Hence $f(x,t)$ has to be expressed as a discrete probability distribution. On the other hand, the service time for a customer can take any positive real value and is not confined to only integral values. Consequently t is a continuous variable and $g(t)$ is a continuous probability distribution.

There is a relationship between the Poisson distribution describing the arrival pattern and the exponential distribution describing the service pattern. It can be proved by using statistical methods that if the service time is given

by the exponential distribution $g(t)$, then the associated Poisson distribution $h(x)$ given by

$$h(x) = \frac{\mu^x e^{-\mu}}{x!},$$

represents the probability that x customers can be served per unit time. Note that both $g(t)$ and $h(x)$ are expressed in terms of the same parameter μ. Hence $h(x)$ is called the associated Poisson distribution for the exponential distribution $g(t)$. In addition, assuming λ is replaced by μ, it may be noted that

$$h(x) = f(x,1)\lambda$$

7.4   CAPACITY OF SERVICE

The capacity of service is defined to be n when n servers can serve simultaneously. If $n = 1$, then we have a *single-server* model. If $n > 1$, then we have a *multiple-server* model.

   The total time spent by a customer in a queueing system consists of two parts: waiting time and service time. If the capacity of service is too small, then the waiting time tends to increase, since there are too few servers to serve the customers. On the other hand, if the capacity of service is large, then some of the servers may remain idle at times while the waiting time tends to decrease. The service time, however, is independent of the capacity of service and depends on the type of service required by an individual customer.

   Knowing the famous dictum that time is money, waiting time and service time are associated, respectively, with a waiting cost WC and a service cost SC. The total cost TC is defined as their sum:

$$TC = WC + SC$$

We saw in Section 3.6 that the objective of a queueing model is to minimize TC. An increase in WC normally leads to a decrease in SC, and vice versa, because a lower WC implies a shorter waiting time for a customer in queue and hence an availability of more servers, resulting in an increase in SC.

7.5   QUEUEING DISCIPLINES

Three general type queues are possible:

   FIFO (First In First Out).   Each newly arrived customer joins the queue, and service is provided in the order in which the customers arrive.

LIFO (Last In First Out). Service is next offered to the customer who has arrived most recently, for example, passengers getting in and out of a crowded train. This discipline is used in reading data out of a stack through the POP operation that removes the top element of the stack and returns it as a function value.

Random. Random choice of customers is made at the time of providing the service. Each customer has an equal opportunity of being served.

It is assumed that customers join the queue and stay until served. If a customer leaves before his turn for service comes, the situation is referred to as *reneging*. If a customer refuses to join the queue because of its length, then we have *balking*. When there is more than one line formed for the same service, the sharing of service among the lines is called *polling*. In data communication, when the host computer scans all the input terminals to determine if there is data/message to be transmitted by the teminals, we have the polling situation. The polling discipline is specified according to:

☐ The order in which the lines are served.
☐ The number of terminals served at each polling session.
☐ The time in transferring service among the lines.

Sometimes a queue may have a *priority scheme* whereby a high-priority customer gets service before all lower priority customers who are already in the queue. There may be several levels of priority. Since there can be several members in the same priority class, a queueing discipline (e.g., FIFO) must be specified for members within a class.

In a prioritized queueing system, two possibilities occur when a higher priority customer arrives while a lower priority customer is being served:

1. Service is continued to the lower priority customer until he is finished and then the natural order of the queue may be distorted by serving the higher priority customer. This is called *nonpreemptive priority*.

2. Service is disrupted to the lower priority customer, who is pushed back into the queue, and the higher priority customer is served. This is *preemptive priority*.

7.6 MEASURES OF QUEUES

Let

$$T_a = \text{mean interarrival time}$$
$$\lambda = \text{mean interarrival rate} = 1/T_a$$
$$T_s = \text{mean service time}$$
$$\mu = \text{mean service rate} = 1/T_s$$

Then *traffic intensity* is defined as the ratio $T_s/T_a = u$, say. If we assume that there is no reneging or balking, so that no customer refuses to join the queue and whoever joins the queue gets served, then u is called the *utilization ratio* ρ and is defined by

$$\rho = \frac{1/\mu}{1/\lambda} = \frac{\lambda}{\mu}, \quad \text{assuming a single server}$$

In case of reneging or balking, however, u is different from ρ. If there are n servers, then ρ is defined as

$$\rho = \lambda/n\mu$$

It is intuitively clear that if $\rho < 1$, then the system can keep up with the traffic flow. But as ρ approaches the value 1, the queue becomes long and undesirable. If $\rho > 1$, then the queue is said to be *unstable* and often leads to loss of customers. A normal trade-off situation is to select a value of n such that $\rho < 1$ and still cost is minimized.

7.7 EXAMPLES OF QUEUEING MODELS

Earlier in this chapter we discussed the example of customers coming to a bank and being served by the tellers to illustrate a queueing situation. We now discuss two more examples of queueing models.

7.7.1 Admission of Inmates to a Prison

After an offender is sentenced to serve a prison term, he/she is sent to the appropriate prison. However, before being admitted to the general prison population, the offender spends a "waiting period" in the evaluation or diagnosis and treatment unit of the prison. A team of counselors, psychologists, and physicians examine the new inmate, determine what kind of prison program should be arranged for him/her (e.g., a certain number of hours of individual and/or group counseling, employment for a certain period of each day in a prison industry program, etc.), to which specific prison ward he/she should be assigned, whether there are any specific medical concerns, and so on. Depending on the number of offenders being sentenced to a prison and the number of persons working in the evaluation unit team, a queueing environment originates in which the queue members or "customers" are the newly sentenced inmates and the "servers" are the members of the evaluation team.

The arrival pattern of the new inmates and the service pattern of the evaluation team members can be determined by analyzing the historical data. If

there is a tendency on the part of the courts to clear up backlogs of pending cases, then a queue can form at the evaluation unit. The waiting time in the queue can be reduced by increasing the number of members of the evaluation unit. The issue of trade-off arises here in that a longer queue of waiting inmates leads to a highly volatile situation and may result in prison riots, while an increase in the number of servers causes a rise in the personnel cost. The prison authority has to decide upon the optimal balance between these two "costs" and determine a way to minimize the total cost, to keep at a minimal level both the risk of inmate disturbance and the personnel cost to run the evaluation unit. The queueing discipline is normally FIFO, although under some special situations priorities can be assigned.

A similar queueing situation prevails in the emergency room of a hospital to handle the admission of new patients.

7.7.2 Repair of Machines at a Shop

So far we have seen examples of queues where both customers and servers are human beings. We now look at a situation where a "customer" is an inanimate object.

Fantastic Electronics is an electronics repair shop specializing in fixing color television sets. It normally employs three repairmen but contracts an additional repairman if a large number of television sets await repair. In this example, the customers are the television sets to be repaired and the servers are the repairmen fixing the sets. The service cost consists of the salaries of the repairmen, the cost of the machines and tools used for repairing, and other overhead maintenance costs. The company wants to minimize this cost. However, such minimizing cannot be done simply by reducing the number of repairmen and machines, because then the owners of the televisions requiring the repair work may get dissatisfied and take their sets to the competitors of Fantastic Electronics. Thus, a waiting cost is involved here in the form of loss of business due to a long repair time. Hence Fantastic Electronics would want to minimize the total cost, which in this case is the sum of the waiting cost and the service cost.

If repair work on television sets is not seasonal in nature, then the arrival pattern can be described by a Poisson distribution and the service pattern by an exponential distribution. The capacity of service ranges from 3 to 4 so that we have a multiple-server model. The queueing discipline is FIFO. However, Fantastic Electronics can change the priority if the owner of a television set agrees to pay an extra charge for priority service.

At the end of this chapter we shall discuss two more examples of queueing models. Both are related to computer applications. One model deals with computer performance evaluation, while the other involves timesharing systems. Since both of these examples require a higher degree of mathematical sophistication, they are postponed until the end of this chapter and may be omitted at first reading.

7.8   GRADE OF SERVICE

We have already seen that the objective of a queueing model is to minimize total cost, which consists of waiting cost and service cost. The latter is easier to measure since it involves such items as personnel cost, equipment maintenance, plant maintenance, and overhead. Waiting cost is more difficult to quantify. Accordingly, various techniques are used to address this issue. One method uses the grade of service as a restriction on the waiting time for customers.

The *grade of service* places some limits on the length of time that a customer has to wait for service. This is an important characteristic for a telephone system or for a data communication system. The grade of service is normally measured by a probabilistic criterion, for example, assuming a value of the probability that at most 10% of the customers will wait more than 3 minutes to be served.

In the case of a telephone system an important design criterion is that there be enough servers in the form of available circuits to avoid having customers wait for service. A message-switching system without the ability to store delayed messages must meet the same stringent conditions.

In a data communication system the grade of service is defined as the probability P (line for data transmission is busy). The grade of service is directly tied to the availability of the line. Thus, a grade of .10 indicates that under dial up connection line the customer will get a busy signal for 1 out of 10 dialings. In designing a network for data communication the analyst must be careful to keep the grade of service low so that the users are not demoralized, due to long waits.

7.9   USE OF QUEUEING MODELS IN DISCRETE SIMULATION

It was noted in Section 6.5 that in a discrete system simulation model the simulated time changes in a stepwise discrete manner. If the clock representing the simulated time is updated at regular time intervals, then the simulation is *time-oriented*. If, however, the clock is up-dated at scheduled occurrences of events, then the simulation is *event-oriented*. Both types of simulation can be handled by using a queueing model.

An important aspect of discrete system simulation is the generation of customer arrivals. If the simulation is time-oriented, then the arrival of the next customer occurs after a fixed interval of time. The arrival pattern is deterministic and the interarrival time is a constant. In an event-oriented simulation, the next customer arrives according to a probability distribution and the interarrival time is no longer constant.

The same considerations apply to the simulation of service times, which can be deterministic or probabilistic. However, a time-oriented simulation where the interarrival time is constant can have probabilistic service times.

Similarly, an event-oriented simulation can have constant service times. In other words, the deterministic or probabilistic nature of the arrival patterns does not determine the corresponding characteristics of the service patterns. A discrete system simulation is characterized as time-oriented or event-oriented depending on whether the interarrival time of customers is constant or variable.

As was noted earlier in Sections 3.6 and 7.7, the purpose of a queueing model is to minimize total cost by striking a proper balance between the waiting cost and service cost for the system. Often an explicit mathematical solution is not available. In such situations, the discrete system simulation technique is applied to determine on a trial-and-error basis the optimal solution to the problem. Let us illustrate the situation with the example of customers coming to a bank for the service of a teller. This represents an event-oriented discrete system simulation. The simulation model can be designed accordingly and can be implemented by using a simulation program written in a high-level language such as FORTRAN or PASCAL or a special purpose simulation language such as GPSS or SIMSCRIPT.

For the example of Sections 7.2 and 7.3, the arrival pattern follows a Poisson distribution with the parameter

$$\lambda = \text{mean arrival rate} = \frac{35}{60} = .58$$

The service pattern follows an exponential distribution with the parameter

$$\mu = \text{mean service rate} = .21$$

The simulation model starts with the simulated clock time initialized to zero. The arrival time of the next customer is determined from the Poisson distribution, and the simulated clock is updated when the next customer arrives. Similarly, the service time is determined by using the exponential distribution. By combining the arrival time, the waiting time in queue (if any), and the service time of a customer, the model calculates his/her departure time. This process is repeated for a prespecified period of time, say one workday of 6 hours, or for a prespecified number of customers. At the end the model stops running.

A part of the simulation program is devoted to the report-generation function. Thereby the model reports values of such statistics as

Average utilization rate of each server.
Total number of customers during simulation.
Maximum number of customers standing in queue at a given instant.
Average length of queue during simulation.
Total number of customers who did not have to wait in queue.
Average waiting time in queue.

The simulation model can be run as often as one likes by varying the number of servers and observing its impact on the average service time per customer, average waiting time in queue, and so on. When the bank management is satisfied with the average server utilization rate (which is desired to be high) and the average waiting time in queue (which should be low), the model can be stopped and the findings can be implemented in the actual daily business.

The process of discrete system simulation will be explained in much more detail in the next chapter. The foregoing example merely illustrates the relation between queueing theory and discrete system simulation.

7.10 APPLICATIONS OF QUEUEING MODEL IN COMPUTER SYSTEMS

The rest of this chapter explores two specific computer applications of queueing models. The treatment assumes a higher level of mathematical maturity on the part of the reader.

The concepts of queueing theory have direct applications in two computer-related areas: (1) computer performance evaluation and (2) timesharing systems. Let us discuss each one separately.

7.11 COMPUTER PERFORMANCE EVALUATION

Every performance study first requires a way to describe the workload and then shows the method of handling the data. The description of the workload involves a sampling of actual jobs that are run. Such a sample is called a *benchmark*. A benchmark should include:

☐ Jobs that are run most frequently.
☐ Jobs that account for most of the system's time and resource use.
☐ Jobs whose completion time requirements are most critical to the system's mission.

The use of a real benchmark job stream is appropriate for a system that already exists.

7.11.1 Type I and Type II Workload Models

Hellerman and Conroy ([2], Chapter 4) have developed two workload models, called type I and type II, to describe the queueing characteristics of a job stream scheduled for execution on a computer system. Any job belonging to the benchmark is characterized by three parameters: A_i, the arrival time of job i for execution; X_i, the execution time for job i, and a scheduling algorithm, such as FIFO or random.

Each job's performance can be analyzed by using queueing theory, where the execution time of each job is interpreted as the "service time."

A *type I workload model* characterizes each job i by an ordered pair of numbers (A_i, X_i), $i = 1,. . ., n$ (assuming n jobs in the benchmark). A *type II workload model* is characterized by an ordered triplet of numbers (A_i, X_i, S_i), where S_i is the setup time for job i, where $i, = 1,. . ., n$. Thus, the only difference between type I and type II models is that the latter includes a setup time for each job and also assumes a setdown time equal to the setup time.

The arrival times A_i and the execution times X_i can be deterministic or probabilistic. In the deterministic case, these times are explicitly specified, whereas in the probabilistic case they are generated from corresponding frequency distributions constructed from historical data gathered from the system or from another similar system.

Both types are concerned *only* with the *time characteristics* of the jobs. In a computer system, every job also requires *space* (storage)—both main storage and auxiliary storage. However, space scheduling is not considered here. Space scheduling is called for mostly in a multiprogramming environment.

Consider a single-server type I model where job requests characterized by a pair (A_i, X_i) flow into a queueing area holding up to q jobs. Assume q to be large enough to hold whatever queue builds up. Following the FIFO algorithm, the jobs are processed and finished. Figure 7-1 illustrates this situation.

A type I job with parameters (A_i, X_i) arrives for processing. Since the model is single-server the job has to wait in a queue if the CPU (central processing unit) is busy. When the CPU becomes free, job (A_i, X_i) leaves the queue and gets processed. It leaves the system when the processing is complete.

7.11.2 Stretch Factor for Job

Let us assume that the job stream consists of n jobs. For a given job i characterized by the parameters A_i, X_i, let us introduce a new variable

$$Q_i = \text{job completion time}, \quad i = 1,2, . . ., n$$

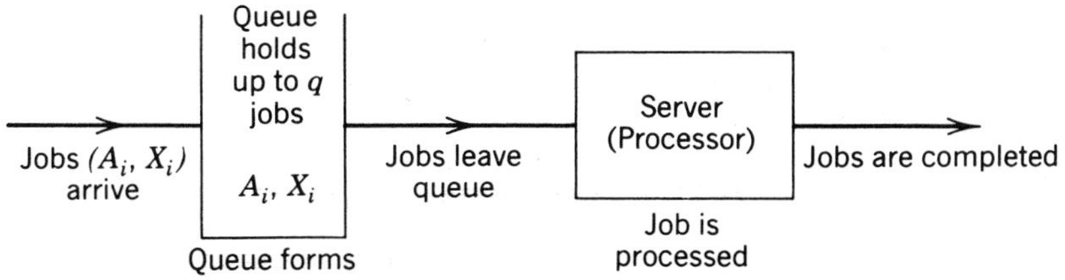

FIGURE 7-1 Single-server model.

Since A_i is the arrival time for job i, it follows that

$$Q_i - A_i = \text{response time or job elapsed time.}$$

Further, since X_i is the job execution time, we get

$$Q_i - A_i - X_i = \text{job waiting time.}$$

The objective is to minimize this job waiting time, the ideal situation being

$$Q_i - A_i - X_i = 0, \quad \text{or} \quad Q_i - A_i = X_i$$

We now define the *stretch factor* for job i to be the ratio

$$\frac{Q_i - A_i}{X_i}, \quad i = 1,2 \ldots , n$$

If the stretch factor equals 1, then there is no waiting for job i. As the stretch factor increases, the job performance relative to time gets poorer.

Note that the stretch factor is the factor by which the minimum possible elapsed time X_i for job i is "stretched" into the actual elapsed time $Q_i - A_i$.

7.11.3 Performance Parameters for Jobs

We now introduce three parameters to measure the performance of a job stream consisting of n jobs $1,2,\ldots, n$.

(a) Mean Response Time. This is defined as the average of all the response times $Q_i - A_i$ for all the jobs i. It is denoted by $\overline{T}$ and is given by the formula

$$\overline{T} = \frac{1}{n}\sum_{i=1}^{n}(Q_i - A_i)$$

$\overline{T}$ is also called the *mean elapsed time* or the *mean wait time*.

(b) Throughput. The *throughput* of a job stream is defined as the number of jobs in the stream divided by the total execution time for all the jobs. It is denoted by P and is given by the formula

$$P = \frac{n}{\sum_{i=1}^{n} X_i}$$

(c) Short Job Figure of Merit. This parameter is denoted by M and is defined by the formula

$$M = \frac{n}{\Sigma_{i=1}^{n} (Q_i - A_i)/X_i}$$

Since the formula for P is independent of A_i, the arrival time of job i, the throughput is independent of the scheduling algorithm. But T is highly sensitive to scheduling, especially for jobs with unequal execution time. M is a sensitive measure of the system's ability to give good service to short-run jobs.

Owing to the high cost of CPU time it is desirable to have no idle time for the server. A criterion for no idle time over an n-job stream is given by

$$A_i \leq A_1 + \sum_{j=1}^{i-1} X_j, \quad i = 2, 3, \ldots, n$$

that is,

$$A_2 \leq A_1 + X_1$$
$$A_3 \leq A_1 + X_1 + X_2$$
$$A_4 \leq A_1 + X_1 + X_2 + X_3$$
$$\vdots$$
$$A_n \leq A_1 + X_1 + X_2 + \cdots + X_{n-1}$$

Let us examine the first inequality,

$$A_2 \leq A_1 + X_1$$

The job completion time for job 1 is $A_1 + X_1$. Hence if job 2 arrives before or exactly when job 1 is completed, then the CPU does not remain idle, although job 2 may have to wait in queue if it arrives before job 1 is finished. Such a situation requires that the arrival time for job 2 must not exceed the completion time of job 1, or

$$A_2 \leq A_1 + X_1$$

The inequalities for $A_3, A_4, \ldots, A_n$ are similarly explained by noting that at each stage we need to add the execution times of *all* the preceding jobs.

7.11.4 Concluding Remarks

Once the benchmark is designed with n jobs in the job stream, a simulation model can be built to run the jobs in the queue and calculate the job stream parameters $\overline{T}$, P, and M. Changing the scheduling algorithm from FIFO to another type (shortest job first, round robin, etc.), the corresponding performance parameters are computed, and the optimal time scheduling is determined.

Note that we have used only a type I workload model. Type II workload models are more complex, and the formula for P becomes more involved.

Through simulation the process can be repeated using different benchmarks as more representative samples of the actual job stream.

7.12 TIMESHARING SYSTEM

A *timeshared computer system* is a collection of resources and a population of customers who compete at various times for the use of these resources. This requires a typical queueing model, as diagramed in Figure 7-2.

The most familiar example of a timesharing system is that of students of a college or university accessing the main computer via their terminals. Each student logs in at his or her own terminal and interacts with the main computer by typing appropriate instructions and then hitting the Return key. In this way many users at many locations gain access to the computer simultaneously as each one goes through a cycle of thinking and typing instructions. The principle behind timesharing is that considerably more time is devoted by a typical user to the thinking phase than in the actual instruction-entering phase. Since the computer works much faster than an individual user, it can process a number of user requests while most of the users are still in their individual thinking phase. If properly handled, a timesharing system can provide excellent response time to many users while maintaining high utilization efficiency for the many resources of the computer facility through concurrent use of devices. Each user of a timesharing system feels that he/she is the only user and is getting the undivided attention of the computer, although in reality the computer is serving many users simultaneously. Timesharing systems were introduced in the early 1960s.

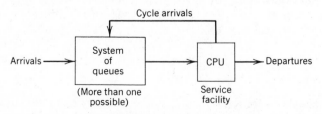

FIGURE 7-2 Timesharing System.

In conformity with the terminology of queueing models, let us call each job of a timesharing system user a *customer* and the CPU a *server*. The capacity of service is n, where n CPUs are available for use. The queueing discipline can be prioritized according to the type of service or be a round robin algorithm whereby each customer accesses the CPU for a small predetermined interval of time and is then transferred back to the queue.

The interval of time during which a customer is provided service is referred to as its *quantum*. The quantum size may vary, and it may or may not be sufficient to meet the customer's demand. If it is sufficient, the customer leaves the system; otherwise, it reenters the system of queues as a partially completed task and waits within that system until it is given a second quantum under the scheduling algorithm, and so on. Eventually, after a sufficient number of visits to the service facility, the customer will have gained enough service and will leave. This is a highly preemptive reentrant queueing rule and is called a *feedback queueing system* by Kleinrock ([3], Chapter 4).

The rest of the discussion in this chapter is adapted from Kleinrock ([3], Chapter 4).

Initially we do not know how large a demand each arriving customer places on the CPU. By continually testing the collection of jobs demanding service, we eventually discover the short-run jobs. By varying the scheduling algorithm it is possible to effect various degrees of preferential treatment for the short jobs.

7.12.1 Parameters of Timesharing Systems

Using Kleinrock's notations, let us assume

t is a time variable representing arrival time of a customer.

x is a time variable representing the service time required by a customer.

$A(t)$ is the interarrival time distribution.

$B(x)$ is the service time distribution.

q_{pn} is the quantum assigned to a customer from priority class p upon its nth entry into service.

$T(x)$ is the response time for a customer requiring x seconds of service.

$W(x)$ is $T(x) - x$ is the waiting time.

$T(x)$ is the single most important performance measure for timesharing systems. $W(x)$ is normally called the *wasted time*. The overhead in time required to remove a customer from the queue when its quantum expires is called the *swap time*.

It may be noted here that most of the above notations have their counterparts in Sections 7.11.1 and 7.11.2. Thus, t, x, $T(x)$, and $W(x)$ correspond to the variables A_i, X_i, $Q_i - A_i$, and $Q_i - A_i - X_i$, respectively, of Sections 7.11.1 and 7.11.2. This correspondence merely stresses the fact that both

computer performance evaluation and timesharing systems are special applications of queueing models.

7.12.2 Analytical Models for Timesharing Systems

Various analytical models are available for timeshared computer systems. Kleinrock has discussed the following algorithms:

- ☐ Batch processing
- ☐ Round robin
- ☐ Last come, first served
- ☐ Foreground-background
- ☐ Multilevel processor sharing
- ☐ Selfish scheduling

All these models make two basic assumptions:

1. A job's exact service time is not known; only the distribution of service time is known.

2. Swap time is a fixed percentage of the customer's quantum.

The *round robin (RR) scheduling algorithm* is probably the most well-known and widely used model. Accordingly the rest of this section is devoted to a brief discussion of this algorithm.

We assume that $q_{pn} = q \rightarrow 0$, that is, all quanta are of the same size and shrink to zero. A new customer (i.e., a job) arrives and joins the queue, works its way up to the head of the queue on a FIFO basis, and gets a quantum of service time. When the quantum expires but the job needs more service, it goes to the tail of the queue and repeats the cycle. Thus, a customer makes repeated cycles each extremely quickly, each time receiving infinitesimal service, until finally its attained service equals its required service and the job departs. In general, when there are k customers in the system, each is receiving service at the rate of $1/k$ second per second. Such a system is called *processor-sharing* because all the customers are sharing the same CPU on an equally proportionate basis.

Kleinrock and others investigated the round robin algorithm extensively and came up with the following properties:

1. Discrimination is *linear*: that is, response time depends on the service time in a strictly linear fashion. A job twice as long will stay on the system twice the time.

2. Mean response time is *independent* of the service time distribution $B(x)$ and depends only on the mean value of the service time. Thus, the round robin algorithm eliminates any dependence of the average response time on the variance of the service time.

3. If we form the ratio of wasted time to service time, we obtain

$$\frac{W(x)}{x} = \frac{\rho}{1 - \rho}$$

where ρ is the utilization factor λ/μ (see Section 7.6). This ratio is independent of the service time x. Normally, we define this ratio as a *penalty function* imposed upon a customer for receiving x seconds of service, because the ratio measures how much time must be sacrificed in waiting for each unit of service time received. Since under the round robin algorithm the penalty function is independent of x, all customers are treated equally irrespective of their service time demands. Under FIFO, the penalty function decreases as x increases. Hence customers often pool many jobs together to form one enormously long job and thereby enjoy preferred treatment. Similarly, if the penalty function increases as x increases, the tendency would be to split a single job into several smaller jobs and thereby enjoy preferential treatment. Short jobs first is an example of this algorithm. Such customer tactics typically tend to increase the overhead on the system and so are undesirable.

4. If the service time has an exponential distribution with mean λ, say, then a customer requiring λ seconds of service time will spend as much time on the system as under the FIFO algorithm. Hence jobs requiring less than λ seconds of service time will be completed more quickly under the round robin system than under the FIFO system.

7.13 SUMMARY

This chapter discusses the basics of queueing theory and its impact on discrete system simulation. A *queue* is charcterized by four parameters: the arrival times of customers, the service times of customers, the number of available servers, and the rule by which a customer is served after arrival. If the interarrival time, that is, the time elapsed between two consecutive arrivals, is a constant, then the arrival pattern is deterministic. If it follows a given frequency distribution, then the arrival pattern is probabilistic or stochastic. The same classification applies to the service pattern. For probabilistic models it is customary to assume that the random arrival pattern follows a Poisson distribution and the associated service pattern is given by an exponential distribution.

Several examples have been provided to show how queueing models appear in everyday life. Customers coming to a bank to be served by the tellers, people standing at a checkout counter in a supermarket, machines sent to a shop for repair, patients coming to the emergency room of a hospital for treatment are all examples of queueing models. Each of these examples exhibits the feature that a certain number of "customers" (e.g., hospital patients, machines in a repair shop) arrive at a service facility and then are

served immediately if a server is available; otherwise they join a queue and wait until a server is available.

Since no customer likes to wait in a queue for service, a waiting cost is associated whenever a queue is formed. In order to minimize this cost, more serves may be employed, but that leads to an increased service cost. Accordingly, the queueing model tries to minimize the total cost, which is the sum of the waiting cost and the service cost. This objective can be achieved analytically by solving explicitly the mathematical model representing the queueing process. If an explicit solution is infeasible, then the process of discrete system simulation is followed. Under this process, several possible values of such variables as the number of servers, the average rate of utilization of the servers, the average waiting time for the customers in queue, and average service time for the customers are input into the simulation model and the resulting output is examined until a satisfactory solution is achieved.

The chapter closes with two computer applications of the queueing model: computer performance evaluation and timesharing systems. The treatment of these two topics is heavily mathematical and may be omitted at the first reading.

KEY WORDS

The following key words are used in this chapter:

arrival pattern

balking

capacity of service

deterministic model

feedback queueing system

grade of service

mean service rate

multiple-server model

polling

probabilistic model

quantum

queue

queueing discipline

reneging

round-robin algorithm

service cost

service pattern

single-server model

stochastic model

utilization ratio

waiting cost

workload models: type I, type II

REFERENCES

1. G. Gordon, *System Simulation*, Prentice-Hall, Englewood Cliffs, NJ, 1978

2. H. Hellerman, and T. F. Conroy, *Computer System Performance*, McGraw-Hill, New York, 1975.

3. L. Kleinrock, *Queueing Systems*, vol. 2, Wiley-Interscience, New York, 1976.

REVIEW QUESTIONS

1. Define a queue and identify its four characteristics.
2. Define a deterministic queueing model and a probabilistic queueing model. Explain their differences.
3. In a probabilistic model, why is it customary to represent the arrival pattern by a discrete distribution and the service pattern by a continuous distribution? How can you represent the service pattern by a discrete distribution?
4. Explain clearly the objectives of a queueing model. What trade-off issues are involved here?
5. Define the terms reneging, balking, and polling.
6. What is the utilization ratio of a queue? How does it determine whether a queue is stable or unstable?
7. Define grade of service. How is it related to the objective function of a queueing model?

FORMULATIONAL PROBLEM

Rig Me Insurance Incorporated (RMII) started 30 years ago as a small Boston-based insurance company providing health and life insurance coverages. Recently it acquired another similar insurance company. As a result of this expansion of business, RMII feels that it has to increase the number of its claim processors. Too few claim processors result in delayed claim processing leading to dissatisfied policyholders, while too many claim processors cost extra money for RMII. The president of RMII wants to study this situation with the help of an analytical model to determine the optimal number of claim processors for handling the claims. Address the problem by performing the following tasks:

(a) Formulate a queueing model describing the above situation. Identify the customers and the servers in the model.
(b) Describe the objective function of the model.
(c) Outline a method to determine the arrival pattern and the service pattern, both assumed to be probabilistic in nature.
(d) What kind of queueing discipline do you recommend and why?

COMPUTATIONAL PROBLEMS

1. A job stream consists of six jobs with the following arrival and execution times, A_i and X_i,

i	A	X
1	0	10
2	4	1
3	15	4
4	17	7
5	22	9
6	32	2

(a) Compute the stretch factor for each job.

(b) Compute the mean response time, the throughput, and the short-job figure of merit.

(c) Determine what jobs have to wait for service, and calculate the corresponding waiting times.

(d) Change the ordering of the given X values so that they are in ascending order. Now repeat steps (a) through (c).

(e) Change the X values to descending order of magnitude. Now repeat steps (a) through (c).

2. A certain assembly process requires two separate assembly machines M and N. Each product is to be processed first by M and then by N. A queue develops at N if a product already processed by M finds N busy. The output of items from M is Poission with the rate of 10 per hour. N processes each item with an exponential service time at the rate of 12 per hour. Three items have arrived for processing at M at times 1, 5, and 8 minutes, respectively. Calculate the length of time that each item has to wait at N.

8

Discrete System Simulation

8.1 TYPES OF DISCRETE SYSTEM SIMULATION

In Section 6.6 we briefly introduced the two main types of simulation models: discrete and continuous. In a discrete system simulation model the simulated time changes in a stepwise discrete fashion. If the clock representing the simulated time is updated at regular time intervals, then the discrete simulation is said to be *time-oriented*. If, on the other hand, the clock is updated whenever the next event occurs, then the discrete simulation is said to be *event-oriented*.

In a time-oriented simulation, the simulated time is incremented by a fixed amount for each transaction; for example,

$$t = t + L$$

where t represents the current simulated time and L is fixed for each transaction. In an event-oriented simulation, the simulated time is updated according to the distribution of the transactions.

Accordingly, a time-oriented simulation is *deterministic* (e.g., stock market simulation on a daily basis, prescheduled inventory reorder process), whereas an event-oriented simulation is *probabilistic*. The probability distribution of the events can be *uniform* or *nonuniform*.

The main emphasis in discrete system simulation is placed on event-oriented simulations. That topic will occupy a major portion of this chapter. However, we shall discuss examples of time-oriented simulation as well. Finally, we shall address the issue of validation of a simulation model. Since simulation is essentially a trial-and-error process, the validation of a simulation model is necessary in order to provide accurate results.

8.2 EVENT-ORIENTED DISCRETE SYSTEM SIMULATION

The model used in a discrete system simulation uses a set of variables to represent the state of the system at any given time. These variables are called *state descriptors*. Some state descriptors range over values such as the number of customers waiting in line for service at a ticket counter. Others represent a flag, such as an indicator that the queue length has reached a limit and hence an additional ticket counter should be opened.

A *discrete event* is defined as a set of circumstances causing an instantaneous change in one or more system state descriptors. For example, the arrival of a customer to join the queue increases the length of the queue by 1, and scheduling the service time of the next event changes the time status of the clock.

The passage of time is recorded by a number referred to as *clock time*. Initially clock time is set to zero, and its subsequent updates indicate how many units of the simulated time have passed since the beginning of the simulation. There is no direct connection between the unit of simulated time and the unit of real time. For example, if the simulation represents job processing by a CPU, then one unit of simulated time may be 100 or 1000 times longer than one unit of CPU processing time. On the other hand, if we are simulating the processing of customers at an airline reservations counter, then one unit of simulated time can be much smaller than one unit of real time, which is measured in minutes and hours, say. The transactions of one full day may be simulated by the model in a few minutes. In event-oriented discrete simulation, each time the next event is scheduled to occur, the simulated clock time is advanced to that instant.

Queueing theory (see Chapter 7) provides the mathematical foundation for discrete system simulation. The arrival pattern, the service pattern, the capacity of the service, and the queueing discipline all enter into the discrete simulation model. Depending on the nature of the arrival and service patterns, we can have a deterministic or time-oriented simulation, or a probabilistic or event-oriented simulation. As noted in Section 7.9, a discrete system simulation is time-oriented or event-oriented according as the interarrival time of "customers" to the model is constant or variable.

We suggest that the reader review, Chapter 7 (especially Section 7.9) before proceeding further in this chapter.

8.2.1 Components of a Discrete Simulation Model

In Section 7.7 we have seen examples of event-oriented discrete simulation models. If we analyze them, we find the following major activities in such models:

1. The model is set up.
2. An event arrives and either joins a queue for waiting or receives service right away.

3. The service period ends for the event.

4. The event either reenters the waiting line (if the service is not yet finished) or leaves the system (if the service is finished).

5. The model is terminated if the desired simulation is over; otherwise, steps 2 through 4 are repeated for the next event.

6. Necessary statistics are gathered at each of the steps 1 through 5 in order to analyze the results of the simulation.

In order to automate a simulation model an appropriate program has to be written to implement steps 1 through 6. Each step can be written as a separate module with steps 1 and 5 together functioning as the control module for the simulation program. The five modules are now presented conceptually, with program flowcharts given in Figures 8-1 through 8-5.

1. *Initialization and Termination. (Fig. 8-1.)*
Set up the model.
Declare the simulation parameters.
Initialize these parameters.
Allocate storage accordingly.
Schedule the arrival of the first event.
Update the simulated clock to the time of arrival of the first event.
Test if the simulation is complete, and if so terminate the model.

2. *Event Arrival. (Fig. 8-2).*
Record the arrival of the first event.
Check status of the server.
If server is busy, then send event to waiting queue.
If server is not busy, then send event to server.
Schedule arrival of next event.

3. *Event Servicing. (Fig. 8-3.)*
Record beginning of service for an event.
Record end of service for the event.
Check the service status, that is, complete or incomplete, for the event.
Record the status of server as free.

4. *Event Departure. (Fig. 8-4.)*
Schedule the departure of the event from server.
If the service status was determined to be complete, then remove the event from the model.
If the service status was determined to be incomplete, then reenter the event into the waiting line for next scheduled service.

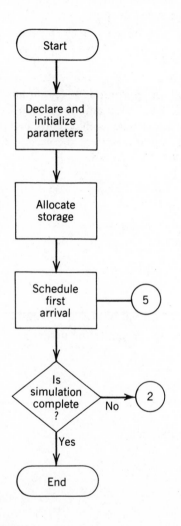

FIGURE 8-1 Initialization and termination.

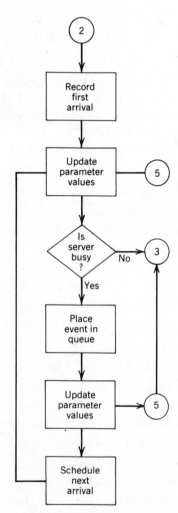

FIGURE 8-2 Event arrival.

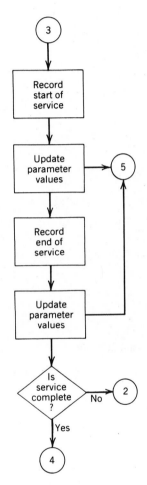

FIGURE 8-3 Event servicing.

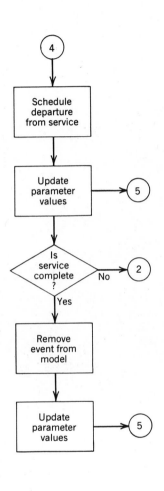

FIGURE 8-4 Event departure.

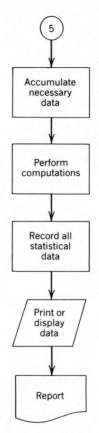

FIGURE 8-5   Statistics collection and report generation.

5. *Statistics Collection and Report Generation. (Fig. 8-5.)*

Interface with each of the other four modules.

Accumulate necessary statistics such as arrival and departure of an event, waiting time for an event, length of waiting queue at the arrival of an event and status of server.

Perform computations to determine such statistics as mean waiting time, mean service time, and frequency of the server being busy.

Record all statisitical data.

Print all data in the form of a nice, usable report.

8.2.2 Generation of Arrival Patterns

The operation of an event-oriented discrete system simulation model involves three major interactions with events processed by the model: arrival of an event, servicing an event, and departure of an event. The first phenomenon is truly exogenous in that the event enters the model from outside. Once it is within the model, the service and departure are controlled internally by the simulation process. Hence the crucial element in the model is the generation of exogenous arrivals. Since an event-oriented model is probabilistic (as opposed to deterministic), the interarrival times of events are given by a probability distribution, which may be uniform and nonuniform. The associated cumulative distribution function is then used to calculate the arrival time of each event.

The initialization and termination module (see Section 8.2.1) determines the arrival time of the first event. Then the interarrival time determined from the distribution is added to the first arrival time to yield the arrival time of the second event. This process is then repeated for each sucessive event. The simulation thus proceeds by creating new arrivals as needed. When the clock time reaches the next arrival time, the event of entering the entity into the system is executed, and the arrival time of the next event is calculated immediately from the interarrival time distribution. The term *bootstrapping* is often used to describe this process of making one entity create its successor.

Since events are assumed to occur randomly in the outside world, the table of random numbers is used to simulate the arrival of an event. The arrival time of the event is computed as follows, depending on whether the interarrival time is distributed uniformly or nonuniformly.

Uniform Distribution. Let μ and σ be the mean and the standard deviation of the distribution, and let N be a random number selected from the table of random numbers. Then the arrival time is given by

$$\mu - \sigma + N(2\sigma + 1)$$

Nonuniform Distribution. Let $F(t)$ be the cumulative distribution function for the interarrival time, and let a table of random numbers X be given. We then form a new table of random numbers $F^{-1}(X)$. Note that X is a uniformly distributed random number while $F^{-1}(X)$ is a random number distributed acccording to the distribution of the interarrival times (see [3], Section 6-10). We use the random numbers $F^{-1}(X)$ to generate the arrival times of succeeding events.

Let us now illustrate this latter process with an example taken from Gordon ([3], Section 7-4). Assume that the interarrival times are exponentially distributed with mean λ. Then

$$F(t) = 1 - e^{-\lambda t}$$

so that

$$F^{-1}(X) = -\frac{1}{\lambda} \ln(1 - X)$$

We take a table of uniformly distributed random numbers X and compute $F^{-1}(X)$ with $\lambda = 1$. We then get a set of exponentially distributed random numbers with mean 1. Multiplying these numbers by λ we get the interarrival times with mean λ. Table 8-1 illustrates the situation for $\lambda = 12$.

In practice, the simulation is always done by computer programs. Simulation programming languages like GPSS automatically take care of determining successive arrival times so that the user need not worry about the detailed algorithm to compute the simulated arrival times. However, if a general programming language like FORTRAN or PASCAL is used, then the user must provide all the algorithms for computing the arrival times.

8.2.3 Generation of Service Patterns

If the service time is given as deterministic, then the next service time is directly computed. However, if the service time is given by a probability distribution, then the procedure of Section 8.2.2 can be used to determine the next event's service time. The appropriate tables of random numbers are used in this case. The service time must be added to the arrival time of an event to determine the completion time of that event. At this time the event either reenters the queue or leaves the model.

TABLE 8-1   Event Arrival Times

Uniformly Distributed Random Numbers (X)	Exponentially Distributed Random Numbers $[F^{-1}(X), \lambda = 1]$	Interarrival Times $(\lambda = 12)$	Simulated Arrival Times
0.100	0.104	1.25	1.25
0.375	0.470	5.64	6.89
0.084	0.087	1.04	7.93
0.990	4.600	55.20	63.13
0.128	0.137	1.64	64.77
0.660	1.086	13.03	77.80
0.310	0.370	4.44	82.24
0.852	1.963	23.56	105.80

The departure time of an event from the model is computed by the following formula:

Departure time from model = Arrival time into model + sum of all service times + sum of all waiting times, if applicable

8.2.4 Statistics Collection

As indicated in Section 8.2.1, a variety of statistics must be collected during a simulation run. Since the simulation is used to determine an optimal or near-optimal solution by systematic trial and error, these statistical data are used to arrive at the desired solution. Figures 8-1 through 8-4 show how all the necesssry statistical data are gathered during the simulation run. The connector symbol ⑤ in each figure provides the interface of each module to the final module, statistics collection, shown in Figure 8-5.

Most simulation programming systems include a report generator to print out statistics gathered during the run. Commonly needed statistics are:

Counts: Number of entities of a particular type, or number of times some event occurred.

Summary Measures: Extreme values, mean, standard deviation, etc.

Utilization: Fraction of time some entity is engaged.

Occupancy: Fraction of a group of entities in use on the average.

Distributions: For example, queue lengths or waiting times.

Transit Times: Time taken by an entity to move from one part of the system to some other part.

The formulas of counts and summary measures are fairly straightforward in that they are collected as values of appropriate counters or are given by the formulas of mean and standard deviation. The other four statistics are explained below.

Utiliztion is given by the formula

$$U = \frac{1}{T} \sum_{r=1}^{N} (t_f - t_b)_r$$

where T is the total simulation time, N is the total number of times the entity has been used, t_f is the time when the entity becomes free, and t_b is the time when the entity was last busy.

If there is an upper limit on the number of entities, then *occupancy* is given by the average number in use as a ratio to the maximum. The formula is

$$B = \frac{1}{NM} \sum_{r=1}^{N} D_r(t_{r+1} - t_r)$$

where N is the number of times the entity has been used, M is the upper limit on the number of entities, n_r is the value of the entity at time t_r, and t_r, t_{r+1} are two consecutive times when the entity changes its value.

The *distribution* is given by a table whose elements are collected during the simulation run and will depend on three items: the lower limit of the table, the size of the intervals used in the table, and the number of intervals in the table.

The *transit time* is measured by means of the time elapsed on the clock during the interval when the entity moves from one part of the system to another.

8.2.5 Simulation of a Telephone System

Gordon ([3], Chapter 8) has discussed in detail the simulation of a telephone system as an example of a discrete event-oriented simulation process. The system has a number of telephones connected to a switchboard by lines. The switchboard has a number of links that can connect any two lines. However, only one connection can be made at a time. If a call cannot be connected, then it is abandoned. When a call is abandoned because the called party is engaged, the call is said to by *busy;* if, on the other hand, the call is abandoned because no link is available, then it is said to be a *blocked* call. The objective of the simulation can then be described as follows: Process a given number of calls, and determine how many of them are completed, or found busy, or blocked.

The simulation model uses the following entities with their associated attributes:

Link. Availability (0 = free, 1 = busy), maximum number (e.g., 3), number in use (e.g., 2)

Clock. Simulated time, which is updated when an event occurs (e.g., call is finished, next call arrives).

Next Call. Origin, destination, length.

Calls in Progress. Origin, destination, completion time.

Call Counters. Number of calls processed, completed, blocked, busy (used to generate summary satistics).

The simulation proceeds by performing five steps:

1. Scan the events to determine the next event.
2. Select the activity that will cause the event.
3. Test whether the event can be executed.
4. Change the records to reflect the effects of the event.
5. Collect necessary statistics for the simulation run.

To illustrate the telephone simulation process, Gordon ([3], Chapter 8)

has shown three snapshots of the system at three distinct simulated clock times. At the end of the simulation run the system prints several statistical data, such as the total number of calls received, found busy, or processed.

8.2.6 Simulation of Toll Booth Operation

We now describe another example of an event-oriented discrete simulation model. The statement of the problem is taken from Gordon ([3], p. 195).

Cars arrive randomly at a toll booth and pay the toll. If necessary, they wait in queue to be served in order of arrival. The interarrival time, measured to the nearest second, is assumed to be uniformly distributed between 0 and 9, inclusive. The time taken to pay is also random and between 0 and 9 seconds, but with the following distribution:

$$f(t) = \begin{cases} \frac{1}{6}t^{-1/2}, & 0 < t < 9 \\ 0, & \text{elsewhere} \end{cases}$$

In this model each car is an event, and the service process consists of the payment of toll to the server at the booth. The complete processing of an event consists of four steps:

1. Car arrives at the toll booth.
2. Car waits in queue if the booth is not free.
3. Car pays the toll whenever the booth is free.
4. Car leaves the booth.

Note that step 2 is omitted if the booth is free.

In order to run this simulation model, we must record the time for each of the following six activities:

1. Car arrives at booth.
2. Waiting in queue starts.
3. Waiting in queue ends.
4. Service starts.
5. Service ends.
6. Car leaves booth.

If the server at the booth is free, then activities 2 and 3 do not occur and time for 1 equals the time for 4. Also, we have the following equalities

$$\text{time for step } 3 = \text{time for step } 4$$
$$\text{time for step } 5 = \text{time for step } 6$$

To run the model we need to generate the arrival times, whose distributions are given by a table of uniformly distributed random numbers, and the service times, whose distributions are given by the function $f(t)$. As noted in Section 8.2.2 in order to produce random numbers with a given distribution $f(t)$ it is necessary to evaluate the inverse of its cumulative distribution function at a sequence of uniformly distributed numbers between 0 and 1. Hence we first compute the cumulative distribution function $F(x)$ of $f(t)$. By definition,

$$F(x) = \int_0^x f(t) \, dt = \int_0^x \frac{1}{6} t^{-1/2} \, dt = \frac{1}{3} \sqrt{x} = y, \text{ say}$$

Then,

$$x = 9y^2$$

and thus,

$$F^{-1}(y) = 9y^2$$

where F^{-1} is the inverse of the cumulative distribution function of $f(t)$.

Let us simulate the model for the first six cars. Using a table of uniformly distributed random numbers, we generate the interarrival times t and the corresponding service times of these cars. The latter uses the function $F^{-1}(y)$, where y is a uniformly distributed random number. Table 8-2 shows all these numbers.

Let us now simulate the model by recording the clock times for the six activities listed at the beginning of this section. The simulated clock time is initialized at $t=0$. Table 8-3 shows the result of running the model, each row of the table representing the processing of a car.

We can run the model for more cars and gather the necessary statistics mentioned in Section 8.2.4. If we write the simulation program in a simulation

TABLE 8-2 Arrival and Service Times for Cars

Interarrival Time t	Cumulative Interarrival Time	Uniformly Distributed Random Number y	Service Time $F^{-1}(y)$
3	3	.876	7
9	12	.560	3
2	14	.653	4
3	17	.614	3
5	22	.818	6
3	25	.548	3

TABLE 8-3 Simulation Run for Six Cars

Car No.	Car Arrives	Wait Starts	Wait Ends	Service Starts	Service Ends	Car Leaves
1	3	—	—	3	10	10
2	12	—	—	12	15	15
3	14	14	15	15	19	19
4	17	17	19	19	22	22
5	22	—	—	22	28	28
6	25	25	28	28	31	31

language such as GPSS (see Chapter 10), then most of these statistics are automatically gathered during the run of the model and are printed at the end of the simulation run. These numbers can then be analyzed to improve the efficiency of the toll booth operation. For example, if we find that the average waiting time for a car is too great, say 50 seconds, then we can recommend that additional booths be opened. We shall pursue these issues in more detail in Chapter 10, when we discuss the GPSS language to write programs for running event-oriented discrete system simulations.

8.3 TIME-ORIENTED DISCRETE SIMULATION

We now discuss the other type of discrete simulation model, namely, time-oriented simulations. As noted earlier in Section 6.5, in a time-oriented discrete simulation the simulated time changes in fixed increments, usually one at a time. Hence the model is deterministic. If the simulated clock currently records a time t, then at the end of one iteration of the simulation process the clock records $t + 1$. This operation continues until the entire simulation is complete. The critical factor here is the updated time, as opposed to the next event in an event-oriented simulation. The arrival time of an event is inconsequential, because two consecutive events are assumed to arrive always at one time unit apart. The concepts of event servicing and event departure are likewise of no real significance since they do not occur conspicuously. Instead, certain prescheduled decisions are made or algorithms are computed at every time value $t, t + 1, t + 2, \ldots$. The model starts at the initialized time $t = 0$.

Wagner ([4], Section 21.3 and 21.5) has discussed two examples of time-oriented discrete simulation: a stock market simulation and an inventory model. Both examples utilize the basic features of a time-oriented simulation:

1. Initialize simulation parameters.
2. Establish decision criteria, if any.
3. Formulate algorithms to be computed at each distinct simulated time unit.

4. Test the decision criteria, if applicable, at time t.
5. Perform algorithms, as needed, at time t.
6. Increment the simulated time by 1; that is, change t to $t+1$.
7. Repeat 4 through 6 until t reaches the preestablished limit of the total simulation time.

Figure 8-6 shows the flowchart for a time-oriented simulation.

In the next two sections we shall discuss two examples of time-oriented simulations.

8.3.1 Simulation of the Stock Market

This example is adapted from Wagner ([4], Chapter 21). An investor wants to test the following strategy for buying and selling common stocks:

If you own the stock, then sell it whenever the price falls two days in a row.

If you do not own the stock, then buy it whenever the price rises two days in a row.

Here we take the simulated time unit to represent one day. Thus, at the beginning of each day the time variable t changes to $t+1$. We start the simulation at $t=0$ and record the daily operation of the model until $t=20$; that is, the model simulates the stock market behavior for 20 days. At the beginning the investor has 100 shares of the stock with a value of $10 per share. Hence the initial amount held by the investor is $1000. The decision criteria are given above. The fluctuation of the stock prices follows the probabilities given in Table 8-4. These values have been derived after analyzing the past historical data.

The investor utilizes the price movements in Table 8-4 as follows: If the price on Monday and Tuesday are both $10, then he believes that the price on Wednesday will be $11 with probability ¼, $10 with probability ½, and $9 with probability ¼, as can be seen in the second row of Table 8-4. If, instead, Tuesday's price is $9, then he believes that the share price on Wednesday will be $10 with probability ¼, $9 with probability ¼, and $8 with probability ½, as can be seen in the third row of Table 8-4. Notice that as the stock price increases, the investor thinks there is probability ½ that it will increase again, and analogous statements hold if the price share remains the same or decreases.

In order to run the simulation we first generate a specific history of stock-price movements according to the probabilities of Table 8-4. Using a table of uniformly distributed random numbers we get the simulated price movements of Table 8-5. Now we apply the decision criteria to the prices in the

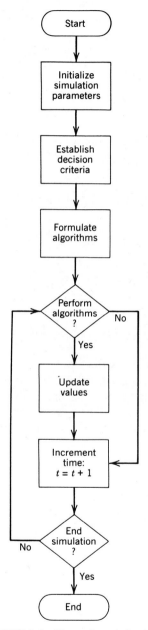

FIGURE 8-6 Time-oriented simulation.

TABLE 8-4   Stock Price Movement Probabilities[a]

Yesterday's Stock Price	Today's Stock Price		
	Increases	Stays the same	Decreases
Increased	½	¼	¼
Stayed the same	¼	½	¼
Decreased	¼	¼	½

[a]Harvey M. Wagner, *Principles of Operations Research,* 2nd Ed. © 1975, p. 911. Reprinted by permission of Prentice-Hall, Englewood Cliffs, NJ.

second and fourth columns of Table 8-5. We observe the following facts:

Days	Price Movements
5, 6	Rises
9, 10	Rises
11, 12	Falls
14, 15, 16	Rises
17, 18, 19	Falls

Accordingly, the investor owns the stocks up to day 12, sells them on day 13, buys them on day 16, and again sells them on day 19. As a result, on day 20 he does not own any stock and has cash of $815.50.

To arrive at this final cash balance, we assume that the investor pays a 2% commission whenever he buys or sells and that he makes at most one transaction per day. Table 8-6 summarizes in tabular form the complete simulation run.

Looking at Table 8-6 we find that the investor sells the 100 shares at $11 per share on day 13. This yields a sell price of

$$\$11 \times 100 = \$1100$$

He pays a commission of 2% on $1100, which amounts to $22. Hence he holds cash of

$$\$1100 - \$22 = \$1078$$

Similarly, when he buys on day 16 he gets 75 shares at $14 per share. The total purchase price is

$$\$14 \times 75 = \$1050$$

TABLE 8-5   Simulated Price Movements

Day	Stock Price	Day	Stock Price
0	10	11	12
1	10	12	11
2	9	13	11
3	10	14	12
4	10	15	13
5	11	16	14
6	12	17	13
7	12	18	12
8	11	19	11
9	12	20	11
10	13		

and a 2% commission on $1050 amounts to

$$\$1050 \times 2\% = \$21$$

Thus, he pays $1050 + $21 = 1071 to buy the stock and is left with a cash balance

$$\$1078 - \$1071 = \$7$$

A similar computation shows that on day 19 he is left with a cash balance of $808.50 after selling the 75 shares at $11 each and the paying a 2% commission on that. Adding to this sum his previous cash balance of $7.00, we find that his final cash balance is $815.50.

8.3.2   Simulation of an Econometric Market Model

This example is adapted from Gordon ([3], Chapter 8). It illustrates the interaction between supply and demand for a commodity in the market and examines the impact of this interaction on the price of that commodity.

In marketing a commodity there is a balance between the supply and demand for the commodity. Both factors depend upon price. A simple market model simulated over a given time period can show the price level at which the balance occurs. Demand for the commodity will be low when the price is high, and it will increase as the price drops. The relation between demand D and price P can be linear or nonlinear depending upon the commodity involved. For the sake of simplicity we assume that D and P are linearly related. On the other hand, the supply can be expected to increase when the price rises, because the suppliers see an opportunity for more revenue. We assume that supply S and price P are also linearly related. Finally, at the end of each simulation period, the market should be cleared completely or

partially. We can therefore formulate the market model mathematically as follows:

$$D = a - bP \qquad (8.1)$$
$$S = c + dP_{-1} \qquad (8.2)$$
$$D = (N\%) \times S \qquad (8.3)$$

The coefficients a, b, c, and d are constants and N is a uniformly distributed random number between 80 and 99 inclusive. By properly defining the values of a, b, c, d, we can make the market model stable or unstable. In a stable market, the price P eventually settles to a fixed value. In an unstable market, P fluctuates with increasing amplitude. Also, Eq. (8.2) shows that supply S depends upon the price P_{-1} from the previous marketing period. This assumption is obviously more realistic. Equation (8.3) shows that at the end of each marketing period only $N\%$ of the market is cleared, where $80 < N < 99$ and N is random.

This simple econometric model can be run as a time-oriented discrete simulation system. We assume that a, b, c, and d are given by

$$a = 12.4, \qquad b = 1.2, \qquad c = 1.0, \qquad d = 0.9 \qquad (8.4)$$

TABLE 8-6 Stock Price Simulation Results

Day	Stock Price	Decision	Shares Held	Stock Value	Cash Held
0	10		100	1000	
1	10		100	1000	
2	9		100	1000	
3	10		100	1000	
4	10		100	1000	
5	11		100	1000	
6	12		100	1000	
7	12		100	1000	
8	11		100	1000	
9	12		100	1000	
10	13		100	1000	
11	12		100	1000	
12	11	Own	100	1000	
13	11	Sell	0	0	1078.00
14	12	—	0	0	1078.00
15	13	—	0	0	1078.00
16	14	Buy	75	1050	7.00
17	13	Own	75	1050	7.00
18	12	Own	75	1050	7.00
19	11	Sell	0	0	815.50
20	11	—	0	0	815.00

so that the market will remain stable. We initialize P to the value P_0, where

$$P_0 = 1.0$$

The simulated time unit is selected as one marketing period. Thus the algorithms (8.1)–(8.3) are computed at the end of each time unit and the clock is incremented by 1. In addition, a table of uniformly distributed random numbers is used to determine the value of N. The model is then run for a predetermined time period and the final price P is computed.

Equations (8.1)–(8.3) combined with (8.4) now read as

$$D = 12.4 - 1.2P$$
$$S = 1.0 + 0.9P_{-1}$$
$$D = (N\%) \times S$$

To illustrate how the model is run, it is enough to examine the second row, since the remaining rows are computed similarly. Thus,

$$S = 1.0 + 0.9P_{-1} = 1.0 + 0.9(1.0) = 1.9$$
$$N = .97 \text{ (taken from a random numbers table)}$$
$$D = .97S = .97 (1.9) = 1.8$$

Therefore,

$$1.8 = D = 12.4 - 1.2P$$

or

$$P = \frac{12.4 - 1.8}{1.2} = 8.8$$

Looking at the last column in Table 8-7 we find that P alternately increases and decreases with slowly decreasing amplitude. It tends to settle at a value of 5.2 at the eighth iteration. Figure 8-7 shows graphically the relationship between time and price.

8.4 VALIDATION OF A SIMULATION MODEL

The validation of a simulation model is needed to increase the user's confidence in the results predicted by the model. A simulation model should have two characteristics:

1. It should provide a good representation of the real-world system being simulated.

TABLE 8-7   Simulation Results of Market Model

t	S	N	D	P
0	—	—	—	1.0
1	1.9	.97	1.8	8.8
2	8.9	.96	8.5	3.3
3	4.0	.85	3.4	7.5
4	7.8	.94	7.3	4.3
5	4.9	.81	4.0	7.0
6	7.3	.93	6.8	4.7
7	5.2	.99	5.1	6.1
8	6.5	.96	6.2	5.2
9	5.7	.81	4.6	6.5
10	6.9	.93	6.4	4.9

2. It should provide an acceptable level of detail.

The statistics collected from a simulation model are used to derive conclusions about the real-world system that has been simulated. Some statements must be made about the probability of the true value falling within a given confidence interval containing the estimated value determined from the simulation model. Without such a confidence interval the simulation results are of little value to the user. Accordingly, the statistical methodology should ensure that (1) statistical estimates are consistent so that as the sample size increases, the estimate tends to the true value; (2) bias is controlled in measuring the mean and the variance, since bias causes the distributions of estimates based on finite samples to differ significantly from the true population statistics, event though the estimates may be consistent; and (3) the simulation model is run sufficiently to obtain a given level of confidence in its results.

After the conceptual simulation model has been successfully implemented as a computer program, the validation process starts. Normally three techniques are used:

1. Testing the closeness of the programmed model to the theoretical model.
2. Replication of runs.
3. Batch means

Each of these three methods is highly mathematical.

8.4.1   Testing Closeness to a Theoretical Model

This applies to the case where an analytical solution can be computed under standardized ideal conditions. For example, Gordon ([3], Section 7-12) provides mathematical solutions for a single-server queue with Poisson arrivals

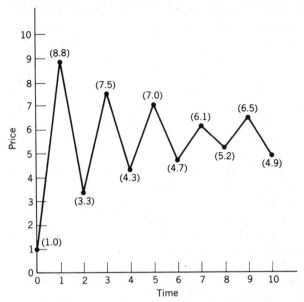

FIGURE 8-7 Price fluctuations in market model.

and with service time distributions being uniform, exponential, Erlang, or hyper-exponential. Hence if we simulate one such system with nonprioritized FIFO queueing discipline, then the results collected from the simulation run statistics can be compared with the analytical results to determine whether the simulated model indeed approximates the theoretical situation. The actual execution of this test is an involved process:

1. The system must be in a steady state, and so we must know when the initial transient phase is over.
2. The construction of confidence intervals assumes that the random variables (waiting time, queue length, etc.) are independently distributed. However, the simulation observations are usually autocorrelated.

The question arises: if an analytical solution already exists, then why is a simulation model needed? The answer is: to determine the various statistical parameters (average length of a queue, average utilization, average time per transaction, maximum number of elements in a queue during the simulation, etc.) that are output by a simulation program but are not normally available by running an analytical queueing model.

8.4.2 Removal of Initial Bias

At the beginning of the simulation experiment a number of model variables are assigned initial values. This procedure establishes a set of initial conditions and, because of the inherent dependence among events, the first observation

is a function of these initial conditions. The second observation is also a function of these values, but usually to a lesser exent than the first. Successive observations are usually less dependent on the initial conditions, so that eventually events in the simulation experiment are independent of them.

Because of their dependence on the initial conditions, observations near the beginning of the simulation experiment are not representative of the process of interest. Accordingly their inclusion in the computation of the sample mean $\bar{x}$ makes it a biased estimator of the true mean μ of the specific variable, such as the length of waiting time in queue, being estimated by the simulation. As the number of observations increases, the bias tends to diminish, since early observations become less influential on the average. However, the bias may be significant for a moderate number of observations. This necessitates the removal, or at least a reduction, of the initial bias.

Transient fluctuations in the system's behavior occur due to starting the system from an idle state. The period at the start of the simulation run, which is unacceptable due to the transient fluctuations, is called the *initial bias period* and is denoted by T_{bias}. We can remove T_{bias} from our consideration in two possible ways: by replication of runs and by batch means. We now discuss each method separately.

(a) Replication of Runs. T_{bias} is estimated by the replication-of-runs method as follows. Start the system from an idle state, and stop after a certain number of observations have occurred. The entities existing in the system at that time are left as they are. The run is then restarted with statistics being gathered from the point of restart. The program for simulation is so written that statistics are gathered from the beginning and then are wiped off for the initial bias period so that the remaining statistics are devoid of transient fluctuations.

Analytically we want to determine a time T_{bias} such that the long-run distributions adequately describe the system for any time $t > T_{bias}$. All results collected prior to time T_{bias} are disregarded. T_{bias} may be expressed in terms of time units or in terms of events, such as number of changes in queue size since the system started, number of completed services.

Consider a single-server queue with Poisson arrivals, exponential services, and FIFO discipline. Assume that there are n customers in each simulation run so that there are n observed values of the simulated events in each batch. Also, assume that there are p such batches. In other words, the n-customer simulation run is repeated p times. Each run is started with a different random number as the Seed of the pseudo-random number generator in order to generate the arrival time of the next event. Let us adopt the following notations:

x_{ij} = ith observation in jth run

$\bar{x}_j(n)$ = sample mean for jth run

$s_j^2(n)$ = sample variance for jth run

$\bar{x}(n)$ = mean for the total simulation consisting of np observations

$s^2(n)$ = variance for the total simulation consisting of np observations

Then we have the following results:

$$\bar{x}_j(n) = \sum_{i=1}^{n} x_{ij}/n$$

$$s_j^2(n) = \frac{1}{n-1} \sum_{i=1}^{n} [x_{ij} - \bar{x}_j(n)]^2, \qquad j = 1, 2, \ldots, p$$

$$\bar{x}(n) = \sum_{j=1}^{p} \bar{x}_j(n)/p$$

$$s^2(n = \frac{1}{p} \sum_{j=1}^{p} s_j^2(n)$$

The variance $s^2(n)$ can be used to establish a confidence interval for $\bar{x}(n)$. By increasing p (i.e., number of runs) we can reduce the size of the confidence interval, but thereby we increase the level of bias.

The time T_{bias} is estimated as that value of n for which $\bar{x}(n)$ demonstrates a definite stabilizing behavior. Gordon ([3], p. 306), for example, has discussed a graphical way to estimate T_{bias}.

The above procedure works well when the observations are uncorrelated. However, for correlated data, $s^2(n)$ is a function of the correlation between observations, a fact that causes considerable difficulty in estimating this variance. In particular, the use of $s^2(n)/n$ as an estimate of the true variance σ^2 may result in significant underestimation of σ^2 when there exists a positive correlation among the observation, because $s^2(n)$ makes no use of the information on correlation.

Fishman ([2], Section 3) has described an estimator of σ^2 that takes into account the effect of correlation. This estimator can be used in a simulation program to estimate how long to run the simulation to estimate the true mean μ with a prespecified degree of statistical accuracy. Fishman has also discussed several criteria for determining sample size ([2], Section 4).

(b) Batch Means. An alternative way to estimate T_{bias} is to make one long simulation run instead of repeating each run by starting from an initial idle state each time. Thus, one complete run consists of N observations that are broken into p batches of size n each so that $N = np$. The experiment is equivalent to repeating an experiment of length n a total of p times such that the final state of one run becomes the initial state of the next. This way of repeating a run is preferable to starting each run from an initial idle state, because the state at the end of a batch is a more reasonable initial state than the idle state. However, the connection between the batches introduces *autocorrelation*. Its effect is that the value of one piece of data affects the value of the following data. The effect usually diminished as the separation between the data increases, and beyond some interval size it may reasonably be ignored. If the batch size n is greater than this interval, the batch means $\bar{x}_j(n)$ can be treated as independent, which assumption is necessary to apply the formulas for $\bar{x}_j(n), s^2_j(n), \bar{x}(n)$, and $s^2(n)$.

It should be noted that both the batch means method and the replication-of-runs method aim at deriving a suitable estimate of T_{bias} so that the observed values of the parameters (mean waiting time, for instance) become reliable. Averill Law ([3], p. 319) tested both methods for many combinations of n and p. The results showed that in almost all cases the batch means method produced a superior result such that the difference was statistically significant.

8.5 SUMMARY

This chapter discusses the two types of discrete system simulations; event-oriented and time-oriented, the emphasis being on event-oriented simulations. The main difference between the two types is that in a time-oriented simulation the simulated clock is updated at regular intervals so that the model is deterministic. In an event-oriented simulation, on the other hand, the simulated clock is updated at the arrival of each event so that the model is probabilistic. However, in both cases the simulated time increases in a step-wise discrete fashion instead of as a continuous variable. Queueing theory provides the mathematical foundation of event-oriented discrete simulation model.

A discrete system simulation model consists of five components, as illustrated in Figures 8-1 through 8-5: initialization and termination, event arrival, event servicing, event departure, and statistics collection and report generation. The crucial activity, however, is the arrival of an event. Depending on the probability distribution of interarrival times, a specific algorithm is provided with illustrative examples to show how the arrival time of the next event can be calculated. A similar discussion is given for computing the service time of an event when the probability distribution of the service time is given.

Since the purpose of running a discrete simulation model is to gather informative statistics about the behavior of the system, the chapter discusses six statistical measures with a formula of computation for each. A simulation program is so written as to collect such statistics automatically as the model runs.

Next the chapter discusses two examples of event-oriented discrete simulations: simulation of a telephone system where each incoming call is an event, and simulation of a toll booth operation on an expressway where each arriving car is an event.

An introduction to time-oriented discrete simulations follows. The basic features of a time-oriented simulation are described; a flowchart illustrates the process graphically. Two examples of time-oriented simulations are given: simulation of a stock market where stocks are bought and sold on a daily basis, and simulation of an econometric market model where the price of a commodity is determined as a result of the interaction between demand and supply of the commodity.

The final segment of the chapter discusses the validation of a simulation

model. Since a simulation is essentially a systematic trial-and-error process, the validation is necessary to increase the user's confidence in the results of the model. As a result of validation it is possible to make statements about the probability of the true value of a variable falling within a confidence interval containing the estimated value of that variable. The main emphasis of the validation process is to eliminate, or at least reduce, the bias in the estimation of the mean and variance determined by the model.

Because of their dependence on the initial conditions, observations near the beginning of the simulation are not representative of the process being simulated. This initial bias can be removed into two ways: by replication of runs or by the batch means method. In either case, we can determine a time T_{bias} such that the simulation represents the system accurately when the simulated time t is greater than the time T_{bias}. An industry study showed that the batch means method gives a better estimate of T_{bias} than the method or replication of runs.

8.6 KEY WORDS

The following key words are used in the chapter:

autocorrelation	occupancy
batch means	probabilistic model
counts	replication of runs
deterministic model	simulated clock
discrete event	state descriptors
distribution	statistics collection
event arrival	summary measure
event departure	time-oriented simulation
event-oriented simulation	transit time
event servicing	utilization
initial bias	validation of simulation
interarrival time	model

REFERENCES

1. W.G. Bulgren *Discrete System Simulation*, Prentice-Hall, Englewood Cliffs, NJ, 1982.
2. Fishman, G. S. "Estimating Sample Size in Computing Simulation Experiments," *Management Science*, 18, Sept. 1971, 21–38.
3. G. Gordon *System Simulation*, Prentice-Hall, Englewood Cliffs, NJ, 1978.
4. H.M. Wagner, *Principles of Operations Research*, Prentice-Hall, Englewood Cliffs, NJ, 1975.

REVIEW QUESTIONS

1. Distinguish between discrete simulation and continuous simulation.
2. Distinguish between time-oriented and event-oriented discrete simulations. Why is the former said to be deterministic?
3. Explain the five components of a discrete event-oriented simulation.
4. Refer to Section 8.2.6. Formulate the five components of the simulation of the toll booth operation.
5. Explain the algorithm to compute the arrival time of an event from the distribution of the interarrival times.
6. Discuss the statistical measures (a) utilization and (b) occupancy.
7. Why is validation necessary for a simulation model?
8. Explain the meaning of initial bias. Why is it necessary to remove it?
9. Define T_{bias}. How do you compute it by replication of runs and by batch means?
10. Is batch means a better method than replication of runs to estimate T_{bias}?

FORMULATIONAL PROBLEMS

1. Formulate the stock market simulation model (Section 8.3) as an event-oriented model by defining the new price of a stock as an event.
2. A machine shop can service one machine at a time out of a total of six machines. When a machine is down, it comes to the shop for repair. It then waits in a queue if the server is busy, or else it is serviced immediately. The queue is FIFO. The interarrival times and the service times are uniformly distributed. The mean and the standard deviation of the interarrival times are 10 and 3, respectively, while the mean and the standard deviation of the service time are 15 and 5, respectively. Now answer the following questions:

a. Does the model represent a discrete system simulation? If your answer is Yes, then specify which type of discrete system simulation it is.

b. Describe the five major subroutines that are needed to simulate this model. (Your desciption must be specific to this model, not generic in nature.)

c. Draw a flowchart of the event arrival module. Be specific relative to the problem described. For example, instead of saying "update variables," specify what variables are to be updated.

d. Given three random numbers 0.545, 0.079, and 0.621, calculate the departure times of the first three machines. Assume that the clock starts at time zero and the queue is of the no-feedback type. For simplicity of calculations, round every decimal to the nearest integer.

9

Continuous System Simulation

9.1 CONTINUOUS SYSTEMS

A continuous system is one in which the predominant activities cause smooth changes in the attributes of the system entities. Such a system is expressed by a set of equations, algebraic or differential. Most of the models that we have discussed in Chapters 4 and 5 are examples of continuous systems, because they are expressed by means of a set of equations. If such a system can be solved explicitly as mathematical functions, then no simulation is involved. However, often an explicit analytical solution cannot be determined, in which case we depend on simulation techniques. The situation is similar to the case of solving a differential equation by successive approximations.

Many simulation studies of continuous systems are concerned primarily with the study of *servomechanisms,* devices that rely upon feedback for their operation. The field of *control theory* provides the theoretical background with which to design such systems, but simulation is used extensively to carry out detailed studies.

A continuous system simulation is quite analogous to the time-oriented discrete system simulation discussed in Chapter 8. In both cases the simulated time clock is updated at regular intervals. However, for a time-oriented discrete system the time increments are discrete and finite, whereas for a continuous system the time increments are continuous and hence are infinitesimal in magnitude.

9.2 SYSTEM DYNAMICS

Continuous system simulation deals primarily with feedback systems that
involve the principle of system dynamics, a concept first introduced by Jay
W. Forrester at MIT in the 1960s. The principal concern of a *system dynamics*
study is to understand the forces operating in a system in order to determine
their influence on the stability or growth of the system, no matter whether
it is a business system or a scientific system. The output of the study suggests
some reorganization or change in policy that can solve an existing problem
or guide developments away from potentially dangerous directions.

Typical examples of system dynamics studies can be found in forecasting
models, especially when such models are used to answer "what if " questions
in corporate planning. Such models incorporate the principle of feedback in
the business environment and capture the fluctuations in the general level
of economic activity caused by business cycles.

A *feedback system* is one in which an action is influenced by the consequences of previous actions. Any such system can be a component of a
more comprehensive feedback system. Within the system boundary the basic
building block is the feedback loop. The *feedback loop* is a path combining
decision, action, level or condition of the system, and information, with the
path returning to the decision point. Thus, a feedback loop consists of two
distinct types of variables, the levels and the rates. Except for constants,
these two are sufficient to represent a feedback loop. The following description of levels and rates is adapted from Forrester ([1], Chapter 4).

The *level* (or *state*) *variables* describe the condition of the system at any
particular time. The level variables accumulate the results of action within
the system. They are represented by the "level equations" (see Chapter 11).
Computing a new value of a level variable involves its previous value, the
rates (actions) that cause the level to change, and the length of time since
the previous computation of the level. The computation of the new value of
a level does not involve the values of any other level variables. The level
variables accumulate the flows described by the rate variables. The level
equations perform the process of integration (the mathematical process defined in calculus). The levels create system continuity between points in
time.

On the other hand, the *rate* (action) *variables* are quite different. The rate
variables tell how fast the levels are changing. The rate variables determine,
not the present values of the level variables, but the slope (change per time
unit) of the level variable values. The rate variables are defined by the "rate
equations" (see Chapter 11). The rate equations are the policy statements
that describe action in a system; that is, the rate equations state the action
output of a decision point in terms of the information inputs to that decision.
Computing the value of a rate variable is done using only the values of level
variables and constants. The rate variable does not depend on its own past
value, or on the time interval between computations, or on other rate variables.

9.3 SYSTEM DYNAMICS DIAGRAMS

A system dynamics view of a system is expressed by using the level equations and the rate equations. A system dynamics diagram resembles a flowchart and describes the structure of a system dynamics model graphically. It uses a set of symbols for indicating the various factors involved in a system dynamics model. The five symbols illustrated in Figure 9-1 are basic to any system dynamics model. We have already discussed *level* and *rate* variables in Section 9.2. A *source* or *sink,* as the name implies, is the beginning or the end of the system flow. A *constant* is independent of time and retains the same value throughout the model. An *auxiliary variable* is defined by combining other variables mathematically in some relationship other than the integration implied by a rate equation and a level. Figure 9-2 illustrates a typical system dynamics model. Solid lines indicate the flow of tangible objects, and dotted lines causal relationships.

Levels are usually dimensionless, since they represent a count. However, the term level is sometimes used for quantities with dimension. Gordon ([2], Section 5-7) provides a simple test to decide whether a quantity can be regarded as level:

Imagine the system brought to rest. Any quantity that is a rate is then automatically zero. But any quantity that maintains a magnitude should be regarded as a level.

We shall pursue the above issue in more detail in Chapter 11, where we

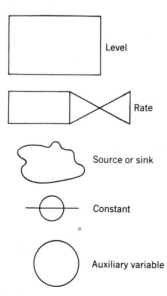

FIGURE 9-1 Symbols used in system dynamics diagrams.

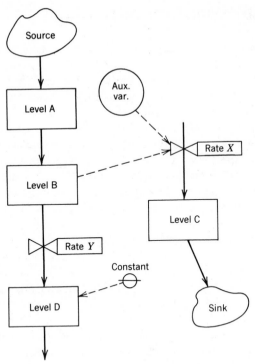

FIGURE 9-2   Structure of a system dynamics model.

shall discuss the language DYNAMO II used for continuous system simulation.

9.4   INVENTORY CONTROL SYSTEM AS A FEEDBACK SYSTEM*

A feedback system is seen in the control of inventories. A retailer usually maintains an inventory of goods, aiming to hold a balance between the cost of holding goods in inventory and the penalty of losing sales if the inventory should become empty. We already examined such a model in Chapter 4. The economic lot size model determined under the principle of continuous review and uniform demand gives us a mathematical model that can be regarded as a continuous system. It can be solved analytically, in which case no simulation is involved. Alternatively, it can be viewed as a time-oriented discrete system simulation, as mentioned in Chapter 8. However, the model mentioned in Chapter 8 assumes a probabilistic demand rather than a uniform

---

*This example is adapted from Gordon ([2], Section 5-11).

demand. As a third alternative, the inventory control system can be designed as a continuous system simulation as follows:
Let

$$X = \text{current inventory level}$$
$$Y = \text{outstanding level of orders placed with the supplier}$$
$$U = \text{rate of ordering from supplier}$$
$$V = \text{rate of delivery from supplier}$$
$$S = \text{rate of sales}$$
$$I = \text{planed inventory level}$$
$$T = \text{average delivery time}$$

Here X and Y are levels; U, V, and S are rates; and I and T are constants.

Then the model is given by the equations

$$\frac{dy}{dt} = U - V, \qquad \frac{dx}{dt} = V - S, \qquad V = Y/T \qquad (9.1)$$

Now, the rate of ordering U is a management decision. Unless the model is of the uniform demand type, the sales rate S will fluctuate. If S increases, then X decreases, because the delivery rate takes time to catch up with the increased value of S. Similarly, if S decreases, then X will increase due to reduced sales. Consequently, U should be estimated as

$$U = S + C(I - X) \qquad (9.2)$$

where C is a constant called the *ordering constant*.
If the demand or sales rate is uniform, then $C = 0$ and we get $U = S$. This agrees with the result from the economic lot size model in Chapter 4. In fact, letting the derivative be approximated by a quotient, we get

$$\text{Rate of ordering} = U \approx \frac{Q^*}{t^*} = \sqrt{\frac{2aK/h}{\dfrac{2K}{ah}}} = a = S$$

However, when the demand is nonuniform, the model gives the solution for U. A computer program will normally be written to solve the system given by (9.1) and (9.2) for given values of I and T, a given functional form for S, and a set of values for the ordering constant C. For each value of C, the program will compute the values of U, V, X, and Y. Plotting X against t, the optimal value of C and hence of U can be determined.
Figure 9-3 shows a system dynamics diagram for the model.

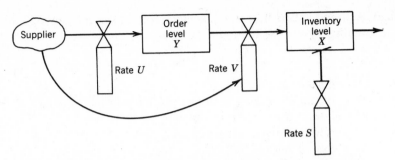

FIGURE 9-3 System dynamics diagram of inventory control system.

9.5 DISCRETE VERSUS CONTINUOUS SIMULATION

A discrete system simulation has the following characteristics:

1. No formal mathematical equations are involved.
2. During simulation the decision variables are updated in a discrete stepwise fashion. The updates are made at regular time intervals for time-oriented simulation or at scheduled occurrences of events for event-oriented simulation.

A continuous system simulation has the following characteristics:

1. The model is described by a set of mathematical equations, algebraic or differential.
2. During simulation the decision variables are updated by a continuous process. For example, rates are expressed as derivatives, which are then integrated with given initial conditions to determine the decision variables.

As an example, let us consider the simulation of the inventory control system. In Chapter 8 we referred to a time-oriented discrete simulation of this system described by Wagner (see Section 8.3). In his work, Wagner does not use any formal equations to describe the model. Instead he uses variables such as INVENTORY ON-HAND, AMOUNT DUE-IN, and TIME DUE-IN to describe the characteristics of the model and updates them at regular time intervals to simulate the flow of data through the model. On the other hand, the same inventory control system has been simulated in this chapter by using the continuous simulation process. Equations (9.1) and (9.2), which include both algebraic and differential equations, adequately characterize the model. Simulation is used to show the outcomes corresponding to different values of the ordering constant C. The two level variables X and Y can be determined by integrating (9.1) with appropriate initial conditions.

However, usually explicit solutions are not possible, and then continuous simulation can provide values of X and Y at small intervals.

9.6 FROM MODELING TO SIMULATION

Now that we have had a glimpse of both modeling and simulation techniques, let us examine how they are related in solving a business or scientific problem. Assume that we want to determine the optimal inventory level under the policy of continuous review with probabilistic demand.

Using the appropriate inventory model, with the distribution for the demand given as a probability distribution, we can calculate the quantity X which represents the optimal inventory level. However, if the distribution of demand is not known explicitly as a continuous function, then an explicit solution is not available. In such a situation using the demand distribution table we can use time-oriented discrete simulation to calculate X on a daily basis, assuming the unit of simulated time to be 1 day.

Alternatively, without knowing the demand distribution we can use the continuous simulation process with several trial values of the ordering constant C and plot the resulting values of X to determine the optimal value of X.

Even in a situation where an analytic solution from the model is available, simulation provides us with the technique of answering "what if " questions by simulating the implementation of a variety of possible scenarios.

9.7 CONTINUOUS SYSTEM SIMULATION FOR SOCIAL SYSTEMS

Since continuous simulation is deeply related to system dynamics, which deals with feedback systems, efforts have been made to apply the continuous simulation process to social systems. We shall discuss two examples of this effort.

The first example deals with the interaction of human beings with society, government, and the environment. The second deals with world dynamics and modeling introduced by Professor Jay W. Forrester at MIT. But first we want to make some general comments about the simulation of social systems.

It is generally believed that social environments and human behavior are too subjective to be amenable to model-building formalism. Societal variables are complex in comparison with variables appearing in the physical sciences. In addition, they are subject to evolutionary changes over which the model builder has no control. Nunn ([3], p. 54) commented as follows:

Social theories are developed as conceptual theories to account for the strong component of meaning in social events. The theorems and hypotheses of phys-

ical science are not appropriate to the social sciences; the former can depend on objective measurement, while the latter must recognize meaning and interpretation. To repeat, the value system and bias of a social engineer are integral parts of his works. To approach a social problem as if it were a physical problem would ignore the involvement of the social engineer and most likely lead to an inadequate solution, such as we have observed in several of our recent governmental social-welfare programs.

Despite such obstacles, Nunn and his group formulated a simulation model for a human-environment system using the continuous simulation technique. This model is described in Section 9.7.1.

9.7.1 Social Simulation Model

The model was built for the Grand Rapids Environmental Quality Demonstration Project in the early 1970s. It consists of five major decision interfaces between the community and its ecological environment: economic, technological, political/legal, physiological, and sociopsychological. The overall relationships among these interfaces are represented as linkages among the corresponding five subsystems: economic, pollution, government, health, and societal (see Figure 9-4). The arithmetic operators (+ or −) indicated on the linkages in Figure 9-4 are general indicators of the nature of the corresponding relationships. For example, skill and education of the labor force

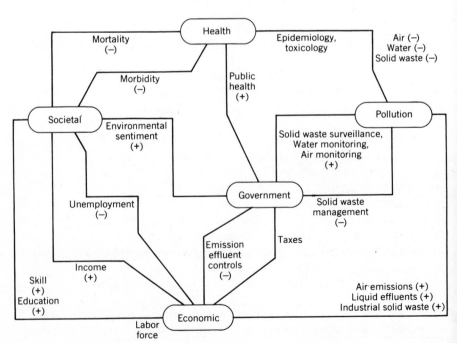

FIGURE 9-4 System diagram for human-environment model.

increase the economic activity and hence appear with positive (+) signs. They imply a positive feedback from the societal subsystem to the economic subsystem. On the other hand, as the pollution increases, the quality of air and water deteriorates and solid waste increases. All three have a negative impact on human health and hence appear with negative (−) signs in the linkage from the pollution subsystem to the health subsystem. All other signs can be similarly explained.

The model depicts the real-world situation at the most general level. It states only the critical human-environmental relationships. It consists of one major outer loop showing feedbacks among the four subsystems societal, economic, pollution, and health. The government subsystem is located in a minor inner loop and interacts with the other four subsystems. For example, as pollution increases, the government subsystem reacts to limit the sources of pollution and to provide additional care and protection of public health. The linkages from government to pollution and health, each with a positive sign, show positive feedbacks.

Nunn ([3], pp. 54–55) has given a very detailed description of the contents of this model. He remarks as follows:

> The entire model is designed, not so much to portray the conditions at a single point in time, but to track the changes as various sectors within the subsystems adapt to changes in other sectors. This provides the ability to simulate the results of changes generated by proposed action programs intended to correct environmental problems.

The model was implemented using DYNAMO (see Chapter 11) as the continuous simulation language. It used earlier data from a simulation study of the Grand Rapids area as baseline data. The model used about 750 equations.

9.7.2 World Dynamics and World Model

During the 1960s, Jay Forrester of MIT introduced the concept of using system dynamics models to address social problems. He proposed that it is necessary to introduce structure into an existing body of knowledge about any given social system in order to build a system dynamics model of that social system. He pursued this idea and eventually developed a model of the world in his book *World Dynamics,* published in 1973. Subsequently, this model was studied under the auspices of the Club of Rome.

The Club of Rome, an informal association of some 85 individuals from over 30 countries, was started in 1968 to study the "predicament of mankind." As noted by its founder Aurelio Peccei ([4], p. 199), the Club wanted to address the "problematique," a cluster of interrelated problems ([4], p. 199):

> Deterioration of the environment, the crisis of institutions, bureaucratisation, uncontrolled urban spread, insecurity of employment and loss of satisfaction

in work, the alienation of youth, questioning of the values of society, violence and disregard of law and order, educational irrelevance, inflation and monetary disruption in the face of material prosperity, the unbridged gap between rich and poor within and between nations.

The Club invited the System Dynamics Group under Forrester at MIT to undertake the construction of a world dynamics model. An international team under Dennis Meadows conducted the study. Their report was published in 1972 under the title *The Limits to Growth*. The world dynamics model used in the study investigated five aspects of global development: population growth, the spread of industrialization, pollution, depletion of natural resources, and the occurrence of malnutrition. The main conclusions from the model indicated that the present trends would place a limit on growth, that growth would stop during the next 100 years, and that disastrous effects would result in the form of reduction of population and deterioration of living conditions. This gloomy nature of the conclusions led people to regard the study as a prophecy of disaster, collapse, and catastrophe. However, the model also noted that it would be possible to establish conditions leading to a state of equilibrium with satisfactory living conditions for everyone if an urgent cooperation among the nations of the world could be initiated to implement some major changes in present practices.

The proponents of the study claimed that the model was to be regarded as the first step in an extremely important new direction, because the only way to gain a better understanding of complex systems like the world and its main subsystems—regions, countries, and large cities—is to construct dynamic models and approach them by systems analysis with the aid of analog and digital computers. Guy Streatfield made the following comments ([6], pp. 210–211):

Meadows' work with the system dynamics world model is an elaboration of Jay Forrester's original invention—a new type of model, based on imperfect data and theories, illustrating the basic dynamic tendencies of the whole world system.

Forrester's model reflects his "impressions" of what is going on in the "real world," and from these it suggests how the real world is likely to develop under alternative policies. Meadows has attempted to add hard facts to Forrester's original impressions and uses three times the number of mathematical equations employed by Forrester. However, as Meadows emphasizes, only about 0.1 per cent of the data required to construct a satisfactory world model are available.

The opponents of the world model provide three main criticisms:

1. The human factor does not appear as a variable in the model.
2. Fluctuations in the level of population increase do not significantly affect the conclusions of the model.

3. Mathematical equations used in the model cannot be changed once the model is started. Consequently the model merely projects an initial state into the future.

Michael Rothkopf summarized as follows ([5], p. 214):

> The level of effect devoted to constructing general world models should be strictly limited to the effort appropriate to provide coherent statements of opinion. Furthermore, such models, if constructed, should be viewed as no more than the sincere opinions of their builders. They should not be presented as scientifically justified conclusions. If they are, decision makers may place excessive trust in them—and this may lead to bad decisions. Whether they are accepted as trustworthy or not, unfounded claims (explicit or implied) of scientific validity will tend to discredit science and call into doubt the truly scientific contributions of scientists.

In a February 1973 report, Peccei, the founder of the Club of Rome, described the MIT work as only the first step and provided a list of areas and projects toward which attention should be focused ([4], pp. 201–205):

> Refining, deepening, and extending the present model.
> New methodologies and steps toward practical action.
> Problems of development and economic justice.
> World population problems.
> New research imperative.
> Lack of enough food for everybody.
> Social problems—the value system and survival.
> Humans and their destiny.
> Institutions and policy making.
> Political consequences.

9.8 SUMMARY

This chapter discusses the concept of continuous system simulation and provides a number of examples of such systems. A continuous system can be characterized by a set of equations, algebraic or differential, along with a set of specified initial conditions. As such it is very close to mathematical modeling discussed in Chapters 4 and 5. However, in a continuous system simulation, results are derived via the simulation process instead of explicit analytical solutions. Time is incremented continuously during the simulation. As such, a continuous system is characterized as a feedback system.

System dynamics provides the basis of continuous system simulation. Accordingly the chapter discusses the principles of system dynamics and il-

lustrates with system dynamics diagrams. The latter resemble flowcharts to some extent and show the interaction among three major components in a system dynamics model: level, rate, and constant. Levels represent the accumulation of various entities in the system, such as inventories of goods, unfilled orders, and number of employees. Rates represent instantaneous flow to or from a level. Constants provide specific initial conditions for the model.

An inventory control system is then discussed to illustrate the process of continuous simulation. Since the inventory system was used earlier in Chapters 4 and 8 as an example of an optimizing model and a time-oriented discrete system simulation, respectively, the relationship among mathematical modeling, discrete system simulation, and continuous system simulation is described with the help of the inventory control system.

The chapter concludes with a reference to the application of continuous simulation processes to social systems. Usually such systems are regarded as not amenable to simulation, since the societal variables are highly subjective in nature. Despite such obstacles the system dynamics principles have been used to simulate social systems. Two examples of such simulation are then provided. The Grand Rapids Environmental Quality Demonstration Project simulates the interaction between a community and its ecological environment. The World Model was conducted under the auspices of The Club of Rome to study the "predicament of mankind." It addresses several aspects of global development related to population growth, pollution, economic and health problems, and the spread of industrialization.

9.9 KEY WORDS

The following key words are used in this chapter:

continuous system	social system
feedback system	societal variable
level variable	system dynamics
linkage in a social simulation model	system dynamics diagram
rate variable	world dynamics
servomechanism	world model

REFERENCES

1. J.W. Forrester, *Principles of Systems*, MIT Press, Cambridge, MA, 1980.
2. G. Gordon, *System Simulation*, Prentice-Hall, Englewood Cliffs, NJ, 1978.
3. P.C. Nunn, "An Approach to the Simulation of Social Systems," *Simulation Today*, no. 14, 53–56 (June 1973).

4. A. Peccei, "The Club of Rome: The New Threshold," *Simulation*, **20**(6), 199–206 (1973).
5. M.H. Rothkopf, "World Models Won't Work," *Simulation*, **20**(6), 213–215 (1973).
6. G. Streatfield, "No Limit to the Growth Debate," *Simulation*, **20**(6), 210–212 (1973).

REVIEW QUESTIONS

1. What is a feedback system? Why is continuous system simulation specially suitable for simulating feedback systems?

2. Explain the concept of system dynamics. How is it related to continuous simulation?

3. Define the terms level variable, rate variable, constant, source, sink, and auxiliary variable, as used in a system dynamics model.

4. How does a time-oriented discrete simulation differ from continuous simulation? Illustrate your answer with an example other than the inventory control system discussed in this chapter.

5. What are some of the advantages and disadvantages of using continuous system simulation to simulate social systems?

6. Explain the concept of positive and negative linkages as used in the example of Section 9.7.1.

7. A company calculates its cash flow at the beginning of each year by the following simplistic model:

Cash flow on Jan. 1,
$$\text{year } X + 1 = \text{Cash flow on Jan. 1, year } X$$
$$+ \text{ total income receipts during year } X$$
$$- \text{ total disbursement during year } X$$

The company wants to project its cash flow for the next five years $X + 1$ through $X + 5$. Explain how this can be done in two possible ways:

   a. Using statistical forecasting with appropriate data collection (see Chapter 5).

   b. Using the continuous simulation technique.

10

Primer on GPSS

10.1 CHARACTERISTICS OF SIMULATION LANGUAGES

In Section 6.8 we made some brief comments about the general features of a simulation language. In the late 1950s and early 1960s a good deal of debate was going on about the need for such special-purpose programming languages. While it is certainly possible to write simulation models in general-purpose languages such as FORTRAN or PASCAL (the latter was not in existence during the 1960s), it is accepted that simulation languages provide some special advantages as built-in features. In addition, different types of simulation languages should be used depending on whether we want to simulate a discrete system or a continuous system.

A simulation language must be able to implement the dynamic process involving interacting entities in the model. Accordingly, specifications of the entities and their interactions are definite requirements. Since the interactions can be described in terms of arithmetical and logical statements involving the model variables, any algorithm-oriented language is capable of implementing a simulation model. However, to make the language more effective, some amount of automatic statistics-collection and report-generation capabilities are needed in addition to the algorithm handling. As a result, various simulation languages were developed in the 1950s and 1960s as modifications of then-existing languages such as FORTRAN and ALGOL as the basic languages. For instance, SIMSCRIPT and CSL were based on FORTRAN, while SIMULA and ESP were based on ALGOL. The flaws of the basic languages invariably entered their offspring simulation languages.

By contrast, GPSS (General Purpose Simulation System) did not have any basic language (see [4], p. 191). Developed principally by Geoffrey Gordon ([2], pp. 197, 221) at IBM and published in 1961, GPSS is used for discrete system simulation, preferably event-oriented. It has a block structure, and

the simultion proceeds by advancing each event through the successive blocks in the program. As with any programming language, execution of statements occurs sequentially, although it is possible to force a conditional or an unconditional transfer of control. A stochastic element is introduced into the program by using a random sample from a probability distribution to forecast the arrival time of the next event.

10.2 OVERVIEW OF GPSS STRUCTURE

A GPSS program consists of a number of different types of blocks representing different kinds of interaction of the system with an event. The blocks of each type require a specification particular to that type and a rule to choose between the possible successor blocks. Unlike most programs, there are no formal statements in a GPSS program. Execution proceeds as a result of different GPSS verbs and their interactions with the data supplied about the blocks. The following briefly summarizes the main language components in a GPSS simulation ([1], p. 60):

Transactions represent traffic in the system.

Blocks cause some basic action to occur.

Facilities can be seized by one or more transactions at a time.

Storages can be entered by one or more transactions.

Logic switches determine the flow of transactions through the model.

Arithmetic variables are used for mathematical relationships.

Boolean variables represent multiple logical conditions.

Functions compute relationships.

Queues are used to accumulate information about delayed transactions.

Tables are used to provide more specific information than is automatically provided by the system.

Savevalues are global storage locations.

Matrix savevalues are used to store selected values arrayed in a matrix.

User chains represent queues and the status of inactive transactions.

Groups represent transactions with common attributes.

GPSS uses 48 types of blocks to represent actions taking place in the system. Each block type is given a unique name. The sequence of events in real time is represented by the movement of transactions through the system in simulated time.

The basic flow through a model is of a transaction created at a GENERATE block moving through the model until it is terminated at a TERMINATE block. Along the way it could SEIZE and then RELEASE a facility, ENTER a storage and then LEAVE it, be placed in a QUEUE and

DEPART the queue, cause a VARIABLE to be evaluated, use a FUNC-TION, and cause logic switches to be set and reset.

GPSS provides a process for each transaction in a system. Each transaction moves through the system and hence through time. As seen by the QUEUE block, it is possible for a transaction to encounter a delay in process and wait. It is because of this time flow within GPSS that it is called a process interaction language.

GPSS automatically accumulates statistics concerning conditions within the model. Furthermore, the programmer has the ability to cause the system to accumulate other information that she or he believes important. All statistics accumulated are output automatically at the end of the simulation run, and they can be output during the run under the control of the programmer.

10.3 GPSS BLOCK DIAGRAM

A GPSS *block diagram* is a collection of characteristically shaped figures (blocks) connected by directed line segments. This plays the same role in a GPSS program that a flowchart plays in a typical high-level language program. A GPSS block diagram can consist of many blocks subject to a limit, usually 1000, imposed by the computer facility.

Each block type is given a name that is descriptive of the block action (for example, ADVANCE, GENERATE, TRANSFER) and is represented by a unique symbol. Each block is assigned an identification number by an assembly program within GPSS. This number is called the *location* of the block. At the time of program execution, a transaction proceeds from one block to another with the next higher location. As in an ordinary program flowchart, the control is transferred sequentially in the block diagram. However, a TRANSFER block can force a bypass of the sequential execution of blocks. The TRANSFER block resembles a decision symbol in an ordinary program flowchart (see Fig. 10-1).

10.4 TRANSACTIONS: DYNAMIC ENTITIES IN A GPSS MODEL

The directed line segments in a GPSS block diagram represent paths along which units of traffic move. Each unit of traffic is called a *transaction*. The forward motion of a transaction continues through the model until one of the following three situations arises:

- [ ] The transaction moves into a block whose purpose is to hold it there (QUEUE).
- [ ] The transaction moves into a block whose purpose is to remove it from the waiting line (DEPART).
- [ ] The transaction stays in its current block because the next block in its path refuses to let it enter.

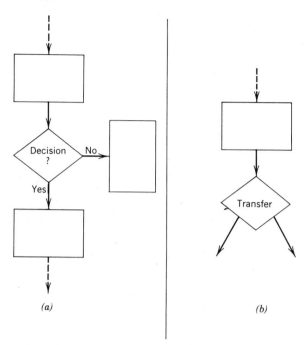

FIGURE 10-1 Decision diagrams. (a) Decision in a program flowchart; (b) decision in a GPSS block diagram.

After a transaction halts for one of these reasons, the forward motion of another transaction is initiated, and so on. Model execution thus consists of a series of subroutine calls that result from movement of transactions. This process is intimately related to the operation of the simulated clock. GPSS logic automatically updates the next event time in the clock, which can register only *integer* values, because GPSS is a "next event" simulator. The time unit for the clock is selected by the analyst.

10.5 GPSS BLOCKS

A block has three attributes: location, operation, and operand.

Location. Locations are designated numerically, starting with 1. The GPSS processor assigns location numbers automatically in the order in which the blocks appear in the program. If the analyst wants to refer to any specific location within the program, he/she can use *symbolic* location names, such as JOE or BYPAS. Names can be three to five characters long with the first three being letters.

Operation. This describes action done by the block and is designated as a verb, for example, GENERATE, QUEUE, ADVANCE.

Operand. A block operand provides the specific information on which the block's action is based. The operands may be regarded as the arguments used in calls on subroutines. Operands are normally denoted A, B, C, D, E, F, G.

10.5.1 GENERATE Block: Arrival Times

The GENERATE block initiates the entry of transactions into a GPSS model. There is no limit to the number of these blocks in a model. When a transaction enters a GENERATE block, the processor schedules the arrival time of the next transaction by sampling from an interarrival time distribution and then adding the sampled value to a copy of the clock's current value. When that future time is reached, another transaction is brought into the model through a GENERATE block, and so on.

The format of this block is

```
GENERATE     A, B, C, D, E, F, G
```

The operands A through G have the following meanings:

A   measures mean interarrival time with default value zero.
B   measures standard deviation or half-width of range over which the interarrival time is distributed uniformly; the default value is zero.
C   measures offset interval, the time when the first transaction arrives. A blank indicates no offset, and the first transaction arrives according to START time.
D   sets a limit to the number of transactions that can enter into a model through a given GENERATE block; the default value is infinity.
E   indicates the priority level of each transaction entering through a GENERATE block; the default is zero. In all, 128 priority levels are possible, numbered from 0 to 127.
F   represents the number of parameters to be attached to each transaction. The maximum number is 100, and the default is 12.
G   indicates the parameter type and can assume the value H or F corresponding to a halfword or a fullword, respectively.

Let us now take some examples.

  (1) GENERATE   3,3,10,5

This block specifies interarrival times which are uniformly distributed between 0 and 6, that is, 3 ± 3. The first transaction arrives at time 10, and the model allows a maximum of five transactions.

(2) GENERATE   5, ,2

This block specifies that the first transaction arrives at time 2 and each next transaction arrives every 5 time units.

(3) GENERATE   8,1, , ,4

This block specifies that transaction arrivals are uniformly distributed between 7 and 9, that is, 8 ± 1. An unlimited number of transactions can enter into the model, all with priority 4.

(4) GENERATE   30,5,1000, ,1,2,H

This block creates transactions with interarrival times uniformly distributed between 25 and 35, that is, 30 ± 5. The first transaction enters at time 1000. Each transaction has priority 1 and two halfword parameters.

Figure 10-2 gives the block diagrams of these four examples.

10.5.2 TERMINATE Block: Departure Times

Transactions are removed from a GPSS model when they enter into a TERMINATE block. Its A operand is a *termination counter decrement,* the

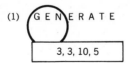

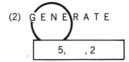

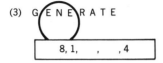

FIGURE 10-2 Examples of GENERATE block.

amount by which the counter is to be decremented each time a transaction enters a TERMINATE block with a default value of zero. Although there may be many TERMINATE blocks in a model, there is *only one* termination counter, which is decremented whenever a transaction moves into any TER-MINATE block. The GPSS processor starts the simulation by using the A operand of the START operation (see Section 10.6) as the initial value of the counter. It is the *only* way to control the duration of a run in the simulated GPSS model. Simulation stops when A reaches the value zero. The format of the TERMINATE block is

```
TERMINATE    A
```

This block works in conjunction with the START statement and the GEN-ERATE block. Figure 10-3 gives an example of this situation. Here the simulation starts with the initial value of the counter as 10. The first transaction arrives at time 30. As it enters the TERMINATION block, the counter is decremented by 1. The next transaction arrives at time 60. When its processing is over, the counter is decremented by 1 again. This cycle is repeated 10 times, since the START statement specifies 10 as the initial value of the counter. Thus, the total simulation runs for 10 transactions, and the total duration of time is

$$30 \times 10 = 300$$

Note that since the default value of A is zero, a statement TERMINATE without A operand will result in an infinite simulation run.

10.5.3 SEIZE and RELEASE Blocks: Facilities

In GPSS, the term *facility* is used as a synonym for server. Names are given to facilities to distinguish them from each other. Names can be numeric or

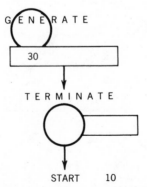

FIGURE 10-3   Example of a TERMINATE block.

symbolic. Numeric names must be positive, ranging from 1 to the maximum number of available facilities, while symbolic names are from three to five alphanumeric characters, the first three of which must be letters.

During the course of simulation the transaction moves from one block to the next. Suppose that, as its next activity, a transaction wants to capture a server. If the server is free, then the transaction captures it, that is, it SEIZEs the facility. If the server is not free, then the transaction waits in its current block until the server becomes free.

The format of the SEIZE block is

```
SEIZE    A
```

where the operand A is the name or number of the facility into which the transaction enters.

Once the transaction finishes being serviced at facility A, it moves to the next block. The format of this block is

```
RELEASE    A
```

where A is the name or number of the facility currently SEIZEd by the transaction. Once A is RELEASEd, it is made available to the next transaction. Figure 10-4 illustrates the use of these two blocks, where A is the name of a facility.

A transaction can be RELEASEd from a facility only if that facility was already SEIZEd. Thus, SEIZE and RELEASE are complementary blocks. GPSS automatically provides information on the following statistics:

☐ What fraction of time was the facility busy?
☐ How many times was the facility captured?
☐ What was the average holding time per capture of the facility?

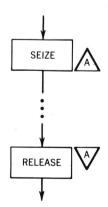

FIGURE 10-4 Example of SEIZE and RELEASE blocks.

10.5.4 ENTER and LEAVE Blocks: Storages

A *storage* is defined as an entity that can be occupied by many transactions at the same time, subject to a predetermined limit. A storage is thus the same as a facility except that it can be occupied by more than one transaction at a time whereas a facility can be used by only one transaction at a time. A transaction occupying a facility or a storage can be interrupted or preempted by another transaction. Also, a facility or a storage can be made unavailable to a transaction, if that is required by the model.

ENTER and LEAVE blocks behave the same as SEIZE and RELEASE blocks, respectively, but with multiple servers instead of a single server. Also, the FACILITY for SEIZE/RELEASE becomes STORAGE in ENTRY/LEAVE. The formats for ENTER and LEAVE are as follows:

```
ENTER    A, B
LEAVE    A, B
```

The operands A and B have the following meanings:

A   indicates the name or number of the storage which is ENTERed or LEAVEd. The name must be three to five alphanumeric characters with the first three characters being letters.

B   represents the number of units in storage. The default value is 1. The value of B cannot exceed the capacity of the target storage. This operand is optional.

GPSS uses an "all or nothing" approach at the ENTER block; a transaction moves into an ENTER block only if the currently available capacity of the STORAGE equals or exceeds the value of the B operand of the ENTER block. The same comment applies to the LEAVE block.

During the simulation run, statistics about the usage of STORAGE units are gathered collectively; that is, different units in a STORAGE have no

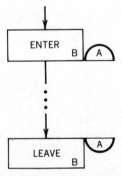

FIGURE 10-5   Example of ENTER and LEAVE blocks.

individual identity. Since a STORAGE simulates a multiple server situation, it follows that users cannot select servers of their own choice. Instead the servers select users by the FIFO discipline within each priority class. In essence, then, a would-be user waiting at a STORAGE goes to the head of the queue and is served by whichever server is then available.

Figure 10-5 illustrates the use of ENTER and LEAVE blocks.

10.5.5 ADVANCE Block: Service Times

Through the SEIZE block the transaction engages a FACILITY in order to get service. While service is being provided, the transaction stops its forward motion in the model. The ADVANCE block accomplishes the task of freezing a transaction's motion for a prescribed length of time, which is normally a random variable, since the service time varies from one server to the next.

The format of the ADVANCE block is

```
ADVANCE    A, B
```

where the operands A and B have the following significance:

A measures the mean interarrival time with default value zero.

B measures the standard deviation or half-width of range over which the interarrival time is distributed uniformly. The default value is zero.

Thus, the A and B operands of the ADVANCE block have the same meaning as those of the GENERATE block. Any number of transactions can wait in the ADVANCE block, and the presence of one transaction does not influence the entry or presence of other transactions.

The ADVANCE block normally appears in the combination SEIZE-ADVANCE-RELEASE or ENTER-ADVANCE-LEAVE, depending on whether a FACILITY or a STORAGE is used. In either case, the typical action consists of three steps:

1. Engage an appropriate unit as server.
2. Get the requested service from the server.
3. Disengage the unit.

Figure 10-6 gives an example of the ADVANCE block

```
ADVANCE    8, 3
```

```
┌─────────────────────────────┐
│  ADVANCE          8, 3       │
└─────────────────────────────┘
```

FIGURE 10-6 Example of an ADVANCE block.

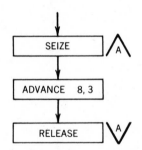

FIGURE 10-7   Example of SEIZE-ADVANCE-RELEASE flow.

Here a transaction stays in a FACILITY or STORAGE for 5–11, that is, 8±3, time units under the uniform distribution.

Figure 10-7 illustrates the following situation. A transaction SEIZEs FA-CILITY A for service; the service time is uniformly distributed over 8±3 time units; and at the end of service the transaction RELEASEs the FA-CILITY. If the transaction uses multiple servers instead of a single server, then SEIZE and RELEASE are replaced by ENTER and LEAVE, respectively, and FACILITY A becomes a multiple-unit STORAGE A.

10.5.6   QUEUE and DEPART Blocks: Gathering Statistics

Statistics about the model can be gathered via the QUEUE and DEPART blocks. The QUEUE block increases and the DEPART block decreases the length of a queue. The maximum number of queues depends on the computer system but is usually about 300. A queue is identified by a number or a symbolic name.

The formats of the QUEUE and DEPART blocks are

```
QUEUE     A , B
DEPART    A , B
```

A   indicates the name or number of the queue.

B   represents the number of units to be added to or subtracted from the queue count according as B is used with QUEUE or with DEPART, respectively. The default value is 1 in either case. This operand is optional.

The following program fragment illustrates this situation:

```
QUEUE      JOE
SEIZE      JIM
DEPART     JOE
ADVANCE    8
RELEASE    JIM
```

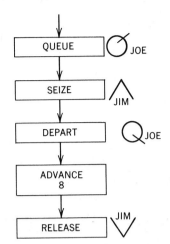

FIGURE 10-8 Block diagram for a program fragment.

Here a transaction enters a queue called JOE and wants to be served by the facility JIM. If JIM is available, then the transaction leaves JOE and gets serviced by JIM for 8 time units. If, however, JIM is not available, then the transaction waits in queue JOE until facility JIM is RELEASEd. Figure 10-8 illustrates the block diagram for the above program fragment.

Thus, QUEUE and DEPART blocks gather statistics describing the involuntary waiting that occurs from time to time at various points in the model. They provide answers to such questions as

- ☐ How many entries were there to the waiting line?
- ☐ How many of these were forced to wait?
- ☐ What was the maximum number of transactions waiting at any one time?
- ☐ What was the average number of transactions waiting during the simulation?
- ☐ For those that had to wait, what is the average time spent in the queue?

There can be many queues in a single model. Four things happen when a transaction moves into a QUEUE block:

1. The total entry count for the referenced queue is increased by 1.
2. The record of the current content of the queue is increased by 1.
3. The transaction is tagged with a copy of the queue's name.
4. The transaction is tagged with the current value of the simulated clock.

Similarly, when a transaction enters a DEPART block:

1. The record of the current content of the referenced queue is decreased by 1.
2. The transaction's tag indicating membership in the referenced queue is removed.

At the end of a simulation the processor automatically prints statistics showing the total entry count, the maximum content, the average content, the current content, and the average residence time in the queue.

There are two types of average residence time in queue, those including transactions with *zero* waiting time and those excluding such transactions.

10.5.7 MARK and TABULATE Blocks: Gathering More Statistics

MARK and TABULATE blocks collect information about the length of time taken by transactions to move through the model. They behave like the QUEUE and DEPART blocks. However, the latter gathers statistics about the "count" information (e.g., how many transactions in a queue), while the former gathers statistics regarding the "duration" information (e.g., how long the transaction stayed in the model).

The formats of the MARK and TABULATE blocks are as follows:

```
MARK        A
TABULATE    A, B
```

The operands A and B have the following meanings:

A   (for MARK block) represents the time of arrival of the transaction.
    (for TABULATE block) represents the name or number of the *table* in which the transit time is recorded.
B   represents the number of times a value is to be entered into the table each time a transaction moves into the TABULATE block.

The MARK block notes the arrival time of a transaction. The TABULATE block subtracts the time noted by a MARK block from the time of arrival at the TABULATE block. This difference is called the *transit time* for the transaction and is entered into the table referenced by the operand A of the TABULATE block. In effect, the transit time of a transaction can be regarded as the duration of time for the transaction's stay in the model, and the MARK block merely resets the transit time to zero.

A table for MARK/TABULATE plays a role similar to that of a queue for QUEUE/DEPART.

10.5.8 TRANSFER Block: Conditional and Unconditional Branching

When a GPSS program is run, the blocks are executed according to their sequential locations in the program. However, branching can be introduced by the TRANSFER block. It plays the same role as IF-THEN-ELSE or GOTO in a high-level language. Thus, the TRANSFER block allows some location other than the next sequential location to be selected. The format is

```
TRANSFER    A, B, C
```

where the operands A, B, and C have the following meanings:

A   indicates the transfer mode explained below.

B, C   represent the addresses of the blocks where the transaction is sent depending on the transfer mode.

The *transfer mode* represented by A is usually a decimal p, $0 < p < 1$, where p can have up to three digits. This means that the transaction moves to the block with address B with probability $1 - p$ and to the block with address C with probability p. If, however, A is left blank, then only one of B and C can be present. In this case, the transaction always moves to the block with address B or C, whichever is present. Thus, the TRANSFER block provides both a conditional and an unconditional branching depending on the value of the transfer mode A.

The transfer mode can have the value BOTH. In this case, the block specified by the operand B is tested. If the transaction is refused access there, then it tries to branch to the block specified in operand C. If it is refused access there too, then it stays in the TRANSFER block until it can enter the first available of the two blocks.

Let us take two examples:

```
(1) TRANSFER    .37, LBL1, LBL2
```

Here the transaction is sent to LBL1 with probability .63 and to LBL2 with probability .37.

```
(2) TRANSFER        , EXIT
```

Here the transaction always branches to the block labeled EXIT. Figure 10-9 illustrates these two examples.

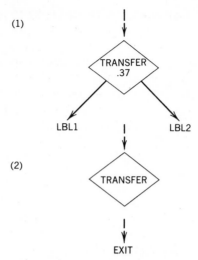

FIGURE 10-9   Examples of TRANSFER blocks. See text for explanation.

10.6   GPSS CONTROL STATEMENTS

GPSS control statements are necessary to run the program. They play the role of JCL statements for a high-level language. There are five GPSS control statements, of which three are essential to run the program. The other two are required for GPSS model validation (see Section 8.4). The five control statements are described below.

SIMULATE is the first statement in any GPSS program. Without this statement the program will be compiled but not executed.

START indicates the end of the problem definition. Its operand A provides the initial value of the termination counter. The simulation stops when operand A becomes zero.

END signifies the end of the model, and terminates all simulation.

RESET is used if we want to rerun the simulation after one run is complete. This statement wipes out all the statistics gathered so far but leaves the system loaded with transactions. The purpose is to gather statistics in the second run with the initial buildup period excluded. A sequence of statements

```
START    10, NP    (NP = No Printing)
RESET
START    1000
```

will run the model for 10 completed transactions, will then suppress the statistics gathered during these 10 runs, and finally will run the simulation

for 1000 more transactions. Suppression of statistics is needed for validation. We can see immediately that the RESET command is used for validation with batch means [see Section 8.4.2(b)].

CLEAR wipes out the statistics gathered so far and also wipes out the transactions in the model. But when the model is rerun, it uses a different random number generator seed. The sequence of statements

```
START
CLEAR
START
```

runs the same problem twice but uses two different seeds. The CLEAR command is needed for validation with replication of runs [see Section 8.4.2(a)].

A typical GPSS program without validation features has the following structure:

```
SIMULATE
Main program statements (GENERATE, SEIZE, TERMINATE,
etc.)
START
END
```

A GPSS program with validation by batch means has the following structure:

```
SIMULATE
Main program statements
START
RESET
START
RESET
⋮
START
END
```

A GPSS program using validation with replication of runs has the following structure:

```
SIMULATE
Main program statements
START
CLEAR
START
```

```
        CLEAR
        :
        START
        END
```

10.7   GPSS Program 1: APPLICANTS IN AN OFFICE

Assume that job applicants come to the personnel department of a company at the rate of one every 5±2 minutes. Two clerks accept their applications and process them at the rate of one every 8±4 minutes. Processed applications are then sent to the supervisor, who talks with each applicant individually and takes 4±3 minutes per applicant. Let us simulate the flow of applicants as a discrete system simulation and run the GPSS program for 1000 applicants.

Figure 10-10 shows the block diagram for the program and Program 1 shows the actual program listing and output.

Note that in the program listing each operation starts in column 8, each operand starts in column 19, and the word STORAGE starts in column 8. A comment line starts with an asterisk in column 1. Also, a comment can be inserted in any line with an operation, provided the comment starts in column 31 or later. GPSS is very sensitive to the column position, and a program will not run if the rules regarding column positions are not followed.

10.7.1   Analysis of the Output of Program 1

The output for Program 1 shows the readings of the RELATIVE and AB-SOLUTE clocks. They show the same value because the RESET statement is not used. If the RESET statement is used, then the RELATIVE CLOCK reading is set to zero at the beginning of each run while the ABSOLUTE CLOCK gives the time since the first run began.

We can now make the following general comments about the characteristics of the model:

☐ The facility STRK was utilized 80% of the time; that is, the supervisor talked with the applicants 80% of the total time.
☐ The average time for the supervisor's interview was 4.004 minutes.
☐ The two clerks were busy 79.9% of the time.
☐ The average time to process an application was 7.981 minutes.
☐ Each applicant joined in two queues, PRCSS and STRKQ. During the simulation run, at most three applicants entered the queue PRCSS and five applicants entered the queue STRKQ.
☐ Of the total 1002 entries in the PRCSS queue, 676 were zero, that is, no waiting was involved for 676 applicants.

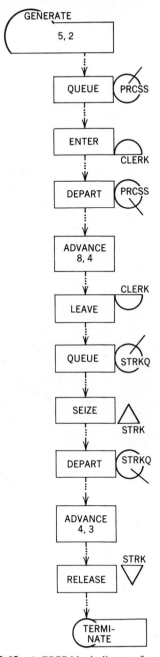

FIGURE 10-10 A GPSS block diagram for program 1.

PROGRAM 1

```
                    ***  G P S S / 3 6 0 / O S   V E R S I O N   2  ***
                    ***  IBM PROGRAM PRODUCT 5734-XS1 ***

BLOCK                                                                      CARD
NUMBER  *LOC  OPERATION  A,B,C,D,E,F,G          COMMENTS                   NUMBER
        *23456789012345678901234567890                                      1
        *   EACH OPERAND MUST START AT COLUMN 19.                           2
        *   A COMMENT STARTS AT COLUMN 31.                                  3
                SIMULATE                                                    4
  1             GENERATE   5,2        APPLICANT ARRIVES                     5
  2             QUEUE      PRCSS      ENTERS LINE FOR CLERK                  6
  3             ENTER      CLERK      CAPTURES A CLERK                       7
  4             DEPART     PRCSS      LEAVES LINE FOR CLERK                  8
  5             ADVANCE    8,4        CLERK PROCESSES APPLICATION            9
  6             LEAVE      CLERK      APPLICANT LEAVES CLERK                10
  7             QUEUE      STRKQ      ENTERS LINE FOR SUPERVISOR            11
  8             SEIZE      STRK       CAPTURES SUPERVISOR                   12
  9             DEPART     STRKQ      LEAVES LINE FOR SUPERVISOR            13
 10             ADVANCE    4,3        SUPERVISOR INTERVIEWS APPLICANT       14
 11             RELEASE    STRK       LEAVES SUPERVISOR                     15
 12             TERMINATE  1          DECREMENT COUNTER BY 1 FOR EACH APPLICANT  16
        *                                                                  17
        *   CLERK STORAGE   2                                              18
        *   CONTROL CARDS                                                  19
        *                                                                  20
                START     1000       RUN MODEL FOR 1000 APPLICANTS         21
                END                                                        22
```

260

FACILITY SYMBOLS AND CORRESPONDING NUMBERS
        1   STRK
STORAGE SYMBOLS AND CORRESPONDING NUMBERS
        1   CLERK
QUEUE SYMBOLS AND CORRESPONDING NUMBERS
        1   PRCSS
        2   STRKQ

             **** ASSEMBLY TIME = .00 MINUTES ****

*23456789012345678901234567890
*   EACH OPERAND MUST START AT COLUMN 19.
*   A COMMENT STARTS AT COLUMN 31.
          SIMULATE
   1   GENERATE   5   2
   2   QUEUE   1
   3   ENTER   1
   4   DEPART   1
   5   ADVANCE   8   4
   6   LEAVE   1
   7   QUEUE   2
   8   SEIZE   1
   9   DEPART   2
  10   ADVANCE   4   3
  11   RELEASE   1
  12   TERMINATE   1
*
   1   STORAGE   2
*   CONTROL CARDS
* *

261

PROGRAM 1 (continued)

```
     START     1000

RELATIVE CLOCK    5004   ABSOLUTE CLOCK    5004
BLOCK COUNTS
BLOCK CURRENT TOTAL   BLOCK CURRENT TOTAL   BLOCK CURRENT TOTAL   BLOCK CURRENT TOTAL
  1      0    1002     11      0    1000
  2      0    1002     12      0    1000
  3      0    1002
  4      0    1002
  5      2    1002
  6      0    1000
  7      0    1000
  8      0    1000
  9      0    1000
 10      0    1000
```

FACILITY	AVERAGE UTILIZATION	NUMBER ENTRIES	AVERAGE TIME/TRAN	SEIZING TRANS.NO.	PREEMPTING TRANS.NO.
STRK	.800	1000	4.004		

STORAGE	CAPACITY	AVERAGE CONTENTS	AVERAGE UTILIZATION	ENTRIES	AVERAGE TIME/TRAN	CURRENT CONTENTS	MAXIMUM CONTENTS
CLERK	2	1.598	.799	1002	7.981	2	2

QUEUE	MAXIMUM CONTENTS	AVERAGE CONTENTS	TOTAL ENTRIES	ZERO ENTRIES	PERCENT ZEROS	AVERAGE TIME/TRANS	$AVERAGE TIME/TRANS	TABLE NUMBER	CURRENT CONTENTS
PRCSS		.191	1002	676	67.4	.955	2.935		
STRKQ	5	.461	1000	415	41.4	2.306	3.943		

$AVERAGE TIME/TRANS = AVERAGE TIME/TRANS EXCLUDING ZERO ENTRIES

***** TOTAL RUN TIME (INCLUDING ASSEMBLY) = .00 MINUTES *****

END

```
*GO
GO
./LIST STRPRS
/LOAD GPSS
*2345678901234567890123456789012345678901234567890
*     EACH OPERAND MUST START AT COLUMN 19.
*     A COMMENT STARTS AT COLUMN 31.
      SIMULATE
      GENERATE    5,2       APPLICANT ARRIVES
      QUEUE       PRCSS     ENTERS LINE FOR CLERK
      ENTER       CLERK     CAPTURES A CLERK
      DEPART      PRCSS     LEAVES LINE FOR CLERK
      ADVANCE     8,4       CLERK PROCESSES APPLICATION
      LEAVE       CLERK     APPLICANT LEAVES CLERK
      QUEUE       STRKQ     ENTERS LINE FOR SUPERVISOR
      SEIZE       STRK      CAPTURES SUPERVISOR
      DEPART      STRKQ     LEAVES LINE FOR SUPERVISOR
      ADVANCE     4,3       SUPERVISOR INTERVIEWS APPLICANT
      RELEASE     STRK      LEAVES SUPERVISOR
      TERMINATE   1         DECREMENT COUNTER BY 1 FOR EACH APPLICANT
*
* CLERK STORAGE    2
* CONTROL CARDS
*
      START       1000      RUN MODEL FOR 1000 APPLICANTS
      END
GO
```

263

☐ Of the total 1000 entries in the STRKQ queue, 415 were zero, that is, these 415 applicants experienced no waiting time in the queue.

☐ Those who waited in the PRCSS queue experienced an average waiting time of 2.935 minutes.

☐ Those who waited in the STRKQ queue experienced an average waiting time of 3.943 minutes.

☐ Since the applicants first entered the PRCSS queue, not all of them could go through the entire simulation. In fact, 1002 entered the model via the PRCSS queue, but only 1000 finished through the STRKQ queue. The remaining two applicants did not finish the simulation when it shut off after processing the 1000th applicant.

10.8 GPSS PROGRAM 2: CALLERS AT A TELEPHONE BOOTH

In a public telephone area two booths are located side by side: one for credit card users and the other for coin operation. The callers come to the booth at the rate of one every 10±5 minutes. They wait in line if the desired telephone is busy; otherwise, they use the phone. An average call takes 6±3 minutes. The callers use the coin-operated phone 90% of the time and the credit card phone the other 10% of the time. We now simulate the model for 1000 callers.

Figure 10-11 shows the block diagram for the model. The actual program listing and the output follow. An analysis of the output can be made as in Section 10.7.1 and is therefore not attempted. However, we make the following observations about the utilization of the queue BOOTH in the model.

The output for Program 2 shows that all of the 1000 entries in the BOOTH are zero entries, that is, no caller has to wait in line. This becomes quite plausible when we find that the average length of a call is 5.936 minutes while the mean interarrival time for the callers at BOOTH is 10 minutes. Obviously, the phones are engaged for a shorter period of time than the time between the arrivals of two consecutive callers at the booth.

The frequency distribution of the callers' interarrival times is next changed to 6±3 from 10±5 minutes (see Program 3). Immediately we notice that BOOTH has zero entries only 97.9% of the time; that is, some of the callers do wait now. This is due to the fact that the callers' arrival frequency is the same as the duration frequency of the calls.

Finally, we change the call duration frequency to 10±5 minutes from 6±3 minutes (see Program 4). As a result, an average call takes 10.057 minutes, while the callers arrive every 6±3 minutes. Consequently, some of the callers have to wait in line at the booth. As a result, BOOTH has zero entries only 56.4% of the time; that is, 43.6% of the callers have to wait on arrival.

Finally, let us look at the TRANSFER block in Figure 10-11. It shows that 90% of the callers should use the coin-operated telephone and 10% should

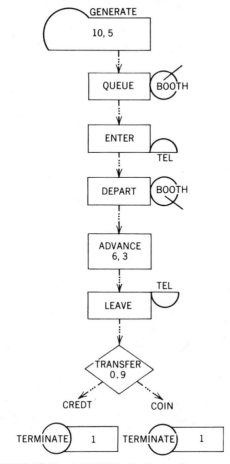

FIGURE 10-11   A GPSS block diagram for program 2.

use the credit card phone. However, the GPSS implementation of this feature uses a random number generator (see Section 10.11.1). Hence in any given run of the model the actual split is only close to the 90–10% division. Thus, from Programs 2, 3, and 4, we find the following breakdown of the credit phone usage versus coin-operated phone usage:

Call Arrival Frequency	Call Duration Frequency	Credit Usage Percentage	Coin Usage Percentage
10 ± 5	6 ± 3	8.3	91.7
6 ± 3	6 ± 3	9.5	90.5
6 ± 3	10 ± 5	9.7	90.3

PROGRAM 2

```
                      ***  G P S S / 3 6 0 /  S   V E R S I O N   2  ***
                      *** IBM PROGRAM PRODUCT 5734-XS1 ***

BLOCK                                                                      CARD
NUMBER   *LOC    OPERATION  A,B,C,D,E,F,G    COMMENTS                      NUMBER
         *23456789012345678901234567890                                      1
         *  EACH OPERAND MUST START AT COLUMN 19.                            2
         *  A COMMENT STARTS AT COLUMN 31.                                   3
                 SIMULATE                                                    4
   1             GENERATE    10,5            CALLER ARRIVES                  5
   2             QUEUE       BOOTH           ENTERS LINE FOR BOOTH           6
   3             ENTER       TEL             CAPTURES PHONE                  7
   4             DEPART      BOOTH           LEAVES LINE FOR BOOTH           8
   5             ADVANCE     6,3             USES PHONE                      9
   6             LEAVE       TEL             LEAVES PHONE                   10
   7             TRANSFER    .9,CREDT,COIN   CREDIT PHONE USED 10% OF TIME  11
   8   CREDITTERMINATE       1                             12              13
   9   COIN   TERMINATE      1                                            14
         *                                                                 15
         TEL   STORAGE       2                                            16
         *                                                                 17
         *   CONTROL CARDS                                                 18
               START        1000            RUN MODEL FOR 1000 CALLERS     19
               END

BLOCK NUMBER    SYMBOL       REFERENCES BY CARD NUMBER
         9      COIN         11
         8      CREDT        11
```

266

STORAGE SYMBOLS AND CORRESPONDING NUMBERS
1   TEL
QUEUE SYMBOLS AND CORRESPONDING NUMBERS
1   BOOTH

**** ASSEMBLY TIME = .00 MINUTES ****

```
*23456789012345678901234567890
*   EACH OPERAND MUST START AT COLUMN 19.
*   A COMMENT STARTS AT COLUMN 31.
        SIMULATE
1       GENERATE    10      5
2       QUEUE       1
3       ENTER       1
4       DEPART      1
5       ADVANCE     6       3
6       LEAVE       1
7       TRANSFER    .900    8       9
8       TERMINATE   1
9       TERMINATE   1
1       STORAGE     2
*
*   CONTROL CARDS
        START       1000
```

RELATIVE CLOCK   10021   ABSOLUTE CLOCK   10021
BLOCK COUNTS

PROGRAM 2 (continued)

BLOCK	CURRENT	TOTAL	BLOCK	CURRENT	TOTAL	BLOCK	CURRENT	TOTAL	BLOCK	CURRENT	TOTAL
1	0	1000									
2	0	1000									
3	0	1000									
4	0	1000									
5	0	1000									
6	0	1000									
7	0	1000									
8	0	83									
9	0	917									

STORAGE	CAPACITY	AVERAGE CONTENTS	AVERAGE UTILIZATION	ENTRIES	AVERAGE TIME/TRAN	CURRENT CONTENTS	MAXIMUM CONTENTS
TEL	2	.592	.296	1000	5.936		2

QUEUE	MAXIMUM CONTENTS	AVERAGE CONTENTS	TOTAL ENTRIES	ZERO ENTRIES	PERCENT ZEROS	AVERAGE TIME/TRANS	$AVERAGE TIME/TRANS	TABLE NUMBER	CURRENT CONTENTS
BOOTH	1	.000	1000	1000	100.0	.000	.000		.000

$AVERAGE TIME/TRANS = AVERAGE TIME/TRANS EXCLUDING ZERO ENTRIES

END

***** TOTAL RUN TIME (INCLUDING ASSEMBLY) = .00 MINUTES *****

*GO

PROGRAM 3

```
              ***  G P S S / 3 6 0 / O S   V E R S I O N   2  ***
                    *** IBM PROGRAM PRODUCT 5734-XS1 ***

BLOCK                                                              CARD
NUMBER  *LOC     OPERATION  A,B,C,D,E,F,G      COMMENTS           NUMBER
        *2345678901234567890123456789012345678901234567890           1
        *   EACH OPERAND MUST START AT COLUMN 19.                     2
        *   A COMMENT STARTS AT COLUMN 31.                            3
                 SIMULATE                                             4
  1              GENERATE   6,3                CALLER ARRIVES         5
  2              QUEUE      BOOTH              ENTERS LINE FOR BOOTH   6
  3              ENTER      TEL                CAPTURES PHONE         7
  4              DEPART     BOOTH              LEAVES LINE FOR BOOTH  8
  5              ADVANCE    6,3                USES PHONE             9
  6              LEAVE      TEL                LEAVES PHONE          10
  7              TRANSFER   .9,CREDT,COIN      CREDIT PHONE USED 10% OF TIME  11
  8     CREDT    TERMINATE  1                                        12
  9     COIN     TERMINATE  1                                        13
        *                                                            14
        TEL      STORAGE    2                                        15
        *                                                            16
        *   CONTROL CARDS                                            17
                 START      1000               RUN MODEL FOR 1000 CALLERS  18
                 END                                                 19

BLOCK NUMBER  SYMBOL      REFERENCES BY CARD NUMBER
          9   COIN        11
          8   CREDT       11
```

269

PROGRAM 3 (continued)

STORAGE SYMBOLS AND CORRESPONDING NUMBERS

   1 TEL

QUEUE SYMBOLS AND CORRESPONDING NUMBERS

   1 BOOTH

```
*2345678901234567890123456789   **** ASSEMBLY TIME = .00 MINUTES ****
*   EACH OPERAND MUST START AT COLUMN 19.
*   A COMMENT STARTS AT COLUMN 31.
        SIMULATE
1       GENERATE    6       3
2       QUEUE       1
3       ENTER       1
4       DEPART      1
5       ADVANCE     6       3
6       LEAVE       1
7       TRANSFER    .900    8       9
8       TERMINATE   1
9       TERMINATE   1
*
1       STORAGE     2
*
* CONTROL CARDS
        START       1000

RELATIVE CLOCK      6043    ABSOLUTE CLOCK      6043
BLOCK COUNTS
```

```
BLOCK CURRENT    TOTAL    BLOCK CURRENT    TOTAL    BLOCK CURRENT    TOTAL    BLOCK CURRENT    TOTAL    BLOCK CURRENT    TOTAL
     1     0     1001
     2     0     1001
     3     0     1001
     4     0     1001
     5     0     1001
     6     0     1000
     7     0     1000
     8     0       95
     9     0      905

STORAGE    CAPACITY    AVERAGE      AVERAGE        ENTRIES    AVERAGE     CURRENT     MAXIMUM
                       CONTENTS     UTILIZATION               TIME/TRAN   CONTENTS    CONTENTS
  TEL         2         1.003          .501          1001      6.059         1           2

QUEUE    MAXIMUM    AVERAGE     TOTAL      ENTRIES    PERCENT    AVERAGE         $AVERAGE         TABLE     CURRENT
         CONTENTS   CONTENTS    ENTRIES    ENTRIES    ZEROS      TIME/TRANS      TIME/TRANS       NUMBER    CONTENTS
  BOOTH      1        .006       1001        980       97.9        .037            1.809

$AVERAGE TIME/TRANS = AVERAGE TIME/TRANS EXCLUDING ZERO ENTRIES

     END

      ***** TOTAL RUN TIME (INCLUDING ASSEMBLY) = .00 MINUTES *****

*GO
```

271

PROGRAM 4

```
                              ***   GPSS/360/OS  VERSION  2  ***
                              ***  IBM PROGRAM PRODUCT 5734-XS1 ***

BLOCK                                                                          CARD
NUMBER   *LOC    OPERATION  A,B,C,D,E,F,G     COMMENTS                          NUMBER
         *2345678901234567890123456789012345678901234567890
         *  EACH OPERAND MUST START AT COLUMN 19.                                1
         *  A COMMENT STARTS AT COLUMN 31.                                       2
                  SIMULATE                                                       3
  1               GENERATE    6,3              CALLER ARRIVES                    4
  2               QUEUE       BOOTH            ENTERS LINE FOR BOOTH             5
  3               ENTER       TEL             CAPTURES PHONE                     6
  4               DEPART      BOOTH           LEAVES LINE FOR BOOTH             7
  5               ADVANCE     10,5            USES PHONE                        8
  6               LEAVE       TEL             LEAVES PHONE                      9
  7               TRANSFER    .9,CREDT,COIN   CREDIT PHONE USED 10$ OF TIME    10
  8      CREDT    TERMINATE   1                                                 11
  9      COIN     TERMINATE   1                                                 12
         *                                                                      13
         TEL   STORAGE     2                                                    14
         *                                                                      15
         *  CONTROL CARDS                                                       16
         START     1000          RUN MODEL FOR 1000 CALLERS                    17
         END                                                                    18
BLOCK NUMBER  SYMBOL   REFERENCES BY CARD NUMBER                                19
         9    COIN        11
         8    CREDT       11
```

STORAGE SYMBOLS AND CORRESPONDING NUMBERS

   1 TEL

QUEUE SYMBOLS AND CORRESPONDING NUMBERS

   1 BOOTH   **** ASSEMBLY TIME = .00 MINUTES ****

```
*23456789012345678901234567890
*   EACH OPERAND MUST START AT COLUMN 19.
*   A COMMENT STARTS AT COLUMN 31.
        SIMULATE
1       GENERATE    6       3
2       QUEUE       1
3       ENTER       1
4       DEPART      1
5       ADVANCE     10      5
6       LEAVE       1
7       TRANSFER    .900    8       9
8       TERMINATE   1
9       TERMINATE   1
*
1       STORAGE     2
*
*  CONTROL CARDS
        START       1000
RELATIVE CLOCK      6057    ABSOLUTE CLOCK      6057
BLOCK COUNTS
```

PROGRAM 4 (continued)

BLOCK	CURRENT	TOTAL	BLOCK	CURRENT	TOTAL	BLOCK	CURRENT	TOTAL	BLOCK	CURRENT	TOTAL
1	0	1002									
2	1	1002									
3	0	1001									
4	0	1001									
5	1	1001									
6	0	1000									
7	0	1000									
8	0	97									
9	0	903									

STORAGE	CAPACITY	AVERAGE CONTENTS	AVERAGE UTILIZATION	ENTRIES	AVERAGE TIME/TRAN	CURRENT CONTENTS	MAXIMUM CONTENTS
TEL	2	1.662	.831	1001	10.057	1	2

QUEUE	MAXIMUM CONTENTS	AVERAGE CONTENTS	TOTAL ENTRIES	ZERO ENTRIES	PERCENT ZEROS	AVERAGE TIME/TRANS	$AVERAGE TIME/TRANS	TABLE NUMBER	CURRENT CONTENTS
BOOTH	4	.336	1002	566	56.4	2.033	4.674		1

$AVERAGE TIME/TRANS = AVERAGE TIME/TRANS EXCLUDING ZERO ENTRIES

END

***** TOTAL RUN TIME (INCLUDING ASSEMBLY) = .00 MINUTES *****

*GO
.

10.9 INTERNAL LOGIC OF A GPSS PROCESSOR

A GPSS processor regards each transaction as being on a current events chain (CEC) or on a future events chain (FEC). The CEC is composed of all transactions that are scheduled to be moved through one or more blocks at the current simulated time or as soon as possible. The FEC consists of those transactions that are either at an ADVANCE block and are being served and so are not scheduled to move to another block, or are scheduled to enter into the model at some future time via a GENERATE block.

Each chain is "open," and a transaction occupies a specific location on the chain relative to the front of the chain. GPSS updates the model by scanning the CEC from front to back, transaction by transaction. The processor picks up the next transaction and moves it forward along the model until one of the following three situations occurs:

1. The transaction is in an ADVANCE block and is served.
2. The transaction cannot enter the next block in its path.
3. The transaction moves into a TERMINATE block.

When a transaction has finally stopped moving, the processor normally moves to the block of the CEC and picks up the next transaction.

Three phases are encountered in the model: the input phase, the clock update phase, and the scan phase. The model starts with the input phase. Next, the processor goes to the clock update phase. After the first clock updating, the processor performs the scan phase. It then moves in a loop between the clock update and scan phases until the simulation run is complete.

10.10 COMMENTS ON MORE COMPLEX GPSS MODELS

The two GPSS programs discussed here illustrate fairly common features of discrete system simulations. Schriber [3] has discussed a wide variety of such problems. Here we mention three more general types of problems that GPSS can handle:

1. A model can handle two types of customers with different distributions of arrival times and service times; if necessary, QUEUE statistics can be collected together or separately as segregated and aggregated statistics; see [3], p. 83.

2. A model can have only one type of customer but can introduce the element of priority classification of customers; it then can show the difference between a no-priority model and a prioritized model and establish that with priority distinction, system performance is improved; see [3], p. 93.

3. A GPSS program can handle an optimizing model by implementing a simple trade-off between the cost of waiting customers and the cost of an idle server. The objective is to determine an optimal number of customers so as to maximize profit. This is an example of an optimizing model obtained through discrete simulation; note that no equations or analytical functions are involved and the optimal solution is reached through a trial-and-error process in simulation; see [3], pp. 97–100.

10.11 SAMPLING FROM A DISTRIBUTION

The GPSS processor uses GENERATE and ADVANCE blocks to determine the next arrival and service times, respectively, for a transaction. If these times are deterministic, then they are represented by statements such as

```
GENERATE    12
ADVANCE     18
```

implying that each new transaction arrives every 12 minutes and is serviced every 18 minutes. However, if such times are probabilistic in nature, then they are computed from a probability distribution, which may be uniform or nonuniform.

In a *uniform* distribution each transaction occurs with equal probability. Thus, the block

```
GENERATE    12,3
```

indicates that the next transaction arrives at any one of the 7 possible time values 9, 10, 11, 12, 13, 14, or 15, and that the probability that it arrives at any one of these time values is $\frac{1}{7}$.

In a *nonuniform* distribution a transaction occurs with different probabilities, which may be given by a frequency distribution table or by a formula (Poisson, exponential, etc.).

Let us now examine how a value is sampled from a given distribution by the GPSS processor.

10.11.1 Sampling from a Uniform Distribution

A uniform distribution in GPSS is given by the formula $A \pm B$, where A is the mean and B is the standard deviation of the distribution. In order to select a specific value from this distribution, GPSS uses random numbers. Thus, the following sequence of actions takes place:

1. The GPSS processor uses *any one* of the eight available sources of random numbers labeled RN1, RN2, . . . , RN8. They are analogous to random number tables.

2. The GPSS processor picks the next available value from the random number source selected, say RN5.

3. The value sampled from the distribution is given by the formula

$$INT(A-B+RN5(2B+1))$$

where INT(X) means the integer portion of the real number X.

4. Finally, GPSS processor adds the value obtained in step 3 to the current value of the simulated clock to determine the next transaction's arrival time or service time.

10.11.2 Sampling from a Nonuniform Distribution

Two possibilities arise here depending on whether the distribution is given by a discrete function or by a continuous function.

Case 1. Discrete Function.   Here the random variable can take only a finite number of values. In order to sample from a nonuniform discrete distribution, the analyst performs the following sequence of actions:

1. Prepare a table with four columns:
   Column 1: Distinct values of the variable
   Column 2: Relative frequency values
   Column 3: Cumulative frequency values
   Column 4: Cumulative frequency intervals

2. Select a random number from a source RN1 through RN8. Suppose he uses RN2 as the source.

3. Determine from column 4 the cumulative frequency interval to which the random number RN2 belongs.

4. Determine the corresponding value of the random variable from column 1.

5. Add the value in column 4 to the current value of the simulated clock to determine the next arrival or service time.

This procedure is implemented by means of discrete GPSS functions. However, a detailed discussion of that concept is beyond the scope of this chapter. The interested reader should consult Schriber's book ([3], Chapter 3).

Case 2. Continuous Function.   Here the random variable can take any value in a continuous interval. The same principle applies as with discrete functions. However, linear interpolation is used between the endpoints of each cumulative frequency interval to select a specific value of the variable. A random number is used from RN1 to RN8 to perform the linear interpolation. For more details the reader should refer to Schriber ([3], Chapter 3).

Finally, suppose that the distribution is given by a formula (e.g., exponential, Poisson, normal). In general, GPSS cannot handle this situation, and so some other high-level language, such as FORTRAN or PL/I must be used. However, IBM developed an approximation function XPDIS to approximate the exponential distribution by a discrete table ([3], p. 164). An analyst who wants to use any other formula (say, normal distribution) has to prepare a table manually beforehand giving the probability corresponding to a random variable value.

10.12 SUMMARY

This chapter provides a brief introduction to the GPSS simulation language. A simulation language is similar to any high-level programming language such as FORTRAN or PASCAL, but it has a built-in capability of collecting statistics from the simulation run. Consequently, the user need not write separate routines to gather relevant statistics.

As a simulation language, GPSS (General Purpose Simulation System) handles discrete system simulations, preferably event-oriented. It has a block structure and the simulation proceeds by advancing each event through the successive blocks in the program. Statements are executed sequentially unless a conditional or unconditional transfer of control occurs. The flow of the model starts with a GENERATE block that simulates the arrival of an event, and then the flow proceeds through the model until it is terminated at a TERMINATE block. During the execution an event can SEIZE a facility and then RELEASE it, ENTER a storage and then LEAVE it, be placed in a QUEUE and then DEPART the queue. A block diagram of a GPSS program takes the place of a program flowchart.

Each GPSS block has three attributes: location, operation, and operand. A brief description of each of these terms is provided in the chapter. Then the chapter discusses the following principal blocks used in a GPSS program: GENERATE, TERMINATE, SEIZE, RELEASE, ENTER, LEAVE, ADVANCE, QUEUE, DEPART, MARK, TABULATE, TRANSFER. Next, we discuss the five control statements SIMULATE, START, END, RESET, and CLEAR.

In order to illustrate the use of GPSS, we next describe two programs that use most of the block statements described above. Relevant comments are made to analyze the program output of each program. A brief description of the internal logic of the GPSS processor then follows. Some comments are made regarding more complex types of GPSS models.

The last three sections of this chapter discuss the sampling process for a uniform or a nonuniform probability distribution. The basic tool used in such samplings is the random number generator. This introduces a stochastic element into a GPSS program, which is necessary because GPSS has to simulate the arrival time, service time, and departure time of each event from a frequency distribution provided by the user who runs the simulation.

10.13 KEY WORDS

The following key words are used in this chapter:

absolute clock
ADVANCE
block
block diagram
CLEAR
clock-update phase
continuous function
control statement
current events chain (CEC)
DEPART
discrete function
END
ENTER
facility
future events chain (FEC)
GENERATE
GPSS (General Purpose
  System Simulation)
input phase
LEAVE
location
MARK

nonuniform distribution
operand
operation
optimizing model
probability distribution
QUEUE
relative clock
RELEASE
RESET
scan phase
SEIZE
SIMULATE
simulation language
START
storage
TABULATE
TERMINATE
transaction
TRANSFER
transfer mode
uniform distribution

REFERENCES

1. W.G. Bulgren, *Discrete System Simulation,* Prentice-Hall, Englewood Cliffs, NJ, 1982.
2. G. Gordon, *System Simulation,* Prentice-Hall, Englewood Cliffs, NJ, 1978.
3. T.J. Schriber, *Simulation Using GPSS,* Wiley, New York, 1974.
4. K.D. Tocher, "Review of Simulation Languages," *Operational Research Quarterly,* **16,** 189–217 (1965).

REVIEW QUESTIONS

1. What is a simulation language? What are its advantages over a high-level language in programming a simulation model?
2. Describe the basic structure of a GPSS program.

3. Define a block in GPSS. How is the flow of logic represented by a block diagram?

4. Explain the difference between an absolute clock and a relative clock in a GPSS program.

5. What are the three attributes of a GPSS block?

6. Discuss the possible meanings of operands A through G of a GEN-ERATE block.

7. What is the difference between a facility and a storage?

8. How does a GPSS program implement the simulation of arrival times and service times?

9. How does a GPSS program handle conditional and unconditional branchings?

10. What is the function of GPSS control statements?

11. Explain the terms: current events chain and future events chain.

12. How does GPSS sample from a uniform distribution?

FORMULATION PROBLEMS

1. During the morning rush hours (6:30 to 9:00 a.m.), both AMTRAK passenger trains and B&M commuter rail trains arrive at Boston's South Station at a rate of one every 28 ± 9 minutes. AMTRAK trains arrive at track category A, while B&M trains arrive at track category B. Of the total number of trains arriving between 6:30 and 9:00 a.m., 85% are B&M while 15% are AMTRAK. A single signal determines whether the appropriate track category is available for a train, and on that basis it either halts the train or lets it go. The signal takes 2 minutes to process each train. Simulate the model for 20 trains.

2. Customers arrive at a bank and are served by tellers according to the following schedule:

9:00 to 11:00 a.m.: Arrival at the rate of one every 10 ± 4 minutes; service by two tellers, each taking 6 ± 2 minutes.

11:00 a.m. to 2:00 p.m.: Arrival at the rate of one every 5 ± 2 minutes; service by four tellers, each taking 4 ± 1 minutes.

2:00 to 4:00 p.m.: same as for 9:00 to 11:00 a.m.

a. Simulate the system for 500 customers.

b. Suppose that the management wants no customer to wait for more than 3 minutes and no teller to be idle for more than 15% of the time. Does your model meet either of these specifications?

11

Primer on DYNAMO II

11.1 CONTINUOUS SYSTEM SIMULATION LANGUAGE

We have seen in Chapter 9 that continuous system simulation deals primarily with feedback systems that involve the principle of system dynamics. A system dynamics model characterizes a feedback loop by means of two types of variables: *level* or state variables and *rate* or action variables. Continuous models are useful when the behavior of the system depends more on aggregate flows than upon the occurrence of discrete events. When the top management of a company is involved in long-range corporate planning, events are aggregated into a continuous flow and then their impact upon the future behavior of the company is studied. Such systems exhibit special characteristics that cannot be examined by studying the components of the system in isolation.

A simulation language that can describe a continuous system must have all the characteristics that are unique to a continuous system. Consequently, the language must be capable of representing the level and rate variables, both of which are essential for a continuous system characterization. While several programming languages are currently available to simulate a continuous system, the language DYNAMO was developed especially for system dynamics models. In this chapter we shall discuss the primary characteristics of DYNAMO with some suitable examples.

11.2 FEATURES OF DYNAMO

In 1959 Phyllis Fox and Alexander L. Pugh III introduced the continuous simulation language DYNAMO. It was successfully used to study business, social, economic, biological, psychological, and engineering systems, to name but a few. Subsequently, in 1965 DYNAMO was revised and updated to

DYNAMO II. Error analysis in DYNAMO II is thorough, and error messages are expressed in user-friendly form.

A model written in DYNAMO is a view of a feedback system as if it were *continuous* over time. DYNAMO chops up time into tiny but discrete intervals. Within each interval it is assumed that the varying rates are constant. Thus, the continuous process is approximated by successive discrete steps. This is analogous to solving a differential equation by finite difference methods or replacing the integration process by successive summations. The name DYNAMO stands for DYNAmic MOdeling.

To simulate the passage of time, DYNAMO uses the letters J, K, L to refer to three instants:

$$J = \text{past instant}$$
$$K = \text{present instant}$$
$$L = \text{future instant}$$

The increment in time is denoted by DT so that

$$DT = \text{constant interval of time from J to K,}$$
$$\text{or from K to L (these are equal)}$$
$$= \text{length of interval JK or KL}$$

Any quantity is either a *constant* (e.g., DT) whose value does not change or a *variable* whose value changes with time and so is written with a time subscript J, K, L, JK, or KL. Also, DYNAMO accepts names of up to six characters, with the first character being alphabetic. No blanks are allowed.

11.3 EQUATION TYPES IN DYNAMO

There are seven types of equations in DYNAMO. Each equation type is characterized by a letter, which must be written in the DYNAMO code to indicate the type of the equation. The seven codes are:

$$L = \text{level equation}$$
$$R = \text{rate equation}$$
$$A = \text{auxiliary equation}$$
$$C = \text{equation assigning a value to a constant}$$
$$N = \text{equation assigning an initial value}$$
$$X = \text{equation continued from the previous line}$$
$$T = \text{equation assigning Y values in a table function}$$

We now explain each type of equation.

11.3.1 Level Equation

A variable that accumulates over time an inflow and/or an outflow is called a *level* variable, and the equation that computes the accumulation is called a *level equation*. Such equations are really the integral equations in DYNAMO.

A level equation is always written in the same form preceded by the letter L. Examples of such equations are

```
L    LEVEL.K=LEVEL.J+DT*(INFLOW.JK-OUTFLOW.JK)
L    INV.K=INV.J+DT*(ORDRCV.JK-SHPMNT.JK)
```

The label L must be followed by one or more blanks. However, no blanks are allowed in the main body of the equation.

The second equation above indicates that the inventory level at present equals the inventory level in the past *plus* the accumulation over time of the difference between ORDRCV = rate of receiving orders into inventory and SHPMNT = rate of shipping items from inventory.

11.3.2 Rate Equations

The variables representing inflows and outflows in level equations are computed in *rate equations*. An example of a rate equation is

```
R    ORDRS.KL=AVSHIP.K+(DSINV.K-INV.K)/TAI
```

where ORDERS = orders in units/month, AVSHIP = average shipments in units/month, DSINV = desired inventory in units, INV = actual inventory in units, and TAI = time to adjust inventory in months.

Rate equations have no standard format. However, the dimension must be the same on both sides of the equation. In conformity with the terminology of calculus, a rate equation computes some or all of the derivatives of a level. The subscript KL on the left-hand side indicates that the rate is computed from the present instant to the next instant. However, the right-hand side of a rate equation can contain different variables depending on the model being simulated.

Since no single form applies to all rate equations, they are often difficult to write. The exact structure of a rate equation must be determined from the context of the problem. Some authors ([3], p. 80) claim that a major portion of the effort in formulating a continuous system simulation model is expended in writing the rate equations in their appropriate forms.

11.3.3 Auxiliary Equations

These equations, as their name implies, aid in the formulation of rate equations. It is often very difficult to write rate equations without doing some

prior computations to simplify the appearance of the rate equations. These additional algebraic computations in DYNAMO are termed *auxiliary equations,* and the variables appearing in them are called *auxiliaries.* Auxiliary equations have no standard format. However, auxiliaries are always computed in the present instant from the present values of other variables. Hence the subscript on the left side of an auxiliary equation is always K, and that on the right side is either K or, occasionally, JK.

As an example, let us consider the rate equation of Section 11.3.2.

```
R    ORDRS.KL=AVSHP.K+(DSINV.K-INV.K)/TAI
```

Here DSINV represents the desired inventory in some unit. But DSINV is itself determined by another rate variable AVSALE. Hence we use the auxiliary equation

```
A    DSNV.K=DIC*AVSALE.K
```

where DIC = desired inventory coverage in number of weeks and AVSALE = average sales rate in units/week.

11.3.4 Constant Equations

An entity in a DYNAMO model is either a *variable* or a *constant.* The value of a variable can change in the model, but the value of a constant never changes. As a result, a variable is always written with a subscript J, K, JK, or KL, whereas a constant does not have any subscript.

An equation assigning a value to a constant is written as follows:

```
C    DIC=4        (see Section 11.3.3)
C    TEMP=32
```

The letter C on the left side shows that the equation assigns a fixed value to a constant.

11.3.5 Initial Value Equations

An equation with label N assigns an initial value to a level variable, that is, a variable used in an L equation. All level variables in a model must be assigned initial values, so that for each L equation there must be an N equation. Variables in an N equation appear without such timescripts as J, K, L, JK, or KL. An N equation may assign a constant value to a level variable or may involve auxiliaries and rates on the right as well as constants. DYNAMO will work through these equations and computations in the model to determine the initial value. If it eventually finds that not enough information

about constants and initial values has been provided in the model, it will say so in an error message.

For example, consider the following program segment:

```
L    INV.K=INV.J+DT*(ORDRCV.JK-SHPMTS.JK)
N    INV=1000
```

This can be replaced by

```
L    INV.K=INV.J+DT*(ORDRCV.JK-SHPMTS.JK)
N    INV=DIC*AVSHIP
C    DIC=4
A    AVSHIP=TOTORD*NWKS
C    TOTORD=2500
C    NWKS=10
```

N equations can also be used to calculate the value of a constant, which need not be the initial value of any level variable.

11.3.6 Continuation of Equations

As noted in Section 11.3.1, DYNAMO allows no blanks in any equation. The character indicating the equation type (e.g., A, or L, or R) is followed by one or more blanks. But once an equation starts, no blanks are permitted. Also, the equation must not be written beyond column 72. An equation requiring more space is continued to the next line by using a letter X in the left column. For example,

```
L  CITPOP.K=CITPOP.J+DT*(BRTHS.JK-DTHS.JK+
X                        INMIG.JK-OUTMIG.JK)
```

The break in the equation can be made anywhere, but it is good practice to break right after an arithmetic operator.

11.3.7 Table Functions

An auxiliary (see Section 11.3.3) in a DYNAMO program need not be an algebraic function involving other variables in the model. Sometimes an auxiliary is expressed in the form of a two-dimensional table consisting of ordered pairs (x,y) such that each y value represents the value of the auxiliary corresponding to an x value from the table. Such a tabular relationship is expressed by means of the TABLE function and table equations. The latter are always labeled with the letter T on the left side.

As an example, suppose that the annual profits of a company over a 5-year period are given by the following table:

Year (X)	PROFIT (Y) (in millions)
1	20
2	25
3	27
4	32
5	38

We can represent the auxiliary PROFIT.K by the following auxiliary equation using the TABLE function:

```
A    PROFIT.K=TABLE(TPRFT,YEAR.K,1,5,1)
```

Here TPRFT is the name of the table giving the five annual values of PROFIT corresponding to the five values 1, . . ., 5 of YEAR. The entries 1,5,1 appearing within parentheses represent the minimum value, the maximum value, and the increment between two consecutive values of YEAR.

The actual table is then represented as follows:

```
T    TPRFT=20,25,27,32,38
```

The TABLE function has the format TABLE (-,-,-,-,-) where the five dashes represent five arguments of the function:

$$\text{First argument} = \text{name of the } y \text{ variable in the table}$$
$$\text{Second argument} = \text{name of the } x \text{ variable in the table}$$
$$\text{Third argument} = \text{minimum } x \text{ value}$$
$$\text{Fourth argument} = \text{maximum } x \text{ value}$$
$$\text{Fifth argument} = \text{increment of the } x \text{ values}$$

The T equation completes the specification of the table by giving in order the y values of the successive specified points on the graph, beginning with the y value corresponding to the minimum x value and ending with the y value for the maximum x value. A y value between two consecutive table entries for y is computed by linear interpolation.

To summarize, an auxiliary variable can be specified in a table function by using the following format:

```
A  var.K=TABLE (y-value name, x-value name, min-x,
              max-x, x-increment)
T  y-value name=y₁, y₂, · · · yₙ
```

where $y_1, y_2, \ldots, y_n$ are the values of y in the table.

If "TABLE" is used, DYNAMO notes every time the input value leaves or returns to the specified range. The compiler prints messages to that effect before showing the results of a simulation. The messages about table overruns are for information only. DYNAMO goes ahead and computes in spite of them. If the input value is above the maximum specified, the last y value listed in the table is used. If the input is less than the minimum specified, the first y value is used.

11.4 SYMBOLS FOR FLOW DIAGRAMS IN DYNAMO II

In Section 9.3 we discussed a set of flow diagram symbols used in system dynamics (see Fig. 9-1). Since DYNAMO II implements any system dynamics model, it uses the same symbols in its own flow diagrams. Figure 11-1 shows the additional symbols used in DYNAMO II that were not included in Figure 9-1.

11.5 EXAMPLE OF A DYNAMO II PROGRAM

Now that we have introduced the basic features of DYNAMO II, let us illustrate the capabilities of the language by means of an example.

In Section 5.9.1 we introduced the concept of postcensal population, the estimated population figure based on the most recent census data and the annual rates of births and deaths. The formula for population in year $t + 1$ can be written as follows:

Population in year $t + 1$
  $=$ population in year t
  $+$ total number of births between years t and $t + 1$
  $-$ total number of deaths between years t and $t + 1$

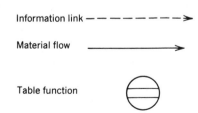

FIGURE 11-1 Flow diagram symbols in DYNAMO II.

The program fragment written in DYNAMO II to simulate the above formula is as follows:

```
L POP.K=POP.J+DT*(BFREQ.JK-DFREQ.JK)
NOTE      BFREQ IS FREQUENCY OF BIRTHS
R BFREQ.KL=BIRTHS.K/YR
NOTE        DFREQ IS FREQUENCY OF DEATHS
R DFREQ.KL=DEATHS.K/YR
L YEAR.K=YEAR.J+DT*YR
A BIRTHS.K=TABLE(TFB,YEAR.K,1,9,1)
T TFB=100,200,300,400,500,600,700,800,900
A DEATHS.K=TABLE(TFD,YEAR.K,1,9,1)
T TFD=10,20,30,40,50,60,70,80,90
NOTE      MODEL STARTS WITH AN INITIAL POPULATION OF
NOTE        100,000
N POP=100000
N YR=1
N YEAR=1
```

The first equation is a level equation and so is labeled L. It describes the population in terms of two rate variables BFREQ and DFREQ, which are given by two rate equations each labeled R. The two auxiliaries are BIRTHS and DEATHS defined by the seventh and ninth equations. Both of them use the TABLE function. The two tables, TFB (table for BIRTHS) and TFD (table for DEATHS), are given by the eighth and tenth equations. The entries of the two tables are given in Table 11-1. The model starts with an initial value of 100,000 for the variable POP. If we assume that DT = 1, then the values of POP corresponding to time 0,1,. . ., 9 are computed by the model as illustrated in Table 11-2.

A flow diagram for this model is shown in Figure 11-2.

TABLE 11-1

Year	TFB	TFD
1	100	10
2	200	20
3	300	30
4	400	40
5	500	50
6	600	60
7	700	70
8	800	80
9	900	90

TABLE 11-2. Sample Output of Population Simulation

Time	POP
0	100000
1	$100000 + 1*(100 - 10) = 100090$
2	$100090 + 1*(200 - 20) = 100270$
3	$100270 + 1*(300 - 30) = 100540$
4	$100540 + 1*(400 - 40) = 100900$
5	$100900 + 1*(500 - 50) = 101350$
6	$101350 + 1*(600 - 60) = 101890$
7	$101890 + 1*(700 - 70) = 102520$
8	$102520 + 1*(800 - 80) = 103240$
9	$103240 + 1*(900 - 90) = 104050$

11.6 RUNNING PROGRAMS AND OBTAINING OUTPUT IN DYNAMO II

Once a continuous simulation model is formulated conceptually and then programmed in DYNAMO II, we need a few control statements to run the model and get output. The three essential statements are SPEC, PRINT, and PLOT. Also, each DYNAMO statement must start in column 1.

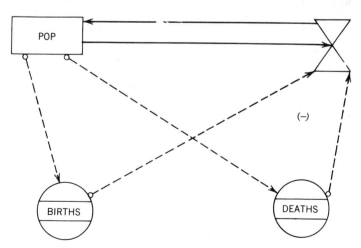

FIGURE 11-2 Flow diagram of population simulation.

11.6.1   SPEC Statement

In the SPEC statement, values are assigned to DT, LENGTH, PRTPER, and PLTPER, where

DT is the computation interval or solution interval. Normally take DT between one-half and one-tenth of the smallest time constant in your model.

LENGTH is the time instant when simulation should stop (similar to the A operand of START in GPSS).

PRTPER is the print period representing the time interval between successive prints of numerical output from the simulation. Unless told otherwise, DYNAMO assumes PRTPER to be zero. Whenever PRTPER has a nonzero value, a PRINT statement should be included specifying what quantities are to be printed.

PLTPER is the plot period representing the time interval between successive points plotted on the graphical output from the simulation. If PLTPER is nonzero, then it must be accompanied by a PLOT statement specifying what quantities are to be plotted.

11.6.2   PRINT and PLOT Statements

The PRINT statement lists the variable names, separated by commas, whose values are to be printed in the output in tabular form. The PLOT statement names the variables to be plotted together on a single graph. As an example, let us consider the following control statements.

```
SPEC    DT=0.5,LENGTH=100,PRTPER=10,PLTPER=2
PRINT   INV,ORDCRV,SHPMTS,AVSALE
PLOT    INV=I/ORDRCV=0,SHPMTS=S/AVSALE=+
```

Here we want to simulate the model in every half time unit up to a total of 100 time units; in all, 200 iterations of the model are made. However, in the tabular printout only 10 sets of values of the variables INV, ORDRCV, SHPMTS, and AVSALE are printed, since PRTPER is taken as 10 and the total simulation time is 100.

Slashes in the PLOT statement indicate a separate scale for plotting the variables. Thus INV will be plotted in one scale using the letter I; ORDRCV and SHPMTS will be plotted in a different scale, and so on. However, in this chapter we shall not discuss graphical output and hence we shall make no use of PLOT statements.

In order to run the program in Section 11.5 we need the following control statements:

```
SPEC    DT=1.0,LENGTH=10,PRTPER=1
PRINT   POP
```

We now introduce three additional statements that are useful in running DYNAMO II models.

11.6.3 NOTE Statement

This statement is used for comments and documentation purposes. Examples are:

```
NOTE
NOTE            **INVENTORY   MODEL**
```

11.6.4 RUN and RERUN Statements

Identifying individual simulation runs is made possible by the RUN statement. Thus, a statement

```
RUN  BASE  SIMULATION
```

appearing after the SPEC, PRINT, and PLOT statements in the source listing will cause the first simulation results to be labeled with the phrase BASE SIMULATION. This heading will be automatically dropped for subsequent runs of the model.

After the model is run for the first time, DYNAMO II shifts into rerun mode, and produces the prompt

```
TYPE RERUN
```

The user can then change any constants or tables appearing in the model. If no reruns are needed, the user types QUIT and thus returns to the computer's operating system.

The RUN statement is the last statement of the model and is used to identify the run. It must be used if the results are being saved for later comparisons and reruns.

11.7 SAMPLE DYNAMO II PROGRAM

Now that we have discussed the DYNAMO II program statements, let us write a complete program. Using the example of Section 11.5 with appropriate control statements, we obtain the program given in Figure 11-3. Note that the output for POP is identical with that given in Section 11.5.

```
PAGE 1          POSTCENSAL POPULATION ESTIMATE      1/10/85 15:21
                * POSTCENSAL POPULATION ESTIMATE
                NOTE        RECURSION EQUATION FOR VARIABLE POP
                L POP.K=POP.J+DT*(BFREQ.JK-DFREQ.JK)
                NOTE        BFREQ IS FREQUENCY OF BIRTHS
                R BFREQ.KL=BIRTHS.K/YR
                NOTE        DFREQ IS FREQUENCY OF DEATHS
                R DFREQ.KL=DEATHS.K/YR
                L YEAR.K=YEAR.J+DT*YR
                A BIRTHS.K=TABLE(TFB,YEAR.K,1,9,1)
                T TFB=100,200,300,400,500,600,700,800,900
                A DEATHS.K=TABLE(TFD,YEAR.K,1,9,1)
                T TFD=10,20,30,40,50,60,70,80,90
                NOTE        MODEL STARTS WITH AN INITIAL POPULATION OF
                NOTE        100,000
                N POP=100000
                N YR=1
                N YEAR=1
                PRINT POP,BFREQ,DFREQ,BIRTHS,DEATHS,YEAR
                SPEC DT=1.0/LENGTH=9/PRTPER=1
                RUN BASE SIMULATION
       ABOVE TFD,  TIME=9.
       ABOVE TFB,  TIME=9.
       PAGE  2        POSTCENSAL  POPULATION  ESTIMATE   1/10/85
       15:21    BASE SIMULATION
          TIME      POP     BFREQ     DFREQ    BIRTHS      DEATHS      YEAR
          E+00      E+03     E+00      E+00      E+00        E+00      E+00
           .0     100.00   100.00    10.000    100.00      10.000    1.000
           1.     100.09   200.00    20.000    200.00      20.000    2.000
           2.     100.27   300.00    30.000    300.00      30.000    3.000
           3.     100.54   400.00    40.000    400.00      40.000    4.000
           4.     100.90   500.00    50.000    500.00      50.000    5.000
           5.     101.35   600.00    60.000    600.00      60.000    6.000
           6.     101.89   700.00    70.000    700.00      70.000    7.000
           7.     102.52   800.00    80.000    800.00      80.000    8.000
           8.     103.24   900.00    90.000    900.00      90.000    9.000
           9.     104.05   900.00    90.000    900.00      90.000   10.000
```

FIGURE 11-3 Sample DYNAMO II program.

11.8   SUMMARY

This chapter discusses DYNAMO II, an updated version of the DYNAMO (for DYNAmic MOdeling) which is a programming language introduced in 1959 for implementing continuous system simulation models. It represents three instants of time—past, present, and future—by the three letters J, K, and L, respectively. The time increment is denoted by DT, which measures the length of time from J to K or from K to L.

A continuous system involves two basic types of variables: level and rate. In order to simulate this situation, DYNAMO uses seven types of equations: level, rate, auxiliary, constant, initial value, continuation, and table functions. A TABLE function enables the user to input the entries of a two-dimensional table as pairs of (x,y) values. The minimum, maximum, and increment of the x values define the domain of the table, and the corresponding y values then span the range of the table.

DYNAMO II uses the same flow diagram symbols as a continuous simulation model. These symbols are utilized to draw a flow diagram for a given problem.

As an example of a DYNAMO II program the chapter simulates the postcensal population estimation problem using two TABLE functions. Finally it discusses a set of six control statements that are needed to run programs and produce output.

The chapter does not discuss graphic output of a DYNAMO II program.

11.9   KEY WORDS

The following key words are used in this chapter:

auxiliary equation	level equation
constant	rate equation
continuous system simulation	system dynamics
control statement	table function
DYNAMO	variable

REFERENCES

1. G. Gordon, *System Simulation*, Prentice-Hall, Englewood Cliffs, NJ, 1978.
2. A.L. Pugh, III, *DYNAMO Users Manual*, MIT Press, Cambridge, MA, 1980.
3. G.P. Richardson and A.L. Pugh, III, *Introduction to System Dynamics Modeling with DYNAMO*, MIT Press, Cambridge, MA, 1981.

REVIEW QUESTIONS

1. Name and describe the two types of variables that characterize a feedback loop.
2. How does DYNAMO II represent three instants of time?
3. How does DYNAMO II distinguish a constant from a variable?
4. Describe the seven types of equations used in DYNAMO II.
5. What are the functions of SPEC and PRINT statements in DYNAMO II?
6. The source listing of a DYNAMO II program is as follows ([3]), p. 96):

```
SIMPLE EPIDEMIC MODEL
*NOTE
  L           SUSC.K=SUSC.J+DT*(-INF.JK)
  N           SUSC=988
  NOTE        SUSCEPTIBLE POPULATION (PEOPLE)
  R           INF.KL=SICK.K*CNTCTS.K*FRSICK
  NOTE        INFECTION RATE (PEOPLE PER DAY)
  C           FRSICK=0.05
  NOTE        FRACTION OF CONTACTS BECOMING SICK
  NOTE        (DIMENSIONLESS)
  L           SICK.K=SICK.J+DT*(INF.JK-CURE.JK)
  N           SICK=2
  NOTE        SICK POPULATION (PEOPLE)
  A           CNTCTS.K=TABLE(TABCON,
              SUSC.K/TOTAL,0,1,0.2)
  NOTE        SUSCEPTIBLE CONTACTED PER INFECTED
  NOTE        PERSON PER DAY (PEOPLE PER PERSON PER
              DAY)
  T           TABCON=0/2.8/5.5/8/9.5/10
  NOTE        TABLE FOR CNTCTS
  N           TOTAL=SUSC+SICK+RECOV
  NOTE        TOTAL POPULATION (PEOPLE)
  R           CURE.KL=SICK.K/DUR
  NOTE        CURE RATE (PEOPLE PER DAY)
  C           DUR=10
  NOTE        DURATION OF DISEASE (DAYS)
  L           RECOV.K=RECOG.J+DT*CURE.JK
  N           RECOV=10
  NOTE        RECOVERED POPULATION (PEOPLE)
  NOTE
  SPEC        DT=0.25, LENGTH=50, PRTPER=5, PLTPER=1
  PRINT       SUSC, SICK, RECOG, INF, CURF
  PLOT        SUSC=W, SICK=S, RECOV=R/INF=I,
              CURE=C(0,200)
```

Answer the following questions ([3], pp. 97–98):

a. What kind of variable is SICK? Why?

b. Why does INF.JK appear in the level equation for SUSC with a negative sign?

c. Why doesn't DUR have a timescript such as J or K?

d. What values of the variables SUSC, SICK, and RECOV are used to compute TOTAL?

e. How many people had already had this disease and recovered at the time the simulation began?

f. What is the computation interval in this model?

g. Why are there only two scales for the five plotted variables?

h. Why does INF have the timescript KL in the rate equation in which it is computed, but the timescript JK in the level equations where it is used?

i. Sketch the table function used in the auxiliary equation for CNTCTS.

7. The following problem is adapted from Richardson and Pugh ([3], pp. 69–73). A cup of coffee is placed in a room and is allowed to cool according to Newton's law of cooling:

Rate of change of coffee temperature
= (constant)* (room temperature − coffee temperature)

The following DYNAMO program implements this law and generates the associated table. Complete *all* the entries in the last *five* lines of the table. Show *all* your calculations.

```
L        COFFEE.K=COFFEE.J+(DT)*(CHNG.JK)
R        CHNG.KL=CONST*(ROOM-COFFEE.K)
C        ROOM=20
C        CONST=0.2
N        COFFEE=90
SPEC     DT=0.5,LENGTH=20,PRTPER=0.5
PRINT    COFFEE,ROOM,ROOM-COFFEE,CHNG
```

TIME	COFFEE	ROOM	ROOM-COFFEE	CHNG
0.0	90	20	-70	-14
0.5	83	20	-63	-12.6
1.0				
1.5				
2.0				
2.5				
3.0				

EXAMPLES AND CONTEMPORARY ISSUES OF DECISION SUPPORT SYSTEMS

Part IV describes some of the DSS packages used in actual practice and also examines some of the contemporary issues in DSS. Chapter 12 completes two case studies, IDSS and D/T DSS, that were introduced in Chapter 2. In addition, it discusses two more decision support systems: EXPRESS and BRANDAID. Chapter 13 explores three miniature DSS packages: The Executive Game, FINANSIM, and The Management Game, all of which are used as instruction tools. Chapter 14 continues this theme of building a DSS as a term project in a classroom environment. Finally, Chapter 15 examines two definitely discernible future trends in the DSS market: to include expert system features of artificial intelligence in DSS, and to develop microcomputer versions of mainframe DSS.

Decision Support Systems in Practice

12.1 Building a DSS: Plan for the Chapter

In Section 2.7 we discussed the five phases of a DSS building process. These processes are implemented through four basic modules (see Section 1.8): the control module, the data storage module, the model-building module, and the data manipulation module.

Parts II and III provided a digression into mathematical modeling and simulation techniques. These are essential for designing the model-building module. In this chapter we shall examine a series of examples and case studies of real-life decision support systems in order to show how the theoretical design process discussed earlier is carried into practice.

In Chapter 2 we introduced two case studies: the Investment Decision Support System (IDSS) and the Distribution/Transportation Decision Support System (D/T DSS). There we discussed the analysis phase of each DSS by describing the background and objectives and then outlining the overall plans. In this chapter we shall complete these two case studies by providing their technical design details, feedback control loops, and evaluation by management. Next, we shall discuss two DSS packages, one dealing with financial analysis and the other dealing with marketing strategy. Finally, we shall briefly mention a number of DSS packages available in the market.

12.2   IDSS: OVERVIEW OF SYSTEM DESIGN PHASE

In Section 2.14.5 we listed the overall functional capacitites of IDSS. The design phase is prepared for providing these capabilities. We feel that IDSS must provide support in four basic areas and thus contain the following subsystems:

Client portfolio information
Security selection analysis
Investment timing analysis
Portfolio analysis techniques

As a result, after its implementation IDSS functions will include maintaining well-organized investment information, reacting to unexpected short-term crises, spotting potentially rewarding investments, and comparing alternative investments.

Reports generated by the system will be designed either for the user or for his/her client. The following options are normally available: daily analysis and summary of client portfolio trends, weekly summary, monthly summary, annual summary, and user exception reports. The system will also generate graphics on both portfolio and other investment trends, computations analyzing expectations for future activity, financial reports on firms issuing securities in the database, and other helpful investment information.

We now discuss in more detail the four subsystems listed above and also indicate how they are incorporated into the four basic modules of any DSS. Figure 12-1 gives a system flowchart for the overview of IDSS.

12.3   IDSS: FOUR SUBSYSTEMS AND THE CONTROL MODULE

The first subsystem, client portfolio information, allows the investment manager to quickly retrieve information concerning a client's portfolio. This would be particularly useful when the user receives a call or an unexpected visit from one of his clients.

The second subsystem, security selection analysis, involves direct access to a substantial database of investment information. The types of information that will be made available to the portfolio manager will include investment price data, characteristics of the user, SEC 10K financial reports, and macroeconomic variables.

The third subsystem, investment timing analysis, deals with the user's need to estimate the trend of price fluctuations at future points in time.

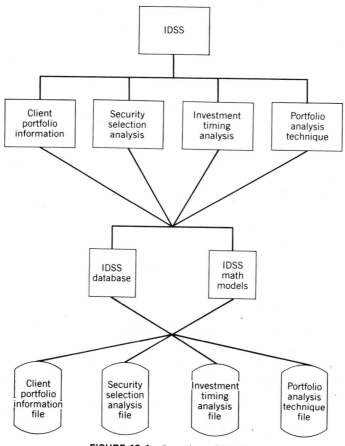

FIGURE 12-1   Overview of IDSS.

The fourth subsystem, portfolio analysis techniques, includes methods for looking at portfolios as a whole to determine the relationship between return on investment, risk, and diversification of the portfolio.

The four subsystems are implemented via the four component modules. The control module (CM) provides entry to IDSS and is menu-driven. It consists of five sample screens, the first of which is shown in Figure 12-2. The remaining four screens will be illustrated as we come to more detailed descriptions of the other subsystems.

The other three modules—data storage, model building, and data manipulation—support the functions provided by the screens of the control module. We shall discuss these modules after describing the four subsystems in more detail.

```
                            I D S S

                        M A I N   M E N U


IDSS can be used by management consultants and portfolio managers
to maximize efficiency in investment decision making. It is
suitable for both short- and long-term decision making. Avail-
able options are;


   1.   CLIENT PORTFOLIO INFORMATION
   2.   SECURITY SELECTION ANALYSIS
   3.   INVESTMENT TIMING ANALYSIS
   4.   PORTFOLIO ANALYSIS TECHNIQUES
   E    EXIT FROM SYSTEM
   H    HELP INFORMATION



SELECT OPTION AND PRESS RETURN KEY.
```
FIGURE 12-2   Screen for the main menu.

12.4 CLIENT PORTFOLIO INFORMATION

When a client calls a portfolio manager asking for an update on her portfolio, a problem sometimes arises in manual systems where the data have been changing rapidly and the maintenance of manual records is not as effective as it should be. This may result in the misplacement of papers, the inability to find the information, and a very embarrassing situation for the manager.

```
                            I D S S

                    CLIENT PORTFOLIO INFORMATION

                                        Investment Type
                                        Codes are

   CLIENT NAME ?                          1 - Common Stocks
   INVESTMENT TYPE CODE ?                 2 - Preferred Stocks
   EARNINGS PER SHARE REPORT (Y/N) ?      3 - Bonds
   DETAILED INVESTMENT REPORT (Y/N) ?     4 - Money Market
   NEWS REPORT (Y/N) ?                        Mutual Funds
   PRESS RETURN KEY .                     5 - Other Mutual Funds
                                          6 - Commercial Paper
                                          7 - Others
                                          8 - All Investments
```
FIGURE 12-3   Screen for client portfolio information.

CLIENT PORTFOLIO

INVESTMENT TYPE RESTRICTED TO: 1 - Common Stocks

CLIENT NAME: HARRY A. WHITE, (202) 567-9876

NAME	EPS	P/E Ratio	Earnings
U.S. Steel	$12.67	4.56	+12.0%
General Motors	$10.34	3.24	- 3.4%
IBM	$ 9.67	2.23	+ 2.3%
McGraw-Hill	$ 4.56	5.67	- 6.7%
LTV	$12.78	6.78	+ 4.5%
General Dynamics	$ 3.78	3.45	- 1.2%

FIGURE 12-4   EPS report.

To overcome this problem, the IDSS will enable the user to obtain a client portfolio report online at request. The portfolio report will list securities in the portfolio, annual yield on an updated basis, date purchased, and most recent price quotation from the stock market exchange on which the stock is traded.

Figure 12-3 shows the screen for the client portfolio information subsystem. Figures 12-4 and 12-5 give examples of an earnings-per-share report and a multipage detailed investment report, respectively. All the data used there are fictitious.

The news report option is a novel feature that provides additional information on a company if the user so desires. Such information may affect the company's stock price.

Figure 12-6 shows a sample news report for Pittsburgh Steel Production Company, a fictitious company. It represents a typical listing of 1982 news for the company. When first announced, the news of October 1, 1982, would be expected to have a positive influence on the stock price. The news of September 15, 1982, for example, is expected to have a negative influence on the stock price. Comparison of the actual results of these news items with their expected results can help the analyst in forecasting future change in price. The analyst can use historic news records of this type along with price trend information and graphic information to improve his analysis of changes in prices and yields.

Obviously, industrywide information is also very important to the stock analyst. The rate of change in durable goods orders, retail sales, GNP, interest rates, consumer prices, inventories, and other macroeconomic variable are necessary for effective investment analysis. Such information will also be available as part of the news function. This will include announcements such

CLIENT PORTFOLIO

PRIMARY KEY: INVESTMENT TYPE . . . . ASCENDING
SECONDARY KEY: CURRENT YIELD . . . . DESCENDING
NUMBER: ALL
INVESTMENT TYPE RESTRICTED TO: 1 - Common Stocks

Investment Type Code: 1, Common Stocks; 2, Preferred Stocks; 3,
Bonds; 4, Money Market Mutual Funds; 5, Other Mutual Funds 6,
Commercial Paper; 7, Other; 8, All Investments

CLIENT NAME: HARRY A. WHITE, (202) 567-9876.   Page 1.

NAME	VALUE	YIELD	PURCH.	PRICE	Pu. PRICE	NEWS
U.S. Steel	67,889.89	12.67	01/12/67	32.5	16.5	Y
General Motors	3,876.54	10.45	12/16/78	12.6	6.5	N
IBM	34,654.90	7.89	07/12/75	123.5	103.5	N
McGraw-Hill	3,456.98	7.56	12/06/79	34.7	23.6	N
LTV	12,432.98	7.43	08/07/80	21.0	16.5	N
General Dynamics	23,456.98	7.21	12/30/65	32.0	12.5	N
TOTAL						

Do You Want To See Page 2, Common Stocks(1) (Y or N)? Y

CLIENT NAME: HARRY A. WHITE, (202) 567-9876   PAGE 2.

NAME	SHARES	TRADING	
U.S. Steel	1000	9/23/82	$-^1{}_2$
General Motors	154	10/12/82	$+^1{}_2$
IBM	123	10/12/82	$+1^1{}_2$
McGraw-Hill	321	10/11/82	$-2^1{}_2$
LTV	200	10/10/82	$+^1{}_2$
General Dynamics	100	10/12/82	$+^1{}_2$

Do you want to see Page 3, Common Stocks(1) (Y or N)? N

FIGURE 12-5   Detailed investment report.

as: "New York, October 5, 1982. The National Association of Home Builders
announced today that sales of new homes declined by 5% in September.
. . ."

The sources of information on the news function can include the many
wire services and financial news organizations, including Dow-Jones,
Moody's, Standard and Poor, AP, UPI, and Barron's.

NEWS

PITTSBURGH STEEL PRODUCTION COMPANY

October 1, 1982 - PITTSBURGH, PA. (UPI) United Steelworkers President, Joe Bonanza, announced today that the threatened strike against the Pittsburgh Steel Production Company had been averted. He announced that agreement had been reached on a new contract which will go into effect on November 1, 1982.

September 15, 1982 - PITTSBURGH, PA(AP) Pittsburgh Steel Production President Sam Enterprise announced a 5% decline in second quarter profits for Pittsburgh Steel. Attributing the drop to a national recession, combined with foreign competition, he predicted a turnaround in the third quarter. Sales for the period fell 4%.

FIGURE 12-6 News report.

I D S S

SECURITY SELECTION ANALYSIS

NAME OF ISSUING FIRM   ?

SECURITY TYPE CODE   ?

CONSOLIDATED BALANCE SHEET (Y/N) ?

RATIO ANALYSIS REPORT (Y/N) ?

PRESS   RETURN   KEY.

Security Type Codes are

    1 - Common stocks
    2 - Preferred Stocks
    3 - Bonds
    4 - Money Market Mutual Funds
    5 - Other Mutual Funds
    6 - Commercial Paper
    7 - Others

FIGURE 12-7 Screen for security selection analysis.

PITTSBURGH STEEL PRODUCTION COMPANY

CONSOLIDATED BALANCE SHEET

BALANCE SHEET, CONSOLIDATED   DEC 31,

	1979	1980	1981
Cash	$ 12,378	$ 33,113	$ 44,144
Short-Term Investments, at cost	182,682	177,814	201,876
Accounts Receivable, Net	173,467	197,361	212,987
Inventories	186,866	204,151	215,987
Prepaid Expenses	59,358	60,496	65,987
TOTAL CURRENT ASSETS	614,751	672,935	786,987
Associated Companies, at equity	180,997	221,659	309,123
Other Investments, at cost	7,889	7,225	7,099
TOTAL INVESTMENTS	188,886	228,884	234,987
Land	15,430	15,768	16,098
Buildings	184,010	187,292	198,099
Equipment	691,760	784,534	805,987
Accumulated Depreciation	(488,958)	(521,702)	(554,877)
TOTAL PLANT AND EQUIPMENT	402,242	465,892	476,456
GOODWILL	8,899	8,006	8,988
OTHER ASSETS	9,663	9,446	9,766
TOTAL ASSETS	$1,224,441	$1,385,163	$1,453,899

306

Loans Payable	24,877	55,217	56,788
Accounts Payable	55,210	79,163	79,988
Taxes on Income Payable	36,579	65,895	67,988
Wages and Employee Benefits Accrued	62,364	66,930	67,988
Other Accrued Liabilities	49,405	66,636	68,766
Advance Payments on Long-Term Contracts	9,553	528	654
TOTAL CURRENT LIABILITIES	237,988	334,369	342,765
Accrued Repairs on Equipment	26,560	19,630	15,767
Other Liabilities and Deferred Credits	17,334	27,971	29,734
Loans Payable Beyond One Year	163,398	147,146	154,723
Deferred Investment Credit	34,596	23,020	22,143
and Income Taxes	2,848	5,063	5,145
Minority Interest in Subsidiaries	2,848	5,063	4,231
TOTAL LIABILITIES			
Common Stock, 25,000,000 shares			
Par $5 per share	100,281	95,956	97,788
Retained Earnings	641,436	732,008	765,121
TOTAL COMMON STOCKHOLDERS EQUITY	741,717	827,964	876,876
LIABILITIES AND STOCKHOLDERS EQUITY	$1,224,441	$1,385,163	$1,434,786

FIGURE 12-8 Consolidated balance sheet.

RATIO ANALYSIS OF SELECTED STOCKS OR BONDS

Security Type: Common Stock   Issuer: Pittsburgh Steel Pro-
                                        duction Company

Ratio Analysis:

		1970	1980	1981
1.	Market Price	$ 89.76	$ 95.78	$ 94.67
2.	Earnings Per Share	3.78	4.12	4.23
3.	Price/Earnings Ratio	5.89	6.78	5.89
4.	Yield	9.80%	10.34%	8.78
5.	Return on Owner's Investment	8.90	9.76	8.76
6.	Return on Total Invest.	8.56	9.56	8.54
7.	Financial Leverage	6.78	7.89	7.99
8.	Profit Margin	9.66	10.32	10.45
9.	Working Capital Ratio	3.45	5.76	5.34
10.	Quick Ratio (Acid Test)	3.32	4.67	4.45
11.	Receivable Turnover	32.75	35.87	32.56
12.	Ave. Age of Receivable	12.45	15.78	15.89
13.	Inventory Turnover	3.67	4.67	4.45
14.	Debt/Equity Ratio	3.67	4.56	4.87
15.	Owner/Total Equity	7.89	8.97	8.87
16.	Creditor/Total Equity	8.95	9.76	9.95
17.	Dividend Yield Ratio	1.32	3.45	3.24
18.	Book Value per Share	$456.78	$567.89	$495.67
19.	Net Worth	$ 12.67M	$ 13.56M	12.78M
20.	Days Sales Uncollected, Annual % Change in	34.56	42.67	32.87
21.	Assets	7.85	8.97	7.86
22.	Liabilities	6.89	7.98	6.89
23.	Owner's Equity	2.34	3.45	3.21
24.	Current Assets	7.98	8.97	7.89
25.	Fixed Assets	6.78	7.89	6.98
26.	Long-Term Liabilities	4.56	5.67	4.32
27.	Sales (Revenues)	9.78	10.34	9.65
28.	Cost of Goods Sold	3.45	4.56	4.78
29.	Net Income	5.67	6.78	5.32
30.	Expenses	4.32	5.78	4.56

FIGURE 12-9 Ratio analysis report.

12.5 SECURITY SELECTION ANALYSIS

The security selection analysis subsystem will enable the user to see historical information available in the database and to analyze the financial statements of firms that may be potential investments. The types of data that will be extracted, computed, and displayed include corporate financial statements, historical security prices and dividends, and interest rate information. It will also include a company news file that can retract corporate information from the news services and display it on request.

In order to generate the reports requested by the user, this subsystem allows access to corporate financial reports that have been obtained from the Securities and Exchange Commission 10K reports. These must be made public by the firm if its shares are traded publicly. Private corporations do not need to reveal this information.

Figure 12-7 shows the screen for this subsystem. Figures 12-8 and 12-9 show two sample reports generated by this subsystem.

12.6   INVESTMENT TIMING ANALYSIS

This subsystem involves heavy interfacing with mathematical modeling. An important area of need for analysis by investment managers is the timing of future upward and downward swings in the stock market. Investors can make money whether securities rise, fall, or remain unchanged if they can predict those changes accurately. This is done by buying stocks low and selling high in a rising market, selling short in a falling market, and buying financial futures in a flat market. For these reasons, the prediction of future trends is very important for portfolio managers. This subsystem involves a forecasting element, graphic techniques, and breadth-of-market analysis.

Figure 12-10 shows the screen for accessing the investment timing analysis subsystem. Since this subsystem is highly mathematical, its components are discussed in more detail with the model-building module. Consequently, no sample reports are shown here.

```
                              I D S S

                    INVESTMENT TIMING ANALYSIS


You can access the model-building module through this subsystem.
Available mathematical models are

1 - LONG RANGE FORECASTING
2 - SHORE RANGE FORECASTING
3 - GRAPHICS
4 - BREADTH OF MARKET ANALYSIS


SELECT YOUR OPTION AND PRESS RETURN KEY.
```
Figure 12-10   Screen for investment timing analysis.

12.7   PORTFOLIO ANALYSIS TECHNIQUES

This subsystem examines the relationship between the risk and return of a portfolio as a whole. As such it analyzes the trade-off issues involved in maximizing the portfolio returns. Like the investment timing analysis subsystem, this subsystem is heavily mathematical. Figure 12-11 shows the screen for this subsystem. Its options are discussed in more detail with the model-building module, and no sample reports are shown here.

While both investment timing analysis and portfolio analysis techniques subsystems are limited to the model-building module, the emphasis of the former is on nonoptimizing statistical models, while that of the latter is on the optimizing mathematical models.

12.8   IDSS: DATA STORAGE MODULE

The data storage module of IDSS contains the necessary data to support all four subsystems of IDSS. It is implemented by using a relational DBMS package, preferably ORACLE, with a user-friendly query language, a report writer, and a graphics package.

The module contains four major files corresponding to the four subsystems. We describe here the basic contents of each file but make no attempt to convert them into a set of appropriate relations for a database. The actual database design should be undertaken after a DBMS package is procured.

12.8.1   Client Portfolio Information

The master file here is used by a manager to view all of his/her clients' accounts at once. Its major data elements are:

☐ Account number.
☐ Portfolio return rate.

I D S S

PORTFOLIO ANALYSIS TECHNIQUES

You can access the model-building module through this subsystem.
Available mathematical models are

1 - CAPITAL ASSET PRICING
2 - INVESTMENT RISK AND RETURN

SELECT YOUR OPTION AND PRESS RETURN KEY.

FIGURE 12-11   Screen for portfolio analysis techniques.

☐ Risk level of portfolio.

☐ Clients' objective (manager's numeric code to indicate client's preferences, if any).

☐ News (used to store any verbiage that the client or portfolio manager finds necessary).

12.8.2 Security Selection Analysis

The security file will be the largest file in our database. It will keep current as well as historical data for each of the securities in the DSS. (Note: Historical data will be stored by date.)

Current data elements:

☐ Name of security
☐ Current market price/per hour
☐ Risk level of security

Historical data elements:

☐ Closing market price/day (available from Dow Jones Reporting Service or Standard and Poor's 500 Stock Price Index).

☐ Price/earnings ratio per/day (available from Dow Jones or S&P 500).

☐ Earnings/share/day [calculated as (market price) / (P/E)].

☐ Balance sheet information (e.g., sales) (available from Securities and Exchange Commission).

☐ Income statement information (e.g., earnings, dividends) (available from Securities and Exchange Commission).

☐ Number of shares traded at an increasing/decreasing/unchanging price (available from the New York Stock Exchange).

12.8.3 Investment Timing Analysis

Several smaller files will be set up and stored by date:

☐ The GNP file will receive its information from the U.S. Department of Commerce.

☐ Business indicators (leading, coincident, lagging) will be obtained from the National Bureau of Economic Research.

☐ Interest rates including treasury notes and prime interest rates will be obtained from the Federal Reserve Bank.

☐ The Federal Reserve Bank will also supply the information of money supply

☐ The consumer price index (CPI) is received from the Department of Labor.
☐ The GNP deflator is obtained through the Department of Commerce.

12.8.4 Portfolio Analysis Technique

Each portfolio client will have his/her own file. Included in each file will be securities information relative to that file only.

☐ Account number.
☐ Security name.
☐ Current price/earnings, (P/E) ratio (see securities file).
☐ Current market price (see securities file).
☐ Current estimate earnings/share (see securities file).
☐ Highest P/E ratio to date.*
☐ Lowest P/E ratio to date.*
☐ Yield on dividend (see securities file).
☐ Individual securities data:
  Security name
  Rate of return on security
  Date purchased
  Original cost
  Number of shares

12.9 IDSS: MODEL-BUILDING MODULE

IDSS uses two types of models: statistical nonoptimizing models and optimizing mathematical models. The former is used in the investment timing analysis subsystem and consists of the following tools:

☐ Forecasting: both short-range and long-range.
☐ Graphics: economic indicators graphing and point-and-figure charting.
☐ Breadth-of-market technique.

The optimizing mathematical model is used in the portfolio analysis technique subsystem and consists of two types of tools:

☐ Capital asset pricing.
☐ Investment risk and return.

We now discuss each item separately.

*Calculated: Every night the closing P/E ratio is compared to the current high/low. Will be updated if necessary.

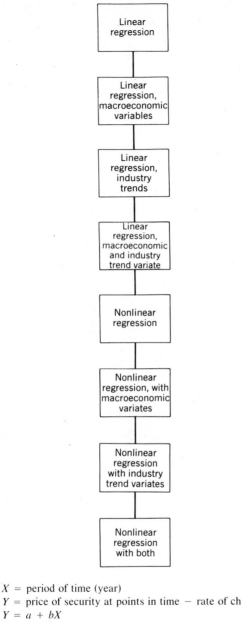

X = period of time (year)
Y = price of security at points in time $-$ rate of change
$Y = a + bX$

$Y = a + bX + cZ,$ Z = macroeconomic variable
$Y = a + bX + dW,$ W = industry average
$Y = a + bX + cZ + dW$
$Y = a + bx + fx^2 + gx^3 + e/x$
$Y = a + bx + fx^2 + gx^3 + e/x + cz$
$Y = a + bx + fx^2 + gx^3 + e/x + dw$
$Y = a + bx + fx^2 + gx^3 + e/x + dw + cz$

FIGURE 12-12 Long-term regression model.

```
RANK  Confidence  TYPE         COEFFICIENTS FROM REGRESSION AND      Y=A+B*X+C*Z+D*W+E/X+F*X**2+G*X**3
      Level                    (CONFIDENCE INTERVALS +/-)
      in %
                               A           B          C            D          E          F          G
1.*** 95%  Linear(2)7.05(1.10)  3.21(.01)   -          -            -          -          -

      Regression Equation:  Y = a+b*X

2.    75%  Nonlinear(6) 4.21(.09)  3.23(.34)  -5.40((1.09)  6.23(.09)  7.12(.02)  -12.3(.01)   -

      Regression Equation:  Y = a+b*x+c*z+d*w+e/x+f*x**2

***Selected as the best predictor of Y.
All other relationships are not statistically significant at the 5% confidence level or above
```

FIGURE 12-13   Sample report from the regression model.

12.9.1   Forecasting

The forecasting model includes two components, one long-term and one short-term. The long-term component enables users to estimate future prices, and thereby return on investment, for 2–10 years in advance. The short-term model is used to forecast prices on a month-to-month basis. The time unit of the short-term model is a week. This model does not estimate price fluctuations from hour to hour or day to day because of the magnitude of the database that would be needed to track such information and the huge number of computations that would be required. For example, one 10-year period will have 520 weekly data elements, 2600 daily elements, and 20,800 hourly elements, less holidays and weekends. Using daily and hourly data for forecasting would also require assumptions to be made to correct for year-to-year changes in the days on which weekends and holidays fall and other year-to-year differences.

If the short-term model used the month as its time unit, it would not be precise enough to allow adequate analysis by the user on a regular basis. It would also require a correction for the differing number of days per month and for leap years.

The long-term model begins with a simple linear regression analysis of stock prices and time. Each time a regression is run, it is tested for statistical significance at several selected confidence levels. The coefficient of determination is also examined to test for the amount of variation explained by the regression. The user may be able to select the exact parameters of these tests. If he/she fails to do so, however, a default value will be used. The tests for statistical significance include t tests on the coefficients and an F distribution test of the equation.

The forecasting model operates in two modes. An interaction mode allows the user to proceed through the analysis, making decisions as he/she proceeds (concerning which relationship best predicts future price levels). The other mode simply allows the user to set minimum requirements of the relationship and the computer tests all of the possible relationships and selects the one which best meets the criteria.

The short-term model utilizes the long-term model for the basis of the yearly projection and applies a seasonality factor to obtain a weekly estimate.

Figures 12-12 and 12-13 describe the long-term forecasting, and Figure 12-14 deals with the short-term model.

12.9.2   Graphics

IDSS requires two types of graphics: (a) economic indicators graphing tcehnique and (b) point-and-figure charting technique.

(a) Economic Indicators Graphing Techniques.   Graphics uses leading, coincident, and lagging economic indicators to foresee and verify changes in the general economic activity.

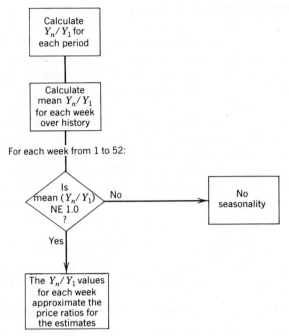

FIGURE 12-14   Short-term regression model.

The user can trace any of the 13 leading economic indicators during the specified time frame. If a change is indicated by the leading indicator (the indicator starts falling), the investment manager can use this information to support a decision to sell stocks and invest in securities less vulnerable to fluctuations in general economic activity.

Coincident and lagging economic indicators can be traced along with leading indicators to verify earlier fluctuations in the leading indicator.

The user can trace the price of an individual security along with one of the economic indicators. The investment manager can see if there exists a lead-lag relationship in past data between the security and the economic indicator. The existence of a lead-lag relationship can be useful in foreseeing stock price performance and improve a manager's buy and sell decisions.

The investment manager can view the graph on the terminal or receive a printed report of the graph.

The economic indicators are monthly data. Their median lead and lag times for both peaks and troughs are also available for printout with the graph.

The price data of individual securities is a monthly price average.

(b) Point-and-Figure Charting Techniques.   Point-and-figure charting is a tool that attempts to forecast how far a price swing of a particular security

will carry. It attempts to answer the question of what price a particular stock or market average is likely to achieve.

The investment manager decides in advance what price changes are significant. The manager also indicates the period of time over which the price changes will be calculated. For each significant price change, a mark is entered on the chart at the price level:

X for increases
0 for decreases

This technique is designed to reveal price congestion areas. A break in price from the general congestion area indicates a possible new price trend and makes it easy to detect a new trend.

12.9.3 Breadth-of-Market Technique

The breadth-of-market technique is a tool used to study major turning points of the market as a whole. The analysis focuses on a change in price of a market average such as the Dow Jones Industrial (DJI) in relation to the net number of stocks traded on a rising price.

The calculations follow:

1. Calculate the net advances or net declines on the N.Y. Stock Exchange on a daily basis.

Number of stocks traded on an advancing price
− Number of stocks traded on a declining price
Net advances or net declines

2. Accumulate the daily net advances and net declines. This gives a measure of "breadth."

Graph the breadth-of-market line and the DJI. Normally, the breadth will move as the DJI moves. A significant divergence of these two lines indicates an approaching reversal in the general economic activity. A decline in the breadth-of-market line while the DJI continues to rise indicates that an increasing number of issues are declining in price and a major downturn of stock prices is approaching.

Breadth of market is also used to detect a recovery in general market activity. The technique is to examine the movement of the breadth-of-market line in conjunction with the DJI and the daily trading volume on the New York Stock Exchange. Typically, the indication of recovery is that the DJI and the breadth-of-market line continue to decline while the volume of trading increases dramatically.

The breadth-of-market technique can also be used to study major turning points for individual securities.

The daily net volume (number of shares traded on an increasing price minus the number of shares traded on a decreasing price) of a particular security is graphed along with the daily price and volume traded of an individual security.

Interpretation of major turning points of an individual security is determined by detecting turning points of the general market.

12.9.4 Capital Asset Pricing

The theory of capital asset pricing is a selection technique for managers to develop their desired portfolio positions.

The Standard and Poor's 500 Stock Price Index is used to calculate the efficient frontier of the complete market. This is done by plotting each individual security's risk σ and return μ and applying a quadratic programming technique to create the efficient frontier.

Figure 12-15 shows the market line plotted against the efficient frontier curve of Markowitz (see Chapter 4). If an individual security falls between M and A, then its expected rate of return will be greater than that of the market.

12.9.5 Investment Risk and Return

Investment Risk. This is measured by the standard deviation σ of the portfolio,

$$\sigma = (r - r_0)/s$$

where r = asset rate of return each period, r_0 = pure interest rate, and s = standard deviation of gains or losses about the mean.

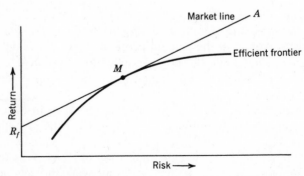

FIGURE 12-15   Capital asset pricing model.

Investment Return. This is measured by the mean μ of the portfolio:

$$\mu = \frac{(\text{current price} - \text{original price}) + \text{dividends}}{\text{price at beginning of period}}$$

Portfolio Return. This is denoted by R_p and is computed as

$$R_p = R_f + \beta (R_m - R_f)$$

where R_f = return of risk-free investment (i.e., 91-day U.S. Treasury note), β is the beta coefficient, and R_m = return of market. β is the slope of the least squares regression line.

12.10   IDSS: Data-Manipulation Module

The data manipulation module of IDSS consists of the query language and data-manipulation language of the relational DBMS that handles the data storage requirements of IDSS. It is possible to generate special reports using these two languages. They provide any user of IDSS with the capability to scan a large database and extract information that meet the user's criteria. We call this specific capability the *screening function.*

The screening function allows the user to select the charateristic, or combination of characteristics, by means of which he/she desires to screen information. For instance, the user might want to know what firms performed best in terms of earnings per share, profit growth rate, or growth in sales. This can be done with the screening function. The screening function can also be used to obtain the worst performances or the average performance (as measured by the median or mean). It can extract either one firm or several. The number of items is user-defined.

In the sample report for the screening function shown in Figure 12-16, the user has selected earnings per share as the criterion. He has asked for the top five elements in descending order by earnings per share. If the user desires additional information concerning these security issuers, he can obtain it by using the select function. For instance, in the example given in the sample report, the user might want more information on General Electric, since it ranks highest in earnings per share. He may then enter the select function and obtain listings for GE's financial statements, ratio analysis, or recent stock price trends.

Screening files will be created dynamically by the relational DBMS as user views. The user will enter all the screening elements and their constraints, if necessary, to obtain a display of all securities in the IDSS database that fall into that category.

```
PRIMARY KEY: EARNINGS PER SHARE
ASCENDING OR DESCENDING: DESCENDING
NUMBER:   5


Earnings Per Share - Top 5 Common Stocks

Rank    Name                               Earnings Per Share
1.      General Electric                        $5.40
2.      TRW                                     $5.23
3.      Honeywell                               $5.10
4.      Litton                                  $4.93
5.      McDonnell-Douglas                       $3.92
```

FIGURE 12-16   Report from screening function.

Example.   An investment manager can request a screening file of all securities whose earnings have increased by 5% over the last 5 years. Then, using this newly created screening file as a basis, a further screening analysis can be done. For example, she may request a search for all those securities whose dividends have increased over the past 3 years. Any sophisticated relational DBMS is specially equipped to handle such queries and then display the result in an attractive report format.

In addition to the report-generation capability, IDSS also requires a graphics function, which should ideally be available from the relational DBMS handling the IDSS data storage. Graphics are a very important part of investment analysis, because "a picture is worth a thousand words." A graph is often even more important than numerical data, since it is easier to see general trends and movements on a graph than on a numeric display.

The IDSS model will utilize two kinds of graphics. One will be time series graphs showing movements of variables over time. The other will be scatter diagrams showing one variable on each axis, with the points indicating the values for each at the same or lagged points in time. Both types are available as standard features with any relational DBMS graphics package.

In addition to the single time series graph of one variable, the graphics function allows the user to select multiple graphs over the same time frame. A useful application of this type of graph is in the technical analysis of the stock market. The graphs for a breadth-of-market analysis can often aid in predicting upturns and downturns in the stock market. Anthony Tabell explained this concept as a divergence of overall indexes with advance-decline differences over time. When the two tend to move together over the short run, prices tend to rise over the long run. However, when the two tend to diverge, the longer term trend is generally down. This is a good use of multiple time series graphing.

12.11   FEEDBACK CONTROL LOOP IN IDSS

The investment decision support system consists of four subsystems: client information, securities selection, portfolio analysis, and investment timing. Since the first two involve access to a database of investment information, they are not concerned with "what if" questions of the feedback control loop. They provide information to financial analysts who use their expertise to make forecasts.

Investment analysts know, from basic economic theory, what general effect certain changes in the economy will have on stock prices. For instance, the Arab oil embargo could be expected to result in an increase in oil prices, oil company profits, and oil stock prices. Increasing interest rates could be expected to reduce stock and bond prices since they improve the yields on alternative investments.

A cut in government spending generally results in falling overall prices. Because this tends to stabilize the economy, in inflationary periods it normally would have an upward effect on the stock market. In deflationary periods, it would tend to have a negative effect on stock prices.

Money supply, interest rates, and inflation affect each other. Because of this, answering "what if" questions on a purely manual basis, without the computer, becomes extremely difficult even for the most brilliant financial analyst.

"What if" questions are thus an essential part of IDSS. They are the key to a competently designed system. Without this feature, the computer would serve only as a large data retreival system: its function would simply be to regurgitate information that it had in its database. With the "what if" functions, the managers can use their expertise to come up with different scenarios, translate them for the DSS, and intelligently view the results. The DSS is not designed to make decisions; its purpose is to help the portfolio manager make better decisions. The "what if" function is a very powerful tool to help the managers make such decisions.

We shall discuss here three separate areas of IDSS where "what if" scenarios are used: (1) sensitivity of leading indicators and securities, (2) single-security pricing versus capital asset pricing, and (3) regression analysis.

12.12   SENSITIVITY OF LEADING INDICATORS AND SECURITIES

After graphing the security and the leading indicator [see Section 12.9.2 (b)], the analyst can use the information to determine the sensitivity of fluctuations in the price of the security to changes in the leading indicator.

The following interaction between computer and manager is used to simulate the reaction of the security, given any variety of user-defined constraints.

Screen I.   (In the investment timing analysis subsystem)

```
>CLEAR (clears screen of previous graphs)
>GRAPH
 ENTER INDICATOR # >    1 0
 ENTER SECURITY CODE > 03865
 START DATE > MM/DD/YY
 END DATE > <CR> (defaults to present date)
```

The system displays the graph of leading indicator #10 along with the security price for the given time frame.

Screen 2.   (In the investment timing analysis subsystem)

```
>Sensitivity
 ENTER PEAK DATES OF INDICATOR
>MM/DD/YY, MM/DD/YY, MM/DD/YY
 ENTER THROUGH DATES OF INDICATOR
>MM/DD/YY, MM/DD/YY, MM/DD/YY
 ENTER PEAK DATES OF SECURITY 03865
>MM/DD/YY, MM/DD/YY, MM/DD/YY
 ENTER THROUGH DATES OF SECURITY 03865
>MM/DD/YY, MM/DD/YY, MM/DD/YY
```

The computer, by simple subtraction, calculates the time lapse between the peak of the indicator and the peak of the security. It also calculates the lead times for the trough of the indicator and the trough of the security. It then calculates the respective

☐ Mean lead peak time and its standard deviation.
☐ Mean lead trough time and its standard deviation.

Next, the percentage change between the peak and trough times is calculated in both the indicator and the security. A ratio of change between peak and trough is calculated as follows:

$$\frac{\% \text{ Change in indicator from peak to trough}}{\% \text{ Change in security from peak to trough}}$$

Finally, it calculates the mean of the percentage change and the standard deviation.

These calculations are used as a measure of "sensitivity."

Note that the number of peak and trough dates is not restricted to three. The analyst can enter the dates of all peaks and troughs that occurred during the time period of interest.

The portfolio manager next enters the future dates and values for peaks

and troughs of the leading indicator. These values are chosen at the manager's discretion.

Screen 3

```
FUTURE DATE > MM/DD/YY
FUTURE INDICATOR PRICE > 600 .
FUTURE DATE > <CR>
```

(all future dates/values are entered)

12.13 SINGLE-SECURITY PRICING VERSUS CAPITAL ASSET PRICING

Three questions a portfolio manager may ask are:

1. Where does security XXX lie relative to the market line based on S&P 500 and the efficient frontier if the security risk and/or return change?
2. How will the market line and efficient frontier be affected by changes in some of their component securities?
3. How does the performance of securities change if the market performance changes and the securities do not?

The scenarios of Figure 12-17 show how the three questions can be answered. Before the manager changes either the security or the efficient frontier, he/she should get into the investment timing analysis subsystem and graph them without any of the changes. Then the portfolio manager enters the portfolio analysis technique subsystem.

Scenario 1 plots the security code with the changes that the manager entered. Scenario 2 recalculates the efficient frontier according to the specifications of the manager and then plots the new efficient frontier. The manager

```
Scenario 1              Scenario 2              Scenario 3
>CHANGE SECURITY        >CHANGE SECURITY        >CHANGE PORTFOLIO
SECURITY CODE> ZZZ      SECURITY CODE> XXX      RISK> 2%
RISK> 3%                RISK> 3%                RETURN> 1%
RETURN> <CR>            RETURN> -2%             >PLOT FRONTIER
SECURITY CODE> <CR>     SECURITY CODE> YYY
>PLOT SECURITY          RISK> 2%
                        RETURN> 2%
                        SECURITY CODE> <CR>
                        >PLOT FRONTIER
```

FIGURE 12-17 Examples of scenarios from IDSS.

now can plot securities from the client's portfolio and compare the performances of the securities with the different frontiers.

Scenario 3 readjusts the ratio changes of the efficient frontier's risk and return and then plots it on the screen. The manager can now select securities to see how the performances of those securities differ when plotted against each of the frontiers.

Figure 12-18 shows the graphic outcome of the three scenarios.

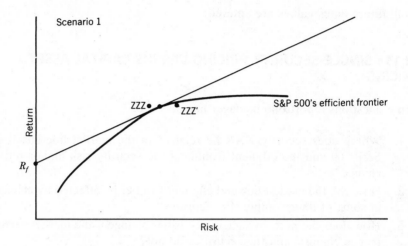

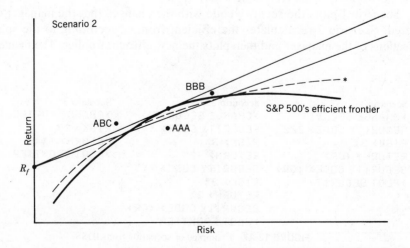

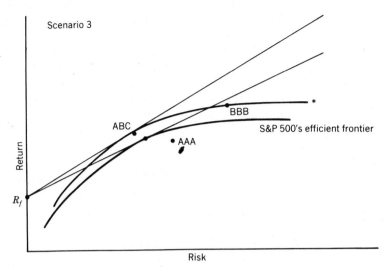

FIGURE 12-18 Three scenarios of "what if".

12.14 REGRESSION ANALYSIS

The forecasting element of the IDSS can be very helpful in aiding the financial analyst to answer "what if" type questions. For instance, the knowledge that the oil embargo would tend to increase prices of oil stocks is a qualitative fact. It does not include "how much" or "when" or what effects the embargo would have on other stock prices or interest rates or the money supply. It is necessary to use quantification processes to answer such questions.

The regression model is useful in analyzing relationships because it tends to quantify "what if" questions. A typical example of this situation follows.

12.14.1 What If Interest Rates Decline?

The investment analyst knows that declines in interest rates tend to reduce costs. Therefore, they can be expected to have an upward effect on corporate profits. Analysts also know that a decline in interest rates tends to make common stocks relatively more attractive as an alternative. The increase in corporate profits can be expected to increase the common stock price of that company as well.

To begin with, historical data, which are included in the IDSS database, are used to find the regression equation that best represents the relationship between time, the price per share of a company's common stock, and the mean prime interest rate (a common benchmark for interest rates).

Let's assume that the relationship is given by the equation

$$Y = 0.191 + 0.056X - 1.011Z$$

where Y is the price per share of common stock, X is the year, and Z is the prime interest rate, with no lags built in.

Assume that all coefficients are statistically significant at or above the 90% level of probability (i.e., 90% of the variation in X and Z can be explained by the regression line) and the F test is positive at the 90% level. Now, assume that the mean prime interest rate is currently 10% per year and the price per share of common stock is $10.

The question is then, what will be the effect of an immediate reduction in the mean prime interest rate from 10% to 7% with no change in the prime rate thereafter?

The solution to the equation would yield the price per share of common stock when the interest rate changes. The regression equation can be rewritten as

$$\Delta Y = 0.056(\Delta X) - 1.011(\Delta Z)$$

where the Δ indicates a change from the current period to the future period. ΔY, therefore, means the stock price at a point in the future minus the current stock price. Since 0.191 is a constant, it disappears from the equation for ΔY.

We now get the equation

$$Y_f - Y_p = 0.056(X_f - X_p) - 1.011(Z_f - Z_p)$$

where the subscripts f and p represent future and present, respectively.

Since all terms in this equation are known except Y_f, it can be solved easily to determine the future stock price. Let us suppose

$$Y_p = \$10.00/\text{share}$$
$$X_f - X_p = 1 \text{ year}$$
$$Z_f - Z_p = -3$$

Solving for Y_f, we obtain

$$
\begin{aligned}
Y_f &= Y_p + 0.056(X_f - X_p) - 1.011(Z_f - Z_p) \\
&= 10.00 + 0.056(1) - 1.011(-3) \\
&= 13.089
\end{aligned}
$$

Thus, an immediate decrease in the prime interest rate from 10% to 7% results in an increase in the price of our stock by $3.09 per share from $10.00 to $13.09, if the regression equation, $Y = .191 + 0.056X - 1.011Z$ represents the true relationship between the prime interest rate and the price of our particular stock with 90% probability.

The regression forecast model can be used for "what if" analyses in many

other ways besides predicting results of changes in the prime interest rate. The model can solve a system of quadratic equations, if the quadratic equations are found to be good estimator. It can also involve the use of variables other than the prime interest rate: the Dow Jones Industrial Average, the money supply, gross national product, personal income, industry averages, and so on. In these cases, the methodology is the same. First, the user will obtain the regression equation that is the best estimator of Y. He then predicts Y_f from the equation. The time interval for these equations need not be a year; it could be a month. If the time basis is a month, however, the regression equation derived must also be carried out with monthly data.

12.15   EVALUATION OF IDSS BY MANAGEMENT

Managers have completed their evaluation of the Investment Decision Support System. Their overall consensus is that the system is effective in supporting the previously used techniques in the decision-making process. Management is also pleased with the added capabilities (e.g., screening) that were previously too time consuming to use. These new capabilities are effective in enhancing the investment managers' approach to decision making.

The following is management's evaluation of the IDSS.

12.15.1   Strengths

1. Managers commented on the effectiveness of the system in reducing the amount of paperwork and calculations that were previously done manually. As a result the managers are able to spend more time with their clients discussing possible investment strategies.

2. Tasks that were previously impossible for a manager to do are now available through the functions of the IDSS. One such function allows the investment manager to have the capability of multilevel screening of securities. Before the IDSS, screening capabilities were limited to wire services, published materials, or manager's time to manually screen securities.

3. With the IDSS, reports (i.e., tables and graphs) are more frequently used due to the ease in generating them. A comparison of the manually written reports and the reports produced by the IDSS reveals the following:

☐ Reports generated by the system contain more complete information.
☐ The data in the system-generated reports contain more current information.

4. Managers are impressed with the limited amount of menu-driven prompts. Once in an analysis mode, the user is allowed the flexibility of

entering commands in any order desired, thereby eliminating unnecessary restraints on the user and verbiage on the screen.

12.15.2 Weaknesses

1. Management wants to include system capabilities that are more portfolio-oriented. An example is allowing a hypothetical portfolio to be created for comparison with a client's portfolio and market.

2. During the calculation of the efficient frontier, management noted that the response time was long enough to concern the user about the status of the system. Managers requested that a message be continuously displayed indicating that calculation is still in progress.

12.15.3 Additional Management Considerations

Management is generally pleased with the forecasting model. Its ability to obtain forecasts automatically with an optional manual override capability is considered an advantage.

Criticism of the forecasting module included disappointment that forecasts could not be carried out for a time frame smaller than a week. Some managers expressed a desire for daily or hourly forecasts. Yet when faced with the cost of storing the increased data necessary for it, they agreed that the added cost would not be justified.

Management also expressed concern about the need for the capability to add macroeconomic variables to the regression model. Some felt that utilizing a maximum of only one macroeconomic indicator at a time did not adequately represent the "real world," where several economic variables often change simultaneously and also interact. However, when the problems such as multicollinearity, serial correlation, and introduction of additional variables were considered, it became obvious that the ability of financial analysts to effectively utilize a model with many macroeconomic variables would be more limited as the number of variables increased.

Management was also concerned about the statistical sophistication needed to operate the regression function manually but is pleased that the IDSS will automatically evaluate several models to obtain one that seems to fit the relationship best. Management feels that the regression model expands their forecasting ability. Yet, to be sure that investment analysts understand the meaning of these statistical tools before using them, an extensive training course is recommended.

Management believes that the user cost must be justified by increased productivity. Looking at the overall capability of the IDSS, management feels that the development costs along with the maintenance costs are justified. Management is now in the process of discussing the possibility of funding the IDSS development group to add more capabilities to the current IDSS to compensate for some of its weaknesses.

12.16   D/T DSS: OVERVIEW OF THE SYSTEM DESIGN PROCESS

We introduced this hypothetical system in Section 2.15. Its main purpose is to provide a means to test various alternative courses of action in order to improve the distribution system. Distribution policies are affected by middle management in the areas of marketing, operations, and accounting, so the system is integrated with these areas to allow the full cost effect of decisions to be reviewed. Since the model is used by middle management, it is designed to be easy to use with a minimal amount of training. The model is designed to provide managers with information on efficient delivery routes, economic inventory levels, and product mix as well as to respond to situational questions such as plant closings, deletion of product lines, and alternative warehouse locations.

Information for the system will be gathered from five different areas:

Information Source	Information Content
Dealers	Current demand
Transportation facilities	Current capacity of the transportation system
Warehouses	Current modes of transportation being used
Plants	Current production level
Accounting department	Cost data for the model objective function

In addition, management will supply constraints and policy-related data for the operation of D/T DSS. Figure 12-19 shows an overview of the system in operation. A typical user can access the system and generate the desired reports.

Descriptions of the four component modules of D/T DSS follow.

12.17   D/T DSS: CONTROL MODULE

The control module provides the entry point for the system and interfaces with the data storage module, data manipulation module, and model-building module. After the user successfully logs in, D/T DSS displays the main menu shown in Figure 12-20. Since the system is online and interactive, the control module allows the user to interface with the system via a set of screens. The three principal groups of users are: Sales and Marketing, Distribution, and Accounting and Forecasting. We now describe the main functions of each group.

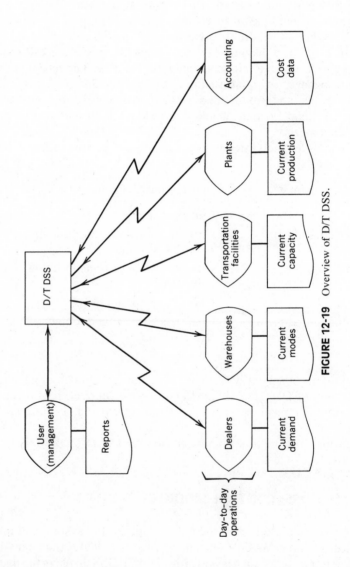

FIGURE 12-19 Overview of D/T DSS.

```
                        D/T   DSS

                      MAIN   MENU


           1   -   SALES/MARKETING

           2   -   DISTRIBUTION

           3   -   ACCOUNTING/FORECASTING

           4   -   HELP

           5   -   EXIT


       SELECT   YOUR   OPTION   AND   PRESS   RETURN
```

FIGURE 12-20   Main menu for D/T DSS.

12.17.1   Sales and Marketing

The sales and marketing department would benefit greatly if given the ability to test out different situations within the D/T DSS. The results from the model that Sales and Marketing would be analyzing would consist of transit cost, the ability of the system to handle an increase or decrease in demand, and average transit time.

Sales and marketing situations can be categorized as a general increase in demand, a general decrease in demand, a specific (within model line) increase in demand, or a specific (within model line) decrease in demand.

Scenarios that would result in a general increase in demand include the following. If the government put import quotas into effect, the general demand for American cars would increase. Also, a rebate or incentive program (i.e., reduced finance rate) would increase demand. A reduction in the transportation cost charges to the customer would likewise increase demand, either across all model lines or within one or several model lines. Another scenario that might increase demand within specific model lines might be the threat of a gasoline shortage. Model lines with high mileage rates (low gas consumption per mile) would experience an increase in demand. Introduction of a new model line would increase the number of units the transportation system would have to handle. Characteristics of the new model line might also affect demand in certain areas of the country. For example, the south would experience a greater increase in demand for a convertible than the colder northern regions of the country. Likewise, the northern part of the country would demand more front- and four-wheel-drive cars.

Decreases in demand would be experienced if automobile imports continued to rise. Increasing the transportation charges to the customer might also decrease the demand for cars and trucks. An increase in the sales tax,

insurance, or excise tax in specific states might have an effect on demand within those states. In general, a decrease in demand would mean that costs would have to be distributed over fewer units, thereby increasing transportation costs per unit. Therefore, the removal of a model line with no replacement line would increase the transportation costs per unit.

A final scenario, which for several reasons is more credible as time passes, is the linking of a foreign manufacturer with an American manufacturer. This scenario would drastically change the sales volume within the transportation model, possibly causing the creation of a fictitious model and its own set of unique scenarios.

Figure 12-21 shows the screen for Sales and Marketing. It enables the user to work in any one of the four scenarios described above.

12.17.2 Distribution

In this company the Distribution Department is responsible for the efficient movement of automobiles from the manufacturing plant to the dealership. The main method or indicator of performance is cost. This can be represented as cost per automobile or cost versus budget.

The Distribution Department acts for the most part in a service role. The main interaction with the model would come about as a reaction to changes instituted by other departments. For instance, Marketing may decide to open new dealerships in a certain area; Distribution must then evaluate the most efficient transportation mode. These types of decisions can be made at any time due to competitive factors, complaints from customers, or poor financial performance. Due to the unpredictable and reactionary type of modifications, it is necessary that Distribution have access to the model and that the model be online.

```
                        D/T   DSS

                   SALES   AND   MARKETING


          1   -   GENERAL INCREASE IN DEMAND

          2   -   GENERAL DECREASE IN DEMAND

          3   -   DEMAND INCREASE FOR A MODEL

          4   -   DEMAND DECREASE FOR A MODEL

          5   -   GO TO MAIN MENU


          SELECT   YOUR   OPTION   AND   PRESS   RETURN
```
FIGURE 12-21 Screen for Sales and Marketing.

There are three major areas of distribution costs that should be manipulated in the model to answer the "what if" questions. The first is change in one or more of the major transportation modes, truck, rail, or barge. A change in mode could result from a price increase or routing requirements. A typical inquiry then would be, "If costs over a certain route for rail deliveries were increased, how would this affect the total costs, and how would it compare with other available transportation modes?" Properly constructed, the model could provide this data by altering the cost factors.

A second area of questioning would revolve around the opening and closing of warehouses. Once the need for the warehouse is established (usually based on nonquantitative criteria, such as, customer satisfaction and prompt delivery) the model can be used to evaluate proper locations for warehouses. A typical scenario would have the model produce possible locations of warehouse A versus warehouse B. This would mean supplying not only cost data but also data concerning the logistics of the proposed warehouse. If the company becomes dissatisfied with the performance of a warehouse, a comparable location may be determined with the help of the model.

The third area is similar to the warehouse problem, and that is the location of dealerships. Here, however, the market determines the location (by market shifts or demand), and the Distribution Department is to determine the most efficient method of transportation. The department would then provide shipping data from selective shipping points. An inquiry then would be, "If inventory requirements dictated that shipments be made from shipping point A, then what are the costs?," and then, "What if shipping point B were used?" With these interrogations and the qualitative factors involved, Distribution will be able to make sound recommendations.

Figure 12-22 shows the screen for Distribution. It describes how a user can employ the system to address the above three areas.


```
                    D/T   DSS

                 DISTRIBUTION


         1   -   TRANSPORTATION MODE

         2   -   OPEN/CLOSE WAREHOUSE

         3   -   DEALERSHIP LOCATION

         4   -   GO TO MAIN MENU


      SELECT   YOUR   OPTION   AND   PRESS   RETURN
```
FIGURE 12-22 Screen for the distribution department.

12.17.3   Accounting and Forecasting

The accounting manager is always concerned with his company obtaining
the lowest possible cost in accomplishing any particular job, and therefore
he must be made aware of the costs incurred or to be incurred on the job.
From the accounting manager's viewpoint, the D/T DSS will serve to provide
the necessary feedback to answer various "what if" questions. This feature
is discussed in more detail in Section 12.21. Figure 12-23 shows the screen
for Accounting and Forecasting.

12.18   D/T DSS: DATA STORAGE MODULE

The data storage module of D/T DSS is designed as a relational database
using a sophisticated relational DBMS package, preferably ORACLE. Its
query language SQL will facilitate data manipulation by users, and its report
writer and graphics packages will be used to produce sophisticated reports
and business graphics.

This module consists of four major data files that may be broken down
into a set of relations and views. The four files are:

1. Customer data file consisting of data about shipment types and product
   mix
2. Warehouse data file consisting of data on labor and rental charges
3. Manufacturing data file consisting of data pertaining to plant capacity,
   resources, and product requirements
4. Transportation data file consisting of data related to transportation
   costs, route information, and transportation modes such as truck, rail,
   and barge

The control module will access the data storage module to retrieve data
required to implement the options selected by a user.

12.19   D/T DSS: MODEL-BUILDING MODULE

The model-building module contains the specifications of two mathematical
modeling techniques used for D/T DSS:

1. Linear programming to determine the minimum cost in transporting
   automobiles from the point of production to the point of sale
2. Linear regression to compute and forecast future fuel cost and labor
   cost (see Fig. 12-23).

```
                        D/T   DSS

            ACCOUNTING   AND   FORECASTING


    1   -   LABOR COST

    2   -   FUEL COST

    3   -   GO TO MAIN MENU


    SELECT   YOUR   OPTION   AND   PRESS   RETURN
```
FIGURE 12-23.   Screen for the Accounting and Forecasting department.

12.19.1   Linear Programming

(a) General Description.   The modeling method chosen by the Distribution/Transportation Decision Support System is linear programming. Linear programming has been chosen because the model needed for Distribution/Transportation is basically a model that will analyze a resource allocation problem. Our D/T DSS model contains characteristics that are fundamental to a linear programming model. The first characteristic that links our D/T DSS model to linear programming is the fact that it has an overall objective. That objective is to minimize the costs incurred in transporting automobiles from the point of production to the point of sale. The second characteristic that links D/T DSS to linear programming is the fact that constraints exist within the model. These constraints must be taken into consideration when attempting to accomplish the overall objective, the minimizing of costs. Finally, our D/T DSS model contains choices regarding the mode of transportation for the automobiles. The three modes that are possible are shipment by rail, shipment by truck, or shipment by barge. These choices are essential to both the D/T DSS and the linear programming model selected.

(b) Constraints.   The constraints within the D/T DSS are essential to meeting the overall objective of minimizing cost. The constraints within the model relate to the modes of transportation, the distribution routes, the production and warehousing facilities, and the point of sale, the dealers. Some of the constraints encountered in the linear programming model for D/T DSS are listed below.

☐ Warehouses   Number of warehouses
                Capacity of each warehouse
                Location of warehouses

☐ Plants   Number of plants
             Production mix per plant
             Production capacity per plant
             Location of plants
☐ Modes of Transportation   Capacity of rail
                              Capacity of truck
                              Capacity of barge
☐ Dealers   Number of dealers
             Capacity of each dealer
             Location of dealers
             Demand from dealers
☐ Unions   Contract agreement with unions

(c) Objective Data.   The objective data within the D/T DSS must be identified and gathered if the model is to produce valid results concerning costs.
Since the objective function of the model is to minimize costs, the objective
data in the model directly relates to costs. In order to gather meaningful
data easily, the accounting department within the company will process all
costs incurred in transporting automobiles from the plant to the dealer. Some
of the objective data in the D/T DSS model are listed below:

Agreements with unions (wages, benefits, etc.)

Cost per mile per unit on rail

Cost per mile per unit on truck

Cost per mile per unit on barge

Warehousing costs

Damage costs per unit per rail

Damage costs per unit per truck

Damage costs per unit per barge

Insurance costs

Interstate fees

Agreements with company employees (wages, benefits, etc.)

(d) Formulation of the Model.   Since the mathematical technique used
in the model will be linear programming, it is important to define the constraints, associated decision variables, and their coefficients.

For a representative part of the model one can look at the choice of transportation modes. There are three available modes of transportation: truck,
rail, and barge. It is the responsibility of the distribution department to decide
which mode should carry how many automobiles to a specific warehouse.

To arrive at cost for each mode the model uses linear regression. The
formula used is

$$Y = Mx + b$$

where Y = transportation costs, x = mileage, M = variable mileage cost, and b = fixed mileage cost.

The variable mileage cost is determined to be $1.20 per mile, and the fixed mileage cost is set at $9.35. For example, if a specified warehouse is 500 miles from the shipping point, the cost would be $609.35, or about $76 per automobile for a standard load of 8 automobiles. This answer is then used as a coefficient in the linear programming model.

The numbers of automobiles carried by truck, rail, and barge are represented by X_1, X_2, and X_3, respectively. The objective function then would be

$$76X_1 + 40X_2 + 25X_3 = Z, \quad \text{minimize } Z$$

The constraints would be as follows:

1. Demand out of the warehouse:

$$X_1 + X_2 + X_3 > 5000 \text{ per month}$$

2. Carrier capacity for deliveries per month:

$$X_1 < 1000$$
$$X_2 < 2000$$
$$X_3 < 3000$$

3. Minimum quantity to be eligible for contract rates:

$$X_1 > 100$$
$$X_2 > 1000$$
$$X_3 > 1000$$

4. Loading capacity at the shipping plant (worker-hours per automobile):

$$1.2X_1 + 0.8X_2 + 0.5X_3 < 6000$$

12.19.2 Linear Regression

D/T DSS uses linear regression in order to compute and forecast values of fuel cost and labor cost under a set of "what if" questions posed by the user. Assuming the line of regression as

$$Y = a + bX$$

where X measures the time in weeks and Y measures the cost in dollars, the coefficients a and b are given by

$$na + b(\Sigma X_i) = \Sigma Y_i$$
$$a(\Sigma X_i) + b(\Sigma X_i^2) = \Sigma (X_i Y_i)$$

The summation is extended over n sets of data values (X_i, Y_i), where n is selected by the user. For example, if a forecast is to be made on the basis of 6-month data, then $n = 26$, since there are 26 weeks in 6 months, and one week is taken as the unit of time.

12.20   D/T DSS: DATA MANIPULATION MODULE

Information for the D/T DSS model is gathered from dealers, transportation facilities, warehouses, plants, and accounting. Each of these five areas is linked to the central computer via telecommunication lines. The dealers, transportation facilities, and warehouses provide the model with information such as current sales, current in-transit movement, current modes of transportation being utilized, and automobile transfers and returns. The plants provide information concerning current and future production levels and movement information about automobiles already built. The accounting department collects and provides the model with the objective data needed, costs that are used by the objective function.

Reports are generated from this collection of information so management can study them and develop "what if" questions. These reports consist of total sales and sales by model lines; total production and production by model lines; and shipments, total and by model lines. Reports are also generated concerning costs incurred in transporting automobiles. Total costs are broken down to show freight costs, warehouse costs, labor costs, and costs from damage and overhead. The information provided in these reports represents the starting point for the model and its ability to answer the "what if" questions.

Figures 12-24 and 12-25 show two sample reports generated by the system. The inventory movement report shown in Figure 12-24 is broken down into two categories, one for dealerships and one for warehouses, both subdivided into five regions, the northeast, midwest, south, Rocky Mountain, and west.

The dealership category consists of opening inventory, closing physical inventory, and closing inventory. The closing physical inventory comprises the opening inventory, plus receipts, sales, transfers out, and returns. The receipts are further subdivided into factory, warehouse, and other dealership receipts. Finally, the dealership closing inventory consists of the closing physical inventory plus any existing in-transit items. All of these dealership inventory amounts are printed on a 12 numeric digit display.

The warehouse category consists of opening and closing inventories. The

XYZ AUTOMOBILE COMPANY
INVENTORY MOVEMENT REPORT
AS OF XXXXXXXXXXXXXX

	NORTHEAST	MIDWEST	WEST
DEALERSHIPS			
Opening inventory	9,999,999,999.99	9,999,999,999.99	9,999,999,999.99
Receipts			
From factory			
From warehouse			
From other dealer			
Total receipts			
Sales			
Transfers out			
Returns			
Closing physical inv.			
In transit			
Closing inventory			
WAREHOUSES			
Opening inventory			
Receipts			
From factory			
From warehouse			
From dealership			
Total receipts			
Transfers out			
To factory			
To warehouse			
To dealership			
Total transfers			
Closing inventory			
Total inventory			

FIGURE 12-24 Inventory movement report.

```
                          XYZ AUTOMOBILE COMPANY
                DISTRIBUTION PROFIT BY REGION RESPONSIBILITY
                       MONTH OF XXXXXXXXXXXXX
                    NORTHEAST           MIDWEST              WEST
                UNITS      % TOT     UNITS      % TOT     UNITS      % TOT
AUTOMOBILES SOLD
  MODEL TYPE 1  9,999,999  999.99    9,999,999  999.99    9,999,999  999.99
            2
            3
            4
            5

  Total

                AMOUNT     $UNIT     AMOUNT     $UNIT     AMOUNT     $UNIT
                9,999,999  999.99    9,999,999  999.99    9,999,999  999.99
Delivery charges
Other income
Total income
Freight costs
  Company owned
    Variable costs
    Depreciation
    Total
  Leased carriers
    Factory to dealer
    To warehouse
    From warehouse
    Detention charges
    Total
  Total freight costs
Warehouse costs
  Company owned
    Handling
    Overhead
    Total
  Leased warehouses
  Total warehouse cost
Total costs
Profit by region
```

FIGURE 12-25 Profit distribution report.

·closing inventory consists of the opening inventory plus receipts and transfers out. The receipts are further broken down into receipts from factory, warehouse, and dealership transfers. These warehouse inventory amounts are then printed on a 12 numeric digit display. Finally, both dealership and warehouse closing inventory totals are combined into the total inventory for each of the five regions.

The other report, Distribution Profit by Region Responsibility, shown in Figure 12-25, is broken down by the five geographic regions, each of which is subdivided into the total income and total costs and, ultimately, profit by region. Before total income is displayed, the number of automobiles sold by model type is shown in both units to seven numeric digits, and as a percentage of the total units to five numeric digits. Total income comprises delivery charges and other income in both amount, to seven numeric digits, and income per unit, to five numeric digits. Next, total costs are shown, which consist of both total freight costs and total warehouse costs. Freight costs comprise both variable costs and depreciation of company-owned freight and leased-carrier charges from factory to dealer, including freight to and from warehouses and detention charges. Warehouse costs consist of both company-owned warehouse handling and overhead charges and leased warehouse charges. Finally, after total costs are displayed, the profit by region is shown.

12.21 FEEDBACK CONTROL LOOP FOR D/T DSS

The distribution/transportation decision support model uses an interactive, user-friendly system to address the "what if" questions. Specifically, the three areas using this system are Sales and Marketing, Distribution, and Accounting and Forecasting. The inquiries made do not change the model's database but, instead, temporarily override the existing parameters to give a modified response. The system then stores the inquiries, and when a final decision is implemented the new parameters become a permanent part of the model's database or they are rejected, depending upon the results of the final decision.

A "what if" session in a particular area starts with the interactive screen for that area. For example, any "what if" question in Sales and Marketing is initiated through one of the options in the Sales and Marketing screen. (Figure 12-21). The system carries on the session by a series of questions and prompts addressed to the user.

Figure 12-26 shows the schematic of a "what if" scenario.

Let us now illustrate the situation with Accounting and Forecasting. Suppose that the accounting manager selects option 1 (labor cost) in Figure 12-23, because the labor unions have negotiated a pay increase to be effective on all applicable employees from the next month. Now the accounting manager will want to know what effect this negotiation will have on next month's

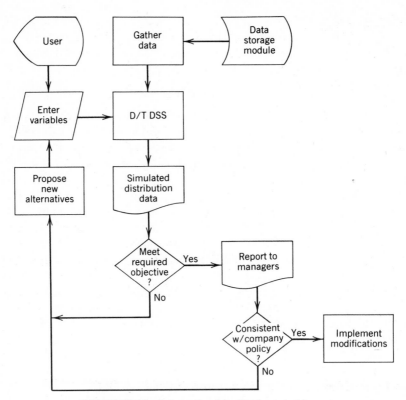

FIGURE 12-26   Schematic of feedback control loop.

costs and, consequently, its effect on net income for the month. The model would be used to apply the differential in the new labor rates, for instance, to a carrier truck driver, to provide the accounting manager with the excess costs that would be incurred the following month on that particular shipment. He would then be able to make recommendations to the controller of the company concerning the amount by which costs will increase and what he feels might be a feasible solution to reduce costs based upon the knowledge he now possesses.

Another example for which the accounting manager would be able to make use of the decision support system would be in the case of rising gasoline prices. For this purpose, he/she selects option 2 in the screen shown in Figure 12-23. Suppose that diesel fuel for the carriers increases by 20 cents per gallon. The accounting manager's staff could then determine the associated increase in cost per mile for the carrier based on its average miles per gallon. After inputting this information into the D/T DSS, the manager would be able to determine whether an alternative mode of transportation would be available for the forthcoming shipments and if so which mode of transpor-

tation would be less expensive. If the alternative transportation mode did not prove to be less expensive, then the accounting manager would also be able to use the D/T DSS to forecast cost increases for the company due to the increase in gasoline prices. This new forecast could then be made available to the controller of the company to aid in making any relative financial decisions.

In summary, when all departments have arrived at acceptable courses of action, the plans must be evaluated on an overall basis to develop one management direction. When implemented, they will become a permanent part of the model. Actual data are then evaluated (i.e., cost, market share and market coverage, gross profit, etc.) to determine if the plan should be reevaluated. Reevaluation takes place at step 1, where each department (or each department that shows poor performance) must go back to the model to evaluate choices. Using this procedure, a feedback control loop will be provided to management.

12.22 EVALUATION OF D/T DSS BY MANAGEMENT

The distribution/transportation decision support system was deemed to be fairly successful by management. The system was able to cover the areas of cost, market share and coverage, and gross profit quite well according to management's expectations. The intent of the design of the D/T DSS was to incorporate the user-friendly concept into the system. Management feels comfortable using the system and thus has not developed the computer phobia associated with the use of some system. The menu displayed on the CRT's as the DSS was being accessed was particularly praised by management in connection with its requirement that the system be user-friendly. Access to the system by authorized personnel was very convenient, as the terminals were physically located in strategic areas throughout the building.

Some of the computer controls developed for the system seemed to leave management a little concerned about the data integrity for the system. However, it was felt that perhaps management did not fully understand some of the technical details of the model's data processing capabilities. To eliminate some of the more technical aspects in this area, it was pointed out to management how the supervisor's input was required in every case before the system would accept any change in the data input. This somewhat alleviated management concern about the integrity of the system.

Management was also a little skeptical about the adaptability of the system to any major changes that may occur in the model. Again, it was thought that this skepticism was due to management's lack of technical knowledge of the system, and consequently management was advised that the system was capable of handling any major change in the model.

In general, there were both positive and negative aspects of the D/T DSS

mentioned by management. However the positive aspects more than out-weighed the negative aspects. Some of the positive aspects of the system not previously mentioned are the following: With the system in force, the information that managers needed for the decision-making function was received on a more timely basis and was therefore more useful. The results obtained from the system were also relevant, and the reports generated were good and thought to be useful for a substantial period of time. Overall, the system was easy to learn how to use, being supported by the menu displays along with the frequent use of prompts that serve to guide the user through the system's procedures. The system was thought to be flexible because it could be used in conjunction with other existing systems and could store scenarios on many levels, such that Distribution could retrieve information from Accounting, say, or vice versa. In addition to the system's short payback period, as a result of the relatively small initial investment, the return on investment figured to be quite promising in terms of the benefits to be derived from the use of the system. Finally, the estimated cost savings after implementing the system have shown up in increased profits along with decreased transit times.

On the negative side, however, it was felt that the system might be too heavily relied upon by management in that they might forget to consider the nonquantitative elements of the decision process. Also, because of the information being exposed to more users, a greater need for security over access devices was mentioned. Management felt that they would like to see locked terminals and more stringent controls on assigning passwords and on security for data storage areas.

In conclusion, although the system was accepted for future use by management, it was deficient in a few areas. Therefore, management directed that one full-time person would be assigned to work on the problem areas. With those problems eliminated, management felt that the system would be a tremendous asset to the company.

12.23 EXPRESS: DSS FOR FINANCIAL ANALYSIS

EXPRESS was developed in 1969 by Management Decision Systems (MDS) to meet the specific needs of financial and marketing managers. EXPRESS uses an English-like language and facilitates not only simple file handling and data aggregation but also extensive modeling and statistical analysis of the data series. The four main components of EXPRESS are:

- ☐ The database.
- ☐ Report and other display capabilities.
- ☐ Analytical capabilities, for example, statistical and financial analysis.
- ☐ Modeling (financial and operational).

1. *Database.* Data are normally collected and stored in a structure with three dimensions: line item, organization division, and time. However, there can be more than three dimensions. Also, the data can be retrieved and changed with very few commands provided by the user, and a user can create his/her own routines in EXPRESS and execute them by typing a single macro command.

2. *Reports and Displays.* EXPRESS can display a wide variety of items, including simple tables of data, customized formal reports, and graphics such as pie charts and histograms. Using TBL and DISPLAY commands, the user can automatically format and label the output.

3. *Analytical Capabilities.* Three separate types of utilities are available: mathematical, financial, and statistical. *Mathematical* utilities include sorting, percent difference, lags and leads, minimum/maximum of a set of numbers, average, year-to-date accumulation, lagged percent difference, and rounding. *Financial* utilities include depreciation (straight-line, sum-of-the-years' digits, and double or multiple declining balance), discounted cash flow techniques, loan amortization, and break-even point of a series of cash flows. *Statistical* utilities include time series analysis and forecasting, causal models and survey analysis, random number generation, risk analysis, and Monte Carlo simulation.

4. *Modeling.* The user can build financial planning models, test alternative scenarios by asking "what if" questions, and perform sensitivity analysis. It is possible to change the model by changing a number of parameters and then simulate alternative decisions. Backward iteration can be done to calculate the figures needed to generate target results.

In November 1982, MDS, the manufacturer of EXPRESS, cut the price of the base system from $130,000 to $50,000. This price includes multidimensional database management, centralized data dictionary maintenance facilities, consolidations and editing, interactive data-manipulation library, customized command capabilities and modeling, prompted data entry, interactive analysis, and output capabilities. A complete financial DSS based on EXPRESS costs about $135,000 (in 1984) compared with the previous price of $228,000.

In February 1983, MDS made the mainframe capabilities of EXPRESS available at the minicomputer level by introducing a version of the product packaged with the PRIME 2250 computer. This minicomputer version is available in 1985 in two configurations: E300 with 2.0MB memory and E600 with 3.0MB memory. The former costs $125,000, and the latter $180,000. Both prices include the hardware PRIME 2250, which sells alone for $39,900 to $48,900.

Both E300 and E600 are available in two versions: finance and marketing. The *finance version* is used for financial reporting, analysis, and modeling. It includes database management capabilities, report and graphics features,

```
→SENSAL
FOR WHICH YEAR(S)>                        81
FOR WHICH DIVISION(S):>                   MACHINE
LINE ITEM(S) TO BE CHANGED:>              UNIT SALE
IMPACT ON WHICH LINE ITEM(S):             NET SALE NET INC.
NUMBER OF SCENARIOS>                      3
PERCENT OR ABSOLUTE CHANGE                PERCENT
FROM BASE>

PERCENT CHANGE FROM THE BASE
DIVISION MACHINE
YEAR YR 81
SCENARIO 1
LINE UNIT SALE:>      -10
SCENARIO 2:>          -20
SCENARIO 3:>           15

SCENARIO 1
UNIT SALES PERCENT CHANGE -10.000
YEAR YR 81
DIVISION MACHINE

                 BASE CASE      CHANGE      DIFFERENCE      %DIFF.

UNIT SALE        84,634.10     76,170.69     -8,463.41     -10.00 %
NET SALES        33,430.00     30,087.00     -3,343.00     -10.00 %
NET INC           1,250.00        889.00     -  361.00     -28.88 %
```

```
SCENARIO 2
UNIT SALE PERCENT CHANGE -20.000
YEAR YR 81
DIVISION MACHINE

UNIT SALES      84,634.10      67,707.28   -16,926.82    -20.00 %
NET SALES       33,430.00      26,744.00   - 6,686.00    -20.00 %
NET INC          1,250.00         528.00   -   722.00    -57.76 %

SCENARIO 3
UNIT SALES PERCENT CHANGE 15.000
YEAR YR 81
DIVISION MACHINE

UNIT SALE       84,634.10      97,329.21    12,695.11     15.00 %
NET SALE        33,430.00      38,445.00     5,015.00     15.00 %
NET INC          1,250.00       1,791.00       541.00     43.28 %
```

FIGURE 12-27 Sample "what if" session of EXPRESS [1].

a set of financial and statistical analyses, and advanced modeling techniques. The *marketing version* supports a variety of applications such as sales planning, sales tracking and control, marketing mix analysis, strategic market planning, market evaluation, new product development, and business planning.

12.24   ROLE OF EXPRESS IN FINANCIAL PLANNING

EXPRESS can be used very effectively in long-range financial planning. It provides a sound basis for evaluating alternative business strategies. It can integrate the year-end financial results, or any previously created consolidation routines and reports, from the company's historical database directly into the planning process.

EXPRESS provides four areas of support in performing financial planning ([1], pp. 23–24):

1. *Investment Analysis.*   The built-in financial utilities and modeling capabilities of EXPRESS allow the user to calculate investment tax credit; discounted cash flow analysis; lease-buy analysis; the ranking, sorting, and classification of capital expenditure portfolios; and sensitivity analysis on capital costs.

2. *"What If" Modeling.*   EXPRESS enables the user to perform analysis using both internal and external data for different divisions, countries, and line of business. The "what if" are handled through user-friendly prompts in an interactive environment. Figure 12-27 (taken from EXPRESS brochure [1]) shows a sample session for sensitivity analysis (SENSANAL).

3. *Risk Analysis.*   The user can perform risk analysis by using the mathematical modeling capabilities of EXPRESS. He/she can model multiple scenarios with comparative probabilities, produce graphs of risk profile outputs, histograms, and probability distributions, and generate statistical measures such as mean and standard deviation to determine trade-offs in risk/return situations.

4. *Forecasting.*   The user can analyze historical data in the EXPRESS database to determine future trends and then forecast results pertaining to future industry growth, revenues, market share, and raw material costs. The basic tools available in EXPRESS include time series analysis, curve fitting, exponential smoothing, regression and correlation, factor analysis, growth rate analysis, and deseasonalization. Figure 12-28 (taken from an EXPRESS brochure [1]) illustrates a sample session on forecasting. The result shows that the data have a linear trend. The user can also get a graph of the trend-fit analysis, if desired.

```
    →          TRENDFIT
TIMES TO BE ANALYZED: >              ACTUALS
DESEASONALIZE BEFORE FITTING TREND? >  NO
FOR WHICH MONTH(S): >                JAN 76 TO DEC 80
FOR WHICH DIVISION(S): >             CHEMICAL
FOR WHICH LINEITEM(S): >             NET SALE
FOR WHICH CURVES?
1-LIN, 2-EXP. 3-PWR, 4-HYP1, 5-HYP2, 6-HYP3>    123


(TSRGMIN) BEST-FITTING CURVE:   LINEAR

(TSRGRSOQ)   COEFFICIENT OF DETERMINATION
(TSC1)       COEFFICIENT   1
(TSC2)       COEFFICIENT   2


TSTYPE          TSRGRSQ    TSC1         TSC2
LINEAR          .909165    5,782.18     72.13123
EXPONENTIAL     .898473    5,922.45     .0093221
PWR FUNCTION    .823134    4,568.72     .1729885
```
FIGURE 12-28   Curve fitting in EXPRESS [1].

12.25   ROLE OF EXPRESS IN MERGERS/ACQUISITIONS ANALYSIS

The user of EXPRESS can analyze the merger/acquisition of other companies in a number of ways ([1], p. 25):

1. *Target Analysis.*   The user can enter and analyze the target company's historical performance and restate its accounts in comparison with the acquiring firm's accounts. He/she can utilize the growth rate, seasonal, and ratio analysis techniques provided by EXPRESS.

2. *Projections.*   The user can project multiple scenarios for the target company and include financial statements, projected market share, cash flow, and expected capital expenditures. It is possible to use several time series forecasting techniques for sales and market forecasts and to evaluate multiple scenarios with "what if" analysis, sensitivity analysis, and risk analysis.

3. *Valuation.*   The user can determine the bid price for the proposed acquisition by using a range of valuation methods such as discounted value of projected cash flows, forecasted book values, and price/earnings ratio analysis.

4. *Consolidated Impact.*   EXPRESS allows the user to consolidate results for all pooling and purchase accounting alternatives; measure the range of debt/equity, liquidity, operating, and other ratios for the consolidated entity; and generate reports and color graphics to represent comparisons and consolidated data for all merger alternatives.

12.26   DSS FOR THE MARKETING ENVIRONMENT

Developing the marketing plan for most consumer products generally involves a preliminary sales forecast and estimate of overall profitability. These figures are then used to specify the budget for the marketing mix: price, advertising, promotion, sales force activities, and so on.

An example of a DSS supporting marketing plan activities is provided by BRANDAID, designed by J. D. C. Little and based on a design strategy he called the decision calculus. This latter term means that a model should be simple (but not simplistic), robust, easy to control, easy to communicate with, and adaptive. A discussion of BRANDAID now follows.

12.27   BRANDAID: A CASE STUDY

12.27.1   Background and Objectives

BRANDAID was introduced by J. D. C. Little in 1975. Its main objective is to develop an annual marketing plan for any product manufactured by a company. As a DSS, then, BRANDAID addresses a semistructured task in which managers are generally successful in intuitive assessments and problem finding. However, they often depend on inefficient heuristics and are unable to integrate the complete analysis involving sales forecast, budgeting, and advertising policy. BRANDAID provides an analytic tool to help managers coordinate the findings. Keen and Scott Morton ([2], pp. 138–147) have discussed the essential features of BRANDAID in their book. The following treatment draws heavily from that work.

12.27.2   Overall Plan and Outline

BRANDAID models the market as consisting of five principal elements: manufacturer, competitors, retailers, consumers, and the general environment. It explores the complex interactions that take place among them. For example, the manufacturer influences the consumers by means of product quality, sales promotion, and prices. The competitors try to hinder the marketing strategy of the manufacturer. Macroeconomic variables such as price trend, level of unemployment, and demand for consumer goods affect the general environment of the market. Managers are usually adept at understanding the interaction of the market by assessing the mutual impact of the five elements taken in pairs. However, in most cases the total picture is too overwhelming to grasp. BRANDAID helps managers to evaluate the overall situation by integrating all its components and allowing them to use their

subjective judgment. Thus, a unique feature of BRANDAID is its incorporation of subjective judgment as well as hard data. As Little puts it ([3], p. 631):

> The approach to calibration, rather than being based on a particular set of data, say, a collection of time series, is unabashedly eclectic. In fact, we would maintain that, for a real decision, exclusive reliance on previous databases will usually be misleading; the calibration task is to estimate what is going to happen, not what has already happened.

BRANDAID is designed to support the decision process for established products and is referred to as an "aggregate response" model since it relates all the major components of a total market system.

12.27.3 Technical Design Components

The main statistical tool used in BRANDAID is forecasting. However, unlike conventional forecasting, BRANDAID combines past data with subjective judgment in calibrating the model. BRANDAID describes the relationships in a marketing system in terms of two parameters: *direct index* and *response curve*. A direct index is a numerical value derived from market tests or historical data. Response curves relate some controllable quantity such as sales to a decision variable such as price. Generally, response curves can be defined only subjectively by the manager specifying a reference value.

To start the process, the manager defines the two decision variables that are to be related by the reference curve and establishes their initial values, which are assigned an index of 1.0 each. Next he defines how changes in the values of one variable will relate to changes in the values of the other variables. These changes are translated into pairs of index values. Only a few sets of these values are needed to determine the full reference curve. Keen and Scott Morton ([2], p. 141) have given an example of a reference curve to connect promotion level with sales figures. Their concluding remark in this respect is quoted below ([2], pp. 141):

> This approach to calibrating the model relies on managers' judgements. The exercise of developing a consensus on the exact shape of the response curve is often valuable in itself for a group of marketing managers. The model combines the individual consensual judgements, on price, advertising and so on; in effect it extrapolates the implications of the manager's beliefs in a way that they themselves cannot, because of the human mind's limited ability to integrate complex masses of data. BRANDAID shows how the computer and the manager can combine their relative strengths in a semistructured task.

12.27.4 Feedback Loop

The feedback loop in BRANDAID is provided by calibration of the model. The process of calibration is really continuous. In order to make it effective it is necessary to get a consensus on managers' decisions. The Delphi technique (see Chapter 5) is normally used to achieve this. A group of knowledgeable people are brought together, and each person makes his/her own estimates of response values. These are then displayed anonymously on a blackboard and the results are discussed. A consensus is attained, and the final recommendations are implemented.

The Delphi technique indeed encourages the feedback loop. After the final recommendations are implemented, the managers review the model's results, compare them with past performance, and, if necessary, redefine parameters. Thereby they can make the parameter values updated and reliable. BRANDAID truly supports managerial decisions in that it depends heavily on the managers' experience, knowledge base, and personalized judgments.

12.28 CONCLUDING REMARKS

So far we have examined four case studies of DSS, two hypothetical examples and two showing DSS in actual use. In Chapter 1 we discussed two other DSS packages, SIMPLAN and CIS. Keen and Scott Morton ([2], Chapter 5) have given several other examples of DSS in use, addressing such diverse applications as portfolio management, financial planning, planning for urban growth, redefining school district boundaries, and assigning city law enforcement personnel to beats. The purpose of this chapter has been to give a flavor of a wide variety of decision support systems in practice.

12.29 SUMMARY

This chapter discusses four specific examples of DSS: Investment Decision Support System (IDSS), Distribution/Transportation Decision Support System (D/T DSS), EXPRESS, and BRANDAID. IDSS and D/T DSS are hypothetical case studies in the sense that they are not used in practice. We introduced both of them in Chapter 2 and described their analysis phases. In this chapter we have continued the study from there and have completed their design and implementation phases.

IDSS provides support in four basic areas, which are its four subsystems: client portfolio information, security selection analysis, investment timing analysis, and portfolio analysis technique. The design phase of IDSS describes its control module as an interactive user-friendly interface that links to the other three modules of IDSS, the data storage, data manipulation, and model-

building modules. The user can access IDSS through a multilevel menu system consisting of one main menu and four detailed menus corresponding to the four subsystems. Sample reports from these subsystems are provided.

The data storage module of IDSS contains file structures for the four subsystems. It is assumed that a relational DBMS such as ORACLE will handle the actual IDSS database and data manipulation including report generation and graphics.

IDSS uses statistical models (forecasting, point-and-figure charting, breadth-of-market technique) in the investment timing analysis subsystem and optimizing models (capital asset pricing and investment risk/return) in the portfolio analysis technique subsystem.

The feedback control loop of IDSS is discussed through three sample "what if" scenarios: sensitivity of leading indicators and securities, single-security versus capital asset pricing, and regression analysis. Sample interactive screens exemplify the "what if" solutions. The discussion of IDSS ends with a management evaluation of its strengths and weaknesses.

D/T DSS provides decision support to improve delivery routes, economic inventory levels, and product mix as well as to respond to situational questions such as plant closings, discontinuation of product lines, and alternative warehouse locations. The control module enables the user to access D/T DSS via the main menu. He/she can then use D/T DSS to address problems in any of the following three areas: sales and marketing, distribution, and accounting/forecasting. Detailed screens are provided in each of these three areas.

The data storage module of D/T DSS uses four major data files: customer, warehouse, manufacturing, and transportation. Two sample reports are shown as examples of the output from the data manipulation module.

The model-building module contains two mathematical models: linear programming to minimize the transportation cost of automobiles, and linear regression to forecast future fuel cost and labor cost.

Finally, sample "what if"scenarios are provided via interactive screens. Comments of an evaluative nature are provided by management to outline the positive and negative aspects of D/T DSS.

EXPRESS is a commercially available DSS for financial analysis. It uses an English-like language and facilitates file handling, data aggregation, mathematical modeling, and statistical analysis. It has report generation and graphics capabilities. It provides four areas of support in performing financial planning: investment analysis, sensitivity analysis in "what if" scenarios, risk analysis, and forecasting. EXPRESS can perform mergers and acquisitions analysis for the user by providing target analysis, projections on cash flow and other financial items, valuations of bid prices for the proposed acquisition, and the consolidated impact of accounting practices.

BRANDAID is a DSS for marketing environment. Its main objective is to develop an annual marketing plan for any product. It models the market

as consisting of five principal elements: manufacturer, competitors, retailers, consumers, and the general environment. It helps managers to evaluate the overall situation by integrating all the components of the markets and then allowing the managers to use their subjective judgment.

The main statistical tool in BRANDAID is forecasting. It describes the relationships in a marketing system in terms of two parameters: direct index and response curve. The latter relates some controllable quantity such as sales to a decision variable such as price. The feedback loop is then provided by calibration of the model. Calibration is really a continuous process. It is implemented in practice by using the Delphi technique. The latter enables managers to arrive at a consensus on their decisions. A case study by Keen and Scott Morton shows that BRANDAID helps the managers to test the various alternative strategies on price and advertising budgets.

12.30 KEY WORDS

The following key words are used in this chapter:

BRANDAID
breadth-of-market technique
calibration
capital asset pricing
client portfolio information
control module
D/T DSS
data manipulation module
data storage module
dealership category
Delphi technique
direct index
distribution profit
distribution/transportation decision support system (D/T DSS)
EXPRESS
feedback loop
financial planning
forecasting
IDSS

inventory movement
investment decision support system (IDSS)
investment risk and return
investment timing analysis
linear programming
linear regression
long-term regression model
merger/acquisition analysis
model-building module
point-and-figure charting
portfolio analysis technique
portfolio return
response curve
risk analysis
screening function
security selection analysis
sensitivity of leading indicators
short-term regression model
warehouse category

REFERENCES

1. *EXPRESS for Finance*, Mangement Decision System, Waltham, MA.
2. P. Keen and M. Scott Morton, *Decision Support System: An Organizational Perspective*, Addison-Wesley, Reading, MA, 1978.
3. J.D.C. Little, "BRANDAID," *Operations Research*, **23**, 628–673 (May 1975).

REVIEW QUESTIONS

1. Describe the functions and contents of the four component modules of a DSS.
2. Refer to the descriptions of SIMPLAN and CIS given in Chapter 1. For each of them, describe how you would design the four component modules.
3. Discuss the functions of the four subsystems of IDSS.
4. Why is it desirable to implement the control module via a set of interactive screens?
5. Explain the difference between a long-term and a short-term regression model, as used in IDSS.
6. What are the functions of an economic indicator? How many types of economic indicators are there? Describe their use.
7. What is a screening function? What role does it play in the data manipulation module of IDSS?
8. Describe the five information sources for D/T DSS.
9. Discuss how linear programming is used in the model-building module of D/T DSS.
10. Descibe the four main components of EXPRESS.
11. What are the four areas of support provided by EXPRESS in performing financial planning?
12. Define direct index and response curve, as used in BRANDAID.

FORMULATIONAL PROBLEMS

1. Assume that you have a relational DBMS package such as ORACLE. Describe in detail how you would design and implement the data storage modules of IDSS and D/T DSS.
2. With the same assumption as in problem 1, write the DBMS commands that will generate the reports of Figures 12-24 and 12-25.

DSS Games as Instructional Tools

13.1 GAMES SIMULATING THE BUSINESS ENVIRONMENT

In recent decades, especially during the late 1970s, several new instructional methods have been developed in the area of decision support systems. This is called *business simulation* or *business gaming*. It involves a dynamic and sequential decision-making exercise structured around a model of business operation in which the participants assume the roles of managers of a simulated firm. The purpose of such instructional aids is to provide the students with a planned learning experience in dealing with financial management problems. The overall scenario can be depicted as follows:

Participants operating in a simulated environment start with some historical data on the firm.

For each period of play (e.g., one quarter, one year), the participants make decisions and supply them as input to the model.

The software package supporting the model evaluates the decisions and provides output for the participants.

The participants analyze this information to determine how well or how poorly their initial objectives have been met.

In a typical financial environment, two objectives of basic concern are profitability and liquidity. *Profitability* can be measured by two criteria:

1. Return on investment (ROI) $= \dfrac{\text{income after taxes}}{\text{total assets}}$

2. $\quad$ Return on equity (ROE) $= \dfrac{\text{income after taxes}}{\substack{\text{common and preferred stocks} \\ + \text{ surplus } + \text{ retained earnings}}}$

ROI is concerned with the productivity of all the firm's assets, while ROE provides a measure of the productivity of the capital contribution of common stockholders.

Liquidity is measured by the *current ratio,* which is computed by dividing the current assets by the current liabilities:

$$\text{Current ratio } = \frac{\text{current assets}}{\text{current liabilities}}$$

The instructional aids supported by the software packages concentrate on achieving the objectives through simulation of business experience. We shall discuss three such packages here:

1. The Executive Game
2. FINANSIM
3. The Management Game

13.2 OVERVIEW OF THE EXECUTIVE GAME

The Executive Game is designed as an educational tool for college students and business managers. It is not a typical simulation or modeling package such as GPSS or SPSS. Rather, the Executive Game uses the science of simulation to present an imaginary business environment to the game participants. This environment allows the game players to practice top-level management planning and decision making in a dynamic business situation.

A single multifirm, hypothetical industry is the focus of the game. Single players or small teams of participants make the top management decisions in the simulated industry. These decisions include quarter-year action concerning budget items such as product selling price and production volumes; marketing, R&D, and plant maintenance budgets; and dividend payments on company stock. Players' decisions are fed to the computerized game model, which simulates the internal operations of the firms, interactions with other firms, and effects of the economy on the firm. Quarterly business reports are prepared by the computer for the players, as are year-end reports for each business "year" the game is simulating. The game, being computer based, is essentially deterministic. However, realistic uncertainty appears because the program includes general economic conditions, inflation, seasonal demand cycles, and the unpredictable behavior of other firms.

The goal of the game is for the players to maximize their firm's return on investment. The game instructions emphasize the importance of planning in decision making both for short-range quarterly decisions and long-range full-game planning. Teaching the players to make these decisions in a well thought out manner is the actual goal of the game's authors.

The game allows the participants to deal simultaneously with production, marketing, finance, market competition, economic fluctuations, inflation, and so on. Practice at coping with these factors will help to develop insight and appreciation for the importance of considering the company as a whole.

The real winners of the Executive Game are those who learn the most. These fortunate persons need not be the managers of the most profitable firms: As in the real business world, luck is an important factor, along with ability, knowledge, and hard work. Your success as a learner is far more important in the end.

Realism in the simulation of the game is achieved by means of three interrelated ingredients:

1. *The Decision Set.* Decisions are made each period, spanning all major business functions. For example, marketing includes product development, pricing, promotion and distribution, plus credit and sales force management. Personnel includes hiring and firing, structuring sales and labor compensation, and labor union relations. Manufacturing covers production, maintenance, and plant expansion. Inventory includes both purchasing and distribution. Within finance, the decision areas include cash management, insurance, the raising of capital, and dividend policy.

2. *The Management Report.* A concise report provides the type of information top management requires and in a desirable format. This includes financial statements, cost accounting and cash flow analyses, raw materials and product flows, sales and market analyses, and audited financial statements of the industry.

3. *The Simulated Environment.* The complex interactions of the competing firms are processed through a simulated marketplace. Insofar as possible, it reflects the behavior of any oligopolistic industry, be it a product or service in manufacturing or in retail, or wholesale marketing. Customers respond to a mix of several marketing appeals. Supplies, capacity, employees, and capital must be acquired in competitive markets. Common business conventions are included, such as:

Recruitment expenses and severance pay.

Plant capacity and raw materials lead time.

Floating prime and long-term interest rates.

Credit sales and bad debits.

Market research estimates.

Real economic growth and an inflation index.

Stocks and bonds underwriting costs.

Investment tax credits.

FIFO, LIFO, and weighted average inventory accounting.

A wide selection of "exogenous events" such as wildcat strikes, antitrust lawsuits, and wage and price controls.

13.3 ESSENTIALS OF THE EXECUTIVE GAME

The objective of the Executive Game is for management, in this case the players or teams of players, to maximize return on investment (ROI) by making effective quarterly decisions on how their company resources—cash, plant, employees, and so on—will be utilized. Quarterly decisions, primarily in terms of dollar amounts, are required for (1) the selling price of the firm's product, (2) the marketing budget, (3) the research and development budget, (4) the plant maintenance budget, (5) the scheduled production volume, (6) the plant investment budget, (7) the raw materials purchases budget, and (8) dividends per share.

To be successful in the game requires planning and coordination among the various decisions and such built-in factors as any significant inflationary trend and the total market potential for the product, which is affected by the overall level of economic activity, seasonal fluctuations, price index, and competitors' decisions. Each of the decision variables has an effect on one or more of the variables. To explain each decision variable would require too much depth for this overview of the game. However, the raw materials purchases budget will be used as an illustration of the interrelationships among the variables.

The supply of raw materials limits the production volume of the firm. Raw materials are purchased at an established price, which increases with the price index but at a lesser rate. Each order incurs various administrative costs (referred to as ordering costs). These costs are not dependent upon the size of the order and will increase with inflation but not as rapidly. The ordering costs must be balanced against the raw materials carrying cost—storage, insurance, and so on—which is related to the value of the firm's raw materials inventory. The most crucial factor to remember concerning raw materials is that they must be ordered a full quarter ahead of when they will be needed for processing. The raw materials to be used in production in the current quarter must come from the firm's inventory at the end of the preceding quarter. Available raw materials affect the production volume, which in turn affects plant maintenance, which in turn affects the plant investment budget. No decision as to the dollars to be spent in any one area can be made without influencing other areas of the firm. Since business decisions are not made in a vacuum, the Executive Game has been designed to make players consider how their decisons impact upon other areas of the

business. All players must familiarize themselves with the interrelationships among the decision variables.

One of the mathematical relationships concerning raw materials purchases involves selecting frequency of ordering so as to minimize the sum of the average ordering cost (X) and the raw materials carrying costs (Y). The problem is somewhat simplified compared to the possibilities that exist in the real business world, since in the game the intervals between orders can only be multiples of one quarter (it is impossible to space orders 75 days apart, say) and the quantity ordered is always supplied on time. The average ordering cost originates at \$50,000, while the average raw materials carrying cost is 5 percent of the value of the raw materials inventory. The basic formulas involved in the calculation if the order is being placed every quarter are:

$$X = \$50,000$$
$$Y = 0.05V \quad (V = \text{value of raw materials inventory})$$

therefore,

$$\text{SUMI} = X + Y = 50,000 + 0.05V$$

If an order were placed every second quarter, the ordering cost per quarter would be \$25,000. The order must be large enough to leave enough raw materials to meet the production needs of the next two quarters. Thus, the average amount of raw materials inventory at the end of the quarter will be enough for $(2 + 1)/2$ or 1.5 quarters. Therefore, the basic formulas involved, if an order were placed every second quarter, are:

$$X = \$25,000$$
$$Y = 0.05 \times 1.5V = 0.075V$$

therefore,

$$\text{SUM2} = X + Y = 25,000 + 0.075V$$

As the order interval increases from 1 quarter to 2 quarters, the cost per order (per quarter) decreases, from \$50,000 to \$25,000, while the carrying cost increases, from 5 percent of the inventory value to 7.5 percent.

Suppose that V is estimated to be \$800,000. The cost can be determined as follows:

$$\text{SUMI} = 50,000 + 0.05(800,000) = 90,000$$
$$\text{SUM2} = 25,000 + 0.075(800,000) = 85,000$$

Under the present assumption, if $V = 800,000$, it would be better by $5000 to order every second quarter.

If $V = 1,300,000$, then costs would be:

$$SUM1 = 50,000 + 0.05(1,300,000) = 115,000$$
$$SUM2 = 25,000 + 0.075(1,300,000) = 122,500$$

Thus, in this instance it will be $7500 better per quarter to place an order each quarter.

These very simple calculations illustrate how decisions must be coordinated and balanced but are not indicative of the complexity of the mathematical models used throughout the game.

Once the required decisions are made, they are entered on a decision sheet, which serves as an input document. Worksheets for analysis of operations are provided so the players can estimate the results of their decisions and compare the estimates with the actual numbers produced by the game. See [2] for examples of the Decision Sheet and the Worksheet forms. It is assumed that an analysis of the actual versus estimated figures will help the players make better decisions in the future.

The essential ingredient for successful management of an Executive Game business is balance and coordination among the various decisions. The need for planning, in addition to quarter-by-quarter balance and coordination, is emphasized by the fact that a logically organized sequence of decisions generally produces better results than erratic fluctuations.

13.4   OUTPUT ANALYSIS

An important thing to remember about the Executive Game is that participants are pitted against one another rather than being pitted against the computer. The Executive Game attempts to simulate the real world. All participants in the simulation are given the same information about the current state of the economy, their company's product prices, their competitors' prices, their market share, and their competitors' market shares.

Let's take a close look at the output from the simulation by examining Figure 13.1. The first two lines tell each team the current state of the economy and give predictions of economic conditions in the next quarter.

The next few lines in the output tell how each firm compares with its competitors in the marketplace, providing players with information about competitors' prices, dividends, sales, and net profit. This information can be used to determine in what direction competitors are moving and whether they are being successful in whatever terms success is being measured.

The last section of the output contains operating, income, cash flow, and financial statements. These are used to determine the areas of weakness for the particular firm.

MODEL 1 PERIOD 1 JAS PRICE INDEX 101. 0 FORECAST, ANNUAL CHANGE   5. 3 0/0
SEAS. INDEX   95. NEXT QTR. 115.   ECON. INDEX 101. FORECAST, NEXT QTR.   95.

INFORMATION   ON   COMPETITORS

	PRICE	DIVIDEND	SALES VOLUME	NET PROFIT
FIRM 1	$ 26. 00	$ 56000.	111071.	$ 158682.
FIRM 2	$ 27. 00	$ 57000.	89124.	$ 31125.
FIRM 3	$ 28. 00	$ 58000.	68640.	$ -121713.
FIRM 4	$ 27. 50	$ 50000.	77523.	$ -50823.

FIRM 7 1
OPERATING STATEMENTS

MARKET POTENTIAL	111071.
SALES VOLUME	111071.
PERCENT SHARE OF INDUSTRY SALES	32.
PRODUCTION, THIS QUARTER	120000.
INVENTORY, FINISHED GOODS	21679.
PLANT CAPACITY, NEXT QUARTER	108913.

INCOME STATEMENT

RECEIPTS, SALES REVENUE		$ 2887849.
EXPENSES, MARKETING	$ 200000.	
RESEARCH AND DEVELOPMENT	150000.	
ADMINISTRATION	333943.	
MAINTENANCE	70000.	
LABOR(COST/UNIT EX. OVERTIME $ 5. 79)	739658.	
MATERIALS CONSUMED(COST/UNIT ' 6. 32)	758197.	
REDUCTION, FINISHED GOODS INV.	-107147.	
DEPRECIATION(3. 125 0/0)	228906.	
FINISHED GOODS CARRYING COSTS	43358.	
RAW MATERIALS CARRYING COSTS	60000.	
ORDERING COSTS	50000.	
SHIFTS CHANGE COSTS	0.	
PLANT INVESTMENT EXPENSES	25000.	
FINANCING CHARGES AND PENALTIES	0.	
SUNDRIES	85343.	2637258.
PROFIT BEFORE INCOME TAX		250591.
INCOME TAX(IN. TX. CR. 10. 0/0, SURTAX 0. 0/0)		91908.
NET PROFIT AFTER INCOME TAX		158682.
DIVIDENDS PAID		56000.
ADDITION TO OWNERS EQUITY		102682.

CASH FLOW

RECEIPTS, SALES REVENUE		$ 2887849.
DISBURSEMENTS, CASH EXPENSE	$ 1757301.	
INCOME TAX	91908.	
DIVIDENDS PAID	56000.	
PLANT INVESTMENT	500000.	
MATERIALS PURCHASED	1750000.	4155210.
ADDITION TO CASH ASSETS		-1267361.

FINANCIAL STATEMENT

NET ASSETS, CASH	$ -245361.
INV. VALUE, FINISHED GOODS	260147.
INVENTORY VALUE, MATERIALS	2191803.
PLANT BOOK VALUE(REPLACE. VAL. $ 7907897.)	7596094.
OWNERS EQUITY(ECONOMIC EQUITY 10114485.)	9802682.

FIGURE 13-1 Sample output from the Executive Game.

While the second section of the output tells each firm where it stands vis-à-vis its competitors, the third section provides specific information on the firm's own position.

There is a worksheet to use in conjunction with the output from the simulation. This worksheet allows each firm's "managers" to fill in information on the position of the firm and on the position of the competition. This allows the managers to focus their thinking. It helps them realize the impact of some of the options available to them

Through the use of the worksheet, the simulation tries to prevent the managers from just guessing at numbers. Although some guesswork is necessary, because firms never know what decisions the other firms will make, the worksheet may help them make an educated guess about what the competition may be doing next quarter.

The use of the worksheet also prevents firms from attempting actions that are beyond the capabilities of their plant and equipment. The worksheet does this by showing the calculations for the maximum that the firm can achieve in the next quarter given certain constraints, such as current investment in plant and equipment or levels of raw materials inventory or finished goods inventory.

13.5 PERFORMANCE CRITERIA

When the Executive Game was first designed, it was accepted that profit maximization would be the basic criterion for measuring performance. However, as the game evolved, many believed that the owner's rate of return on investment was a more precise measure of performance.

Strictly speaking, the Executive Game's large measure of uncertainty makes it almost meaningless to attempt to maximize any specific quantity (profit, ROI, etc.). It is more likely, as in the real world, that you would think of maximizing "most likely" gains or "hoped-for" gains or minimizing the "worst case" difference between possible and actual gains. Gains can be thought of as standing for whatever basic measure is deemed appropriate.

It can be seen that the general idea is to conceptualize the uncertainty of the business environment as a set of possible general economic and competitive conditions, each with a numerical probability, and each of which will affect the gains to be had from any particular policy. The expected value of the gains from a particular policy is the probability-weighted average of the gains it will yield under the various possible conditions. The goal is therefore to make "average" gains as large as possible.

It should be noted that it is not really viable to apply decision theory methods formally except to subproblems of the total problem posed by the Executive Game. The decision theory perspective can be used, however, to conceptualize problems up to and including the total problem of managing your total firm. By aiming to maximize the "average gains," you can get

away from the idea that you must somehow predict exactly how things are going to work out.

The case for profit maximization stems from the fact that most business firms want to maximize long-run gains. In fact, if the game went on indefinitely, it might be fitting to think of long-run profits as the primary criterion of managerial performance. This can be seen even more clearly when you think of long-run profits more specifically as average profits over an indefinitely long period of time. In the indefinitely long run, maximizing average profits comes to the same thing as maximizing the expected value of profits per quarter. Thus, the profit maximization theory seems to head you in the right direction.

The profit maximization theory fails, however, if the question of dividends is addressed. If one were to maximize retained earnings, no dividends would be declared. This would allow as much cash as possible to be kept to avoid the risk of cash shortages. On the other hand, firms with such a financial posture appeal only to investors who can forego current personal income in the anticipation of delayed dividends or capital gains. This is not the sort of firm represented in the Executive Game. The stockholders of firms in the game hope for a large and consistent income. They want at least a reasonable part of their money now, not at some indefinite future date. With this in mind, return on investment was introduced as the primary criterion for the evaluation of management.

The return on investment concept was devised to reflect the preference for receiving a given amount of money now rather than later. This preference may stem from the desire for current consumption or from the fact that a sum received now can be reinvested and return a larger sum at a future time. The players must decide when to declare dividends. Two firms can have the same profits and pay the same total dividends; but, for instance, if one of them has a steady stream of dividends throughout play while the other hoards cash until the last few quarters of play and then issues a few large dividends, then the first firm will score higher than the second. This can best be illustrated with an example.

Firms 1 and 2 compete against each other in the same industry. Each starts with owners' equity of $10,000,000 and earns a net profit of $1,300,000 over 2 years of play. Each also pays out three dividends of $100,000 cash. But Firm 1 declares dividends in the first three quarters of play, while Firm 2 distributes dividends in the last three quarters. The calculation by the computer reveals that Firm 1 has earned an ROI of 6.44%, while Firm 2 has earned only 6.32%. The illustrative difference is small, but much larger differences could occur in similar examples if larger portions of total profits were distributed or if the duration of the game were 3 or 4 years.

In general, then, it can be seen that the desire to play it safe with respect to the possibility of cash shortages will motivate the player to keep unused cash on hand rather than distributing it as dividends. One of management's jobs, as in real life, is to strike a proper balance between these opposing forces.

13.6 FINANSIM: AN OVERVIEW

The simulated business environment of FINANSIM is an abstract one; it does not replicate that of any real industry. Each firm in the model produces and sells an unnamed and unidentified product. For each period of play, namely 1 year, the FINANSIM managers make the following decisions:

1. Determine the number of production units to be manufactured.
2. Purchase or sell marketable securities.
3. Float new or retire existing debentures.
4. Obtain bank loans to help finance company operations.
5. Issue new common stocks.
6. Make dividend payments on existing common stock.
7. Maintain or expand the firm's plant and equipment capacity.
8. Invest in any or all of three types of capital improvements each period that will result in future savings for the firm by reducing its operating costs.

Each FINANSIM firm begins the simulation by operating a going concern and making decisions for period 2. Decisions for period 1 have already been made. The results of these decisions are given by three computer outputs:

FINANSIM Income Statement.
FINANSIM Position Statement.
FINANSIM Supplemental Information.

See [1] for examples of these forms and statements. At the beginning of period 2 and each succeeding period, the firm's decisions are entered into the FINANSIM model through the FINANSIM decision form blank (see [1]).

13.7 OBJECTIVES OF FINANSIM

FINANSIM managers work with two objectives:

1. Maximize profitability (measured by ROI and ROE).
2. Maximize liquidity of assets (measured by the current ratio).

These terms have been discussed in Section 13.1. In order to meet these objectives, each manager makes numerous decisions and takes into consideration not only their effect on attaining the current objectives but also their implications for the future. For example, it may be desirable to undertake

plant expansion even though it yields a lower ROI in order for a firm to be more profitable in the long run.

The decision problems faced by the FINANSIM manager can be classified into three major categories:

1. *Investment of Funds in Income-Producing Assets.* The FINANSIM firm has several kinds of income-producing investments available to it each period. First are capital improvements, which effect savings in per-unit production costs and/or fixed manufacturing expense in the future. Second and third are investments in plant and equipment capacity. Fourth is the utilization of funds for production. Fifth is an opportunity to invest its funds in marketable securities. The first important task of the FINANSIM manager is that of evaluating the profitability of the utilization of funds for each of these types of investments. This evaluation involves examining both the cost of each investment alternative and the income that it will produce.

2. *Acquisition of Funds.* The FINANSIM manager must evaluate the alternative sources of funds available each period. In addition to financing operations from either cash on hand or cash to be generated during the period, the manager may resort to the following sources of funds: sales of marketable securities, notes payable, bank loans, debentures, and common stock. In evaluating these sources in light of the firm's profitability and liquidity objectives, numerous considerations may have to be taken into account, for example, the cost of funds, restrictions placed on management (such as that long-term debt cannot exceed 60% of total equity), and the risk of being unable to (1) meet both interest and principal payments on borrowed funds and (2) pay the amount of dividends to the firm's common stockholders that management considers desirable.

3. *Timing of Cash Inflows and Outflows.* The manager must plan the timing of cash outflows (for example, production expense, interest payments, and income taxes) and cash inflows (such as fund generated from cash sales and the collection of accounts receivable) in such a way that an adequate liquidity position is maintained without the firm's profitability being adversely affected. Such planning involves forecasting the effect that decisions each period will have upon all cash inflows and outflows during the period. A basic tool commonly utilized in projecting a firm's cash position is the cash budget.

13.8 FINANCIAL PLANNING USING FINANSIM

FINANSIM managers use three tools of financial planning: (1) the pro forma income statement, (2) the cash budget, and (3) the pro forma position statement. We now discuss each tool separately. For a more detailed treatment refer to [1], Chapter 4.

13.8.1 Pro Forma Income Statement

This statement is simply a projection of what the firm's income position will be at the end of any particular period, given any planned set of decisions. Preparation of such projections will enable the FINANSIM manager to estimate each period the impact of any sets of decisions being considered on the firm's sales revenue, expenses, and profits. If the projections for certain decision sets under consideration are adverse, the manager can examine the impact of other possible decision choices that may prove more desirable for the firm. Thus, the pro forma income statement can serve as a useful means of evaluating numerous alternative strategies available to the manager.

13.8.2 Cash Budget

The cash budget is a projection of the firm's ending cash balance for the period; it is based on all cash inflows and outflows expected to result in the period from any given set of decisions. By preparing a cash budget, the FINANSIM manager can help answer such questions as the following about any planned set of decisions:

1. Will the decisions result in an excessively large ending period cash balance? If so, will it be more desirable to invest in additional marketable securities? Should larger dividends be paid out to the firm's common shareholders?

2. Conversely, will such little cash be available that notes payable will have to be obtained? If so, should certain expenditures planned for the period be reduced so that the firm's liquidity position will be less strained?

Projection of the firm's ending balance for the period is a relatively simple task once the FINANSIM manager has prepared a pro forma income statement. This is because (1) much of the data required for the cash budget can be drawn directly from the pro forma income statement; and (2) relatively few calculations, other than simple addition and subtraction, are necessary in making cash projections.

13.8.3 Pro Forma Position Statement

The pro forma statement is a projection of the firm's asset and liability position at the end of the current period. Preparation of the pro forma position statement will enable the manager to answer the question; What effect will my planned set of decisions have upon the firm's retained earnings, current ratio, and long-term debt/equity ratio?

As discussed above, each tool involves financial projections for the firm. The managers determine the degree to which the financial objectives of the

firm will be realized as a result of their decisions. Normally, this happens by developing complete projections in the following order:

1. Pro forma income statement.
2. Cash budget.
3. Pro forma position statement.

However, there are several other ways in which the financial projections can be sequenced. For example, it is possible to begin the evaluation by preparing the cash budget first, then the income statement, and finally the position statement. It is not possible, however, to begin the firm's projections with the position statement. This projection must always be prepared last, since completion of the cash budget is necessary to obtain the firm's ending cash balance, and a completed pro forma income statement must first be developed to obtain income transferred to retained earnings.

We should also point out that sometimes, in the process of preparing financial projections, the manager may find that a particular series of decisions have been poor ones and may reject them without completing all three financial statements.

13.9   INVESTMENT DECISIONS IN FINANSIM

In making investment decisions for capital equipment, the manager must determine how profitable his/her decision will be for the company. Three considerations should be mentioned in this context:

1. The net returns from any given investment must exceed the initial cost of that investment; otherwise, the firm will be worse off financially by making the investment.

2. Costs are associated with any investment even if the firm utilizes its own funds rather than any obtained from external sources to finance the investment. This is because when a firm utilizes its funds for any investment it in effect forgoes the opportunity of realizing returns on the funds by investing them elsewhere.

3. When several available investment opportunities exist for each of which the net return exceeds the investment cost, but funds are not available for undertaking all the investments, the manager must develop some method of ranking the investments by degree of profitability. The manager finally chooses those that are most profitable.

The *profitablility index* (PI) is often used as a measure for ranking alternative investment decisions:

$$PI = \frac{\text{Present value of future returns}}{\text{First cost of investment}}$$

The alternative with the highest PI is selected.

Various models are available for evaluating investment decisions for capital equipment. FINANSIM uses four such items:

Paycheck.
Accounting rate of return.
Net present value.
Internal rate of return.

In addition, FINANSIM managers can use risk models (applicable particularly to net present value), because actual sales in the future are not known for certain in FINANSIM.

The next issue that concerns a manager is the acquisition of funds for capital investment. Four external sources of funds are available to the FINANSIM manager—notes payable, bank loans, debentures, and common stock—and each has important, distinctive characteristics. The first three sources are forms of debt financing; they have fixed maturity dates and call for fixed tax-deductible interest payments. Common stock, the only form of equity financing available to the manager, has no maturity date and requires no fixed dividend payments to the firm's shareholders. Common stock is not cost-free, however; in fact, if the firm's previous price/earnings ratio is taken as the cost of common stock, it is the most costly of all forms of external financing.

In choosing from among alternative sources of financing, one generally appropriate guide is to match the duration for which the funds are to be acquired to the duration for which they will be utilized. Also basic in deciding upon funds acquisition is the cost of alternative sources. Because the firm's various financing and investment decisions are interrelated, utilization of a weighted cost of capital ([1], pp. 196–201) is appropriate for FINANSIM decision making.

13.10 THE MANAGEMENT GAME

In July 1974 the Sloan School of Management at MIT introduced the Management Game as a course under information and decision systems. The purpose of the course was to let the students "understand the complex interrelationships among functions within an operating company" ([3], pp. 1–2).

The Management Game is very similar to the Executive Game. Accordingly, it is not necessary to discuss it in detail: an overview, as given below, will suffice.

The class is divided into six firms competing in a consumer nondurable goods industry with domestic and foreign markets. Each firm is required to diagnose the characteristics of the industry, set corporate goals, develop a strategy, make quarterly operating decisions, and comply with governmental

regulations. When the game begins, each firm has historical data on 11 quarters of activity for its firm and the industry.

The quarterly operating decisions consist of various marketing, production, and financial factors such as price, advertising, inventory, capacity, loans, and dividends. The decisions from all six firms are input to a computer simulation, which returns the resultant interaction of market characteristics, economic conditions, and competition in the form of standard accounting reports. Eight sets of quarterly decisions are made by each firm during the first week of the course, simulating 2 years of activity.

The game concentrates on three principal divisions within the industry: marketing, production, and finance. In *marketing* each firm develops reliable forecasts, largely by analyzing the best available indicators, the previous quarters' results. Overall demand is assumed to be relatively stable. Customers continue to buy the product unless there is a price increase, in which case they reevaluate the product in relation to all its competitors. In *production* the items are produced through a large-scale batch process that is constrained by the labor force and machine capacity. Inventory is not available for sale until the quarter after it is scheduled for production. In *finance*, each firm exercises substantial planning and management control. Timing is important due to the uncertainties of the financial environment. Funds must be transferred to and from the foreign operation; loans may be needed for financing, manufacturing, or inventory build-up; stock may be issued and dividends paid to the stockholders.

Each firm is operated on the basis of thousands of decisions that are made by the managers. Three forms are used to input the decisions:

1. Firm goals I and II.
2. Decision form, used for marketing, production, and finance decisions, and for forecasts.
3. Forecasts and plans form.

On the basis of the input data, the game simulation program is run and generates a wide variety of reports:

Domestic balance sheet
Foregin balance sheet
Domestic profit and loss statement
Foreign profit and loss statement
Domestic sources and uses of funds
Foreign sources and uses of funds
Domestic reconciliation of retained earnings
Foreign reconciliation of retained earnings
Domestic inventory reconciliation
Foreign inventory reconciliation

Domestic cash flow statement
Foreign cash flow statement

The game continues by taking the previous quarter's results and trying to learn from the earlier mistakes. It rewards coherent and reasonable strategies and penalizes extreme decisions.

13.11 SUMMARY

This chapter discusses three business game packages that simulate the decision-making process of managers in a real-world business environment. The three packages discussed here are the Executive Game, FINANSIM, and the Management Game. They give the flavor of the operation of such games. These are used as instructional tools for students.

The overall scenario in each game consists of four phases: (1) Participants start with some given historical data; (2) for each period of game they provide their decisions as input to the model; (3) the software simulates the model and provides output for the participants; (4) the participants analyze the output, learn from their mistakes, and continue.

The objective of each game is to maximize *profitability* and liquidity of assets. The former is measured by the return on investment (ROI) and return on equity (ROE), while the latter is measured by current ratio.

A single multifirm hypothetical industry is the focus of the game. Single players or small teams of participants make the top management decisions in the simulated industry. These decisions include quarterly actions concerning budget items such as product selling price and production volumes; marketing, R&D, and plant maintenance budgets; and dividend payments per share of stock. Players' decisions are fed to the computerized game model, which simulates the internal operations of the firms, interactions with other firms, and effects of the economy on the firm. Quarterly business reports are prepared by the computer for the players, as are year-end reports for each business "year" the game is simulating.

The games allow the participants to deal simultaneously with production, marketing, finance, market competition, economic fluctuations, inflation, and other factors. Practice at coping with these factors will help to develop insight and appreciation for the importance of considering the company as a whole.

The objective of the Executive Game is to maximize the ROI by achieving balance and coordination among various managerial decisions.

In FINANSIM each firm produces and sells an unnamed and unidentified product. For each period of play, which simulates one year, the FINANSIM managers must determine the number of production units to be manufactured, purchase or sell marketable securities, float new debentures or retire existing ones, obtain bank term loans to help finance company operations, issue new common stock, make dividend payments on existing common stock, maintain

or expand the firm's plant and equipment capacity, invest in any or all of three types of capital improvements each period that will result in future savings for the firm by reducing its operating costs.

Each FINANSIM firm begins the simulation by operating a going concern and making decisions for period 2. Decisions for period 1 have already been made. The results of these decisions are given by three computer outputs: the FINANSIM income statement, the FINANSIM position statement, and FINANSIM supplemental information. At the beginning of period 2 and each succeeding period, the firm's decisions are entered into the FINANSIM model through the FINANSIM decison form blank.

As with the Executive Game, the participants in FINANSIM want to maximize both ROI and ROE for profitability and the current ratio for liquidity of assets. The chapter also discusses financial planning using FINANSIM and the process of investment decision making in FINANSIM.

The Management Game, used as a course at the Sloan School of Management at MIT, is very similar to the Executive Game and therefore is not treated in detail. In this package each firm makes decisions for three major areas of industry: marketing, production, and finance. The decisions are input to the model and then 12 different output reports are produced by simulating the business decision environment.

13.12   KEY WORDS

The following key words are used in this chapter:

business games	Management Game
business simulation	marketing
cash budget	production
current ratio	profitability
decision input form	profitability index
Executive Game	pro forma income statement
finance	pro forma position statement
FINANSIM	return on equity (ROE)
liquidity of assets	return on investment (ROI)

REFERENCES

1. P.S. Greenslaw, M.W. Frey, and I.R. Vernon, *FINANSIM; A Financial Management Simulation,* West Publishing, St. Paul, MN., 1979.

2. R.C. Henshaw and J.R. Jackson, *The Executive Game,* 3rd ed., Richard D. Irwin, Homewood, IL, 1978.

3. P.G.W. Keen and J.R. Gordon, *The Management Game,* Massachusetts Institute of Technology, Sloan School of Management, July 1978.

REVIEW QUESTIONS

The best exercises for Chapter 13 consist of actual execution of the three software packages discussed in the chapter. The instructor should form teams with the students and let them play one or more of the games. It is, however, necessary to acquire the appropriate software and instruction manuals. The computer center of the institution must install these packages before the students can participate in the games.

14

Building a DSS as a Term Project

14.1 GENERAL OBJECTIVES OF A TERM PROJECT

The main objective of assigning students to individual DSS term projects is to simulate the process of design and implementation of a DSS in a classroom environment. Any DSS term project should be done on a team basis, with each team composed of four to six students. Since the building of a DSS, even within a simulated environment, is a highly complex job, a nontrivial DSS does not normally result from an individual effort. Also, we have seen in the preceding chapters that a wide variety of expertise is needed to build a DSS. Different members of the team can provide this mixture of knowledge. Thus, the execution of the project on a team basis gives the students in-depth practical experience and insight into the area of designing and implementing a DSS.

The term project has a twofold impact. It benefits the students by giving them practical experience with the DSS building process. It enriches the instructor by giving him/her student feedback on the course material and the student interaction in the teaching process. Normally the instructor should encourage each team to make an oral presentation of its project. When different teams in the course make their presentations, both the students and the instructor get new ideas about decision support systems addressing different topics. Such experience is indeed invaluable.

14.2 CONTENTS OF A TERM PAPER ON DSS

In Section 2.8 we have mentioned five possible areas in which a DSS can be developed. These are:

☐ Investment strategies
☐ Manufacturing
☐ Marketing
☐ Customer service
☐ Job planning and administration

This list is by no means exhaustive. Plenty of additional areas for DSS development can be found.

We now give a tentative table of contents of a DSS term paper, listing the issues involved in each chapter:

Chapter 1   Background and Objectives: *Why* is the DSS needed? *Who* needs it? *When* is it needed?

Chapter 2   Overall Plan and Outline: *What* is involved? Include typical scenarios.

Chapter 3   Technical Details of the Model: *How* is the system designed? Describe modeling method, data collection, data processing, and data display/production. Include sample reports.

Chapter 4   Feedback Control Loop for Dynamic Management: *How* does the system handle "What if" questions?

Chapter 5   Evaluation of the DSS by Management: Is it successful? *Why?* If not, what else is needed?

A DSS is particularly useful for handling "what if" questions. This theme must play a significant role in the term paper.

As indicated in Chapter 2, any information system development has three phases: analysis, design, and implementation. A DSS is no exception to this rule. By examining the proposed table of contents we can easily see that the first two chapters address the analysis phase, the next two chapters address the design phase, and the last chapter addresses the postimplementation evaluation phase.

Any DSS presents two alternative views: the user's and the designer's. The DSS team first familiarizes itself with the user's view of the DSS in order to complete the analysis phase. Next, it changes its perspective and acquaints itself with the designer's view of the same DSS. Thereby the team is able to handle the design phase of building the DSS. Finally, it examines

the user's view once again, but this time from a critical management evaluation perspective.

In my opinion, Chapter 3 of the term paper is the most difficult to write. Here the team must synthesize all the functional requirements of the DSS specified in Chapter 2 and then design the four component modules of the DSS:

☐ Control module
☐ Data storage module
☐ Data manipulation module
☐ Model building module

These modules are described in Section 1.8.

14.3 STUDENT PARTICIPATION IN A TEAM

For a team effort to be truly successful, team members must be cooperative and sincere in their efforts. Normally a team leader is selected and he/she coordinates the efforts of all the members. The team leader should keep an open mind and be totally unbiased in judgment. The leader should not impose his/her wishes on the rest of the team. Work assignments should be distributed equitably among the members so as to utilize each member's greatest potential in this joint approach. Group involvement is an option. It becomes most valuable when there is effective group interaction among the members.

A team approach has the advantage of gathering ideas from people with differing backgrounds to greatly enhance the pool of solution ideas for any given task. In addition, it is much less likely that several workers will overlook a small detail of analysis or design as an individual might. The process of "brainstorming" is, of course, widely used in group settings and can lead to excellent and innovative ideas. Finally, a decision made by group vote or consultation might be considered to be more risk free because of the interaction of several members, as opposed to relying on the opinion of a single person.

However, a team approach is not without disadvantages. Without good leadership and open-minded members, group meetings can become nothing more than arguments, with members not consulting one another but merely defending their own ideas. Defensiveness can develop if a group member feels attacked by other members or feels his/her ideas are not receiving equal consideration. The success of a group depends in large part on the willingness to reach compromise.

14.4 MIS MANPOWER SUPPORT ANALYSIS*

This DSS was a classroom project designed for a "high tech" manufacturing company whose product is sold to industry and is computer related. There are approximately 5000 employees in the company and the MIS department comprises about 100 persons. Growth for the company was very rapid during its first 8 years, but now growth is stabilizing and as we approach the company's tenth anniversary we expect a 10–15% rate of growth this year. This rate of growth may not be directly related to the MIS department's increase in personnel. Historically our company has had strong controls and has tried to keep a lid on the possibility of runaway manpower levels.

SECTION I

Explanation of Need

The need for a Manpower Support Analysis System arises because of the contradiction and complexity of both budgetary requirements and the flexible posture Management Information Systems (MIS) departments must maintain to support the user community. The contradiction is that annual budgets are normally done once a year and are created to fit the responsibility that a particular organization is chartered with. Unfortunately, a nice, neat fixed responsibility and workload cannot be generally applied to the actual responsibility of an MIS organization. Even though MIS organizations do have planned tasks (i.e., Five Year Business Systems Plan), servicing the user is the primary goal and if that means a *hot* item needs completion right away, then MIS resources must be shifted and directed to that new task. This is not to say that MIS jumps around from one thing to another without consideration, but responsiveness is a key. After all, the system is the user's, not MIS's.

We will concern ourselves with professional level staffing excluding operations personnel (computer room staff). Even though support staff such as secretaries, aides, and others are important to the organization as a whole, we wish to limit our decision process to the professional level systems staff.

Our objective is to aid the middle management of the MIS organization in their manpower assessment for a fiscal year. This assessment will consider but not be limited to the following areas.

---

* The rest of this chapter contains an example of a DSS developed on a team basis by three of my former graduate students in computer information system: Mike P. Castonguay, M.C. Cipriano, and Carl R. Katzeff.

    I. Company Growth
   II. User Expectations
       a. Long-term systems planning
       b. Short-term systems planning
       c. Unplanned projects
  III. Staffing Considerations
       a. Maintain current systems
       b. Attrition levels (turnover of help; leaving to competitor)
       c. Accommodate promotional movement
       d. Balancing levels of technical expertise
       e. Use of contract labor
       f. Relate labor to user expectations
  IV. Product Standards
       a. Level of documentation (time and quality)
       b. Level of analysis (time and quality)
   V. Other Considerations
       a. Economic constraints (good or poor business conditions; hiring freezes; layoffs)
       b. Building and space availability
       c. Hardware capacity

Possibly all of the above and more are needed to answer the questions concerning our manpower needs. While we will not be creating an entire budget, we may take into consideration some budgetary information based on previous years' actuals massaged by upper management guidelines.

Who Will Use the System?

The individuals who will use this system are basically of two types, but predominantly of the middle management level of our MIS organization. Some upper-level managers may make use of the system, but at a less detailed level. The upper manager might use the system to gain general overall pictures concerning expectations from his direct reports.

    Middle managers are those who report to or are one level away from divisional directors. They (middle managers) are responsible for functional groups of individuals (Finance and Production or Warehousing and Purchasing).

    A division manager is responsible for a higher level of organization related to a functional segment of the overall business. Such divisions might be Manufacturing, Marketing, or Research and Development.

Frequency of Use

Because this DSS is directly related to the budgeting cycle, its heaviest use will come once a year during the final quarter. It can also be used to give revised personnel estimates and justify or explain manpower problems or needs due to projects that have changed.

We have all experienced the situation where a *hot* item suddenly appears to be the pet project of a finance controller. Quick and correct personnel needs assessment is crucial at these times too, and any tool to aid in the decision process is always welcome. Another example may be sudden business advances, which might necessitate staffing changes. Utilizing the DSS to answer these and other "what if" conditions are possible applications of the Manpower Support Analysis System.

SECTION II

Overall Plan and Outline

The initial steps in the Manpower Analysis Cycle begin with obtaining growth information from the Corporate Planning and Control Department. This data is correlated to historical trends to determine the growth and expansion in MIS for the upcoming year. Coupled with this investigation is the need to examine current industry trends in the area of MIS usage and staffing expectations. For example, specialists in manpower planning have determined that along with a prosperous business environment for the coming year there appears a sharp increase in demands upon corporate data processing departments. When quantified, a 35% increase in programming requests might relate to a 10 or 15% company growth rate. This is an area that we will try to analyze when reviewing long- and short-term requests. At that time it may be possible to show the correlation between user demands and company growth or to show EDP needs rising for some other reason.

Internal to the MIS department in this study will be the need to review the long- and short-term systems projects currently submitted and approved. These requests will be analyzed to create time estimates for expected completion. The time estimates will then be correlated to the long- and short-term plans to compute professional staffing needs necessary to meet the approved user demands. For our consideration we will use the following for project classification:

Short-term projects: current year (fiscal).
Long-term projects: over one year.

Staffing considerations will be analyzed utilizing a Personnel Modeling System that will aid in forecasting attrition levels and promotional movement within our group. Fortunately, the Personnel Department maintains a software package that accommodates this need.

A review of the current levels of support needed to maintain existing systems would reveal actual manhours and percentages of support versus development work currently being done. This will be an important factor when considering available manhours for development using existing staffing levels. Projects due for completion will have an effect on the maintenance hours that will be needed.

Internal guidelines that describe the level of documentation required by technical staff (i.e., job specs; installation requirements; manuals) govern product standards. The level and details required for product standards will directly affect the time analysis that is applied to user expectations.

Other items will be taken into account that may set uncontrollable limits on other decision areas. Some of these other items include:

Space Availability.   As a practical matter you can only fit just so many people into so much space. Our Plant Management department allocates space to functional areas according to a very high level of decision making. Our piece of the pie is therefore not within our control, but we must live within our limits.

Hardware Capacity.   To optimize the existing hardware and give good service to both the user and the systems community, the Technical Services MIS group controls use of the computer system. So that the development work will not bog down the system with compiles and use of the Editor, the systems community is limited to just so many terminals and space allocation.

Our DSS is being created to offer assistance in the area of information management and decision making for personnel needs to the MIS Department only.

Major Use Scenario

During the final quarter of each fiscal year, budgets are due from every functional department of the company. It is at this time that the information gathered during the prior years is summarized and applied to the task of budgeting for the coming year. New information is acquired as needed and combined with prior years' historical data. As part of the budget, an accurate assessment of personnel levels to be used is required. The MIS management must be able to put their arms around all the information needed and assemble it, analyze it, and budget, accurately, personnel levels that will be required.

This annual manpower needs assessment is the primary function of our

DSS and therefore requires review of all constraints and decision variables, particularly the following:

A. Obtain various economic forecasts from the Planning and Control Department (i.e., company growth, effects of competition, current year revenue plans, etc.).

B. Review through "life cycle methodology" the current system's maintenance requirements, and correlate staffing needs accordingly.

C. Through interaction with the Personnel Department we will determine attrition levels, promotional movement, and the optimal balance of technical expertise.

D. User expectations must be analyzed to predict demand on MIS resources.

E. Product standards (documentation, publications, analysis methods) from the MIS Department will be quantified as an added consideration to determine demand on MIS resources in relation to all projects.

F. Other considerations will include building and space availability (information received and controlled by plant management) and hardware capacity (controlled by MIS Technical Services).

G. After considering current MIS Department staffing levels and information supplied from C above, determine short- and long-term staffing goals and/or requirements.

The above information will then be input into the DSS, and a product (output) helping to guide hiring policies for the upcoming fiscal year will be the result. Information such as the number of people needed and the ratio of new hires to contract labor will be included as the product of the DSS.

The following are examples of non-scheduled applications of the DSS. One should remember that there are other examples that may be applied too. Basically any situation that calls for an adjustment in workload or time available to perform a project can call for the use of the DSS.

Economic Scenario

The recession has affected our company too. The cost of money has postponed capital expenditures, and research projects and functional areas of the company are also being hit. We have prior approval to hire three new people, but a freeze on new hires will not allow us to accomplish this. We budgeted our personnel needs at the beginning of the year based on the demand factors at that time.

Now we must adjust our time estimates or workload. A preference is to remain on schedule and accomplish our goals for the year. What do we do first?

   A. Contact users and request feedback as to what projects they can put
   off or reschedule. They should be made aware of how we are being
   affected by these short-term policies.
   B. Obtain information from management as to what other resources are
   being cut.
   C. Replace affected (changed variables) decision variables and constraints. Then rerun the DSS to determine what level of personnel is
   still needed or whether the revised user demands have lowered or
   brought the staffing needs down to current levels.

   In this scenario we are trying to judge whether or not we have adequate
staffing levels to accomplish our jobs with what we have. Or we can use the
DSS output to help justify the fact that we cannot get by without the new
hires we had prior approval for.

Shifting Demands

The vice president of finance is applying pressure on finance directors to
give him information that will relate cost of goods shipped to the revenue-
producing status of those units. He feels very strongly that this type of information will authenticate the Planning and Control Department's revenue
projections by showing their relation to real assets and that the data is correct.
An added attraction is the ability to give more accurate return on investment
information. A very strict deadline has been given. January first of the next
fiscal year he wants to see the first output. This gives us nine remaining
working months to accomplish what he asks. A battle between the directors
has resulted in no real slack given in demands. Two small projects can be
slowed down, one can be postponed, and none can be cancelled.

   A. We must review the projects that time and demands have been altered
   on. We must analyze and determine how many people we can free
   up.
   B. We contact Personnel for a pool of qualified candidates. They give
   us time estimates that suggest it will take one to three months to
   find the needed individuals to hire.
   C. We review availability of qualified contract labor. Possibly this can
   help in the short run.
   D. Building and space availability (information received and controlled
   by plant management) and hardware capacity (controlled by MIS
   Technical Services) are always considered.

E. We must always refer to MIS Department staffing levels and information relating to short- and long-term staffing goals and/or requirements.

F. Replace affected (changed variables) decision variables and constraints. Then return the DSS to determine what level of manpower will be needed to meet the new demands that must be satisfied within this year.

Critical Personnel Leave

A highly skilled individual leaves the company for a competitor. This person was with the company for 8 years. She takes with her a great deal of experience. She functioned as a project leader and was involved in the middle of the development of a new manufacturing accounting and production system. This was a sensitive time to lose this individual. Her understanding (familiarity) of the company, technical expertise with our software, and the project that she was working on all make this a key individual. To make matters worse, a second individual left simultaneously to work for her in the new job. We must shift our resources to keep this project on schedule. It will take added people to accomplish and become familiar with the project to finish it on schedule.

A. We must obtain feedback from users to see if we can postpone other projects. But the response is negative and all projects must be done by promised dates.

B. We contact Personnel for a pool of qualified replacements. They give us a time estimate that suggests it will take 2 months to replace the individuals lost with other candidates of similar qualifications.

C. We review availability of qualified contract labor. Possibly this can help in the short run.

D. Replace affected (changed) decision variables and constraints. Then rerun the DSS to determine what level of manpower will be needed to meet the unchanged demands that must be satisfied within a shorter span of time.

By analyzing the time requirements on the projects in progress, we are able to determine how many individuals can work on different modules at the same time. Even though only two people left, we are faced with the same demands, and by the time we replace the two people *time* has gone by. In this scenario, constraints may govern our decision more than decision variables.

SECTION III

Model Methods

There are two modeling methods used within this first phase of the Manpower Needs Assessment System. Because of the scope of this system as a whole entity, there was a need to modularize the project and deliver it in portions. This is why there are only two mathematical methods used.

Linear Regression

The first model type is a linear regression model. It will be used to forecast three pieces of information: (1) demand hours; (2) head count; (3) sales growth.

These models will utilize historical data that has been gathered over the past 10 years. However, the models only use nine of those years. A forecast of the next year will be the objective (the upcoming budget year).

The sales volume will be a benchmark indicator. This indicator will be used as a mechanism to relate overall sales growth to MIS manpower expectations. The relational data will become the basis for future analysis, possibly a future phase of the MIS-DSS.

Linear Programming

Once the system calculates the above data for this coming year (1983), optimization (allocation) of MIS resources can be determined using the second mathematical model type, which is a linear programming model. This model will show levels of MIS personnel in relation to a desired skill mix (programmer/analyst; senior analyst; project manager).

The model will return values based on some user-defined information, standard information obtained from outside (uncontrollable) sources, and use of the data calculated from the linear extrapolations. This linear programming model can be run more than once depending on the fit of the answer returned from the first pass through (most feasible solution/optimal solution).

The two models are described in more detail in the following pages along with an example.

Model Type One

It is assumed that the overall trend concerning sales volume, users' demand of MIS time, and the personnel growth of the MIS department will continue steadily. The company then needs to predict each of these occurrences for

TABLE 1

YEAR	ACTUAL DATA ($ IN 000'S)	SMOOTHED DATA 3 YR AVERAGE
1974	22,275	
1975	35,034	34,230
1976	45,381	46,974
1977	60,508	57,219
1978	65,769	66,208
1979	72,346	73,529
1980	82,474	81,572
1981	89,896	91,317
1982	101,582	

the next year. This will be accomplished using the following step-by-step forecasting approach:

A. Gather historical data regarding sales volume, head counts, and user demand hours for the past 9 years.

B. Smooth this data over the entire 9-year span so that no individual year will deter the goal of showing a definite trend. The data in Tables 1–3 reflect the actual sales, demand hours, and head counts in MIS for the past 9 years together with their respective smoothed data (using the 3-year moving average method).

C. Both the actual and smoothed data are then plotted graphically showing the contrast in data (Figs. 1–3).

D. Using the graphs in Figures 1–3, the sales, demand hours, and head count trends can be calculated using the smoothed data. As indicated, all three figures show linear trends. Therefore, it will be necessary to use a linear model to estimate sales, demand hours, and head counts for the following year.

TABLE 2

YEAR	ACTUAL DATA (HOURS)	SMOOTHED DATA 3 YR AVERAGE
1974	10,650	
1975	22,540	22,685
1976	34,865	41,781
1977	67,940	67,085
1978	98,450	97,355
1979	125,675	127,150
1980	157,325	157,323
1981	188,970	183,931
1982	205,500	

TABLE 3

YEAR	ACTUAL DATA (MIS EMPLOYEES)	SMOOTHED DATA 3 YR AVERAGE
1974	4	
1975	11	10
1976	16	20
1977	35	32
1978	47	47
1979	60	60
1980	75	73
1981	86	86
1982	98	

YEAR	X	X_2	Y	XY
1974	-4	16	22275	-89100
1975	-3	9	35034	-105102
1976	-2	4	45381	-90762
1977	-1	1	60508	-60508
1978	0	0	65769	0
1979	1	1	72346	72346
1980	2	4	82474	164948
1981	3	9	89896	269688
1982	4	16	101582	406328
	0	60	575265	567838

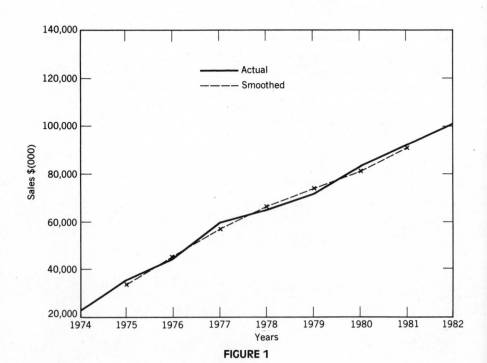

FIGURE 1

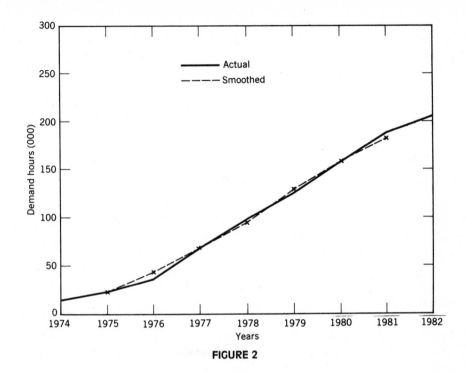

FIGURE 2

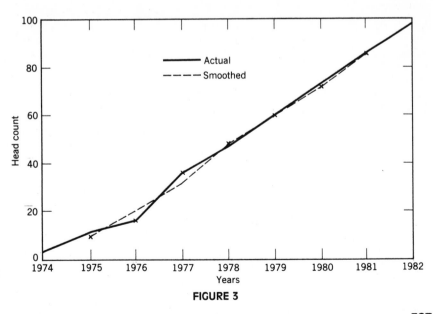

FIGURE 3

```
                    9A = 575,265
                     A = 63,918
                   60B = 567,838
                     B = 9,463

        SALES FOR 1983 :
                A    +    BX    =       Y
              63,918 + 9,463(5) = 111,233
```
FIGURE 4

E. By using the data presented, it now becomes necessary to solve for the coordinates of our linear trends. This will be accomplished where:

$$Y = A + BX$$
$$NA + B\Sigma X = \Sigma Y$$
$$A\Sigma X + B\Sigma X^2 = \Sigma XY$$

The results are presented in Figures 4–6.

Model Type Two

By analyzing past data it has been determined that there are eight major areas concerning MIS personnel requirements that need consideration in supporting the user community:

Combination of job functions: the total mix of job functions in the MIS area.

YEAR	X	X^2	Y	XY
1974	-4	16	10650	-42600
1975	-3	9	22540	-67620
1976	-2	4	34865	-69730
1977	-1	1	67940	-67940
1978	0	0	98450	0
1979	1	1	125675	125675
1980	2	4	157325	314650
1981	3	9	188970	566910
1982	4	16	205500	822000
	0	60	911915	1581345

```
                  9A = 911,915
                   A = 101,324
                 60B = 1,581,345
                   B = 26,356

        DEMAND IN HOURS FOR 1983 :
                A    +    BX    =       Y
             101,324 + 26,356(5) = 233,102
```
FIGURE 5

YEAR	X	X^2	Y	XY
1974	-4	16	4	-16
1975	-3	9	11	-33
1976	-2	4	16	-32
1977	-1	1	35	-35
1978	0	0	47	0
1979	1	1	60	60
1980	2	4	75	150
1981	3	9	86	258
1982	4	16	98	392
	0	60	432	744

$$9A = 432$$
$$A = 48$$
$$60B = 744$$
$$B = 12.4$$

MIS EMPLOYEES FOR 1983 :
$$A + BX = Y$$
$$48 + 12.4(5) = 110$$

FIGURE 6

Combination of people: the total mix of MIS employees per average user request.

Programmer/analysts: minimum number of programmer/analysts needed to support the current user community.

Systems analysts: minimum number of systems analysts needed to support the current user community.

Project managers: minimum number of project managers needed to support the current user community.

Physical capacity: total number of MIS personnel that can perform effectively given current facilities.

Attrition rate: total mix of MIS employees expected to leave the company in the next year.

Promotion rate: total mix of MIS employees expected to be promoted by the company in the next year.

The above eight major considerations will help form the constraints for our linear programming model. Therefore, assume our decision variables to be the types of employees in MIS represented by:

$X1$ = programmer/analyst
$X2$ = senior analyst
$X3$ = project manager

The objective function is to minimize MIS manpower used to service all the needs of the user community subject to the following constraints:

$$5X1 + 2X2 + X3 \leq 110$$
$$3X1 + 7X2 + X3 \geq 116$$
$$X1 \geq 30$$
$$X2 \geq 20$$
$$X3 \geq 5$$
$$1.5X1 + X2 + 2X3 \leq 110$$
$$5X1 + 2X2 + X3 \leq p\ddagger$$
$$2X1 + 3X2 + 2X3 \geq p\dagger$$

Data Processing

Data Entry. The data entry is accomplished through the use of interactive processing. Menu-driven programs control and guide an individual through the process of updating the MIS-MANAGEMENT-DATA-BASE. A separate module controls the entry of data into the DEMAND-RECORD-AREA. This being the first year, a small amount of extra effort will be needed to load the past history. There are extra fields that will be maintained but not used at this time but at some future phase of the project.

DSS Processing. The modeling system is also run interactively. The system controls the normal sequence of events but allows the user options to update or alter information as each portion is reached. Through the use of "program function keys" (PF keys) the user can select options such as modifying the displayed data or printing the screen that they are presently viewing. The user can also back out of the process with an EXIT function.

Normal Sequence	Type	SCR-#
1. Main menu		01
2. Forecast demand hours	Linear extrapolation	03
3. Review demand hours		04
4. Forecast head count	Linear extrapolation	05
5. Review head count		06
6. Forecast sales growth	Linear extrapolation	07
7. Review sales growth		08
8. Linear extrapolation summary	Report	09
9. Define objective function	Linear programming	10
10. Fill in user definitions	LP	11
11. Linear programming report	Report	12
12. End of processing	Return to main menu	01

† Calculated by taking the number of demand hours projected earlier in our linear regression model and dividing by the average number of hours per year per employee to determine number of people needed for user demand:

$$\frac{\text{Demand hours}}{\text{Hours per yr}} = \frac{223,102}{2000} = 112 \text{ employees}$$

‡ Provided by Personnel Department through their own projection analysis.

See Appendix B for general system charts (Informational/General Model).

All the support routines and programs are executed in real time. We have experienced very good response time during initial systems testing.

Reports—Output

As part of the user functions, the user has the capability to print any of the screens desired including the summary screens and linear programming reports. An added function of the system is to automatically concatenate all summaries and reports from the screen and print them out together but in the same format. Because the hard copy reports look so much like the screen output, samples were not included.

You may not be able to get the full effect of the screens as shown in the appendix. The reason for this is that modifiable fields (those which can be input by the user or updated by the programs) show up with an asterisk when printed on the sample screens contained in the appendix. There are numeric fields that show up *as is* because of the editing of the COBOL definition.

SECTION IV

Feedback Control Loop

One of the central themes of our DSS is to provide the manager with flexibility in allowing him/her the tools to answer "what if" questions about manpower needs. Once the initial DSS has been performed, it takes only seconds to reformulate the analysis with "what if" type queries. This will aid in displaying feature conditions and the risk associated with alternative courses of action, which can be clearly understood with a minimal expenditure, of time and effort. With this in mind, a review of the systems capability to accommodate this important function is critical.

The final output of the system reports a summary of the modeled information developed by the forecasting methods used. The system directs the user through the normal path needed to arrive at this output. The modification capability built into the system facilitates changes going through the normal DSS flow.

To highlight the "what if" capability, let's review the normal system flow.

First Modeling Phase

1. The first module involves linear extrapolation. Actual data is retrieved from the DEMAND-RECORD-AREA and the first screen appears showing the actual data accompanied with related calculations. Recognizing the fact that an "off" year might have been erroneously entered into the system, we built in the ability to modify data as needed by the user. This modified data is then processed and redisplayed for inspection by the user. The modify option will remain, never locking the user out.

2. The second screen of each set of linear extrapolation screens (SCR-03 and 04,SCR-05 and 06,SCR-07 and 08) provides the user with the ability to define the year to be solved. The screen is processed and the solution displayed. The user then has two directions that he/she can follow at this point. The first might be to change the year for which he/she wants the model solved. It is important to note that this change can only be done on SCR-04 within the first set of screens. This is because we want all the subsequent forecasts to be performed for the same year. Therefore, we do not consider this a limiting factor, but a control and guide for the user.

The second option open to the user is to go back to the prior screen and modify data as needed, then return to the second screen for final calculations.

Aside from the exceptions noted above, all three sets of screens relating to linear extrapolation have the same modification capability. The final screen of this first modeling type summarizes all three sets. It is here on SCR-09 that the user has a final chance to modify data before proceeding to the second modeling phase.

Second Modeling Phase

1. When you first enter the linear programming model phase, SCR-10 permits the user to define his/her objective function. The user must also choose to minimize or maximize the objective function.

2. The next part of the linear programming phase depends upon more user involvement. It is here that the standard constraints are displayed. The user can fill in the coefficients of the decision variables and the right side of the equation for three constraints (3–5) on SCR-11.

3. It is at this point that the fiinal product of the system is produced. The user is then provided with the capability of solving "what if" conditions. SCR-13 (see Appendix A) controls the areas the user might wish to modify.

Please note that we have received comments from users during unit testing regarding the difficulty with developing the objective function and formulating the coefficients for the constraints and objective function. We will cover this subject along with a full review of the system in Section V Evaluation of the Manpower Needs System.

Also, we assume that the user is manually changing and formulating the coefficients for the examples and discussions contained within this section to remain consistent. It should also be mentioned here that changes in the methodology for formulating coefficients have been requested by the users.

"What If" Scenario 1

The manager of the MIS Departments is reviewing the summary report on screen 12 from the initial run of the DSS. Now, after analyzing the report, he wants to know the effect on the objective function when he changes the forecasted head count from 110 to 125 people.

To continue, the Enter key is depressed while on screen 12. This displays screen 13, the modification menu. Here the manager is given several options from which to choose.

First, he selects PF key 01 to save the data generated from the initial run.

Second, PF key 05 is selected. This function key·allows the familiar user to skip or avoid going to the beginning of the system prompts, bringing him to screen 14. The novice user may have selected PF key 03, to start at the beginning and modify data using the normal system sequence. Screen 14 is a modified version of screen 11. Instead of showing the entire construction of the constraint equations however, only the right side of each equation is displayed with definitions.

The right side variables are displayed in a high-intensity modifiable state on the screen (HIMOD). The only right side variable not modifiable directly is the computed demand head count (Cl). The user may change this field (if desired) by changing Y1 (demand hours), resulting in the system computing the new Cl value.

The manager enters the data desired next to Y2 (forecasted head count) and presses the Enter key, which brings him back to the modification menu (SCR-13). A message is displayed inviting the manager to make further modifications or process the changed data.

The manager is satisfied with the change already made and presses PF key 13 to reprocess the linear programming model with the revised data.

The system displays screen 11 to allow the manager a second review and/ or print option before continuing. The manager presses the Enter key to continue. The DSS follows the standard path and displays screen 12 (the summary report). After the manager reviews the report, the modification menu reappears, allowing the manager to choose additional changes.

The "what if" question is accommodated very well here and the manager seems pleased. He comments on the flexibility of the system to handle both the experienced and novice user. Another good feature was the ability to change several right side variables at the same time, eliminating the need to wait for system responses to each change.

What about changing the coefficients? What if the mix of the job functions needs to be tailored to my department's needs? We request the manager to proceed to the modification menu for a second "what if" scenario.

"What If" Scenario 2

A review of pending projects combined with feedback from the current staff has revealed a weakness in our mix of job functions. An MIS manager has questioned the following results:

```
PROGRAMMER/ANALYSTS (X1) - 85
SENIOR ANALYSTS (X2)      - 33
PROJECT MANAGERS (X3)     -  7
```

The individual feels a need for more qualified, senior people to cover the higher level of projects that his department has committed itself to for the upcoming fiscal year. More specifically, the first run of the DSS contained a constraint of:

$$1.3(X1) + .4(X2) + .1(X3) \geq 116$$

The manager wishes the coefficient of the second decision variable (X2), senior analysts, changed to ".5" (e.g. .5X2). The following are the steps to accomplish this:

1. From SCR-11, depress Enter key, which brings processing to SCR-13 (the modification menu).
2. Once on SCR-13, enter "PF-07," which facilitates changes to the coefficients identifiable on SCR-11. The coefficients are displayed in a modifiable state; the right-hand side of the equation cannot be altered at this point.
3. Enter changes to the desired coefficients (e.g., X2) and depress the Enter key. This returns processing to SCR-13 where more modifications can be made, or the DSS can once again be run.
4. Choosing the latter option (by entering "PF-13") will rerun the DSS. The sytem displays SCR-11 to review/edit the recent changes.
5. The DSS will continue its standard path and calculate a new summary report (SCR-12).

Summary of "What If" Analysis

The two scenarios we went thorugh with our manager showed how a user familiar with the system can easily maneuver data and reprocess the linear programming model with the changed data. If you are uncomfortable, you can always start from the beginning and just follow the standard path.

The first scenario demonstrates how to change the variables in the right-hand side of the constraint equations (referred to as the "right side" variables). Following this example the manager could easily have changed the right side variable to Loss from Attrition or Space Capacity. What if you could change the number of people that will leave your department by some new incentive plan? You could run the modification through screen 14, then reprocess.

The second scenario demonstrates how the coefficients can be changed to fit the needs of a special situation. The area of standard coefficients will be discussed in Section 5, Evaluation of the system. What if your department has a more mature level of individuals who are ready to be promoted in the senior analyst category? You may wish to weight this decision variable heavier for Loss from Promotion by raising the coefficient of X2. Very simple—select that modification function, change the coefficient, and reprocess.

If you have a need to solve for a different year in the future, the system allows you to start at the beginning.

Response from users involved in the unit testing of the DSS has been favorable. By including user involvement, we will be able to satisfy the expected functions of the system more accurately. There are areas that need further analysis, but the system's ability to handle user interaction is strong in the minds of the design team and users.

SECTION V

Evaluation of System

The managers of the MIS department have reviewed the Manpower Support Analysis System both informally and formally. During a review meeting the entire staff put together information relating to their review of the system. They were asked to evaluate the system in relation to the original specifications. Also, they were asked to take into account the next modules that will be installed.

Successful Components

The major success of the system was its ability to aid in the forecasting of manpower needs for budgeting purposes. The system enabled managers to complete Manpower Analysis segment during the budgeting cycle a full 2 weeks ahead of schedule with only one request to bring down the head count levels from upper management. This displayed both the system's ability to decrease the time needed to perform the task, and that the numbers once presented were more credible because of the more logical/scientific approach used to create the manpower needs. In the past, upper management would always question manpower needs more severely, and it was much more difficult to justify increases. This was true partially because the manual approach used involved lots of guesswork and wild plugging of numbers.

The system interfaces well with systems it receives data from (Personnel System, Plant Management System), such as attrition rate, space availability, etc. The system did very well with the data currently available. This can be attributed to the fact that the data was tested before implementation of a modeling technique within the system.

The data entry screens proved to be a friendly and acceptable way to use the sytem. Utilizing a standard sequence of events, the system helped the unfamiliar user, while options to skip to short-cut modification screens during the "what if" phase of the system accommodated knowledgeable users. For example, a change to the "demand hours" could be accomplished from SCR-14 rather than returning to SCR-03 and following through the entire standard system sequence again.

Users commented that response time was exceptional, and this was confirmed when benchmark tests were run against other DSS systems.

Areas for Improvement

There were major areas that needed improvement within the system. Creation and modification of the coefficients and the objective functions caused the biggest headache of all. It was felt that standard coefficients and objective functions should be available through the use of a file. The system would load a standard value based on your cost center or special request and proceed allowing the user to fine tune the values of the coefficients and objective function as special cases required. Modifications to the coefficients would be enhanced further by adding another level to the modification "what if" process. This level would in effect allow the user to define ratios of one type of employee to another. Then the user could choose the change the coefficients across the board or for individual constraints only. The system would then take the ratios and interpret them into the necessary coefficients. This would simplify the mechanics of runningg the DSS.

A second area that will be corrected as other systems are brought up is for all the desired constraints that were not used in the modeling process to be phased in. The reason they were not all initially used was that not all the information was readily available. As an example, product standards need to be taken into consideration when calculating demand hours. It was decided this information would be captured better when the project management system comes online. Hardware limitations were not used because the current system still has excess capacity. However, data collection for system use will be formalized in the coming months so this constraint can be applied to the models. As other management systems are installed with relevant information they can be integrated with the Manpower Support Analysis System too. As needs arise or change, the system will change too.

Another area the system was deficient in was in its ability to handle off-cycle manpower analysis. This was not as urgent as the budget needs, but it relied on the project management system to capture more accurate manpower demand data. Then as long- and short-term goals change, the information will be more readily available. Also the modeling types used would have to be more flexible to handle forcasting for shorter periods than a year, say, in increments of a month.

It was felt that regular batch reporting would be good for the group managers and director. This batch reporting would allow them to see monthly or weekly (whatever is chosen) statuses of the manpower needs as they are being developed at both the detail and summary levels by organization.

For nonfinancial types, the interpreting of numbers is difficult. The managers all agreed that some sort of pictorial presentations would be helpful. Graphics capabilities may be included in a future module. Among the suggestions were bar graphs and pie charts.

Another area that would require further work as the system develops is documentation. The managers felt that they were comfortable with the use of the system, because they were MIS-oriented people. But if future users of the sytem are not as sophisticated, then more internal and external documentation is needed. Internally the system may need some more instruction screens to guide users along the way. The managers liked what was there and stressed keeping the instruction screens optional.

An oversight not caught in the beginning design phases was the fact that the record area needed to be able to handle data at the cost center level for several generations of data. This is so the "what if" questions can be saved for reference until end-of-year initializations and that managers are at the cost center level and not at the top level. To handle this problem the record layout has been changed to include the cost center, a revision number, and a report switch. The cost center and revison number were explained above. The report switch will allow the manager to pick a revision that he/she wishes to officially report, and then the reports that roll up the data can use this switch to select the correct revision; this revison will also be more readily identifiable to the user.

To reflect the philosophy of DSS that we have adopted, our system will not remain stagnant. We anticipate changes in the future to reflect current business needs and trends. This philosophy will slowly be applied to other areas of MIS responsibility, making our system designs more flexible and ready to adapt to the user community. One more improvement that might represent this is building more models into the Manpower Analysis System. Then build the intelligence into the system to diagnose data and inform the user of the modeling alternatives that might be used, select the most appropriate (best suited) model and run the system for the user. The reason model flexibility is necessary is because as time goes by the trends of the data may change. In other words, the use of linear extrapolation to forecast may not be appropriate, so the system should be able to assist the user in recognizing this. This type of improvement is not an immediate need; it is more of a planned improvement to be included in a future phase of the project.

APPENDIX A. SCREEN/REPORT FORMATS

Screen Number	Function
01	Main Menu
02-1	Instruction Screen #1 Page—1
02-2	Instruction Screen #1 Page—2
03	Linear Extrapolation model—Y1
04	Linear Extrapolation Calculation—Y1
05	Linear Extrapolation Model—Y2
06	Linear Extrapolation Calculation—Y2

07   Linear Extrapolation Model—Y3
08   Linear Extrapolation Calculation—Y3
09   Linear Extrapolation Summary
10   Linear Programming—Objective Function Definition
11   Linear Programming—Model Definition
11A*   L/P Variable and Constraint Definitions
11B*   L/P Standard/What If Sequence Instructions
12   L/P Summary Report—Data Summary
13   Modification Menu
13A*   Modification Menu Instructions
14   Modification Screen for Right Side variables

* Nonfunctional Screens—Instructional Only

```
         B E N T L E Y    C O M P U T E R    C O R P O R A T I O N
                    MIS PERSONNEL MANAGEMENT SYSTEM

                VERSION 00          SCR-01


              Function              Function
              Key                   Description

              01                    Manpower Needs Assessment

              14                    Instruction Screen

              16                    EXIT



'ROW 24 IS RESERVED FOR MESSAGES.
```

```
         B E N T L E Y    C O M P U T E R    C O R P O R A T I O N
Version 00              MIS PERSONNEL MANAGEMENT SYSTEM              SCR-02-1
```

Welcome to the MIS Personnel DSS. This system was developed as a tool to help MIS management develop manpower (labor head count) levels during the Budgeting process.

The system is interactive and relies on your responses and review and approval of information as the system develops data. The system will control the sequence of events that will occur. You have the option of changing data in some cases to create a better 'Fit' and make the data 'Reasonable'.

The system uses data from the MIS-MANAGEMENT-DATA-BASE known as the DEMAND-RECORD-AREA. The system uses nine (9) of the past years as data. It then generates a series of screens based on 'Linear Extrapolation' to show you some foundation information that will be used in a second model used with 'Linear Programming'. Reference your 'User Manual' for addition information.

```
Def.:   (1) SUM - means the same as SUMMATION-E and is used as Sigma Notation
        (2) ( * ) - Will indicate arithmetic functions that are user defined.
            *   - A blank space before a variable is a user number.

An example is the Objective Function     ** X1 ( * ) ** X2 ( * ) ** X3  = Y2
          Filled in it might look like     4 X1 ( + )  5 X2 ( + )  2 X3  = Y2
                               or          4 X1 ( - )  5 X2 ( - )  2 X3  = Y2
                        Press ENTER to continue
```

```
         B E N T L E Y    C O M P U T E R    C O R P O R A T I O N
Version 00              MIS PERSONNEL MANAGEMENT SYSTEM              SCR-02-2
```

Definitions continued:
    (3) 'X' Value SCR04 -   This value is entered to complete the equation
                     and allow calculations for the year desired. The
                     System will only do 'Linear Extrapolation at
                     this point, so you must choose a year in future.
                     For the comming year the 'X' value will always be
                     5. For successive years keep adding 1. For the
                     year after this 'X' will = 6.
                      Once you choose the 'X' value it will be carried
                     through to the other 'Linear Extrapolation Models
                     within the system.   Example: X = **

    (4) PF - This stands for Program Function Key. It will be followed by
           a number indicating which key (i.e. PF 1 or PF 16) is to be
           used, along with the function description.
           Standard values: ENTER = ENTER key
                             PF 14 = Print Screen /or Instructions
                             PF 16 = EXIT

                  Press ENTER to continue

```
         B E N T L E Y    C O M P U T E R    C O R P O R A T I O N
Version 00              MIS PERSONNEL MANAGEMENT SYSTEM              SCR-03
                       Linear Extrapolation of Demand Hours
```

Year Used	X	X↑2 'Square'	Y1 Hours	X * Y1
****	4-	ZZZ9-	Z,ZZZ,ZZ9-	ZZZ,ZZZ,ZZZ.99-
****	3-	ZZZ9-	Z,ZZZ,ZZ9-	ZZZ,ZZZ,ZZZ.99-
****	2-	ZZZ9-	Z,ZZZ,ZZ9-	ZZZ,ZZZ,ZZZ.99-
****	1-	ZZZ9-	Z,ZZZ,ZZ9-	ZZZ,ZZZ,ZZZ.99-
****	0	ZZZ9-	Z,ZZZ,ZZ9-	ZZZ,ZZZ,ZZZ.99-
****	1	ZZZ9-	Z,ZZZ,ZZ9-	ZZZ,ZZZ,ZZZ.99-
****	2	ZZZ9-	Z,ZZZ,ZZ9-	ZZZ,ZZZ,ZZZ.99-
****	3	ZZZ9-	Z,ZZZ,ZZ9-	ZZZ,ZZZ,ZZZ.99-
****	4	ZZZ9-	Z,ZZZ,ZZ9-	ZZZ,ZZZ,ZZZ.99-
SUMMATION-E	0	ZZZ9-	Z,ZZZ,ZZ9-	ZZZ,ZZZ,ZZZ.99-

                  Press ENTER to continue
          PF 2 = Modify; PF 14 = Print Screen; PF 16 = EXIT

Row 24 reserved for messages.

```
         B E N T L E Y    C O M P U T E R    C O R P O R A T I O N
Version 00              MIS PERSONNEL MANAGEMENT SYSTEM              SCR-04
                       Linear Extrapolation of Demand Hours
```

```
                    X         X↑2        Y1          X * Y1

       SUMMATION-E  Z99-      ZZZ9-    Z,ZZZ,ZZ9-   ZZZ,ZZZ,ZZZ.99-
```

    Enter a value for X designating year you wish to calculate.
                    X = **

```
                    SUM Y1 = N*A      >>>>   A = Z,ZZZ,ZZZ.99-
            SUM X*Y1 = B*(SUM X↑2)    >>>>   B = Z,ZZZ,ZZZ.99-

     Calculated Demand Hours Y1 = A + B*X   >>>>   Y1 = Z,ZZZ,ZZZ.99-
```

                  Press ENTER to Continue
          PF 02 = Modify 'Prior' Screen and Reprocess
              PF 14 = Print Scree; PF 16 = EXIT
Row 24 reserved for messages.

```
          B E N T L E  Y   C O M P U T E R    C O R P O R A T I O N
Version 00                MIS PERSONNEL MANAGEMENT SYSTEM              SCR-05
                       Linear Extrapolation of Head Count

        Year  !  X   !  X↑2   !    Y2     !    X * Y2
        Used  !      ! 'Square'! Head Count !
     ============!======!========!===========!=================
        ****  !  4-  ! ZZZ9- !  ZZ,ZZ9- ! ZZ,ZZZ,ZZZ.99-
        ****  !  3-  ! ZZZ9- !  ZZ,ZZ9- ! ZZ,ZZZ,ZZZ.99-
        ****  !  2-  ! ZZZ9- !  ZZ,ZZ9- ! ZZ,ZZZ,ZZZ.99-
        ****  !  1-  ! ZZZ9- !  ZZ,ZZ9- ! ZZ,ZZZ,ZZZ.99-
        ****  !  0   ! ZZZ9- !  ZZ,ZZ9- ! ZZ,ZZZ,ZZZ.99-
        ****  !  1   ! ZZZ9- !  ZZ,ZZ9- ! ZZ,ZZZ,ZZZ.99-
        ****  !  2   ! ZZZ9- !  ZZ,ZZ9- ! ZZ,ZZZ,ZZZ.99-
        ****  !  3   ! ZZZ9- !  ZZ,ZZ9- ! ZZ,ZZZ,ZZZ.99-
        ****  !  4   ! ZZZ9- !  ZZ,ZZ9- ! ZZ,ZZZ,ZZZ.99-
     ============!======!========!===========!=================
     SUMMATION-E !  0   ! ZZZ9- !  ZZZ,ZZ9- ! ZZZ,ZZZ,ZZZ.99-


                     Press ENTER to continue
            PF 2 = Modify; PF 14 = Print Screen; PF 16 = EXIT

Row 24 reserved for messages.



          B E N T L E  Y   C O M P U T E R    C O R P O R A T I O N
Version 00                MIS PERSONNEL MANAGEMENT SYSTEM              SCR-06
                       Linear Extrapolation of Head Count



             X        X↑2        Y2         X * Y2

      SUMMATION-E  Z99-      ZZZ9-   Z,ZZZ,ZZ9-   ZZZ,ZZZ,ZZZ.99-

         The value for X designating year you 'are' calculating
                    X = Z9   from SCR-04

                        SUM Y2 = N*A    >>>>   A = Z,ZZZ,ZZZ.99-
               SUM X*Y2 = B*(SUM X↑2)   >>>>   B = Z,ZZZ,ZZZ.99-

      Calculated Head Count  Y2 = A + B*X   >>>>  Y2 =   ZZ,ZZZ.99-



                     Press ENTER to Continue
            PF 02 = Modify 'Prior' Screen and Reprocess
                  PF 14 = Print Scree; PF 16 = EXIT
Row 24 reserved for messages.



          B E N T L E  Y   C O M P U T E R    C O R P O R A T I O N
Version 00                MIS PERSONNEL MANAGEMENT SYSTEM              SCR-07
                       Linear Extrapolation of Sales Growth

        Year  !  X   !  X↑2   !    Y3     !    X * Y3
        Used  !      ! 'Square'!Sales(000's)!  (000's)
     ============!======!========!===========!=================
        ****  !  4-  ! ZZZ9- ! Z,ZZZ,ZZ9- ! ZZZ,ZZZ,ZZZ.99-
        ****  !  3-  ! ZZZ9- ! Z,ZZZ,ZZ9- ! ZZZ,ZZZ,ZZZ.99-
        ****  !  2-  ! ZZZ9- ! Z,ZZZ,ZZ9- ! ZZZ,ZZZ,ZZZ.99-
        ****  !  1-  ! ZZZ9- ! Z,ZZZ,ZZ9- ! ZZZ,ZZZ,ZZZ.99-
        ****  !  0   ! ZZZ9- ! Z,ZZZ,ZZ9- ! ZZZ,ZZZ,ZZZ.99-
        ****  !  1   ! ZZZ9- ! Z,ZZZ,ZZ9- ! ZZZ,ZZZ,ZZZ.99-
        ****  !  2   ! ZZZ9- ! Z,ZZZ,ZZ9- ! ZZZ,ZZZ,ZZZ.99-
        ****  !  3   ! ZZZ9- ! Z,ZZZ,ZZ9- ! ZZZ,ZZZ,ZZZ.99-
        ****  !  4   ! ZZZ9- ! Z,ZZZ,ZZ9- ! ZZZ,ZZZ,ZZZ.99-
     ============!======!========!===========!=================
     SUMMATION-E !  0   ! ZZZ9- ! Z,ZZZ,ZZ9- ! ZZZ,ZZZ,ZZZ.99-


                     Press ENTER to continue
            PF 2 = Modify; PF 14 = Print Screen; PF 16 = EXIT

Row 24 reserved for messages.
```

```
              B E N T L E Y   C O M P U T E R   C O R P O R A T I O N
    Version 00            MIS PERSONNEL MANAGEMENT SYSTEM              SCR-08
                          Linear Extrapolation of Sales Growth


                                      🖉

                        X        XↃ2      Y3         X * Y3

            SUMMATION-E   Z99-    ZZZ9-   Z,ZZZ,ZZ9-   ZZZ,ZZZ,ZZZ.99-

                The value for X designating year you 'are' calculating
                            X = Z9  from SCR-04

                            SUM Y3 = N*A      >>>>   A = Z,ZZZ,ZZZ.99-
                    SUM X*Y3 = B*(SUM XↃ2)    >>>>   B = Z,ZZZ,ZZZ.99-

        Calculated Sales Growth Y3 = A + B*X   >>>>   Y3 =     ZZ,ZZZ.99-




                            Press ENTER to Continue
                    PF 02 = Modify 'Prior' Screen and Reprocess
                        PF 14 = Print Scree; PF 16 = EXIT
        Row 24 reserved for messages.
```

```
              B E N T L E Y   C O M P U T E R   C O R P O R A T I O N
    Version 00            MIS PERSONNEL MANAGEMENT SYSTEM              SCR-09
                          Linear Extrapolation Summary

     *1 Calculated Demand Hours Y = A + B*X  >>>>   Y1 = Z,ZZZ,ZZZ.99-
        Calculated Head Count   Y = A + B*X  >>>>   Y2 = Z,ZZZ,ZZZ.99-
        Calculated Sales Growth Y = A + B*X  >>>>   Y3 = Z,ZZZ,ZZZ.99-

        You may change data here if the numbers do not fit correctly
        into an expected trend. Please remember that any changes you
        make will effect the final outcome of the Controlling Model, but
        the raw data on the Data-Base will not be effected. You can
        recover from changes by simply going back to the beginning and
        use the 'Original Data'.

           The next Phase of the DSS uses a Linear Programming Model

               Note *1  =>   Y1 / 2000 Hrs. = C1 = ZZ,ZZZ.99-

                            Press ENTER to Continue
                    PF 02 = Modify; PF 14 = Print Screen; PF 16 = EXIT

        Row 24 is reserved for messages.
```

```
              B E N T L E Y   C O M P U T E R   C O R P O R A T I O N
    Version 00            MIS PERSONNEL MANAGEMENT SYSTEM              SCR-10
                          Linear Programming
                          Ojective Function Formulation


        The user is required to define the weighting of variables and arithmetic
        functions. Also a minimum or maximum objective is asked. Minimizing is the
        default.    ** X1 - The input in front of X1 is the weighting variable.
                    ( * ) - This is looking for a plus ( + ) or a minus ( - ) sign.


        The Objective Function Is: 'Z' =   ** X1 ( * ) ** X2 ( * ) ** X3

                              Minimize = 1
                              Maximize = 2
                          Choice or Default =  1




                            Press ENTER to Continue
                        PF 14 = Print Screen; PF 16 = EXIT

        Row 24 is reserved for messages.
```

```
         B E N T L E Y     C O M P U T E R     C O R P O R A T I O N
Version 00              MIS PERSONNEL MANAGEMENT SYSTEM                SCR-11
                          Linear Programming Model
```

$C1 = Y1 / 2000$ Hrs. = ZZ,ZZZ.99

```
                          Standard Constraints
===============================================================================
   Mix of People          ** X1 + ** X2 + ** X3  <=  Y2 =  ZZ,ZZZ.99
   Mix of Job Function     ** X1 + ** X2 + ** X3  =>  C1 =  ZZ,ZZZ.99
   Programmer/Analyst      X1                      =>  ***   User Defined
   Senior Analyst                     X2           =>  ***   User Defined
   Project Manager                             X3  =>  ***   User Defined
   Space Capacity         ** X1 + ** X2 + ** X3  <=  S1 =  ZZ,ZZZ.99
   Loss From Attrition    ** X1 + ** X2 + ** X3  <=  P1 =  ZZ,ZZZ.99-
   Loss From Promotion    ** X1 + ** X2 + ** X3  =>  P2 =  ZZ,ZZZ.99-
```

```
                          Press ENTER to Continue
                             PF 2 = Modify Data
         PF 12 = Directions/Definitions; PF 14 = Print Screen; PF 16 = EXIT
   Row 24 is reserved for messages.
```

```
         B E N T L E Y     C O M P U T E R     C O R P O R A T I O N
Version 00              MIS PERSONNEL MANAGEMENT SYSTEM               SCR-11A
                          Linear Programming Model
```

Use Within Model	Definition or Use or Origin
Used to calculate C1	Y1 = Forecasted Demand Hours
Mix of People	Y2 = Forecasted Head Count
NOT used in this model	Y3 = Forecasted Sales Volume
Mix of Job Function	C1 = Calculated from Y1 / 2000 Hrs Per Year Per Employee.
Programmer/Analyst	X1 = Decision Variable 1
Senior Analyst	X2 = Decision Variable 2
Project Manager	X3 = Decision Variable 3
Space Capacity	S1 = Supplied By Facilities Management
Loss From Attrition	P1 = Supplied By Personnel Department
Loss From Promotion	P2 = Supplied By Personnel Department

```
                          Press ENTER to Continue
                       PF 14 = Print Screen; PF 16 = EXIT
```

```
         B E N T L E Y     C O M P U T E R     C O R P O R A T I O N
Version 00              MIS PERSONNEL MANAGEMENT SYSTEM               SCR-11B
                          SCR-11B INSTRUCTIONS
```

Standard Sequence
   During the Standard Sequence the user may only modify user defined
fields and the constraint equation coefficients. These fields will be
displayed in a High Intensity Modifyible state (HIMOD) on the screen.
Other fields will be displayed in a Low Intensity Nonmodifyible state
(LOPRO or Loprotect)on the screen. You will have a chance to change
these fields after the initial sequence is complete. (LOPRO fields are
Y2, C1, S1, P1 and P2).

'What If' Sequence
   The program goes into this phase as soon as the first sequence is
over and you are at the 'MODIFICATION MENU'. Press PFkey 11 to Modify
Coefficients. Now back to SCR-11 only the coefficients are displayed
in a HIMOD state. All other fields are displayed in a LOPRO state on the
screen. To modify the Right Hand Side of the equation you will choose
PFkey 7 (See Modification Menu).

```
                          Press ENTER to Continue
                       PF 14 = Print Screen; PF 16 = EXIT
```

```
              B E N T L E  Y   C O M P U T E R    C O R P O R A T I O N
Version 00              MIS PERSONNEL MANAGEMENT SYSTEM              SCR-12
                        Linear Programming Summary Report

                            For The Year ****

Linear Extrapolation Calculations:

         Demand Hours = Y1 = Z,ZZZ,ZZZ.99-    Y1 / 2000 Hrs. = C1 = ZZ,ZZZ.99
         Head Count   = Y2 = Z,ZZZ,ZZZ.99-
         Sales Growth = Y3 = Z,ZZZ,ZZZ.99-


                    Optimal Solution To     !    Comparison/Analysis Data
                    The Objective Function  !   Current Yr.    Need/Excess
     Programmer/Analysts = ZZ,ZZZ.99-       !    ZZ,ZZZ.99-     ZZ,ZZZ.99-
     Senior Analyst     = ZZ,ZZZ.99-        !    ZZ,ZZZ.99-     ZZ,ZZZ.99
     Project Managers   = ZZ,ZZZ.99-        !    ZZ,ZZZ.99-     ZZ,ZZZ.99-
     Total              = ZZ,ZZZ.99-        !    ZZ,ZZZ.99-     ZZ,ZZZ.99-

                          Press ENTER to Continue
              PF 12 = Directions/Definitions; PF 14 = Print Screen; PF 16 = EXIT

        Row 24 is reserved for messages.
```

```
              B E N T L E  Y   C O M P U T E R   C O R P O R A T I O N
                        MIS PERSONNEL MANAGEMENT SYSTEM
     VERSION 00               MODIFICATION MENU                    SCR-13




                    Function          Function
                      Key             Description


                      01       Save Model As Constructed
                      03       Start From Beginning Of The Standard Sequence
                      05       Modify Right Side Of Equations on SCR-11
                      07       Modify Coefficients On SCR-11

                      13       Reprocess Data

                      14       Instructions
                      16       Exit
```

```
              B E N T L E  Y   C O M P U T E R    C O R P O R A T I O N
                        MIS PERSONNEL MANAGEMENT SYSTEM
     VERSION 00               MODIFICATION MENU                   SCR-13A
                              INSTRUCTIONS

     Function          Function
       Key             Description

       01       The system will save your data and file it to your cost center.
                This allows you to come back at a later time to review or change
                data without having to remember how you got to this point.

       03       Starting with the first Menu the system will retrieve your data
                and start from scratch. (A different year may be solved for.)

       05       This function will go to SCR14 where the changes can be made.
       07       This function will go to SCR11 allowing changes to coeficients
                only.

       13       This function will reprocess the Linear Programming Model with
                the changed data. The system will inform you if you have not
                made changes.

       16       Exit - This will allow you to EXIT the system and log off.
```

```
            B E N T L E Y   C O M P U T E R   C O R P O R A T I O N
Version 00              MIS PERSONNEL MANAGEMENT SYSTEM              SCR-14
                          Linear Programming Model
                               'Right Side'
                           Modification Screen


                   Right Hand Side of Constraint Equations
=============================================================================
        Forecasted Head Count             Y2 =    ZZ,ZZZ.99
        Forecasted Demand Hours           Y1 =    ZZ,ZZZ.99
          To change C1, modify Y1.  System will calculate new C1.
        Programmer/Analyst                X1 =    ZZ9
        Senior Analyst                    X2 =    ZZ9
        Project Manager                   X3 =    ZZ9
        Space Capacity                    S1 =    ZZ,ZZZ.99
        Loss From Attrition               P1 =    ZZ,ZZZ.99-
        Loss From Promotion               P2 =    ZZ,ZZZ.99-

                        Press ENTER to Continue
            PF 14 = Print Screen; PF 16 = EXIT - No Modifications

Row 24 is reserved for messages.
```

APPENDIX B

```
Wang VS Integrated EDITOR - Version 6.06.00          16:49 10/28/82   Page
Input File is DEMANFLE in Library CRKCOPY  on Volume NFDD03

000100 *********************************************************************
000200 *    THE DEMAND FILE CONTAINS STATISTICAL INFORMATION THAT WILL
000300 *    BE USED TO DETERMINE MANPOWER BUDGETING NEEDS.
000400 *
000500 *    RECORD LENGTH    -    105
000600 *    RECORD KEY       -    STARTS POS 1 LENGTH OF 4
000700 *    INDEXED SEQUENTIAL FILE
000800 *
000900 *    DE-SALE; DE-DEMAND-HOURS; DE-HEAD-COUNT; DE-BUDGETED-PEOPLE;
001000 *    ARE FIELDS THAT CAN BE MAINTAINED BY THE USER. VARIANCE
001100 *    FIELDS ARE CALCULATED WITHIN THE MANPOWER-NEEDS-SYSTEM. OTHER
001200 *    FIELDS EXIST AND WILL BE UTILIZED AS PHASES OF THE SYSTEM
001300 *    DEVELOPE.
001400 *********************************************************************
001500  01  DEMAND-RECORD-AREA.
001600      05  DEMAND-RECORD-KEY.
001700          10  DEMAND-YEAR              PIC  X(04).
001710      05  DEMAND-MODELING-FIELDS.
001800          10  DEMAND-SALE-VOL          PIC  S9(11).
001900          10  DEMAND-HOURS             PIC  S9(07).
002000          10  DEMAND-HEAD-COUNT        PIC  S9(04).
002100          10  DEMAND-HRS-TO-HEAD-CALC  PIC  S9(04).
002200          10  DEMAND-BUDGET-PEOPLE     PIC  S9(04).
002300          10  DEMAND-BUDGET-VARIANCE   PIC  S9(04).
002400          10  DEMAND-HOURS-VARIANCE    PIC  S9(04).
002500          10  DEMAND-SPACE-ALLOC       PIC  S9(04).
002600          10  DEMAND-ATTRITION-ACTUAL  PIC  S9(03).
002700          10  DEMAND-PROMO-NET-LOSS    PIC  S9(03).
002710      05  DEMAND-GENERAL-HISTORIC.
002720          10  DEMAND-PROG-ANALYST      PIC  S9(04).
002730          10  DEMAND-SENIOR-ANALYST    PIC  S9(04).
002740          10  DEMAND-PROJECT-MANAGERS  PIC  S9(04).
002750          10  DEMAND-PROG-ANAL-VAR     PIC  S9(04).
002760          10  DEMAND-SENIOR-ANAL-VAR   PIC  S9(04).
002770          10  DEMAND-PROJECT-MGR-VAR   PIC  S9(04).
002800          10  DEMAND-CONTRACT-LABOR-USED PIC  S9(03).
002900          10  FILLER                   PIC  X(09).


*** End of Listing ************************************************************
```

SUMMARY

This chapter outlines a general methodology for building a DSS as a term project in a classroom environment. The students should work on a team basis on separate DSS projects and produce a five-chapter term paper as the end product. The first two chapters of the paper should describe the requirements of the DSS: who would be using the DSS and what end products they would expect from it. The next two chapters of the paper should give the technical design of the DSS, the contents of the four component modules of the DSS. In addition, they should include a number of "what if" scenarios that can be handled by the DSS. The last chapter of the paper should include evaluation comments from the management.

The bulk of the chapter contains a sample term paper on DSS written in a classroom environment. The title of the paper is MIS Management Support Analysis. It takes place in a hypothetical high tech manufacturing company that has to frequently reassign its MIS personnel to address immediate staffing needs that suddenly surface. The budget is done on an annual basis, and some long-range assignments are made, but priorities often change on a short-range basis, necessitating a revision of the earlier plan. The objective of the DSS is to aid middle management of the company in their assessment of personnel needs on both a short-term and a long-term basis.

To start with, the DSS accepts growth information from the corporate planning and control department of the company and correlates it with the current industry trends in the area of MIS usage and staffing expectations. In addition, it analyzes both short-term and long-term company projects to create time estimates for their expected completion. These estimates form the basis of computing professional staff necessary to meet the approved user demands. It also takes into account the availability of office space for employees and the hardware capacity. As three major use scenarios, the paper discusses and economic situation affected by recession, a change of priority situation, and a situation created when a highly skilled individual leaves the company for a competitor.

The DSS uses two modeling methods: linear regression and linear programming. The first is used to forecast three pieces of information—demand hours, head count, and sales growth—by utilizing historical data for a 9-year period. The second method is used to optimize the allocation of MIS resources on the basis of the total projected demand derived by linear regression. The output shows levels of MIS personnel in relation to a desired skill mix (e.g., programmer/analyst, senior analyst, project manager). The user accesses the DSS through menu-driven interactive screens. Appendix A of the report describes all 18 screens used by the DSS. They include such functions as entering and modifying data, running linear regression and linear programming models, generating reports, and performing "what if" analysis. The report closes with some comments of management about the successful components of the system and areas needing improvement.

14.5   KEY WORDS

The following key words are used in this chapter:

analysis phase	long-term project
component modules of DSS	menu-driven system
design phase	MIS
designer view of DSS	postimplementation evaluation phase
DSS term paper	return on investment
feedback from users	short-term project
linear programming	user view of DSS
linear regression	"what if" scenario

15

Current and Future Trends in DSS

15.1 SALIENT FEATURES OF DSS

We have discussed a wide variety of DSS packages including two hypothetical case studies, IDSS and D/T DSS (see Chapters 2 and 12). All of them have the following common features:

1. Control module uses non-procedural English-like commands.
2. Model-building module has optimizing and/or non-optimizing models.
3. Data storage module uses relational database system to store data.
4. Data manipulation module handles report and (optional) graphics generation.
5. DSS permits the user to perform "what if" analysis.

Currently, numerous packages available in the market or under development claim the title of DSS. Such confusion is expected since the DSS discipline is very young and not yet standardized. Out of this chaos we have selected a set of DSS packages that satisfy all five of the above requirements. The list is by no means exhaustive.

15.2 CURRENTLY AVAILABLE DSS PACKAGES

The DSS packages listed below are grouped into three categories:

1. DSS marketed by vendors
2. DSS reported in the literature and already implemented

3. DSS reported in the literature as under development

15.2.1 DSS Marketed by Vendors

1. AUTOTAB II

    Vendor: Capex Corporation/Computer Associates, 1600 Route 208, Fair Lawn, NJ 07410

    Hardware/Software: IBM mainframe with PCM or CMS; also TSO-compatible

    Modeling: No optimization; time series, exponential smoothing, adaptive filtering, financial analysis

    Report generation and graphics displays are available.

2. CEO (Comprehensive Electronic Office) Decision Base

    Vendor: Data General Corporation, Westboro, MA 01581

    Hardware/Software: Eclipse family with ADS, ADS/VS, ADS/WS, and AOS/RT 32

    Modeling: Spreadsheet, charting tool

    Report writer is available.

    DSS is fully intergrated with office automation system.

3. CUFFS

    Vendor: Cuffs Planning and Models Ltd., 201 East 87th Street, New York, NY 10028

    Hardware/Software: DEC-10, DEC-20; IBM 370 under VM/CMS

    Modeling: Optimization, forecasting, financial analysis

    Report writer and graphical displays are available.

4. EMS (Economic Modeling System)

    Vendor: Economic Sciences Corporation, 2150 Shattuck Avenue, Berkeley, CA 94704

    Hardware/Software: IBM 4300 and up

    Modeling: No optimization; forecasting, advanced econometrics, financial analysis

    Report generator and graphical displays are available.

5. EXPRESS

    Vendor: Management Decision Systems, Inc., 200 Fifth Avenue, Waltham, MA 02254

    Hardware/Software: PRIME 250 and up under PRIMOS; IBM 4341, IBM 370/148 and up under VM/CMS

    Modeling: Linear programming; regression, trend analysis, time series, financial analysis

    Report writer and graphics are available.

DSS handles marketing finance and production. See Sections 12.23–12.25 for more details.

A micro version of this DSS is available (see Section 15.6).

6. FCS/EPS

Vendor: EPS, Inc., 8700 Commerce Park Drive, Houston, TX 77036

Hardware/Software: IBM, Burroughs, CDC 6400 and up, PRIME, Data General

Modeling: Optimization, forecasting, correlation, curve fitting, multiple linear regression, financial analysis, risk analysis using Monte Carlo technique

Report writer and graphics are available.

DSS will be available in a personal computer version (see Section 15.6).

7. IFPS (Interactive Financial Planning System)

Vendor: Execucom Systems Corporation, 3410 Far West Boulevard Austin, TX 78731

Hardware/Software: IBM, DEC, CDC, PRIME

Modeling: Electronic spreadsheet, forecasting, financial analysis, optimization

Report writer and graphical displays are available. IFPS is available on mainframes. IFPS/Personal released in April 1983 is the micro version of IFPS and links mainframes and IBM PCs together for data access, consolidation of information, and timely report generation (see Section 15.6).

8. IMPACT

Vendor: MDCR, 760 Highway 18, Suite 120, East Brunswick, NJ 08816

Hardware/Software: IBM 370 and up under VM/CMS, MVS/TSO

Modeling: scanning procedure, forecasting, financial analysis, basic statistical functions

Report writer and limited graphics (bar chart and plotting) are available.

9. MODEL

Vendor: Lloyd Bush & Associates, 1 Battery Park Plaza, New York, NY

Hardware/Software: IBM, PRIME, VAX-11

Modeling: No optimization; forecasting, regression analysis, financial analysis (rate of return, depreciation, mortgage)

Report writer and graphics are available.

10. SIMPLAN

Vendor: Simplan Systems, Inc., 300 Eastowne Drive, Chapel Hill, NC 27514

Hardware/Software: IBM, PRIME

Modeling: No optimization; forecasting, econometrics, financial analysis

Report generation and graphics are available.

SIMPLAN handles finance, marketing, and production planning. See Section 1.10 for more details.

11. STRATAGEM

Vendor: Integrated Planning, Inc., 93 Massachusetts Avenue, Suite 212, Boston, MA 02115

Hardware/Software: IBM mainframe under VM/CMS

Modeling: No optimization; multiple regression analysis, forecasting, financial analysis, analysis of variance, discriminant analysis, correlation

Report writer and graphics are available.

12. TABOL (Tabular Oriented Business Languages)

Vendor: General Electric Information Services, Rockville, MD 20852

Hardware/Software: IBM and IBM plus compatible

Modeling: Optimization, extrapolation technique, forecasting, financial analysis, statistical routines

Report writer and graphical displays are available.

15.2.2 DSS Reported in Literature and Implemented

Keen and Scott Morton ([2], pp. 99–100) have reported six DSS packages, two of which have already been discussed.

1. *BRANDAID*.   This is a marketing model DSS developed by J.D.C. Little using the decision calculus technique. It was implemented in 1975. See Section 12.27 for more details.

2. *CIS (Capacity Information System)*.   This is a graphics-based DSS used in a production planning environment. It was implemented in late 1975. See Section 1.11 for more details.

3. *GADS (Geographic Data Analysis and Display System)*.   This system was developed by IBM Research Division as an interactive graphics system capable of drawing maps by using data from an already existing database. It includes optimization algorithms and statistical analysis of data. Powerful graphics capabilities are its most distinguishing feature. GADS is very user friendly and has been used by nonprogrammers to solve unstructured problems effectively. It was used in 1974 to design a police beat plan for a city

so as to minimize the response time to calls for service and to level out the workload of police officers. In 1976 GADS was used to help a school superintendent and his senior staff design a zoning plan for the school district.

4. *GMIS (Generalized Management Information System).* This system was developed during the early 1970s at MIT by a group led by J.J. Donovan and S.E. Madnick ([2], p. 160). It is based on the concept of a virtual machine, which allows several seemingly incompatible computer programs and databases to be simulated on a real computer. For example, if a project needs to use one model written in FORTRAN and another model written in APL to access data in a relational database that is supported by an SQL-type query language, then GMIS allows that to happen. It includes the modeling languages TROLL (for analysis of econometric time series data), TSP (Time Series Processor), DYNAMO (see Chapter 11), and APL/EPLAN (econometric modeling and forecasting). It also has statistical packages and database management systems. It was used in the NEEMIS (New England Energy Management Information System) during 1974–1976.

5. *PMS (Portfolio Management System).* This is a DSS used by investment managers in a banking environment. The objective is to provide investment services and to manage security portfolios of customers who can be wealthy individuals or trustees of large pension funds. PMS aims at maximizing portfolio return for a given level of risk or minimizing portfolio risk for a given level of return. It employs Markowitz's efficient frontier modeling technique and quantitative risk analysis. It uses three categories of data: portfolio related data, securities related data, and securities price data. PMS examines the entire portfolio rather than individual securities. Reports and graphical displays are available by means of a wide variety of operators. For example, STATUS displays the contents of a portfolio, TABLE diplays portfolio values, HISTO and SCATTER produce histograms and scatter plots, respectively, of the components of a portfolio, and so on. PMS was initially designed by T.P. Gerrity and later was succesfully implemented in one large commercial bank and three other banks during 1974 and afterwards ([2], p. 101).

6. *PROJECTOR.* This DSS supports corporate financial planning. It was developed by C.L. Meador and D.N. Ness in the early 1970s. It offers multiple regression, exponential smoothing, trend and seasonal analysis, goal programming (a linear progamming technique with multiple objectives), and optimization algorithms. The user can specify one or more criteria for evaluating alternatives. PROJECTOR contains four types of models: project analysis, merger/acquisition, forecasting, and cash flow analysis. Interactive dialogue is an important feature. However, PROJECTOR does not provide graphic capabilities. This DSS was used in 1974 by a small New England manufacturing company to study the acquisition of a new subsidiary and assess its financial impact.

15.2.3 DSS Reported in Literature as Under Development

Two packages fall under this catergory:

1. *CAP (Computer-Aided Planning).* This is a DSS for the planning of production levels. It uses monthly sales forecasts for a given product over a time span of 1–2 years and expresses its desired level of inventory as a percentage of annual sales. It then assists production planners to distribute production quotas uniformly over the full year so as to reach target schedules. CAP uses a complicated modeling method known as Mixed Integer Linear Programming (MILP). MILP algorithms are notorious for their unpredictability with respect to required computer time. As a result, CAP is unsuitable when the user requires a fast response time. During its development stage in 1974–1977, CAP was used to improve the decision process related to planning and aggregate production in a Dutch factory. It was developed by C. A. Th. Takkenburg ([5], pp. 249–259).

2. *IDAMS (Integrated Data Analysis and Management System).* This is an APL-based DSS designed to support business and scientific end users. It was developed at the IBM Scientific Center at Heidelberg, Germany, and was tested in 1983 at the IBM Scientific Center in Los Angeles. IDAMS is more a DSS generator rather than a DSS. In other words, IDAMS provides an interactive probem-solving environment by using all five sailent features of a DSS listed in Section 15.1. However, the individual end user must use the IDAMS tools to generate an appropriate DSS for his/her own applications. The scope of IDAMS has been described as follows by J. William Bergquist and Ephraim R. McLean ([5], pp. 190–191):

> In IDAMS, the user views his data as a collection of interrelated tables, a data base with a relational data model as its external view. The menus and descriptions of the data and programs, what is called the "inventory data" in IDAMS, consists of tabular (formatted) and non-tabular (unformatted) information. The formatted part serves primarily for the identification and definition of these tables, while the unformatted part supports the selection of the data and programs.
>
> These inventory data appear as an information network with facilities to guide the user to those nodes that contain the information he is seeking. The nodes of the network carry the actual information, while the arcs express an order relationship, associating one node to the nodes that succeed it. This allows the user to navigate from general menus to more specific ones. By narrowing down the search context through successive selections of menus, one arrives at the node containing the information the user is seeking.

Typically, a user will set up a "query," i.e., his specific data analysis or manipulation requirement, by using the guidance front end to identify the tables and programs required to perform his processing; and then he will use the data analysis front end to set up and execute this query. Online training

is provided for new users to acquaint them with the system's facilities. The user guidance features make it possible to develop an extensive repertoire of user-tailored solution steps customized to the needs of specific applications. The system is thus not application-dependent in any way. Instead, it offers facilities for the inclusion of application-specific information to achieve customization. Information about the system, as well as about data and programs, may be consulted within a uniform language interface.

15.3 RIGHT-BRAINED DSS VERSUS LEFT-BRAINED DSS

The salient features of DSS, as described in Section 15.1, depict the DSS as largely mathematical model-based and quantitatively analytical in its approach. It helps a manager to handle semistructured and unstructured tasks by providing him/her the necessary information from a large database. During this process the DSS uses a set of appropriate mathematical models. It has been postulated that any task requiring quantitative procedures is associated with functions performed by the left side of the human brain, while a task that is more creative and uses qualtitative analysis is performed by the right side of the brain. Accordingly, the DSS packages discussed in this book are labeled *left-brained DSS* by some authors ([5], pp. 47–64). In fact, all the DSS packages commercially available are left-brained. This brings us to the next question: Are *right-brained DSS* packagess at all possible?

L.F. Young ([5], p. 48) has mentioned one example of a right-brained DSS. It was developed at Yale University during 1977–1978 and is called POLITICS. It attempts to model national reactions to international events. In general, a right-brained DSS is best suited to handle such tasks as formulating general policy, determining methods and processes for influencing individual and group behavior, and conceptualizing alternative new products.

Young ([5], pp. 52–53) has proposed four functional levels of a right-brained DSS:

1. Information retrieval.
2. Filtering and pattern recognition.
3. Extrapolation, inference, and logical comparison.
4. Modeling.

Each functional level is implemented by a set of modules that use qualitative analysis such as tapping prior experience, knowledge, and wisdom; using classification and analogy techniques; generalizing on the basis of known facts; and building proper scenarios to formulate policy.

In concluding his paper, Young proposes a total decision support system (TDSS) consisting of a left-brained and a right-brained DSS and their interface. The interface should automatically translate qualitative descriptions

into partially complete mathematical expressions and verbally expressed scenarios into partially complete mathematical or symbolic models ([5], p. 62).

15.4 ROLE OF ARTIFICIAL INTELLIGENCE IN DSS

A right-brained DSS, as envisaged by Young, is still only a concept. However, the first three functional levels of such a DSS enumerated in section 15.3 can be handled by artificial intelligence. These three levels are

☐ Information retrieval from prior knowledge.
☐ Filtering and pattern recognition using classification and analogy.
☐ Inference from known facts.

Artificial intelligence represents a vast domain of methods and algorithms that attempt to use computers to simulate the process of human thinking and human reasoning. It is a study of how to make computers do things that human beings can do more efficiently at present. Problems coming under the purview of artificial intelligence include the following ([4], p. 3):

Game playing.
Theorem proving.
Perception, i.e., vision and speech.
Natural language understanding.
Expert systems.

The last two categories have a significant impact on the design of DSS.

Natural language understanding addresses the problem of communicating with computers via a language (e.g., English) as it is normally written. Even a nonprocedural language is a far cry from a natural language. For example, the SQL query language used by the ORACLE database management system is a de facto industry standard of nonprocedural query languages to be used in a relational DBMS package. But SQL still has its own syntax and instruction delimiters, which must be correctly used to get response from the system. Thus, SQL is *not* a natural language. In order to understand a natural language, the computer must be instructed to understand written text using lexical, syntactic, and semantic knowledge of the language as well as the required real-world information. Currently, several DBMS packages are commercially available that use natural language to handle queries from the user. If we use such a DBMS in designing a DSS, then the user will be able to communicate with the system in natural language. The implementation of the control and data manipulation modules will be much simpler then.

An expert system has been defined as follows by Forsyth ([1], p. 10):

An *expert system* is regarded as the embodiment within a computer of knowledge-based component, from an expert skill, in such a form that the system
can offer intelligent advice or make an intelligent decision about a processing
function. A desirable additional characteristic, which many would consider
fundamental, is the capability of the system, on demand, to justify its own line
of reasoning in a manner directly intelligible to the enquirer. The style adopted
to attain these characteristics is rule-based programming.

Thus, an expert system has four components:

1. Knowledge base
2. Inference engine
3. Knowledge acquisition module
4. Explanatory interface

Collectively these four components correspond to the four modules of a DSS.
In fact, we can set up a table of correspondence between the components
of a DSS and those of an expert system; see Table 15-1. Consequently, several
attempts have been made to design a DSS by using the two techniques of
artificial intelligence, expert systems and natural languages interface. Such
a DSS is not only more versatile than the conventional left-brained DSS but
also provides much greater support for managerial decision making. A manager, for example, can query the DSS in a natural language format and can
also ask the DSS for a justification of the specific course of action suggested
by the DSS. It should be clearly understood, however, that despite the impact
of artificial intelligence on DSS field the final decision is made by the manager.
Even an expert system cannot deprive a human manager of his/her decision-
making authority.

TABLE 15-1

DSS Modules	Expert System Components
Control module	Explanatory interface
Data storage module	Knowledge base
Data manipulation module	Knowledge acquisition module and explanatory interface
Model-building module	Knowledge acquisition module and in-ference engine

15.5 DSS PACKAGES USING ARTIFICIAL INTELLIGENCE

We shall discuss here three DSS packages of which only the first is commercially available in the United States. The list is by no means exhaustive.

1. *REVEAL.* This DSS is marketed by InfoTym, a division of the Information Systems Group of McDonnell-Douglas. It works with IBM machines using VM/CMS, ICL Inc. machines using VME, DEC VAX units using VMS, and IBM PC/XT using PC-DOS. The mainframe software can support microcomputer users who are linked to the mainframe. InfoTym claims that REVEAL is the first package that allows the user to combine DSS techniques with a knowledge-based expert system. The user can quickly create business models and expert systems that can perform algorithmic operations and approximate reasoning. The real strength of REVEAL lies in the synergy of DSS technology and knowledge-based engineering that allows it to handle applications requiring both strategies.

In order to create the knowledge base for the expert system in REVEAL, users write rules using a natural language syntax ([1], p. 146). Each rule contains a linguistic representation of what can be imprecise data or approximate statements. The link between the knowledge base and the DSS is established by using fuzzy sets, which allow the user to create mathamatical models representing imprecise concepts, intuition, experience, and policy statements. For example, a user can define mathematically what is meant by a "low" price or a "high" margin. Note that "low" or "high" as used in our everyday language is an imprecise concept. P.L.K. Jones ([1], pp. 140–144) has given a detailed discussion of the fuzzy sets in REVEAL.

REVEAL uses a relational DBMS, a text editor, a report writer, and a graphics display tool. Thus it includes all the standard tools of a DSS. The user communicates with the system by means of a set of interactive commands that are very close to English. Figure 15-1 gives an example of a simple profit and loss model in REVEAL. It resembles the financial assets model of SIMPLAN (Fig. 1-7) very closely, which illustrates the DSS aspect of REVEAL. Figure 15-2, on the other hand, represents the expert system aspect of REVEAL in that it shows suggested career choices for students on the basis of their performance in a wide variety of academic courses. Figure 15-3 shows how the knowledge-based rules are stored in REVEAL as a set of decision rules. All three figures are taken from P.L.K. Jones' paper ([1], p. 133–150).

2. *DECMAK.* This package is not yet commercially available in the United States. It has been developed and implemented by its designers M. Bohanec, I. Bratko, and V. Rajkovic at J. Stefan Institute of Ljubljana, Yugoslavia ([5], pp. 235–248). DECMAK uses the decision tree analysis method in its design of the DSS part and the notions of fuzzy sets and rule-based programming in its design of the expert system features. The system is interactive and user-friendly. It allows the user to formulate the problem and build the decision-making rules in the knowledge base.

MODE > inspect

```
 1 :  ! Example P&L model
 2 :  ! ------------------
 3 :
 4 :  price=compound (base.price,price.infl,12)
 5 :  cost =compound (base.cost , cost.infl,12)
 6 :
 7 :  margin=price-cost
 8 :  revenue=volume*price
 9 :  profit=volume*margin
10 :  net.profit=profit-fixed.exp
11 :
12 :  profit%sales=net.profit/revenue * 100
```

Profit and Loss Projection

	January 1983	February 1983	March 1983	April 1983	May 1983	June 1983
Selling price / unit	10.00	10.12	10.24	10.36	10.48	10.60
Direct cost / unit	7.00	7.10	7.20	7.30	7.40	7.50
Unit sales margin	3.00	3.02	3.04	3.06	3.08	3.10
Planned sales volume	100	115	110	130	135	140
Gross trading profit	$300	$347	$334	$398	$416	$434
Fixed expenses	$150	$150	$150	$160	$165	$170
Net operating profit	$150	$197	$184	$238	$251	$264
Profit as % revenue	15%	17%	16%	18%	18%	18%

Key assumptions were :
  Selling price inflation of 15% per year
  Direct cost inflation of 18% per year

FIGURE 15-1 Profit and loss model in REVEAL [1]. Reprinted from *Expert Systems* by Richard Forsyth, with permission of the publisher, Chapman and Hall.

```
MODE > input.data
```

	SMITH	BROWN	DAVIES	ARNOLD	JOHNSON	RICHARDS
PHYSICS	.90	.60	.53	.84	.80	.81
CHEMISTRY	.70	.70	.64	.58	.79	.79
MATHS	.95	.65	.81	.64	.80	.96
BIOLOGY	.60	.40	.76	.88	.72	.69
ENGLISH	.10	.60	.63	.25	.39	.42
FRENCH	.05	.10	.29	.71	.60	.28
ECONOMICS	.75	.20	.82	.74	.78	.85
HISTORY	.45	.80	.79	.83	.72	.16
GEOGRAPHY	.30	.70	.75	.68	.59	.42
ART	.60	.05	.20	.75	.40	.80

```
MODE > execute
```

```
..Candidate's name :        SMITH
..Suggested career : RESEARCH

..Candidate's name :        BROWN
..Suggested career : TEACHING
..Alternate career : ADMINISTRATION

..Candidate's name :        DAVIES
..Suggested career : TEACHING
..Alternate career : ACCOUNTANCY

..Candidate's name :        ARNOLD
..Suggested career : MEDICINE
..Alternate career : ADMINISTRATION

..Candidate's name :        JOHNSON
..Suggested career : ACCOUNTANCY
..Alternate career : RESEARCH

..Candidate's name :        RICHARDS
..Suggested career : ACCOUNTANCY
..Alternate career : RESEARCH
```

FIGURE 15-2 Suggested career choices. Example of expert system in REVEAL [1]. Reprinted from *Expert Systems* by Richard Forsyth, with permission of the publisher, Chapman and Hall.

DECMAK uses a *semantic tree* as its basis to solve any problem. The semantic tree consists of three types of entities: performance variables, a set of functions, and a set of equations. One *performance variable* is called the *root variable* and forms the root node of the semantic tree. A nonroot variable is called a *basic variable* if it appears as a terminal node in the tree; otherwise it is called an *aggregate variable*. Each *function* is expressed by means of an equation that defines a performance variable in terms of two or more other performance variables. A variable can take numeric or character values. A character value such as "acceptable," "good," or "low" is defined by means of fuzzy sets.

	SMITH	BROWN	DAVIES	ARNOLD	JOHNSON	RICHARDS
RESEARCH	81				61	63
WRITING						
ADMINISTRATION				65		
TEACHING		85	65	55		
POLITICS						
MEDICINE				65		
LAW						
ACCOUNTANCY			63		57	71
ARCHITECTURE						61

```
 1 : !Career selection policy
 2 : !------------------------

 3 :
 4 :      If math is excellent and physics is excellent then re-
          search is indicated

 5 :
 6 :      If maths is less than average or physics is less then
          average than research is discouraged

 7 :
 8 :
 9 :      If art is more than good and maths is more than average
          then architecture is indicated

10 :
11 :      If maths is more than average and economics is more than
          good then accountancy is indicated

12 :
13 :      If biology is more than good and the worst.science is
          more than average then medicine is indicated

14 :
15 :      If avge. art is less than good and avge.science is less
          than good then teaching is indicated

16 :
17 :
18 :      If english is more than good and maths is more than av-
          erage and worst.science is more than poor then law
          is indicated

19 :
20 :      If english is excellent and worst.art is more than poor
          then writing is indicated

21 :
22 :
23 :      If english is good and economics is good but maths is
          less than average then politics is indicated

24 :
25 :
26 :      If (worst.art is good or worst.science is good) and
          maths is average then administration is indicated
```

FIGURE 15-3 Representation of knowledge in REVEAL [1]. Reprinted from *Expert Systems* by Richard Forsyth, with permission of the publisher, Chapman and Hall.

To solve a decision-making problem, the user starts with a subproblem and inputs the basic variables and the knowledge-based rules. DECMAK then builds the associated semantic tree interactively by computing aggregate variables in terms of the basic variables. Eventually it computes the root variable represented by the root node of the tree. This root variable represents the overall utility and is thus the final decision provided by the situation.

DECMAK has been implemented on PDP-11 under the RT-11 or RSX-11 operating systems as well as on DEC-10 under the TOPS-10 operating system. It is written in PASCAL and consists of 3500 lines of code using about 100 subprograms. It also includes a HELP function.

DECMAK was actually used to select a computer system from a range of alternatives. A factory with about 2000 employees needed a computer system supporting 140 interactive terminals, 10 printers, and 700 MB disk storage. The problem was solved by using the following steps ([5], p. 241) :

1. Establishing a decision-making group.
2. Changing analysis.
3. Identifying alternatives.
4. Identifying the performance variables and constructing a semantic tree.
5. Defining the decision-knowledge functions.
6. Analyzing the alternatives and evaluating them.
7. Explaining the results of the evaluation.
8. Implementing the chosen alternative.

The performance variable SYSTEM was the root variable representing the overall quality of the computer. It had four admissible values: unacceptable, acceptable, good, very good. This again depended on economic conditions, technical features, and personnel. Technical features were defined in terms of hardware and software, and so on. The semantic tree consisted of 20 basic variables and 9 aggregate variables and used 9 knowledge-based rules. During the use of DECMAK it was possible to determine the reasoning behind a decision by using the expert system feature of the package.

3. *IMS (Intelligent Management System).* This package is currently under development at the Robotics Institute of Carnegie-Mellon University. Its goal is to help managers use artifical intelligence in their daily decision-making tasks. IMS explores semistructured and unstructured problems by means of heuristic problem-solving techniques, the latter being a growing segment of artificial intelligence ([4], Chapters 2, 3 and 11). M. S. Fox describes the characteristics of IMS as follows ([5], pp. 106):

> Constraint-directed and rule-based problem-solving architectures are used to perform organized control, management, and analysis. These architectures easily incorporate constriants/heuristics in the performance of control and

management tasks such as job-shop scheduling and trend analysis. And natural language parsers and rule-based arthitectures are used to construct flexible user interfaces.

The modeling system used by IMS provides the following features ([5], p. 11) :

1. The model is composed of declarative objects and relations that match the user's conceptual model of the organization.

2. The modeling system provides a library of objects and relations that the user may use, alter, and/or extend in their application.

3. The model incorporates a variety of representational techniques, allowing a wide variety of organizations to be modeled (continuous and discrete). In addition, it is extensible, which allows the incorporation of new modeling techniques.

4. The user interactively defines, alters, and peruses the model.

5. The model can be easily instrumented. For example, it can be diagramatically displayed on a color graphics monitor at different level of abstraction. The complete organization, or parts thereof, can be viewed with summaries (e.g., queue lengths, state).

6. The modeling system is simple to learn to use because the modeling tools match the concepts people use to think about problems.

The modeling system uses *schema* as the basic unit for representing objects, processes, ideas, and so on. A schema consists of a schema name and a set of slots. The whole mechanism is based on the knowledge representation system called Schema Representation Language or SRL. IMS includes an elaborate user interface that features both the decision-making component and the expert system component. It allows the manager to perform "what if" analysis ([5], p. 108) in a typical DSS environment. It also enables the user to access knowledge-based rules for smooth handling of organization problems and for checking inconsistent information, if any, existing in the model ([5], pp. 107, 111).

15.6 DSS IMPLEMENTED ON MICROCOMPUTERS*

Initially, DSS software was implemented on mainframes because both modeling packages and database systems required in the development of DSS were storage-intensive and needed large memory. However, since 1980 many of the vendors of mainframe DBMS packages have marketed microcomputer versions of these DBMS. This phenomenon is due to the rapid expansion of the microcomputer market accompanied by a downgrading of their prices.

* This section relies heavily on an article by Eric Nee; see [3]).

As a result, micro versions of mainframe DSS packages are becoming increasingly popular. With these new microcomputer-based DSS, anyone with a microcomputer is able to access large data banks and perform sophisticated analysis of multifactored problems such as sales trends, marketing programs, and financial projections. This enables the managers at small companies, which cannot afford mainframes or even minicomputers, to get the benefit of DSS capabilities.

In addition to purely microcomputer-based DSS, a wide variety of DSS packages are now available that have links to mainframe-based DSS. This latter type makes possible both complex modeling and maintenance of large corporate data files. Mainframe DSS software has traditionally been sold to Fortune 1000 companies on an in-house or timesharing basis. Most of the recently released micro-to-mainframe DSS software continues to be sold to these same companies, but now there are more people who can use the DSS because of the greater availability of the micros. Also, data processing managers can relieve some of the burden from mainframes by encouraging DSS users to use the mainframe-to-micro links. With these links, users can download information from the mainframe to the micro and perform various calculations offline from the mainframe.

DSS vendors have taken two main approaches in designing the mainframe-to-micro links :

1. Provide a link to the microcomputer from the mainframe that allows the user to download data to the micro and then manipulate it on a standard micro software product. Management Decision Systems, Inc. used this approach to produce EXPRES-MATE/LINK in the first quarter of 1984. The product connects a micro user to the company's mainframe DSS product EXPRESS and allows him/her to exchange data between EXPRESS and the micro, convert the mainframe data to a format compatible with a micro software such as Visicalc, and operate EXPRESS on the mainframe from the micro.

2. Develop a smaller version of the mainframe DSS with fewer capabilities than the mainframe version. It gives the micro user his/her own DSS package that can operate in a standalone mode. However, with its link to mainframe, the micro version is designed to operate as part of a distributed environment. In designing the downsized micro version, the DSS vendors normally leave most of the DBMS capabilities to the mainframe because of its greater storage capacity and processing power and include as many as possible of the analytical capabilities of the mainframe in the micro version. For example, the standalone micro DSS MICRO W is limited to two-dimensional analysis such as sales and overtime, while its mainframe counterpart can perform up to seven-dimensional analysis.

We now include four representative micro DSS packages to illustrate their scope. The list is by no means exhaustive.

1. **IFPS/PERSONAL** (link to IFPS on mainframe)

   Vendor: Execucom System Corporation, Austin, TX

   Description: Two-dimensional DSS modeling packages, operates as standalone or can exchange models and data between micro and mainframe

   Hardware: Microcomputers—IBM PC, PC/XT Compaq, TI Professional, Mainframes—Burroughs, CDC, DEC, Hewlett-Packard, Honeywell, IBM, Univac, Wang

   Capabilities: Nonprocedural modeling, goal seeking, financial analysis, report writer, data file editing, case management

   Memory: 512KB and two disk drives

   Price: $1,500

2. **MICRO W** (Link to SYSTEM W on Mainframe)

   Vendor: Comshare Inc., Ann Arbor, Mi

   Description: Downsized version of SYSTEM W minus most database management

   Hardware: Microcomputers—IBM PC, PC/XT, 3270 PC. Mainframes—IBM 370

   Capabilities: Two-dimensional analysis, operates standalone or exchanges models and data between micro and mainframe

   Memory: 256KB

   Price: SYSTEM W, $55,000–75,000; with 5 copies of MICRO W, $80,000; additional MICRO W, $200 each

3. **EXPRESS-MATE/LINK** (link to EXPRESS or mainframe)

   Vendor: Management Decisions Systems, Inc., Waltham, MA

   Description: Micro link to mainframe DSS

   Hardware: Microcomputers—IBM PC and all micros 100% compatible with IBM PCs; Mainframes—IBM, PRIME

   Capabilities: Data transfer between micro and mainframe DSS, convert mainframe data to format compatible with micro programs

   Memory: 192KB, one double-sided disk

   Price: $450

4. **MICRO FCS** (link to FCS-EPS on mainframe)

   Vendor: EPS Inc., Windham, NH

   Description: Transfers entire mainframe DSS to micro minus database management and sophisticated consolidation

   Hardware: Microcomputers—IBM PC, PC/XT, IBM-compatibles, DEC Rainbow, HP 150, Wang PC; Mainframes—Amdahl, Data General, DEC, Hewlett-Packard, Honeywell, IBM, PRIME, Univac, Wang

Capabilities: Fully syntax-compatible with main frame DSS; transfers files between micro and mainframe, builds menus on micro and mainframe products, modeling, reporting, graphics
Memory: 192KB, two floppy drives
Price: $2000

15.7 FUTURE TRENDS IN DSS

Two definite trends are currently discernible in the DSS development efforts:

1. Research is intensive in the area of interaction between DSS and artificial intelligence. REVEAL (Section 15.5) is but one example of such an interface. As natural language representation and the development of expert systems progress more and more, there will be an increase in the number of DSS packages featuring an artificial intelligence component. Of course, managers must be reassured that no DSS can ever take the decision-making authority from them.

2. Many DSS vendors are becoming involved in producing micro versions of mainframe DSS. This trend is very similar to the trend of developing micro versions of mainframe DBMS packages. Micro-based DSS software makes the DSS capability available to a larger group of users and also takes some of the workload off the mainframe.

15.8 SUMMARY

There are numerous software packages currently on the market that claim the title of DSS. Consequently, the chapter starts with a list of five salient features that characterize a true DSS package. A package that has all five features can properly be called a DSS. The chapter then gives brief descriptions of 20 DSS packages grouped under three categories: DSS marketed by vendors, DSS reported in the literature and already implemented, and DSS under development. The first group includes 12 DSSs: AUTOTAB II, CEO Decision Base, CUFFS, EMS, EXPRESS, FCS/EPS, IFPS, IMPACT, MODEL, SIMPLAN, Stratagem, and TABOL. The second group includes six DSSs: BRANDAID, CIS, GADS, GMIS, PMS, and PROJECTOR. The third group includes two DSSs: CAP and IDAMS.

Next, the chapter discusses left-brained and right-brained DSS packages. The decision support systems discussed in the book and currently available in the market are called *left-brained* since they are based on quantitative procedures, which are handled by the left side of the human brain. A *right-brained* DSS, on the other hand, handles more creative decision making that is based on a qualitative analysis. However, no right-brained DSS is as yet commercially available. Therefore, we raise the question, Is a right-brained

DSS possible? Although the answer is still unknown, this brings us to the discussion of the role of artificial intelligence in the design and implementation of a DSS.

Natural language understanding and expert or knowledge-based systems are the two areas within artificial intelligence that have a direct bearing on DSS. If the DBMS used in the design of a DSS has a natural language query capability, then the user can access the DSS via its control module by means of plain unstructured English. This makes the DSS front end very user-friendly. An expert system can offer intelligent advice on the basis of its own knowledge base and the conversation with the user. In addition, it can justify its own line of reasoning if requested to do so by the user. These features of an expert system can be very helpful for a DSS. The chapter shows an almost one-to-one correspondence between the modules of a DSS and the components of an expert system. At present, REVEAL is the only commercially available software that features both a DSS and an expert system. REVEAL uses the concept of fuzzy sets to combine the DSS characteristics with those of an expert system. Fuzzy sets allow the user to create mathematical models representing imprecise concepts, intuition, experience, and policy statements. The chapter also discusses two other DSS-cum-expert systems: DECMAK (not available in the United States) and IMS (still under development at Carnegie-Mellon University in Pittsburgh, Pennsylvania).

Due to the rapid expansion of the microcomputer market many vendors are now producing micro versions of mainframe DSS software. There are two main approaches in this effort: (1) Provide a link to the microcomputer from the mainframe that allows the user to download data to the micro and then manipulate it on a standard micro software product; (2) develop a smaller version of the mainframe DSS with fewer capabilities than the mainframe version, which gives the micro user a downsized DSS that can operate in a standalone mode. The chapter discusses four examples of such micro DSSs: IFPS/Personal, Micro W, EXPRESS-MATE/LINK, and Micro FCS.

Two definite future trends in DSS market are to include expert system features in DSS and to develop micro versions of mainframe DSS.

15.9 KEY WORDS

The following key words are used in this chapter:

artificial intelligence	CUFFS
AUTOTAB II	data manipulation module
BRANDAID	data storage module
CAP	DECMAK
CEO Decision Base	EMS
CIS	expert system
control module	explanatory interface

EXPRESS

EXPRESS-MATE/LINK

FCS/EPS

GADS

GMIS

IDAMS

IFPS

IFPS/PERSONAL

IMPACT

IMS

inference engine

knowledge-acquisition module

knowledge base

left-brained DSS

mainframe-to-micro link

micro-based DSS

MICRO FCS

MICRO W

MODEL

model-building module

natural langage

nonprocedural language

PMS

PROJECTOR

REVEAL

right-brained DSS

SIMPLAN

STRATEGEM

TABOL

total decision support system (TDSS)

"what if" analysis

REFERENCES

1. R. Forsyth, ed., *Expert Systems,* Chapman and Hall Computing, New York, 1984.
2. P. Keen and M. Scott Morton, *Decision Support System: An Organizational Perspective,* Addision-Wesley, Reading, MA, 1978.
3. E. Nee, "Reaching Decisions with Micro-to-Mainframe DSS," *Micro Manager,* November 1984.
4. E. Rich, *Artificial Intelligence,* McGraw-Hill, New York, 1983.
5. H.G. Sol, ed., *Process and Tools for Decision Support,* North-Holland Publishing, Amsterdam, 1983.

INDEX

A

Absolute clock, 258, 262, 267, 270, 273
Activity, 80
  parallel, 80
ADVANCE, 251–252
Alexander's filter technique, 105
Analysis phase, 375
Arrival pattern, 183–184
Artificial intelligence, 414
Autocorrelation, 225
AUTOTAB II, 408
Auxiliary equation, 283–284

B

Balking, 187
Batch means, 222, 225
Benefit:
  intangible, 41
  tangible, 41
Beta coefficient, 107–108
Block, 243
  diagram, 244
BRAND AID, 350–352, 410
Breadth of market technique, 317–318
Burst point, 80
Business gaming, 356
  simulation, 356

C

Calibration, 351
CAP, 412
Capacity information system (CIS), 20–24, 410
Capital asset pricing, 103–105, 318
  market line, 103–104
Carrying cost, 88
Cash budget, 367
CEO decision base, 408
CLEAR, 257
Client portfolio information, 302–308
Clock update phase, 273
Constant, 282, 284
Constraint, 61, 63, 79
Control module, 11, 35, 407
  D/T DSS, 329–334
  IDSS, 300–302
  statement, 256–258, 289–291
Corporate planning model, 13
Correlation, coefficient of, 133
Cost/benefit analysis, 32, 41–42
Counts, 211
Critical activity, 80
Cross-impact method, 156–157
CUFFS, 408
Current events chain (CEC), 273
  ratio, 357
Curve:
  asymptotic growth, 141–144

429

M